The VAMPIRE & HIS PLEASANT COMPANIONS

1

MARIMO RAGAWA

ORIGINAL STORY
NARISE KONOHARA

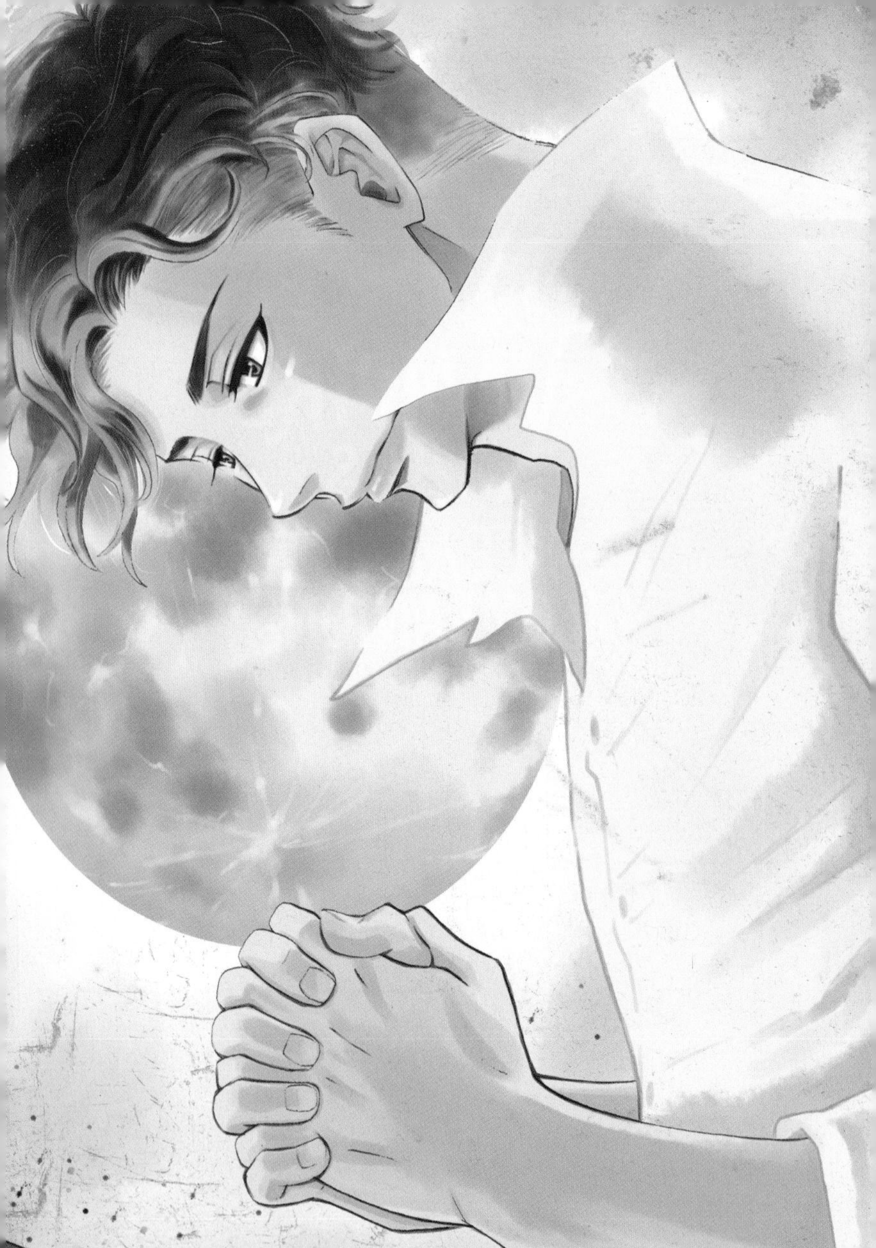

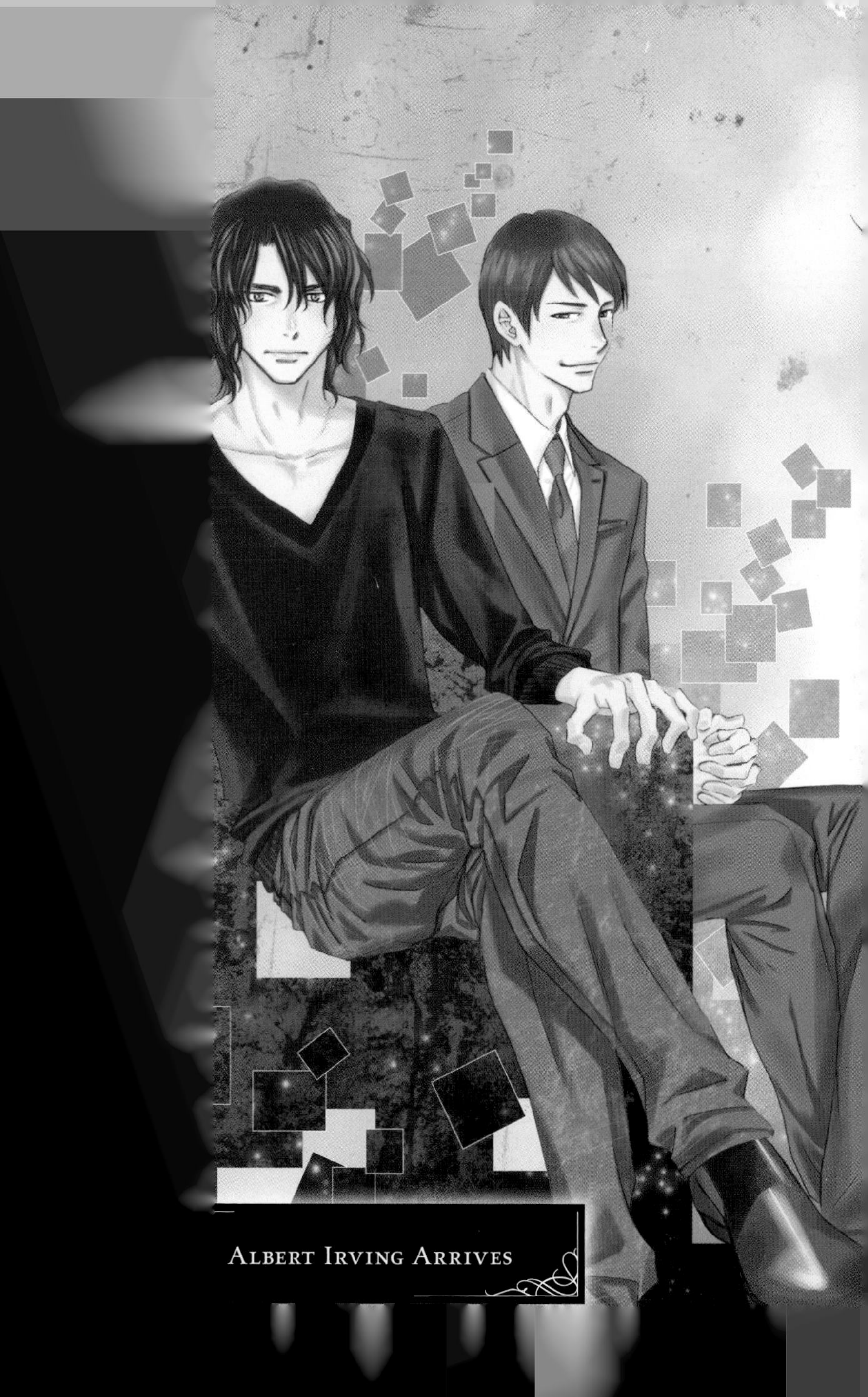
Albert Irving Arrives

CONTENTS

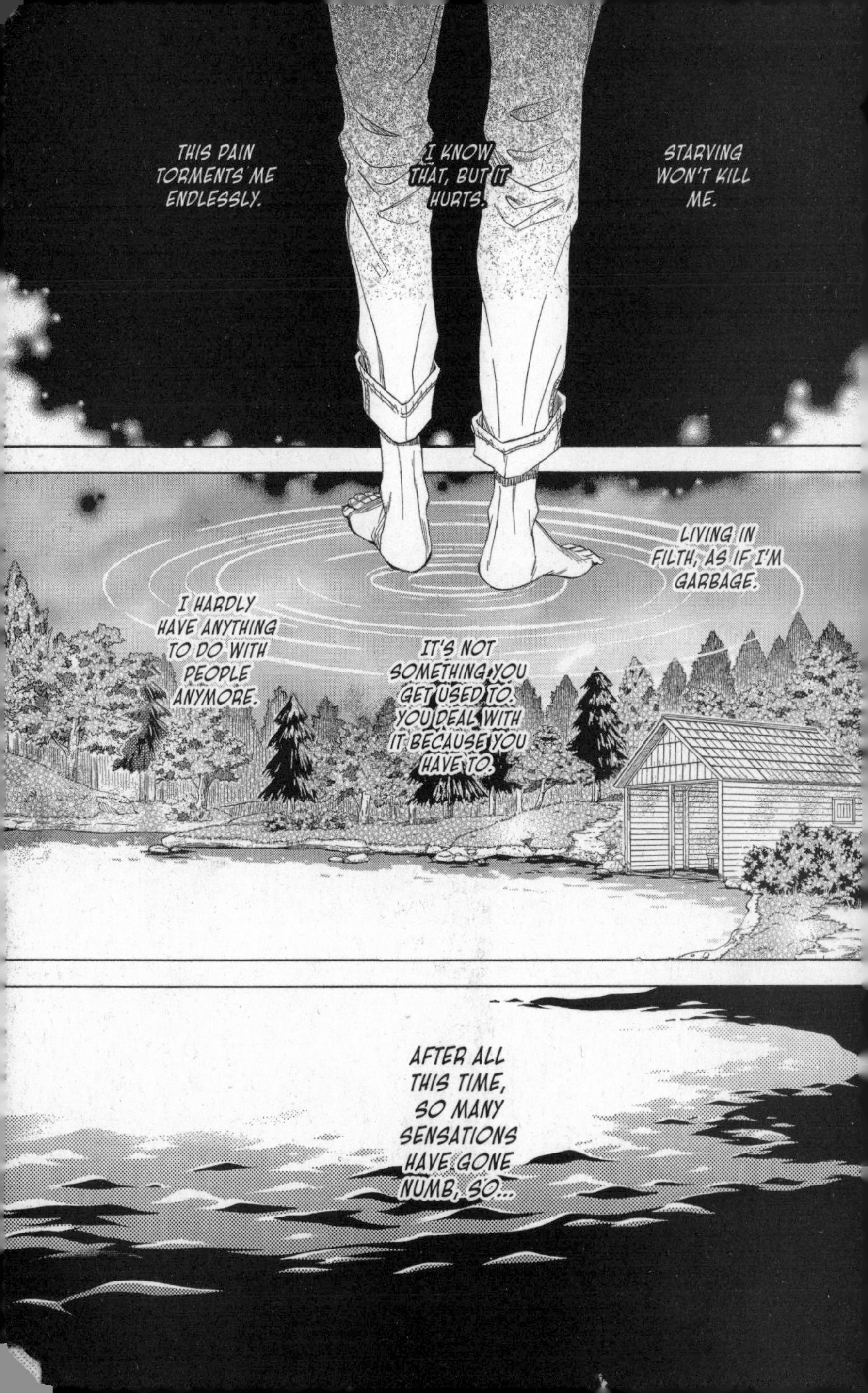
STARVING WON'T KILL ME.
I KNOW THAT, BUT IT HURTS.
THIS PAIN TORMENTS ME ENDLESSLY.
LIVING IN FILTH, AS IF I'M GARBAGE.
IT'S NOT SOMETHING YOU GET USED TO. YOU DEAL WITH IT BECAUSE YOU HAVE TO.
I HARDLY HAVE ANYTHING TO DO WITH PEOPLE ANYMORE.
AFTER ALL THIS TIME, SO MANY SENSATIONS HAVE GONE NUMB, SO...

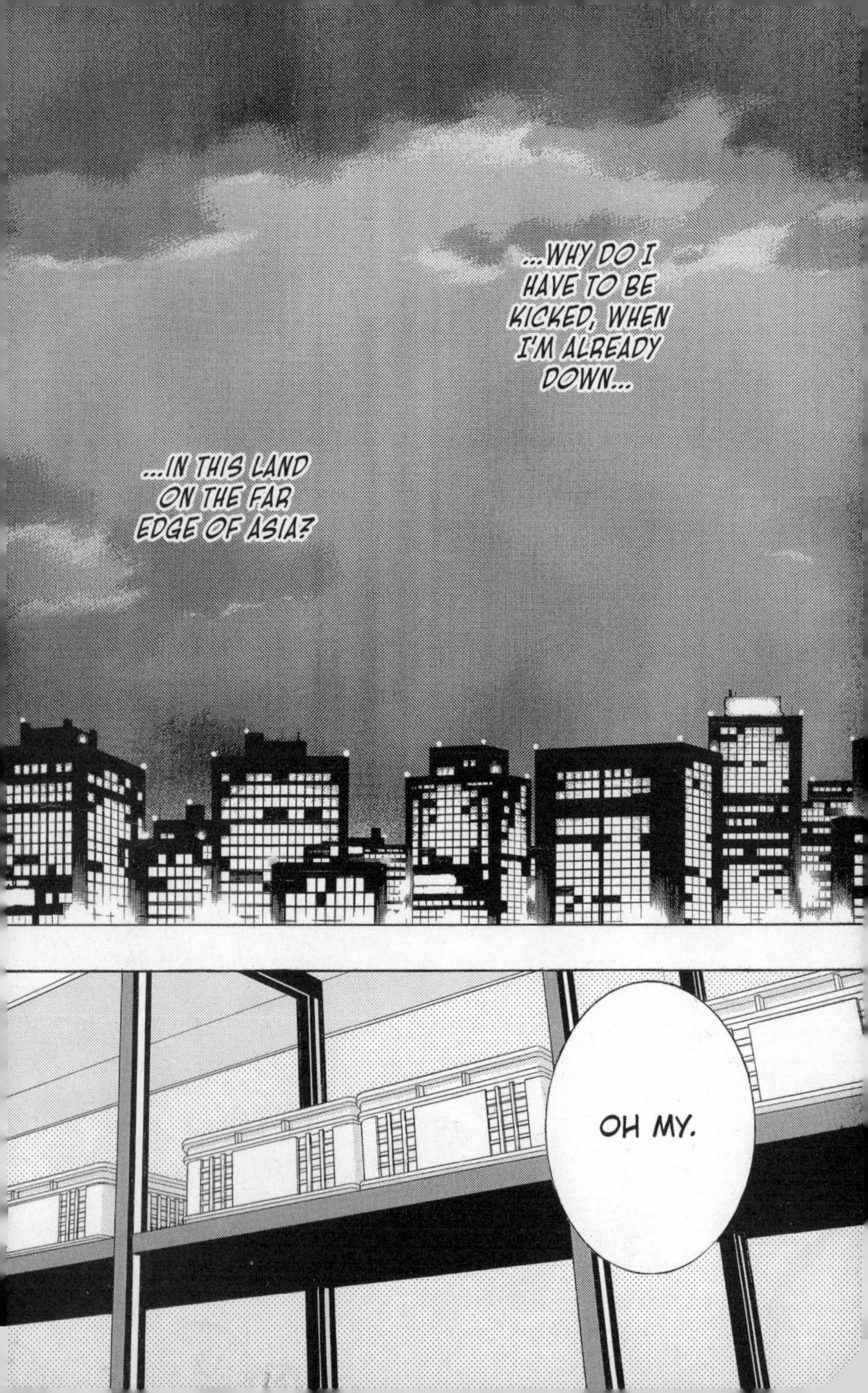
...WHY DO I HAVE TO BE KICKED, WHEN I'M ALREADY DOWN...
...IN THIS LAND ON THE FAR EDGE OF ASIA?
OH MY.

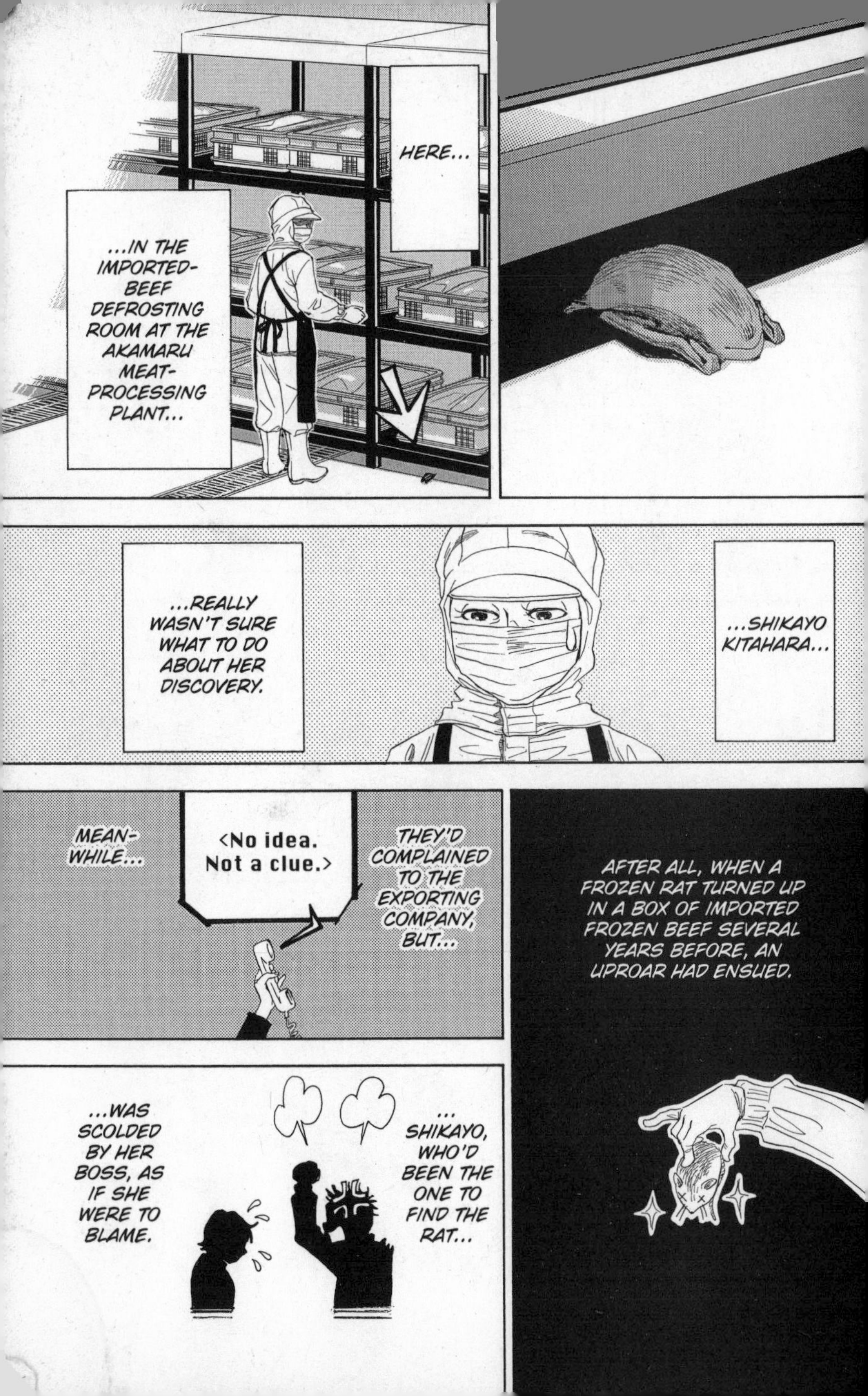
HERE...
...IN THE IMPORTED-BEEF DEFROSTING ROOM AT THE AKAMARU MEAT-PROCESSING PLANT...
...SHIKAYO KITAHARA...
...REALLY WASN'T SURE WHAT TO DO ABOUT HER DISCOVERY.
AFTER ALL, WHEN A FROZEN RAT TURNED UP IN A BOX OF IMPORTED FROZEN BEEF SEVERAL YEARS BEFORE, AN UPROAR HAD ENSUED.
THEY'D COMPLAINED TO THE EXPORTING COMPANY, BUT...
<No idea. Not a clue.>
MEAN-WHILE...
... SHIKAYO, WHO'D BEEN THE ONE TO FIND THE RAT...
...WAS SCOLDED BY HER BOSS, AS IF SHE WERE TO BLAME.

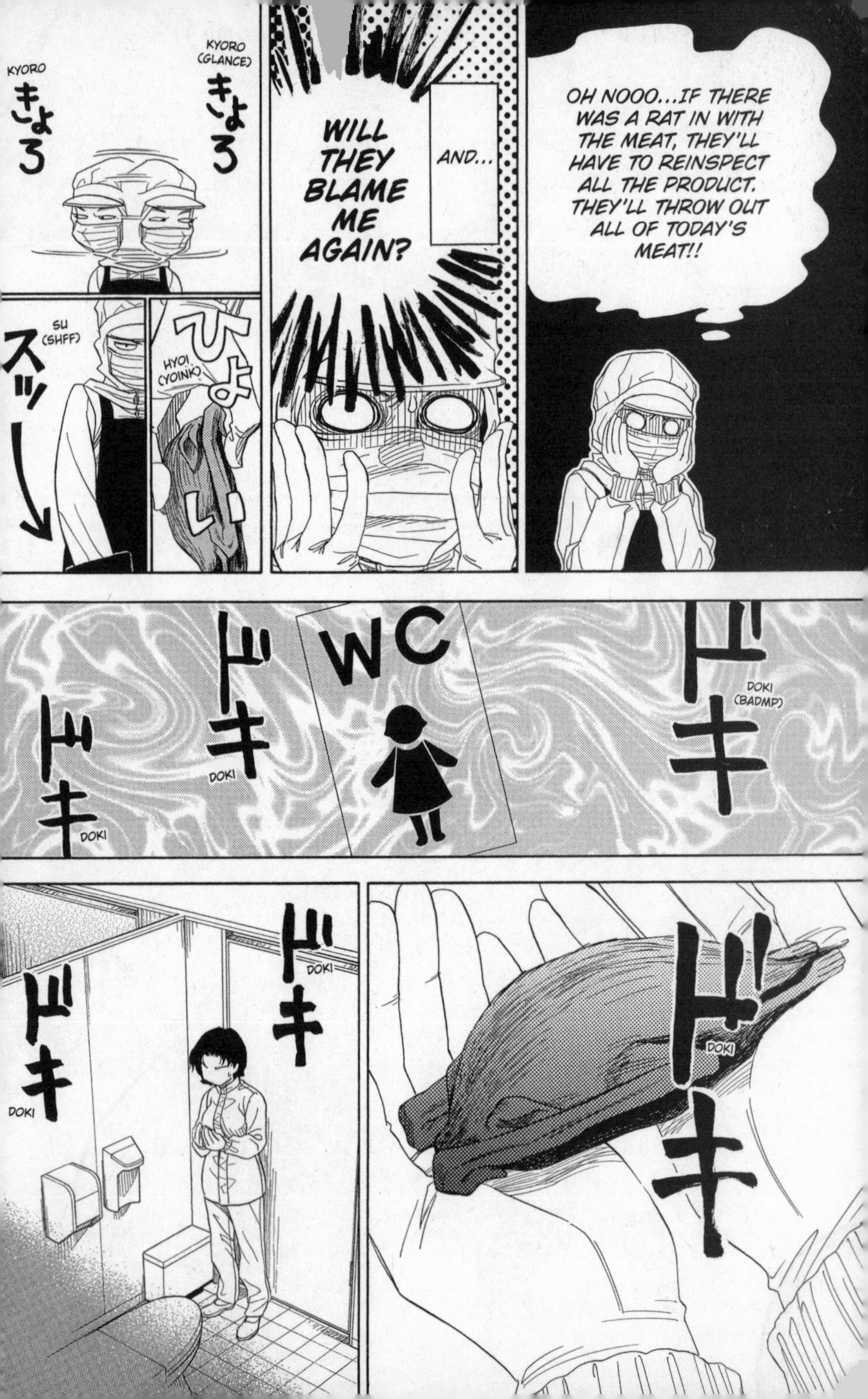

OH NOOO...IF THERE WAS A RAT IN WITH THE MEAT, THEY'LL HAVE TO REINSPECT ALL THE PRODUCT. THEY'LL THROW OUT ALL OF TODAY'S MEAT!!
AND...
WILL THEY BLAME ME AGAIN?
きょろ
KYORO (GLANCE)
きょろ
KYORO
ひょい
HYOI (YOINK)
スッ
SU (SHFF)
ドキ
DOKI (BADMP)
WC
ドキ
DOKI
ドキ
DOKI
ドキ
DOKI
ドキ
DOKI
ドキ
DOKI

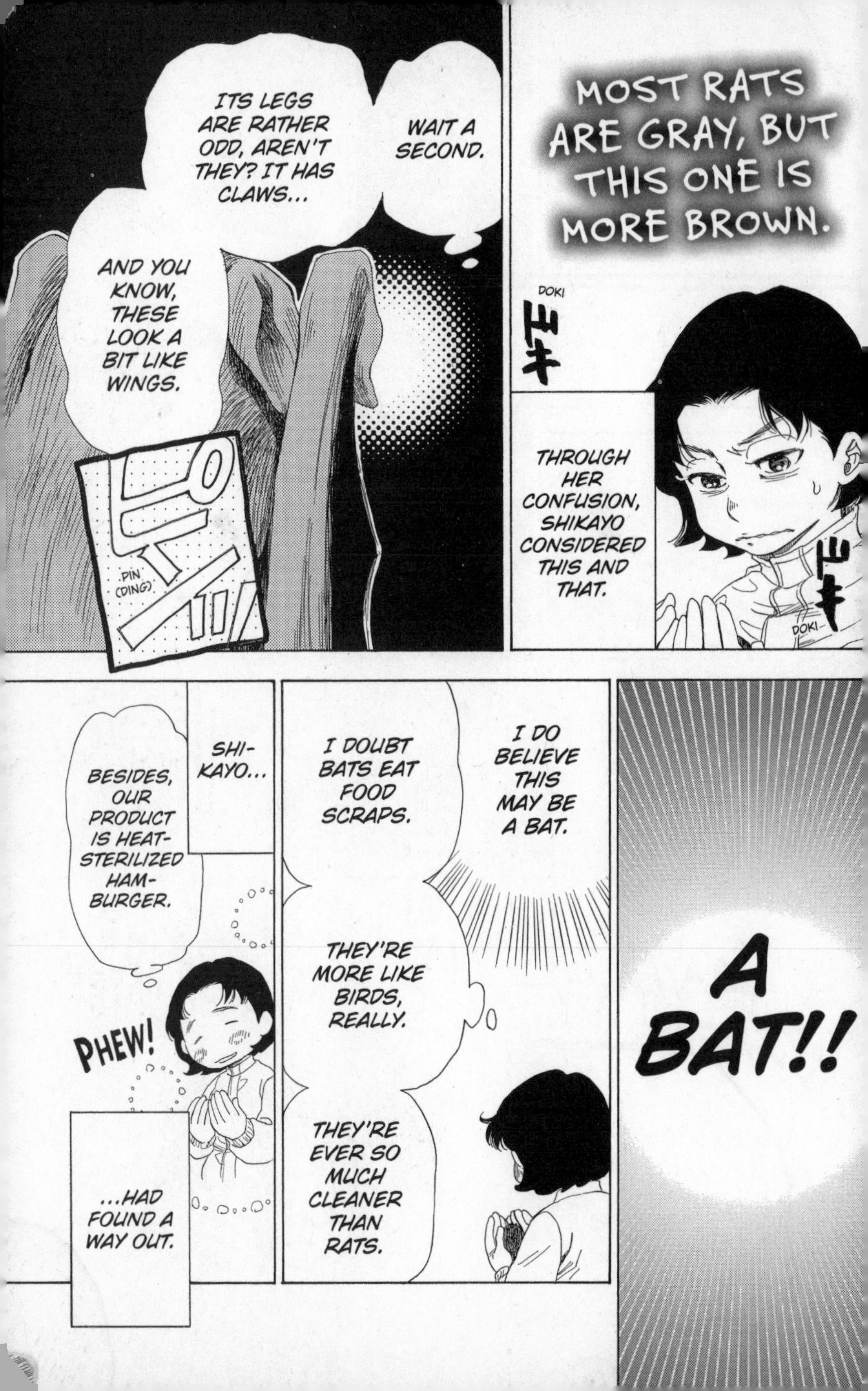
MOST RATS ARE GRAY, BUT THIS ONE IS MORE BROWN.
DOKI
THROUGH HER CONFUSION, SHIKAYO CONSIDERED THIS AND THAT.
DOKI
WAIT A SECOND.
ITS LEGS ARE RATHER ODD, AREN'T THEY? IT HAS CLAWS...
AND YOU KNOW, THESE LOOK A BIT LIKE WINGS.
PIN (DING)
A BAT!!
I DO BELIEVE THIS MAY BE A BAT.
I DOUBT BATS EAT FOOD SCRAPS.
THEY'RE MORE LIKE BIRDS, REALLY.
THEY'RE EVER SO MUCH CLEANER THAN RATS.
SHI-KAYO...
BESIDES, OUR PRODUCT IS HEAT-STERILIZED HAM-BURGER.
PHEW!
...HAD FOUND A WAY OUT.

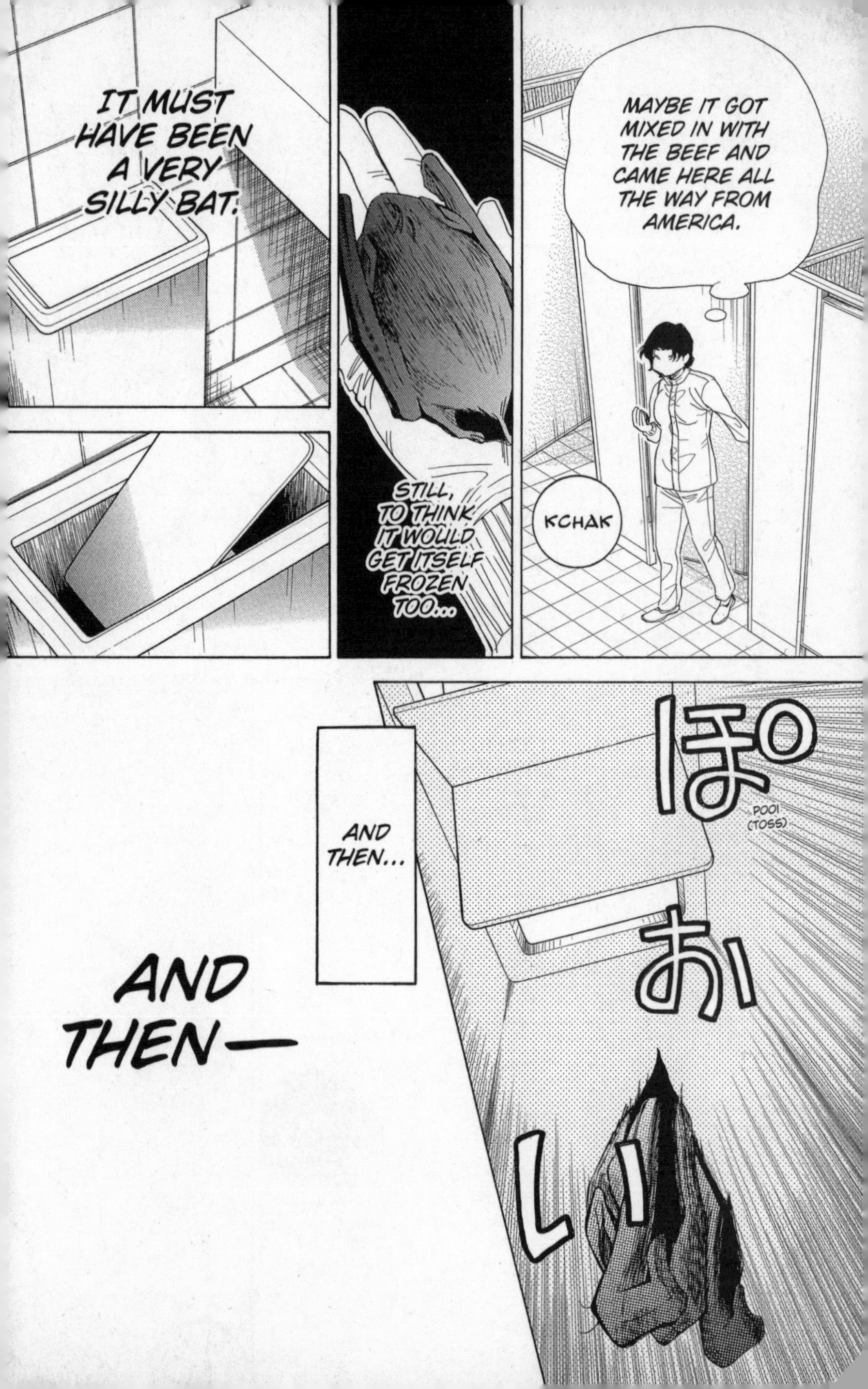
MAYBE IT GOT MIXED IN WITH THE BEEF AND CAME HERE ALL THE WAY FROM AMERICA.
KCHAK
STILL, TO THINK IT WOULD GET ITSELF FROZEN TOO...
IT MUST HAVE BEEN A VERY SILLY BAT.
ぽおい
POOI (TOSS)
AND THEN...
AND THEN—

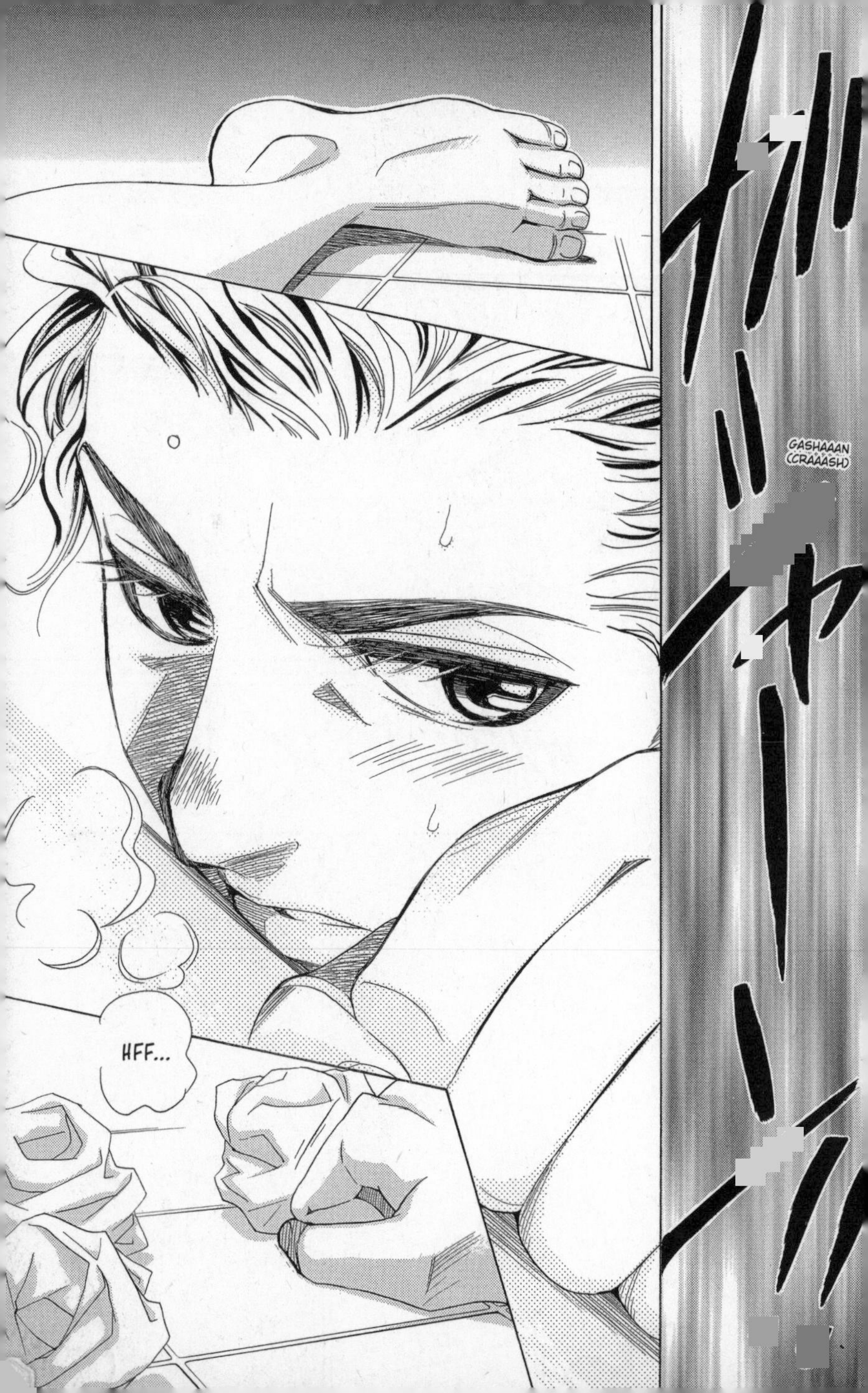
GASHAAAN (CRAAASH)
HFF...

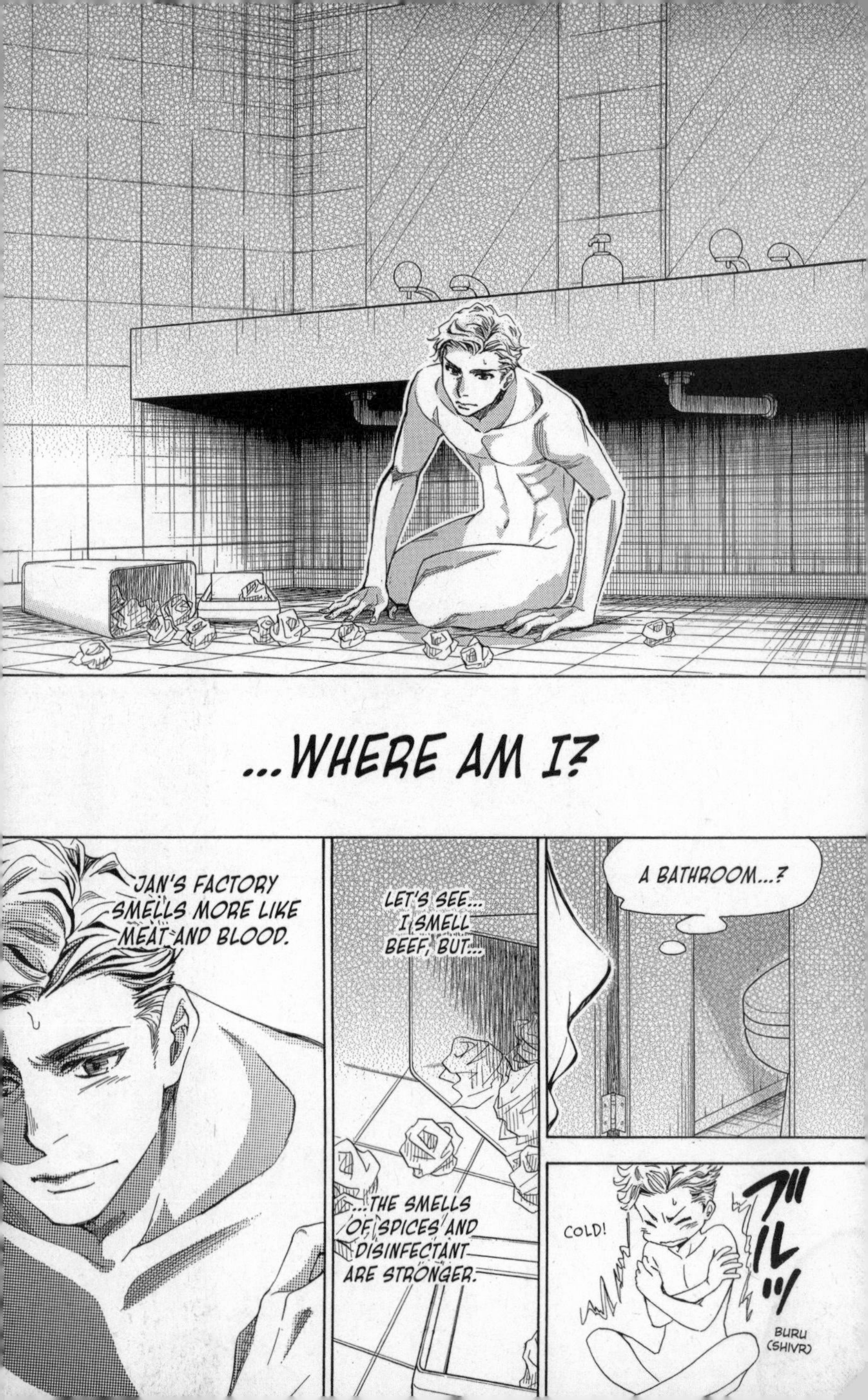
...WHERE AM I?
A BATHROOM...?
COLD!
ブルッ
BURU (SHIVR)
LET'S SEE... I SMELL BEEF, BUT...
...THE SMELLS OF SPICES AND DISINFECTANT ARE STRONGER.
JAN'S FACTORY SMELLS MORE LIKE MEAT AND BLOOD.

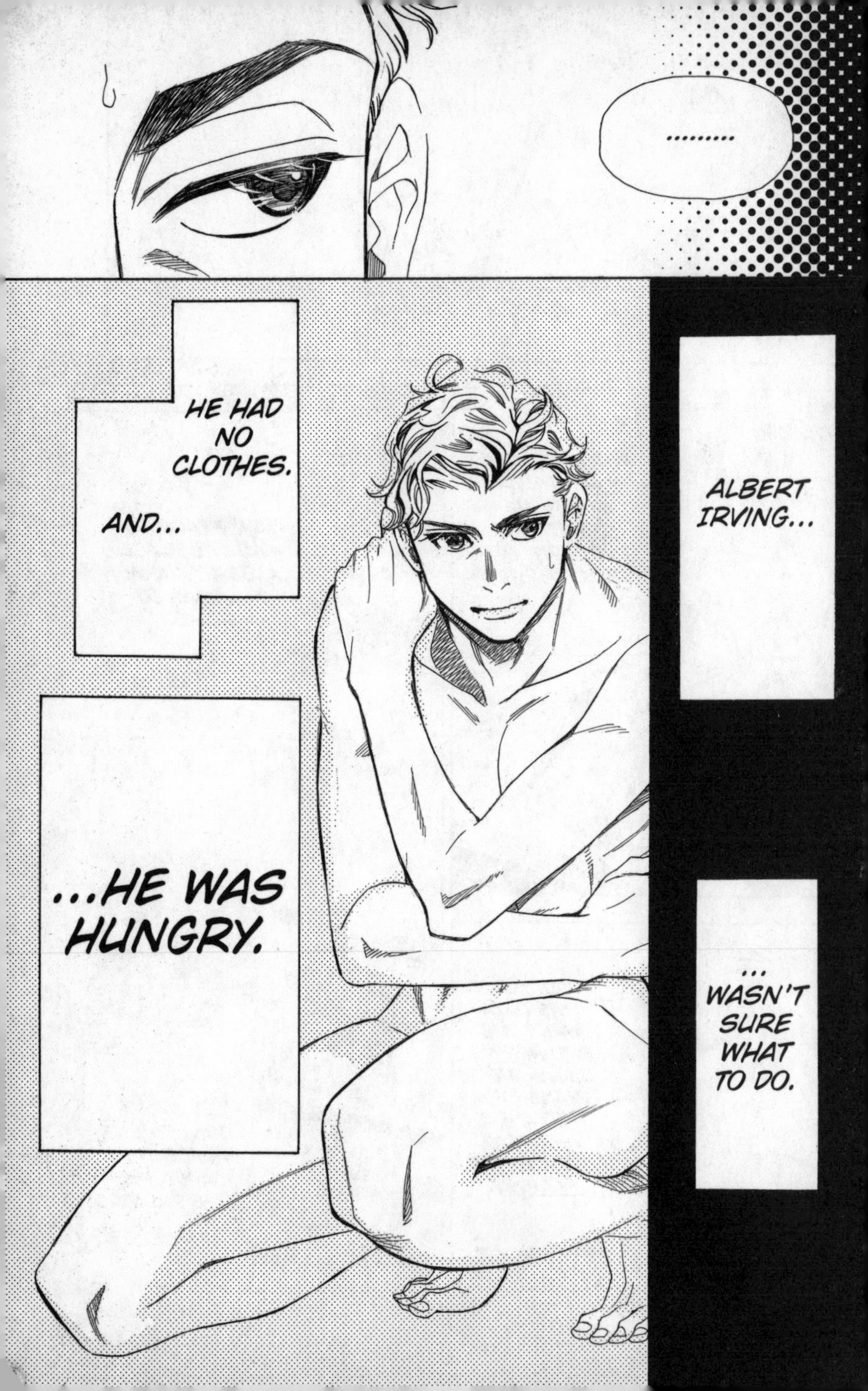
....
ALBERT IRVING...
...WASN'T SURE WHAT TO DO.
HE HAD NO CLOTHES.
AND...
...HE WAS HUNGRY.

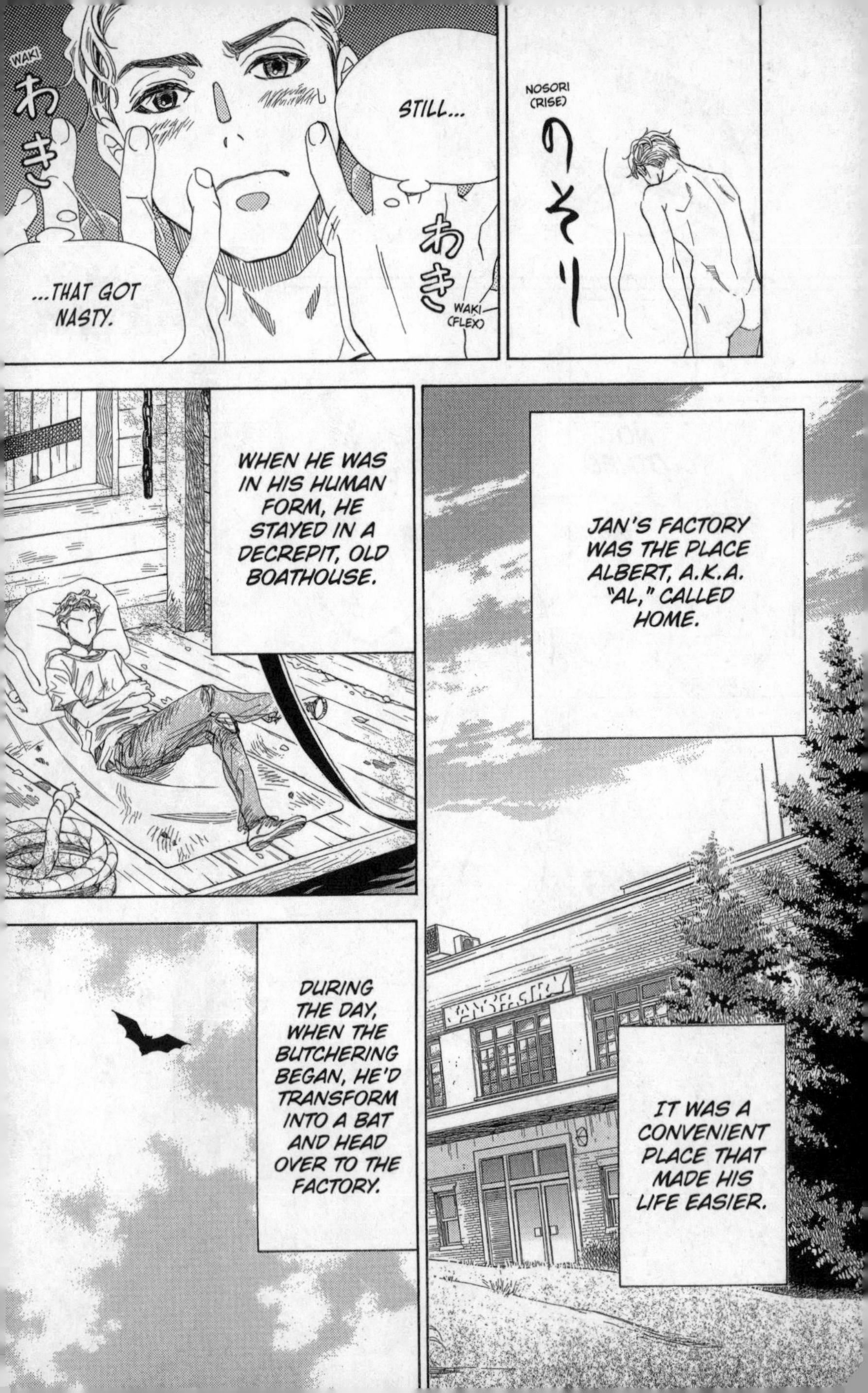
のそり
NOSORI (RISE)
STILL...
わき
WAKI (FLEX)
わき
WAKI
...THAT GOT NASTY.
JAN'S FACTORY WAS THE PLACE ALBERT, A.K.A. "AL," CALLED HOME.
IT WAS A CONVENIENT PLACE THAT MADE HIS LIFE EASIER.
WHEN HE WAS IN HIS HUMAN FORM, HE STAYED IN A DECREPIT, OLD BOATHOUSE.
DURING THE DAY, WHEN THE BUTCHERING BEGAN, HE'D TRANSFORM INTO A BAT AND HEAD OVER TO THE FACTORY.

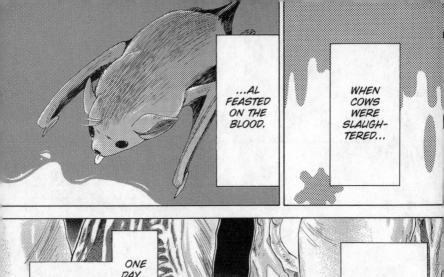

WHEN COWS WERE SLAUGH-TERED...

...AL FEASTED ON THE BLOOD.

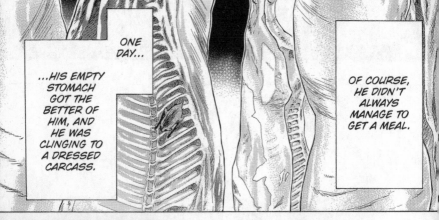

OF COURSE, HE DIDN'T ALWAYS MANAGE TO GET A MEAL.

ONE DAY...

...HIS EMPTY STOMACH GOT THE BETTER OF HIM, AND HE WAS CLINGING TO A DRESSED CARCASS.

LUCKILY, HE WASN'T SPOTTED...

...BUT THEY STARTED BUTCHER-ING THE CARCASS...

DAM

DAM

AND SO...

DAM!

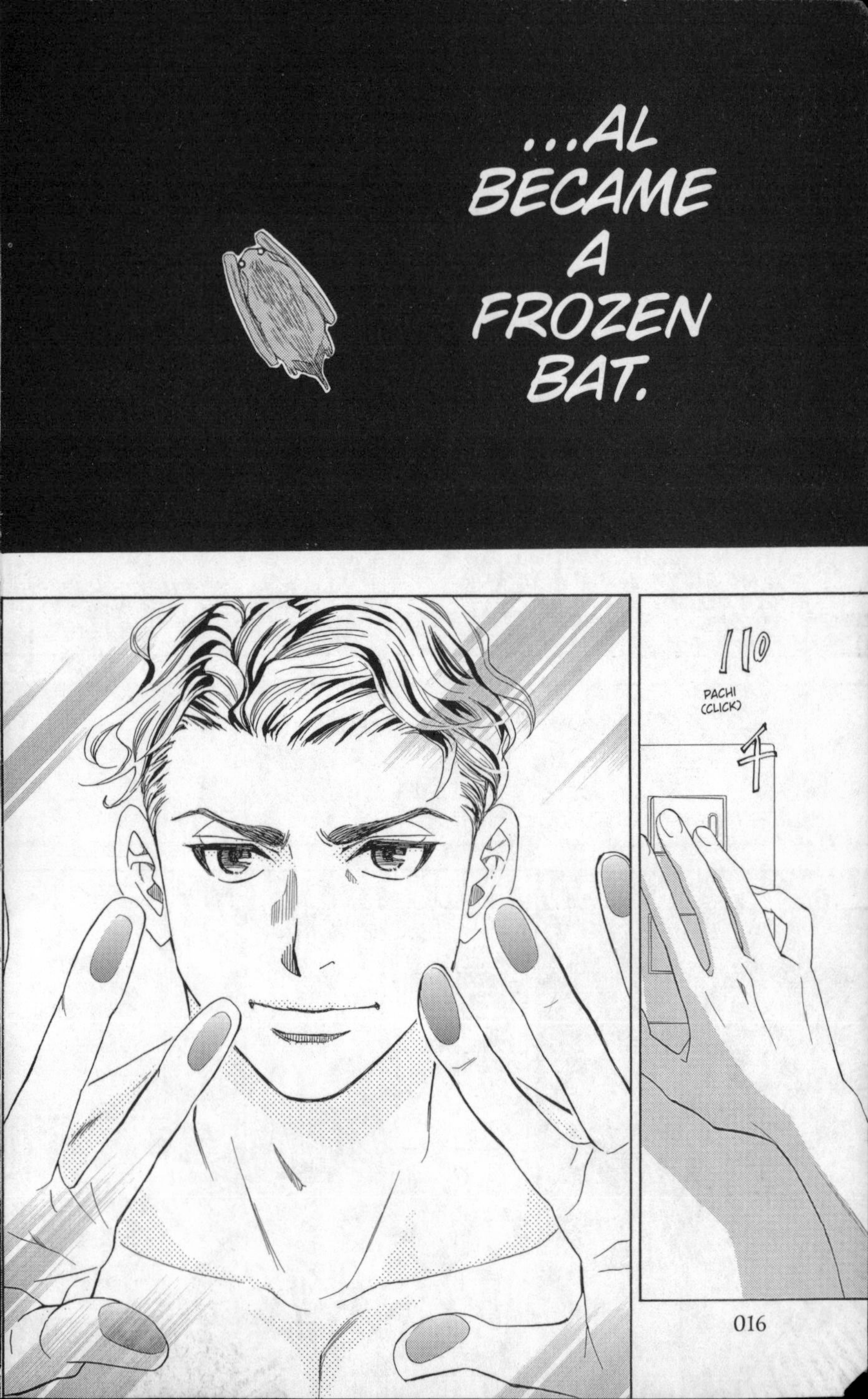
...AL BECAME A FROZEN BAT.
PACHI (CLICK)

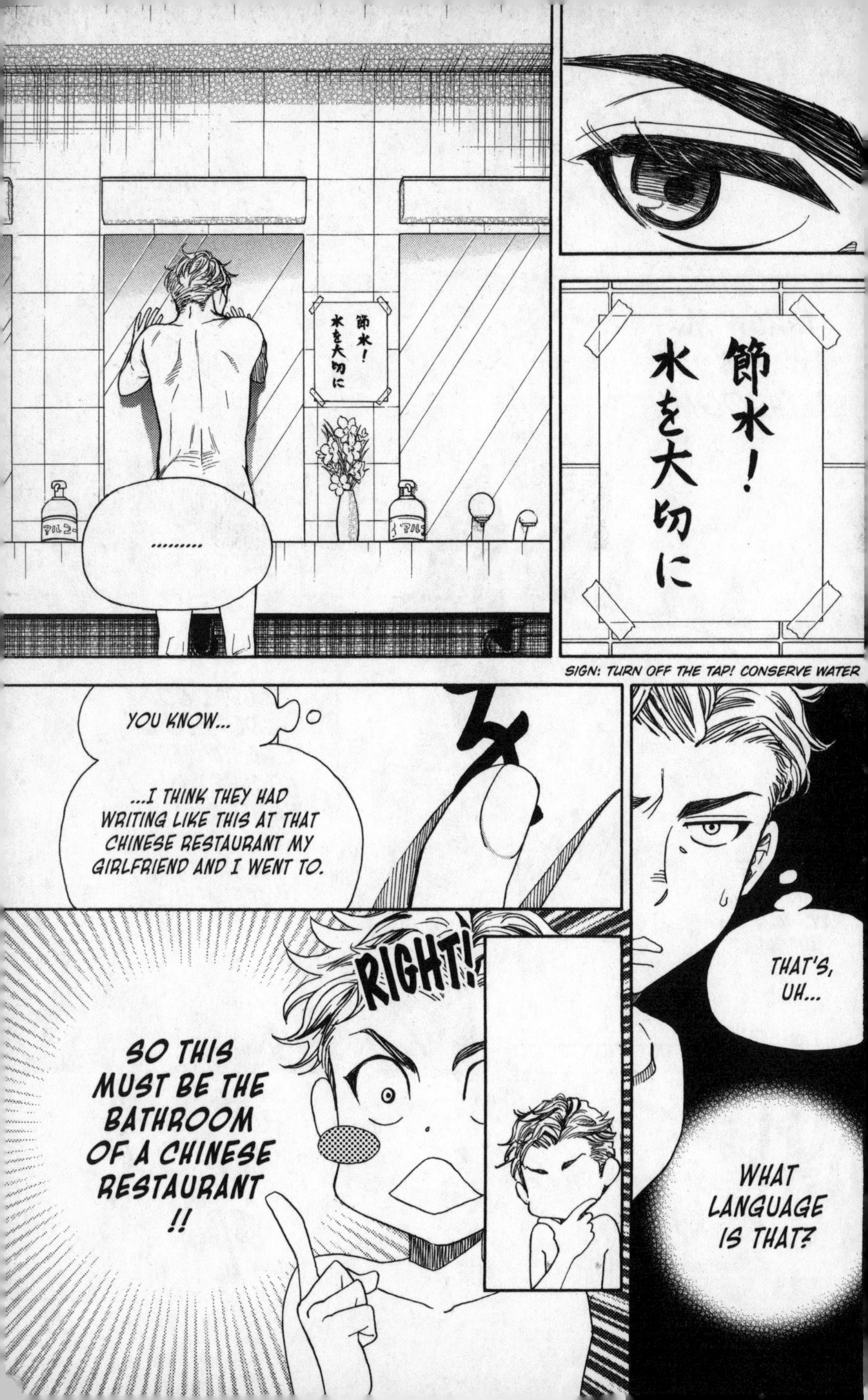
節水！
水を大切に
節水！
水を大切に
....
SIGN: TURN OFF THE TAP! CONSERVE WATER
THAT'S, UH...
WHAT LANGUAGE IS THAT?
YOU KNOW...
...I THINK THEY HAD WRITING LIKE THIS AT THAT CHINESE RESTAURANT MY GIRLFRIEND AND I WENT TO.
RIGHT!
SO THIS MUST BE THE BATHROOM OF A CHINESE RESTAURANT !!

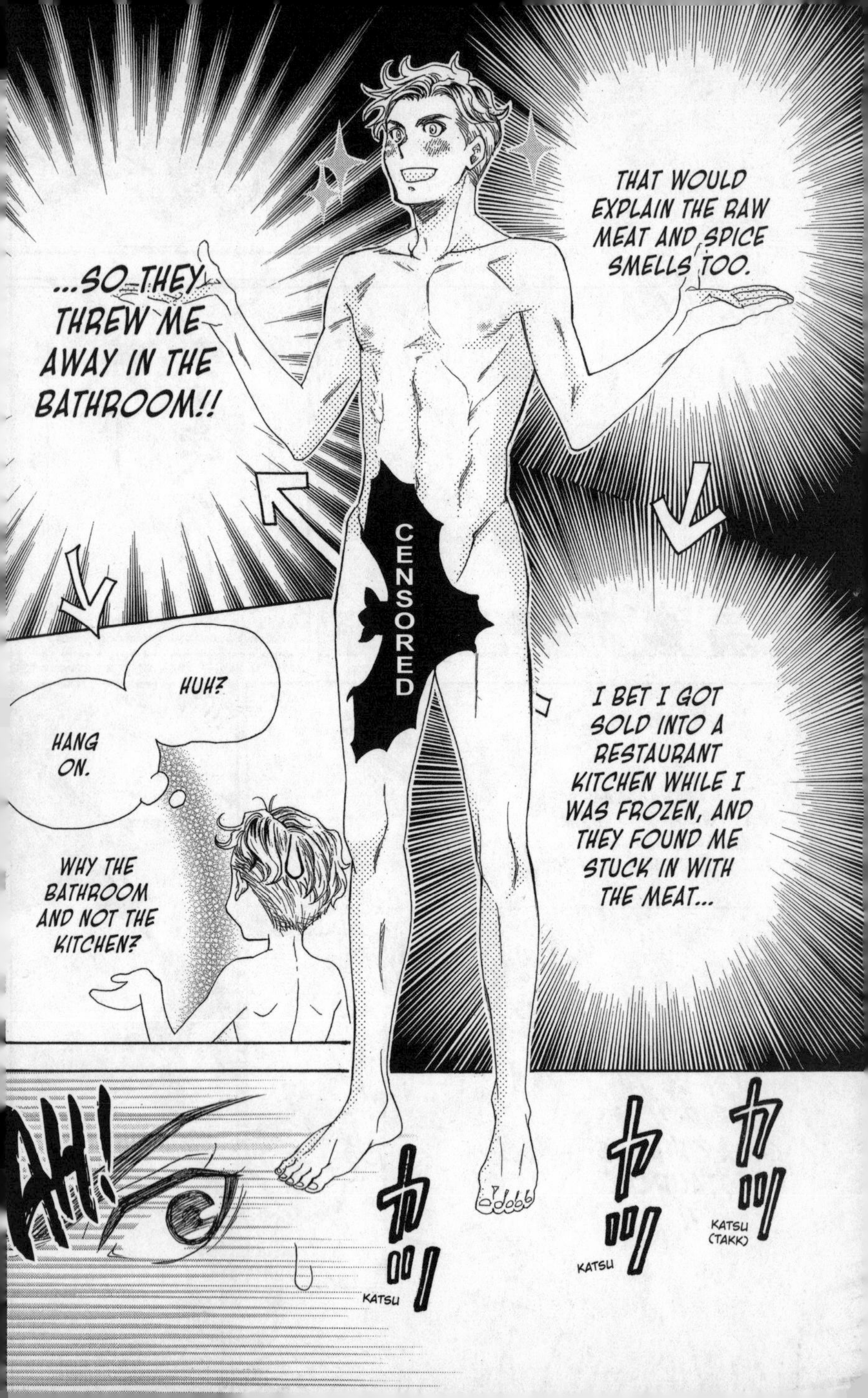
THAT WOULD EXPLAIN THE RAW MEAT AND SPICE SMELLS TOO.
...SO THEY THREW ME AWAY IN THE BATHROOM!!
CENSORED
I BET I GOT SOLD INTO A RESTAURANT KITCHEN WHILE I WAS FROZEN, AND THEY FOUND ME STUCK IN WITH THE MEAT...
HUH?
HANG ON.
WHY THE BATHROOM AND NOT THE KITCHEN?
KATSU (TAKK)
KATSU
KATSU
AH!

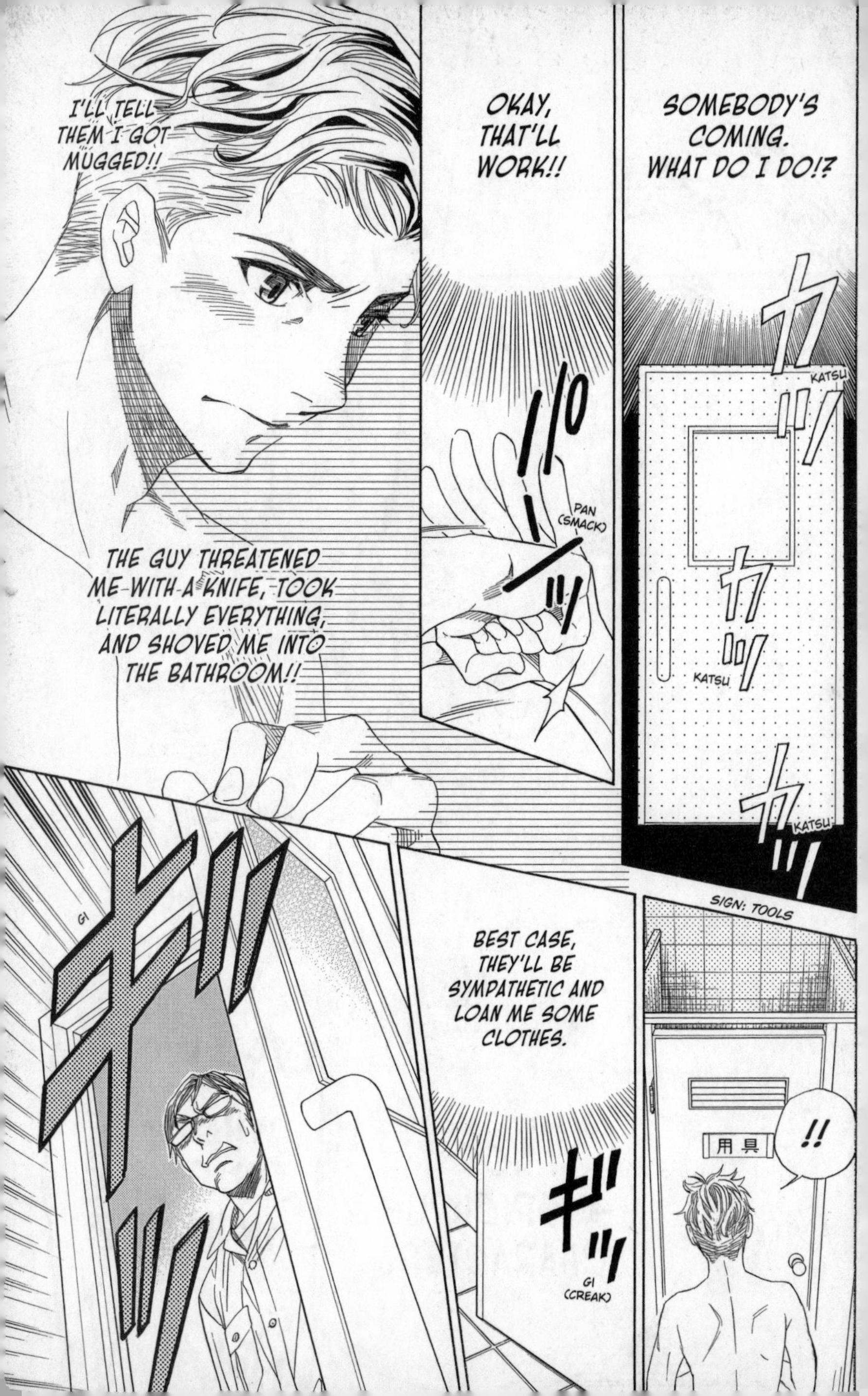
SOMEBODY'S COMING. WHAT DO I DO!?
KATSU
KATSU
KATSU
OKAY, THAT'LL WORK!!
PAN (SMACK)
I'LL TELL THEM I GOT MUGGED!!
THE GUY THREATENED ME WITH A KNIFE, TOOK LITERALLY EVERYTHING, AND SHOVED ME INTO THE BATHROOM!!
SIGN: TOOLS
用具
!!
BEST CASE, THEY'LL BE SYMPATHETIC AND LOAN ME SOME CLOTHES.
GI (CREAK)
GI

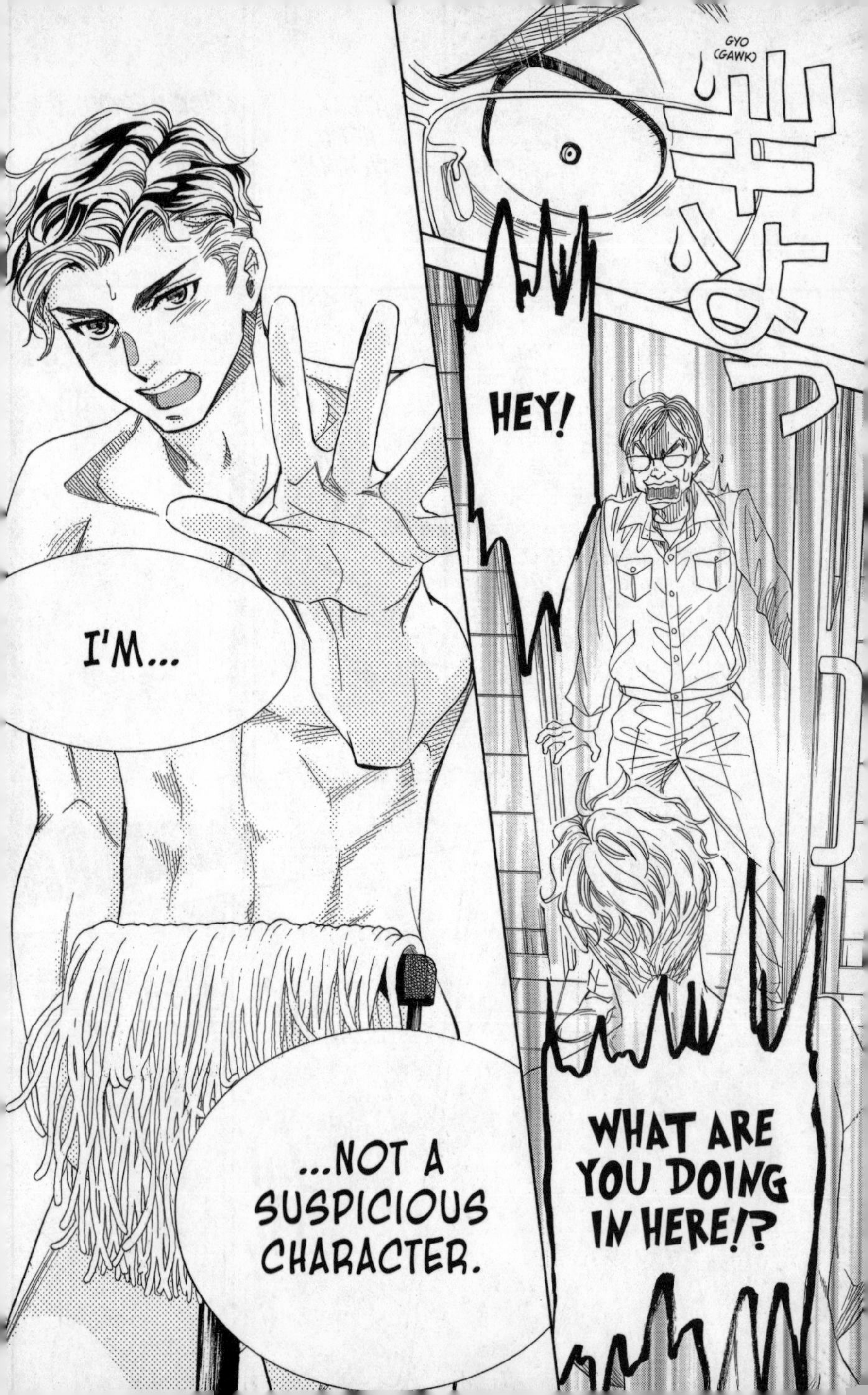
GYO (GAWK)
ギョッ
HEY!
WHAT ARE YOU DOING IN HERE!?
I'M...
...NOT A SUSPICIOUS CHARACTER.

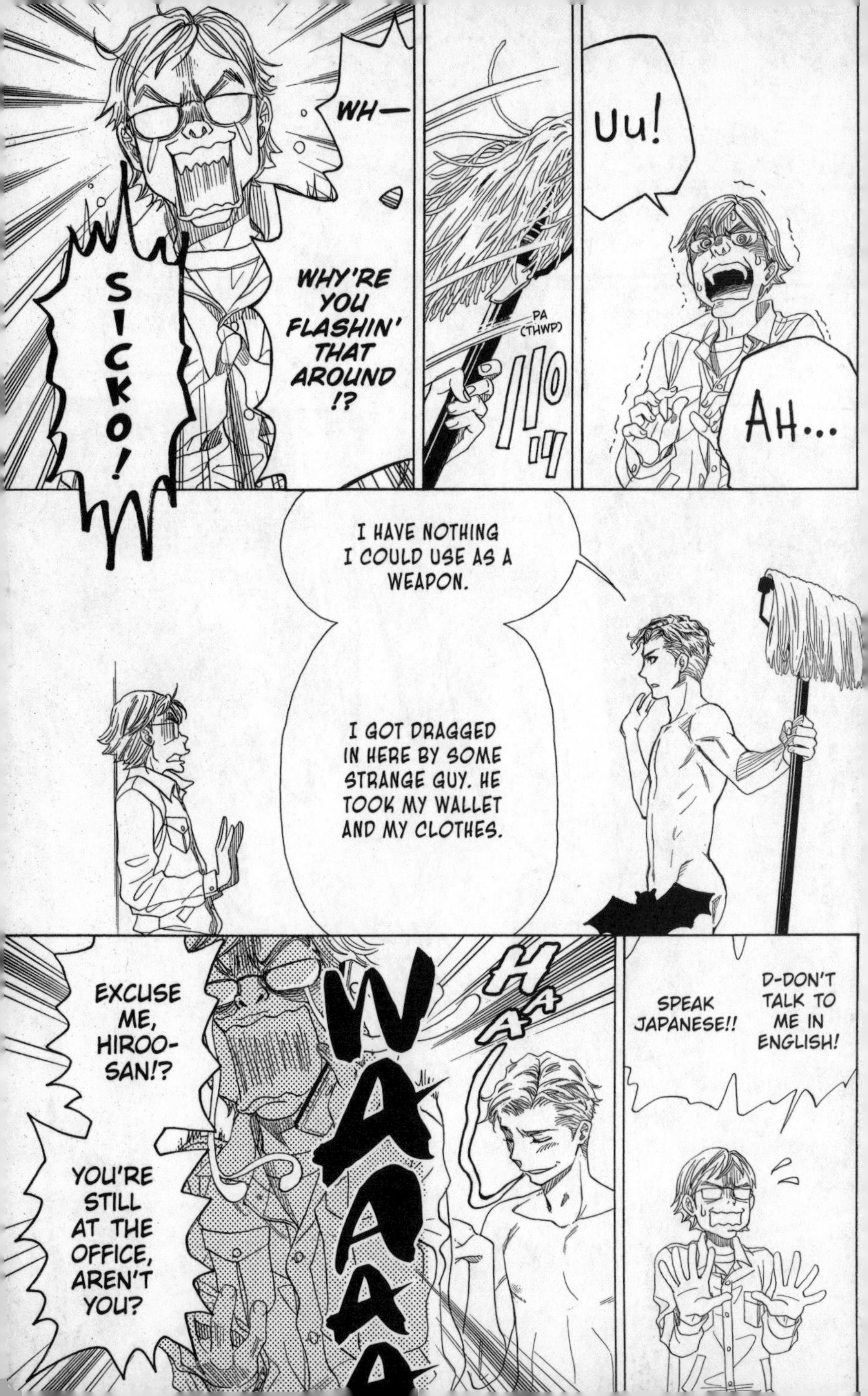
Uu!
AH...
PA
(THWP)
WH—
WHY'RE YOU FLASHIN' THAT AROUND!?
SICKO!
I HAVE NOTHING I COULD USE AS A WEAPON.
I GOT DRAGGED IN HERE BY SOME STRANGE GUY. HE TOOK MY WALLET AND MY CLOTHES.
D-DON'T TALK TO ME IN ENGLISH!
SPEAK JAPANESE!!
HAHA
WAAAA
EXCUSE ME, HIROO-SAN!?
YOU'RE STILL AT THE OFFICE, AREN'T YOU?

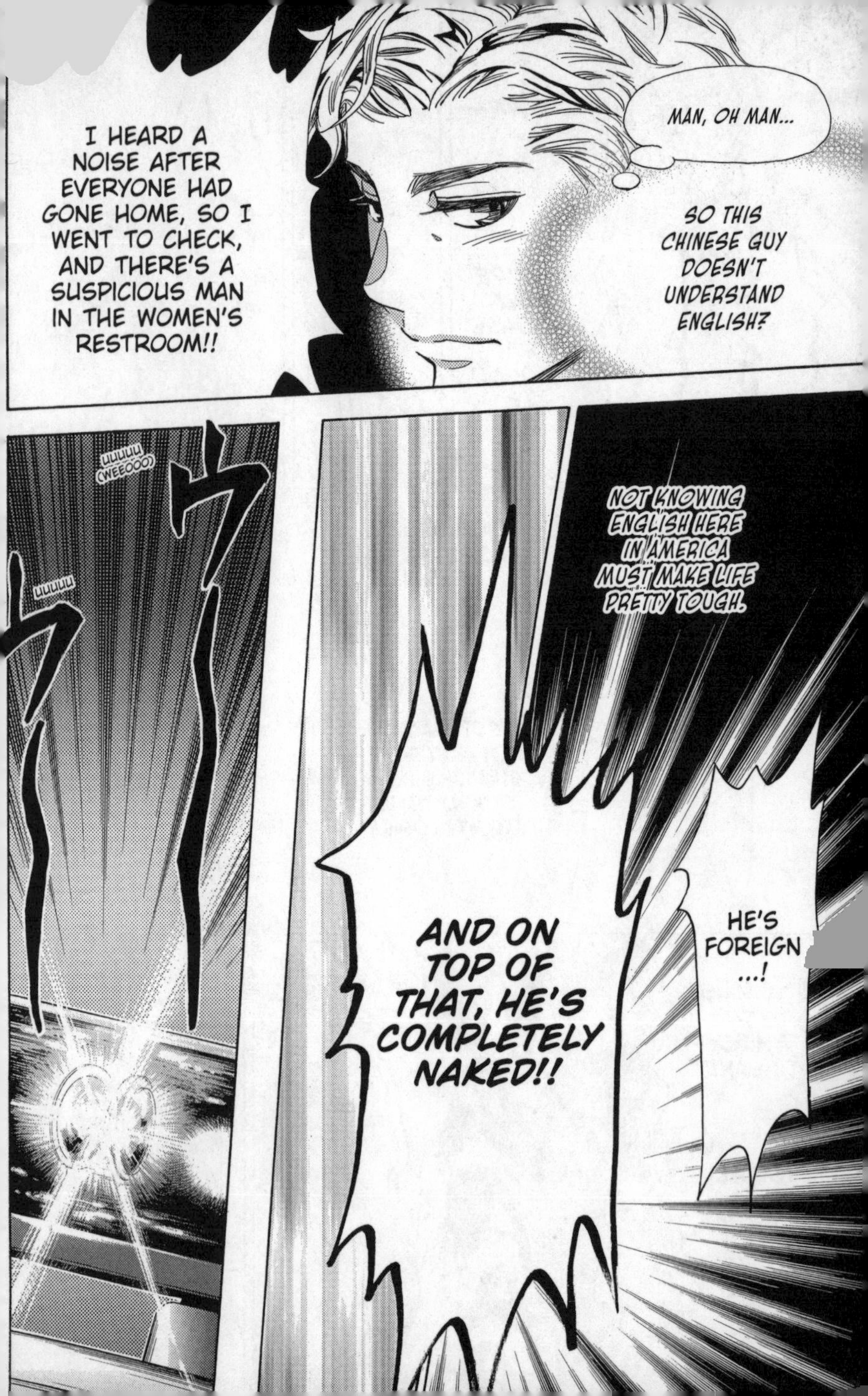
MAN, OH MAN...
SO THIS CHINESE GUY DOESN'T UNDERSTAND ENGLISH?
I HEARD A NOISE AFTER EVERYONE HAD GONE HOME, SO I WENT TO CHECK, AND THERE'S A SUSPICIOUS MAN IN THE WOMEN'S RESTROOM!!
NOT KNOWING ENGLISH HERE IN AMERICA MUST MAKE LIFE PRETTY TOUGH.
HE'S FOREIGN ...!
AND ON TOP OF THAT, HE'S COMPLETELY NAKED!!
uuuuu (WEEOOO)
uuuuu

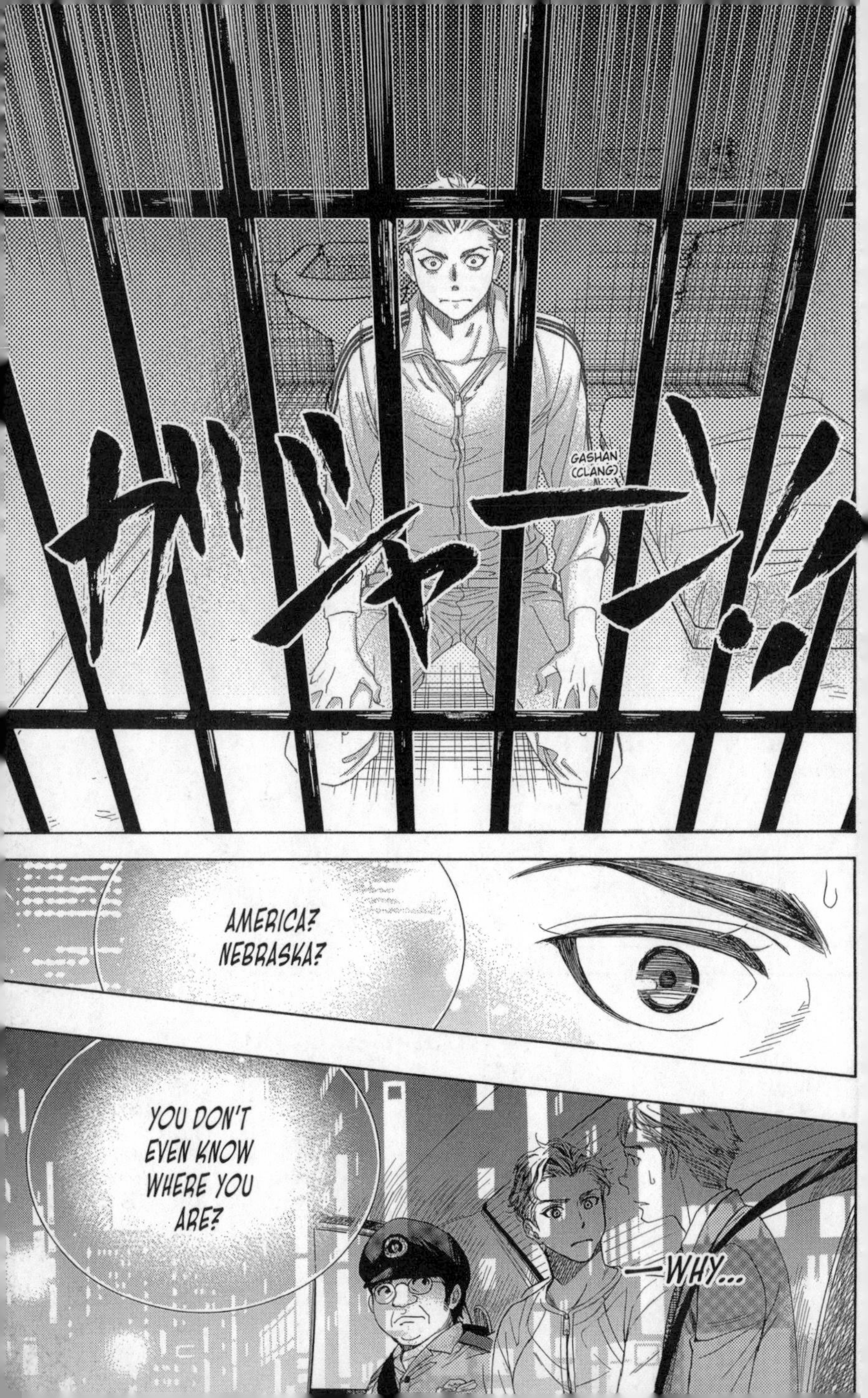
GASHAN (CLANG)
AMERICA? NEBRASKA?
YOU DON'T EVEN KNOW WHERE YOU ARE?
—WHY...

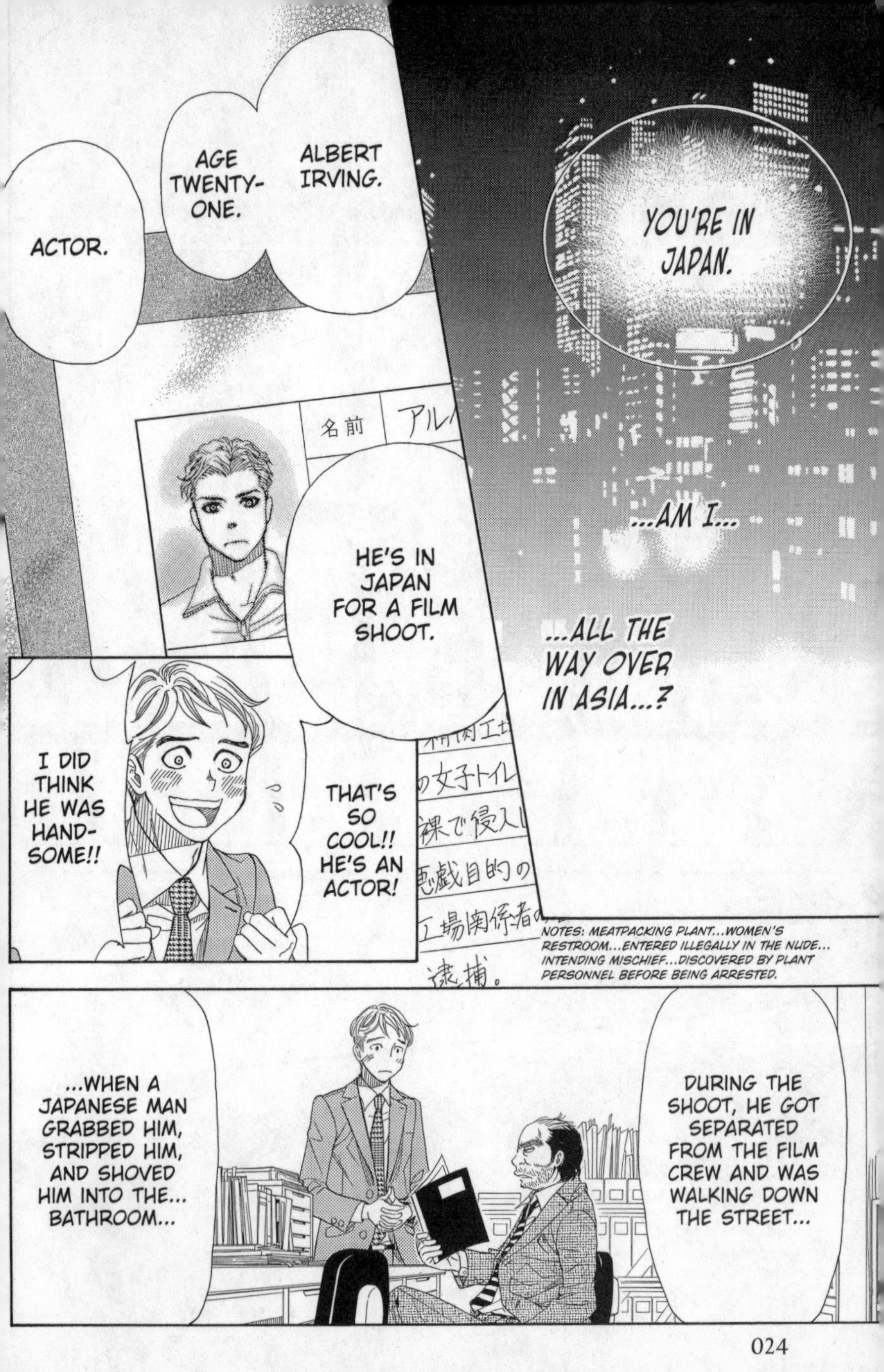
YOU'RE IN JAPAN.
...AM I...
...ALL THE WAY OVER IN ASIA...?
ALBERT IRVING.
AGE TWENTY-ONE.
ACTOR.
名前
HE'S IN JAPAN FOR A FILM SHOOT.
THAT'S SO COOL!! HE'S AN ACTOR!
I DID THINK HE WAS HANDSOME!!
NOTES: MEATPACKING PLANT...WOMEN'S RESTROOM...ENTERED ILLEGALLY IN THE NUDE... INTENDING MISCHIEF...DISCOVERED BY PLANT PERSONNEL BEFORE BEING ARRESTED.
DURING THE SHOOT, HE GOT SEPARATED FROM THE FILM CREW AND WAS WALKING DOWN THE STREET...
...WHEN A JAPANESE MAN GRABBED HIM, STRIPPED HIM, AND SHOVED HIM INTO THE... BATHROOM...

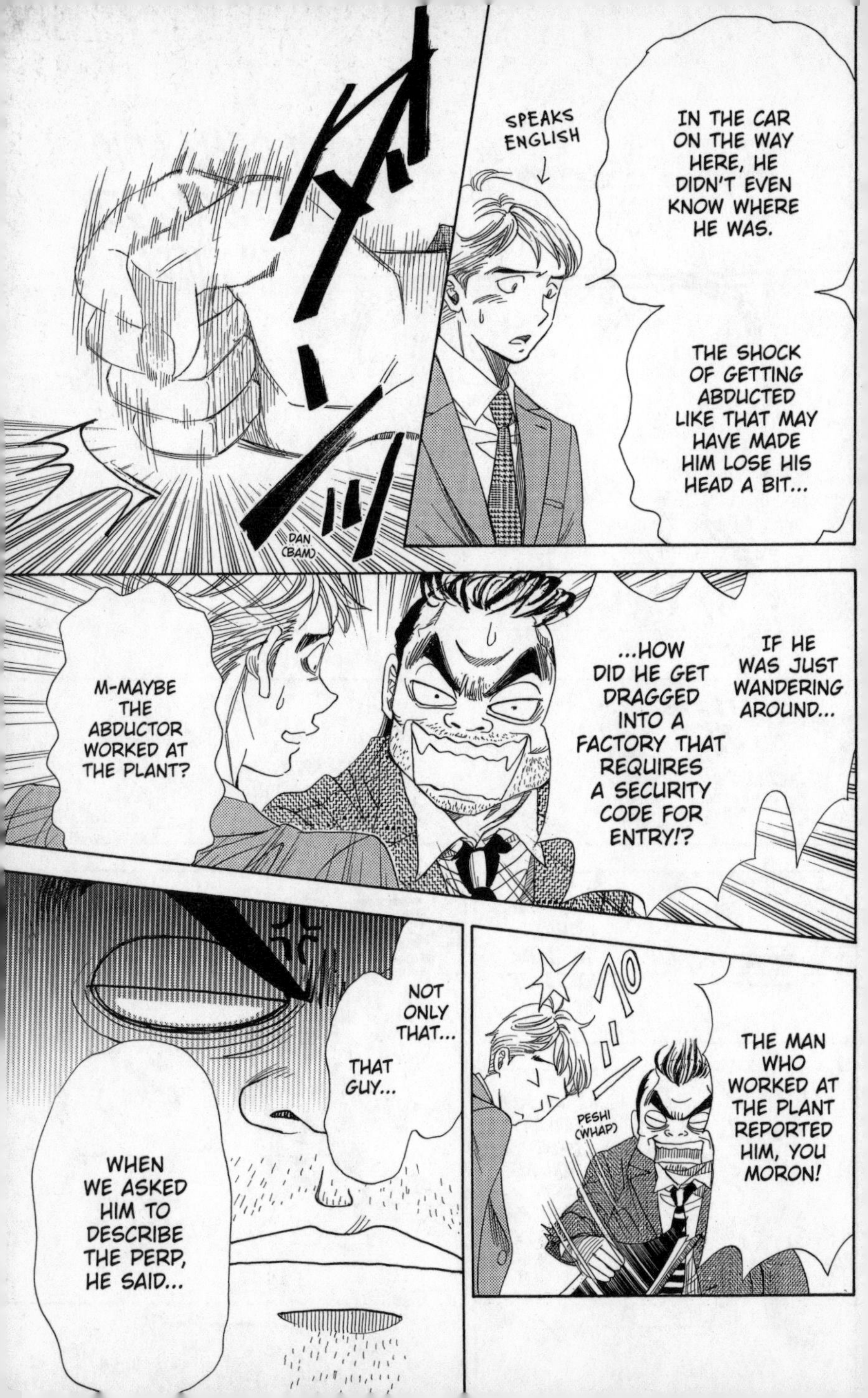

SPEAKS ENGLISH
IN THE CAR ON THE WAY HERE, HE DIDN'T EVEN KNOW WHERE HE WAS.
THE SHOCK OF GETTING ABDUCTED LIKE THAT MAY HAVE MADE HIM LOSE HIS HEAD A BIT...
DAN (BAM)
IF HE WAS JUST WANDERING AROUND...
...HOW DID HE GET DRAGGED INTO A FACTORY THAT REQUIRES A SECURITY CODE FOR ENTRY!?
M-MAYBE THE ABDUCTOR WORKED AT THE PLANT?
THE MAN WHO WORKED AT THE PLANT REPORTED HIM, YOU MORON!
PESHI (WHAP)
NOT ONLY THAT...
THAT GUY...
WHEN WE ASKED HIM TO DESCRIBE THE PERP, HE SAID...

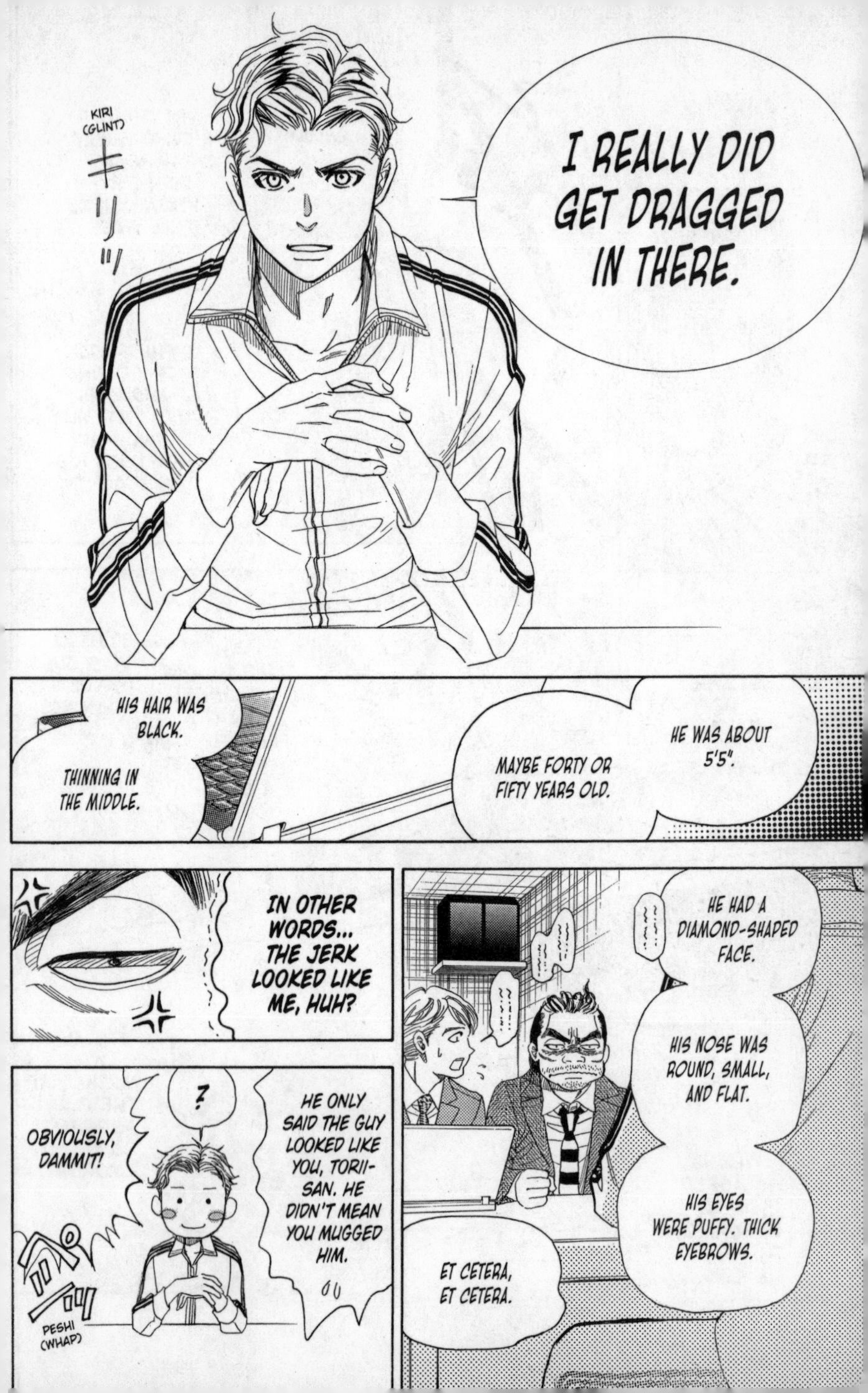
I REALLY DID GET DRAGGED IN THERE.
KIRI (GLINT)
HE WAS ABOUT 5'5".
MAYBE FORTY OR FIFTY YEARS OLD.
HIS HAIR WAS BLACK.
THINNING IN THE MIDDLE.
HE HAD A DIAMOND-SHAPED FACE.
HIS NOSE WAS ROUND, SMALL, AND FLAT.
HIS EYES WERE PUFFY. THICK EYEBROWS.
ET CETERA, ET CETERA.
IN OTHER WORDS... THE JERK LOOKED LIKE ME, HUH?
HE ONLY SAID THE GUY LOOKED LIKE YOU, TORII-SAN. HE DIDN'T MEAN YOU MUGGED HIM.
?
OBVIOUSLY, DAMMIT!
PESHI (WHAP)

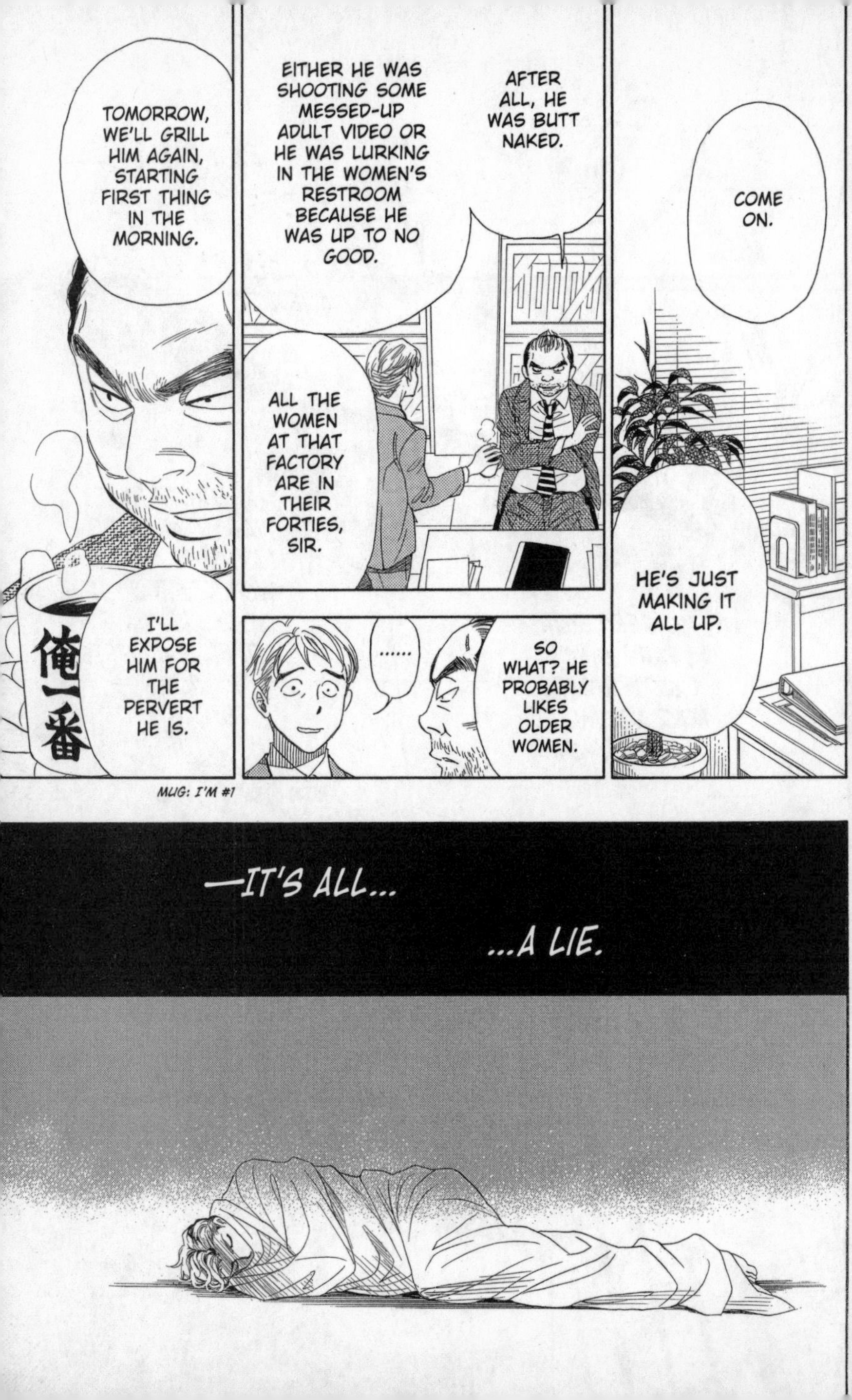
COME ON.
HE'S JUST MAKING IT ALL UP.
AFTER ALL, HE WAS BUTT NAKED.
EITHER HE WAS SHOOTING SOME MESSED-UP ADULT VIDEO OR HE WAS LURKING IN THE WOMEN'S RESTROOM BECAUSE HE WAS UP TO NO GOOD.
ALL THE WOMEN AT THAT FACTORY ARE IN THEIR FORTIES, SIR.
SO WHAT? HE PROBABLY LIKES OLDER WOMEN.
......
TOMORROW, WE'LL GRILL HIM AGAIN, STARTING FIRST THING IN THE MORNING.
I'LL EXPOSE HIM FOR THE PERVERT HE IS.
俺一番
MUG: I'M #1
—IT'S ALL...
...A LIE.

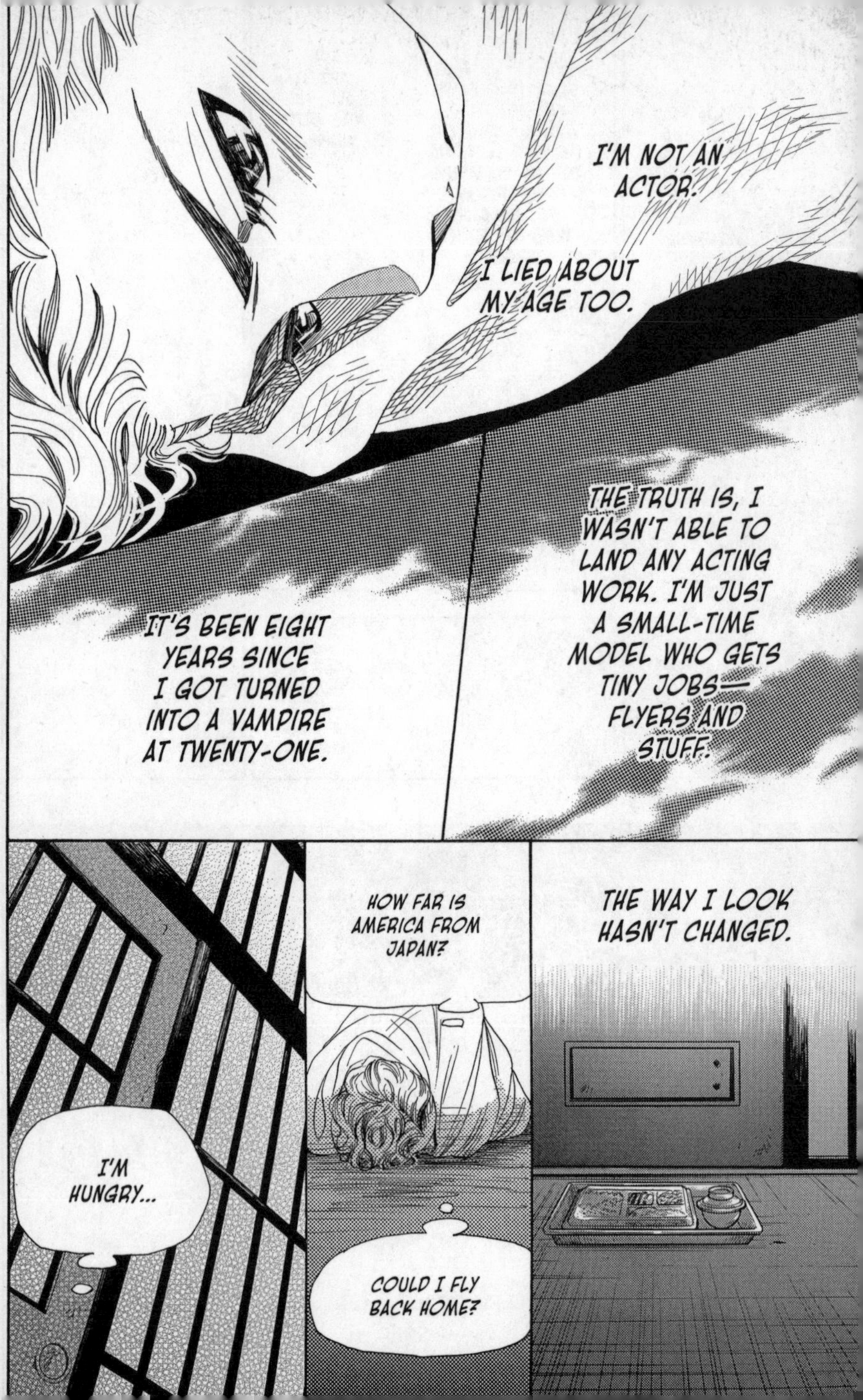
I'M NOT AN ACTOR.
I LIED ABOUT MY AGE TOO.
THE TRUTH IS, I WASN'T ABLE TO LAND ANY ACTING WORK. I'M JUST A SMALL-TIME MODEL WHO GETS TINY JOBS—FLYERS AND STUFF.
IT'S BEEN EIGHT YEARS SINCE I GOT TURNED INTO A VAMPIRE AT TWENTY-ONE.
THE WAY I LOOK HASN'T CHANGED.
HOW FAR IS AMERICA FROM JAPAN?
COULD I FLY BACK HOME?
I'M HUNGRY...

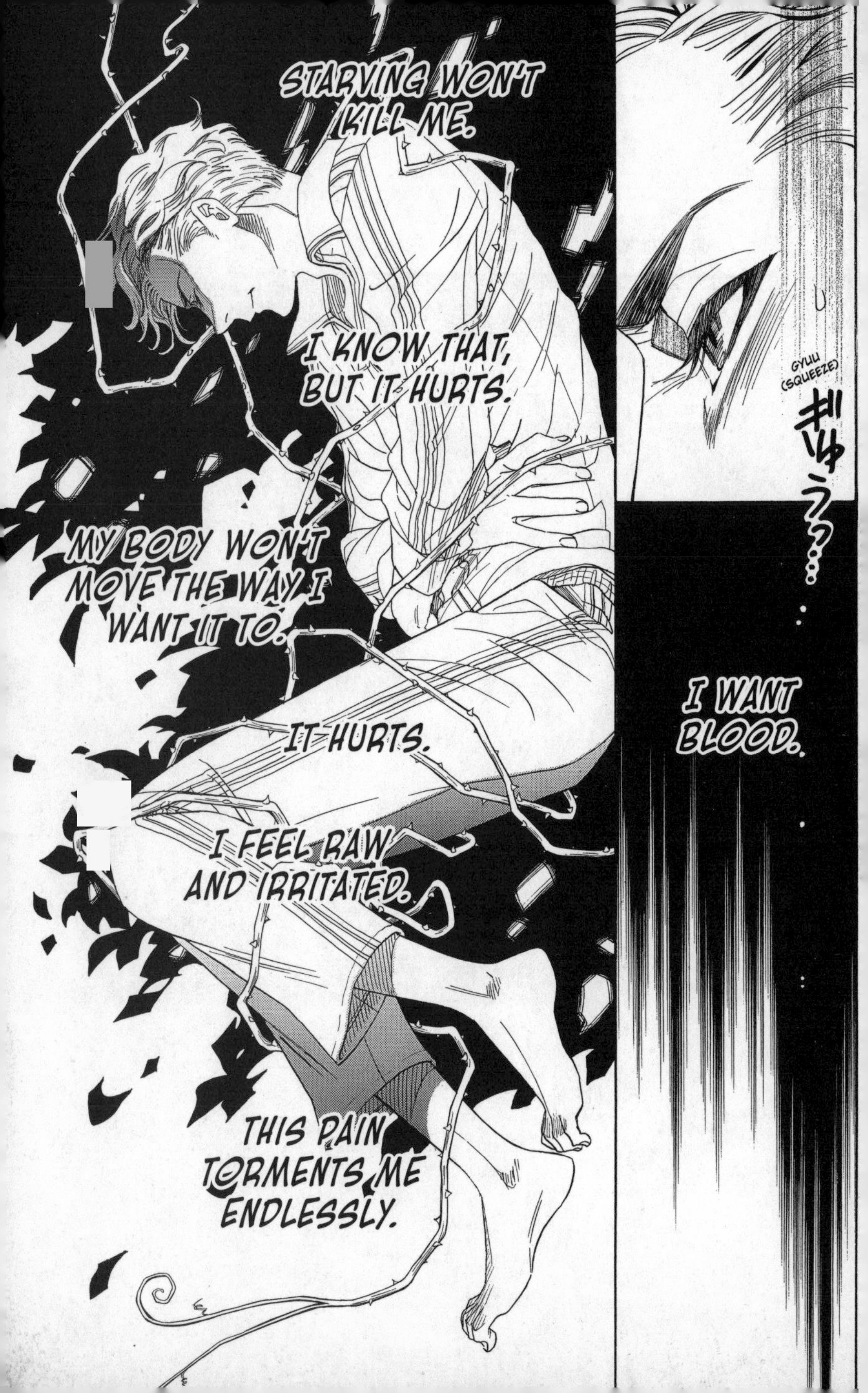
GYUU (SQUEEZE)
ぎゅうっ…
I WANT BLOOD.
STARVING WON'T KILL ME.
I KNOW THAT, BUT IT HURTS.
MY BODY WON'T MOVE THE WAY I WANT IT TO.
IT HURTS.
I FEEL RAW AND IRRITATED.
THIS PAIN TORMENTS ME ENDLESSLY.

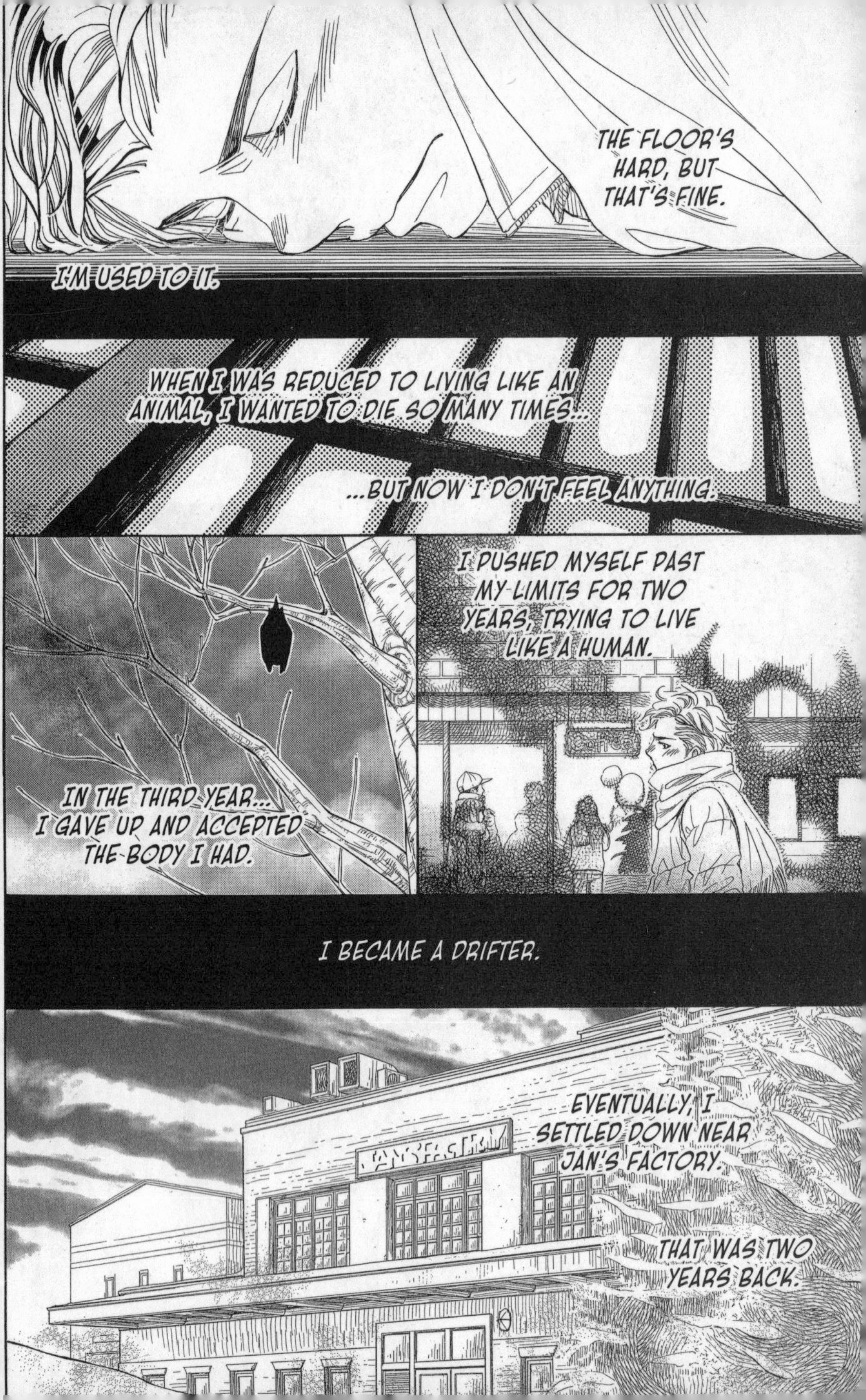
THE FLOOR'S HARD, BUT THAT'S FINE.
I'M USED TO IT.
WHEN I WAS REDUCED TO LIVING LIKE AN ANIMAL, I WANTED TO DIE SO MANY TIMES...
...BUT NOW I DON'T FEEL ANYTHING.
I PUSHED MYSELF PAST MY LIMITS FOR TWO YEARS, TRYING TO LIVE LIKE A HUMAN.
IN THE THIRD YEAR... I GAVE UP AND ACCEPTED THE BODY I HAD.
I BECAME A DRIFTER.
EVENTUALLY, I SETTLED DOWN NEAR JAN'S FACTORY.
THAT WAS TWO YEARS BACK.

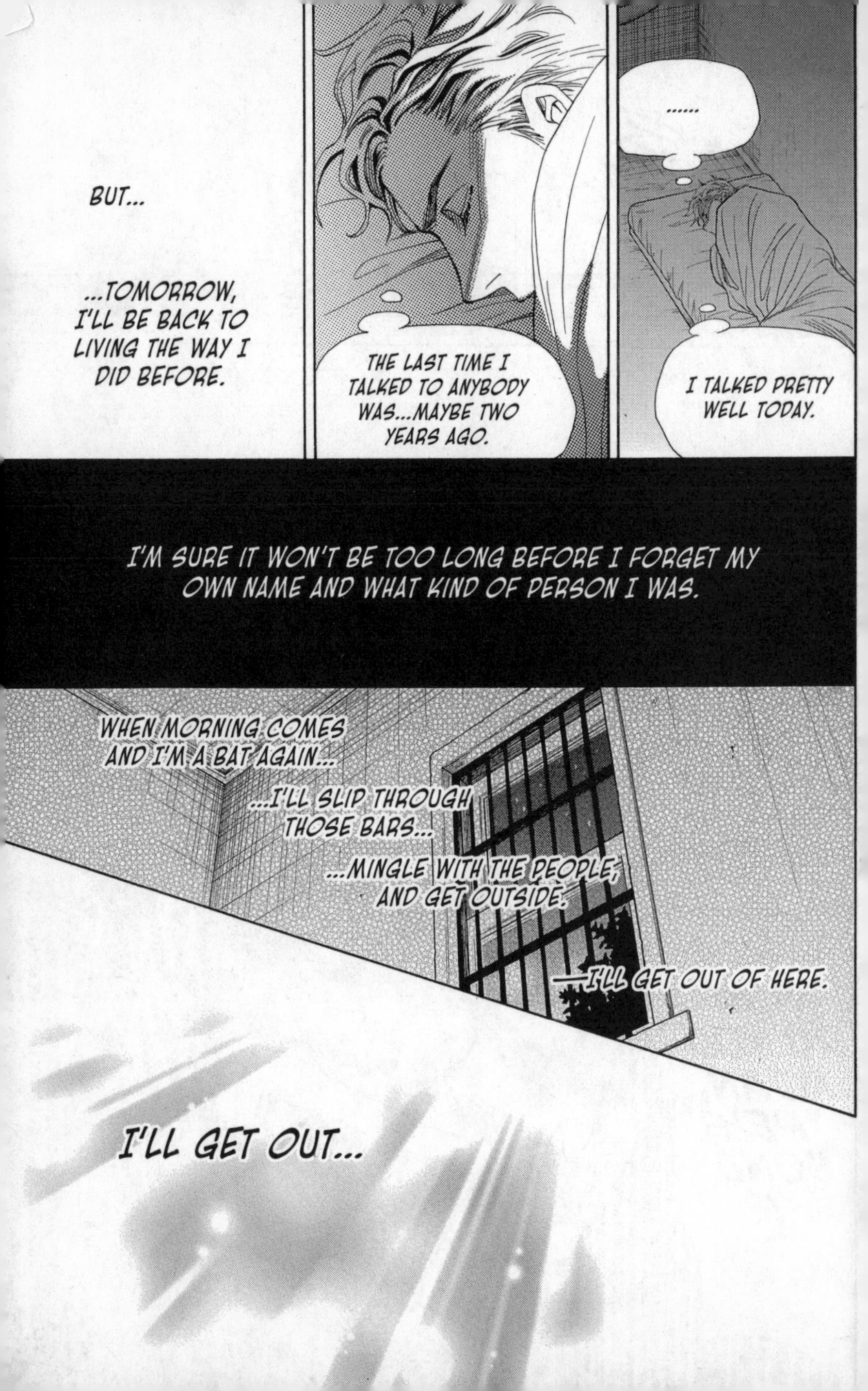
......
I TALKED PRETTY WELL TODAY.
THE LAST TIME I TALKED TO ANYBODY WAS...MAYBE TWO YEARS AGO.
BUT...
...TOMORROW, I'LL BE BACK TO LIVING THE WAY I DID BEFORE.
I'M SURE IT WON'T BE TOO LONG BEFORE I FORGET MY OWN NAME AND WHAT KIND OF PERSON I WAS.
WHEN MORNING COMES AND I'M A BAT AGAIN...
...I'LL SLIP THROUGH THOSE BARS...
...MINGLE WITH THE PEOPLE, AND GET OUTSIDE.
—I'LL GET OUT OF HERE.
I'LL GET OUT...

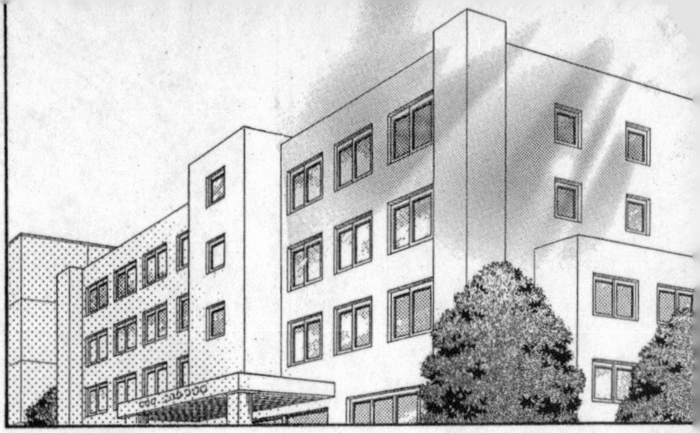

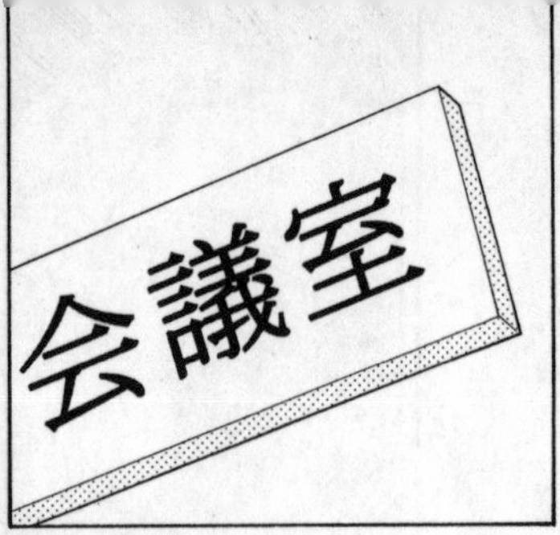
会議室

SIGN: MEETING ROOM

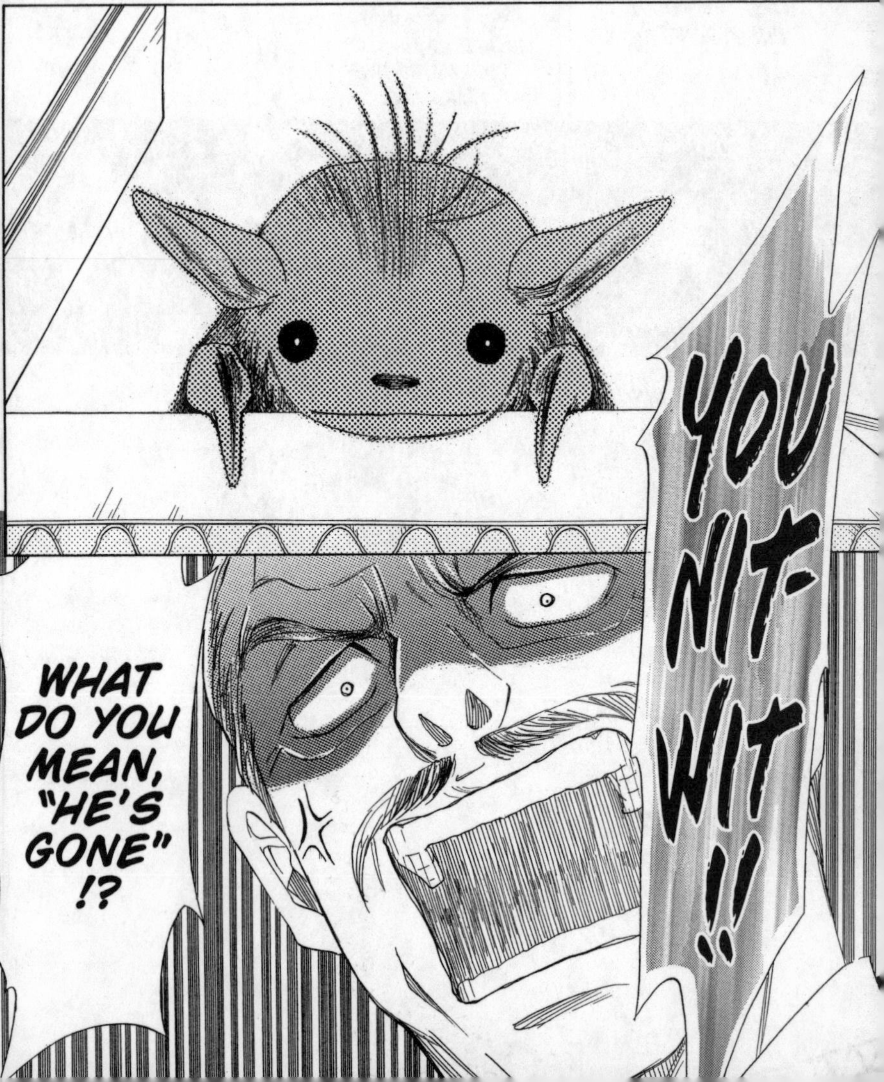
YOU NIT-WIT!!
WHAT DO YOU MEAN, "HE'S GONE"!?

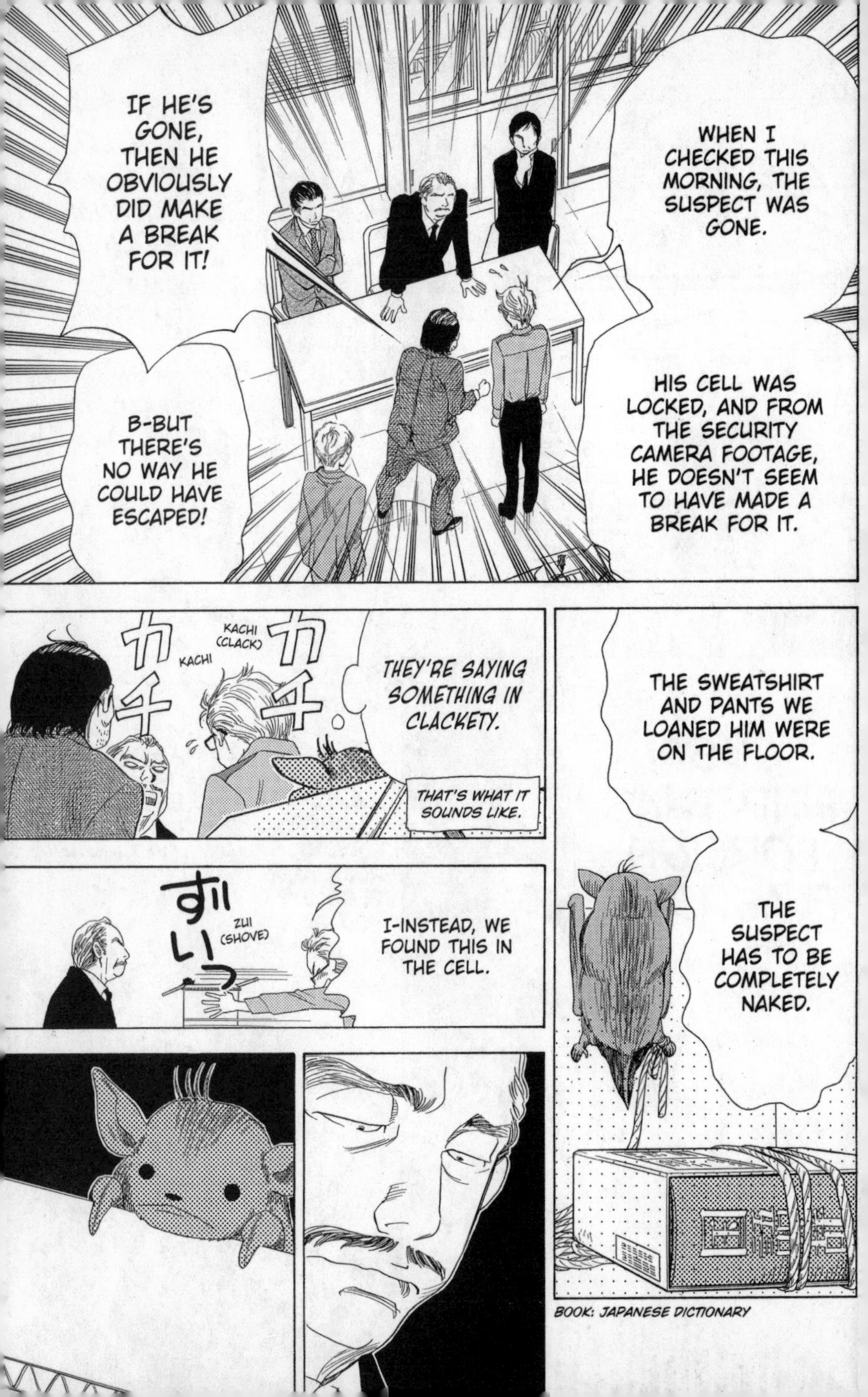
WHEN I CHECKED THIS MORNING, THE SUSPECT WAS GONE.
HIS CELL WAS LOCKED, AND FROM THE SECURITY CAMERA FOOTAGE, HE DOESN'T SEEM TO HAVE MADE A BREAK FOR IT.
IF HE'S GONE, THEN HE OBVIOUSLY DID MAKE A BREAK FOR IT!
B-BUT THERE'S NO WAY HE COULD HAVE ESCAPED!
THE SWEATSHIRT AND PANTS WE LOANED HIM WERE ON THE FLOOR.
THE SUSPECT HAS TO BE COMPLETELY NAKED.
BOOK: JAPANESE DICTIONARY
カチ
KACHI (CLACK)
カチ
KACHI
THEY'RE SAYING SOMETHING IN CLACKETY.
THAT'S WHAT IT SOUNDS LIKE.
I-INSTEAD, WE FOUND THIS IN THE CELL.
ずいっ
ZUI (SHOVE)

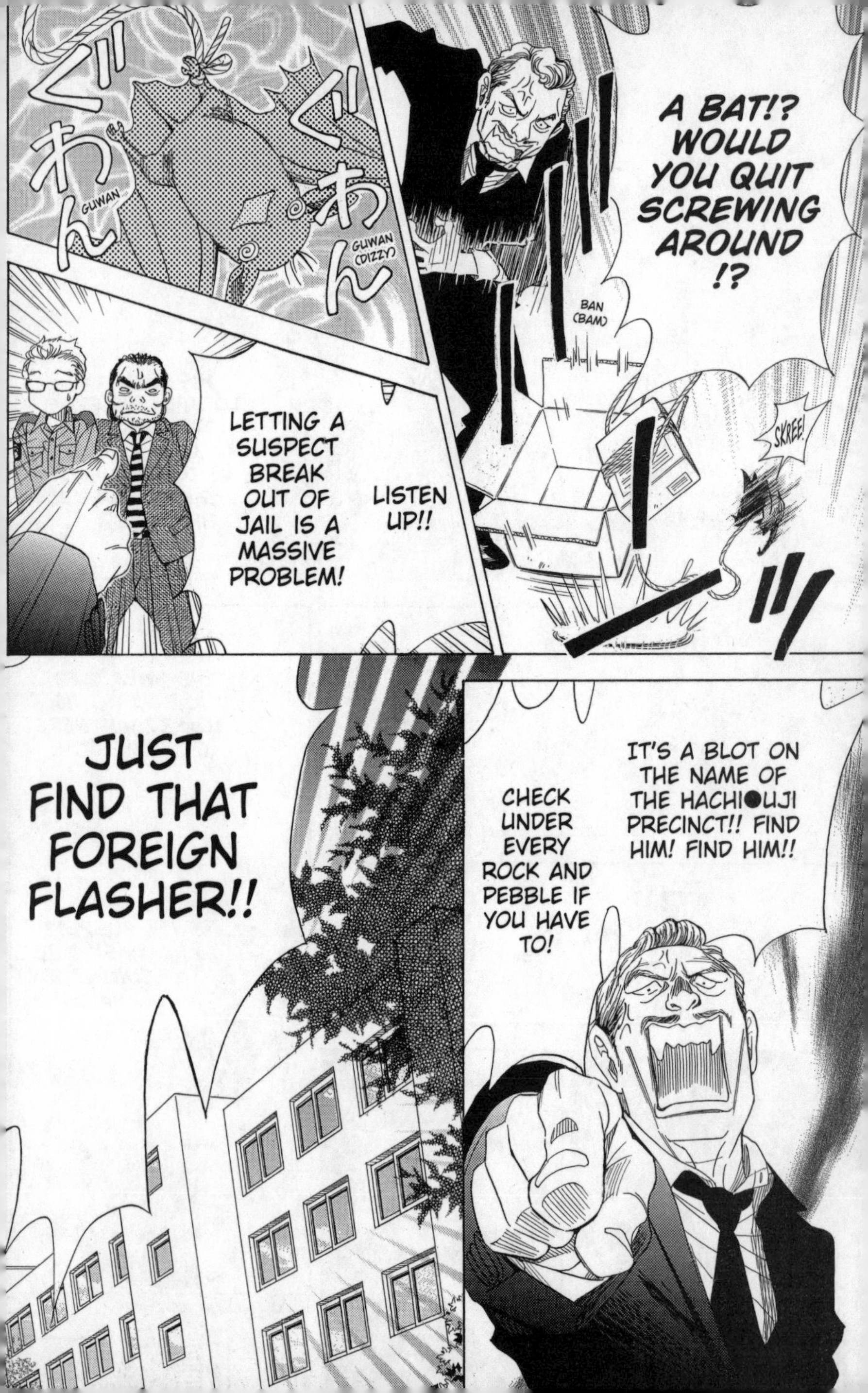
A BAT!? WOULD YOU QUIT SCREWING AROUND!?
BAN (BAM)
SKREE!
ぐわん
GUWAN (DIZZY)
ぐわん
GUWAN
LISTEN UP!!
LETTING A SUSPECT BREAK OUT OF JAIL IS A MASSIVE PROBLEM!
IT'S A BLOT ON THE NAME OF THE HACHI●UJI PRECINCT!! FIND HIM! FIND HIM!!
CHECK UNDER EVERY ROCK AND PEBBLE IF YOU HAVE TO!
JUST FIND THAT FOREIGN FLASHER!!

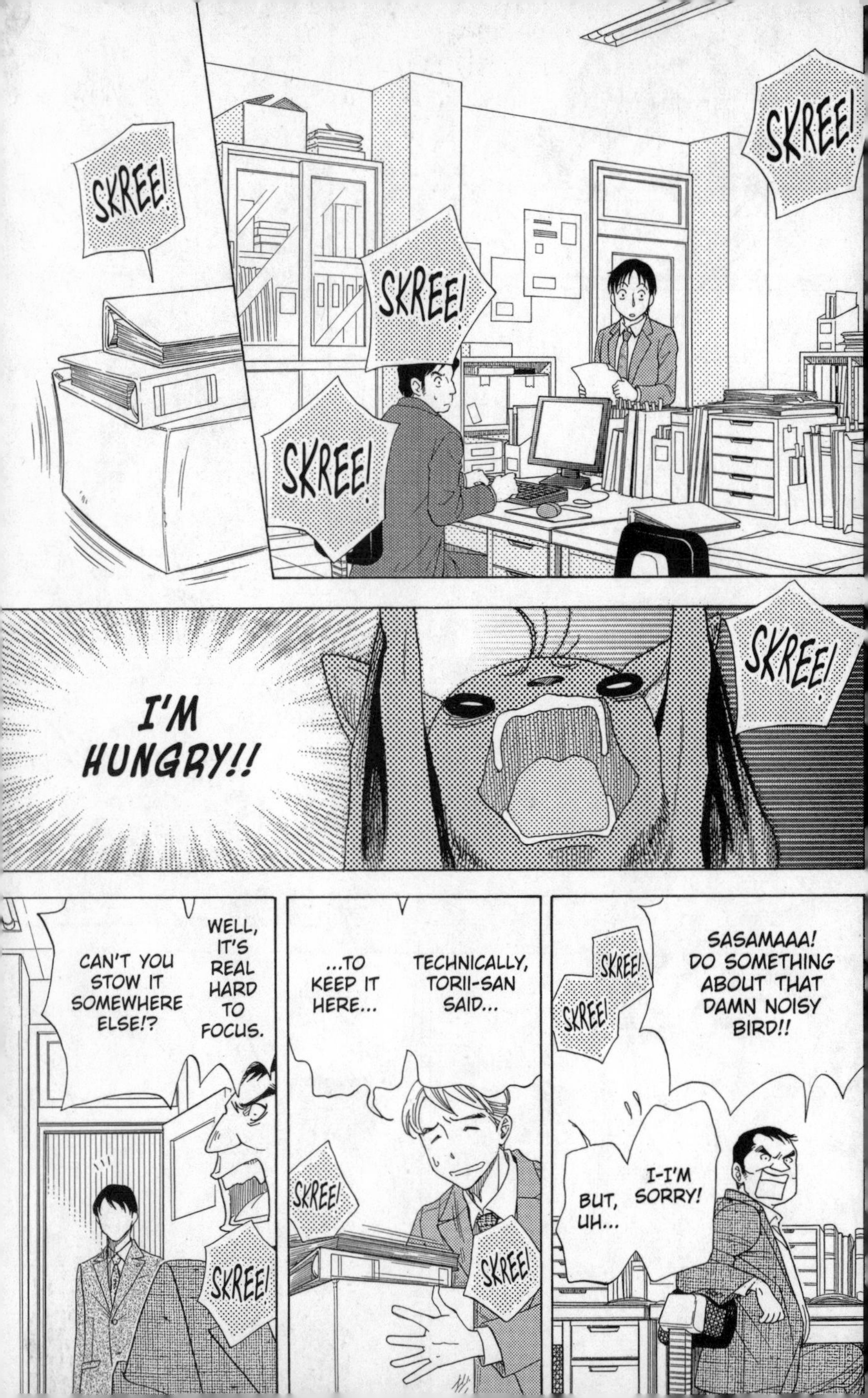
SKREE!
SKREE!
SKREE!
SKREE!
SKREE!
I'M HUNGRY!!
SASAMAAA! DO SOMETHING ABOUT THAT DAMN NOISY BIRD!!
SKREE!
SKREE!
I-I'M SORRY!
BUT, UH...
TECHNICALLY, TORII-SAN SAID...
...TO KEEP IT HERE...
SKREE!
SKREE!
WELL, IT'S REAL HARD TO FOCUS.
CAN'T YOU STOW IT SOMEWHERE ELSE!?
SKREE!

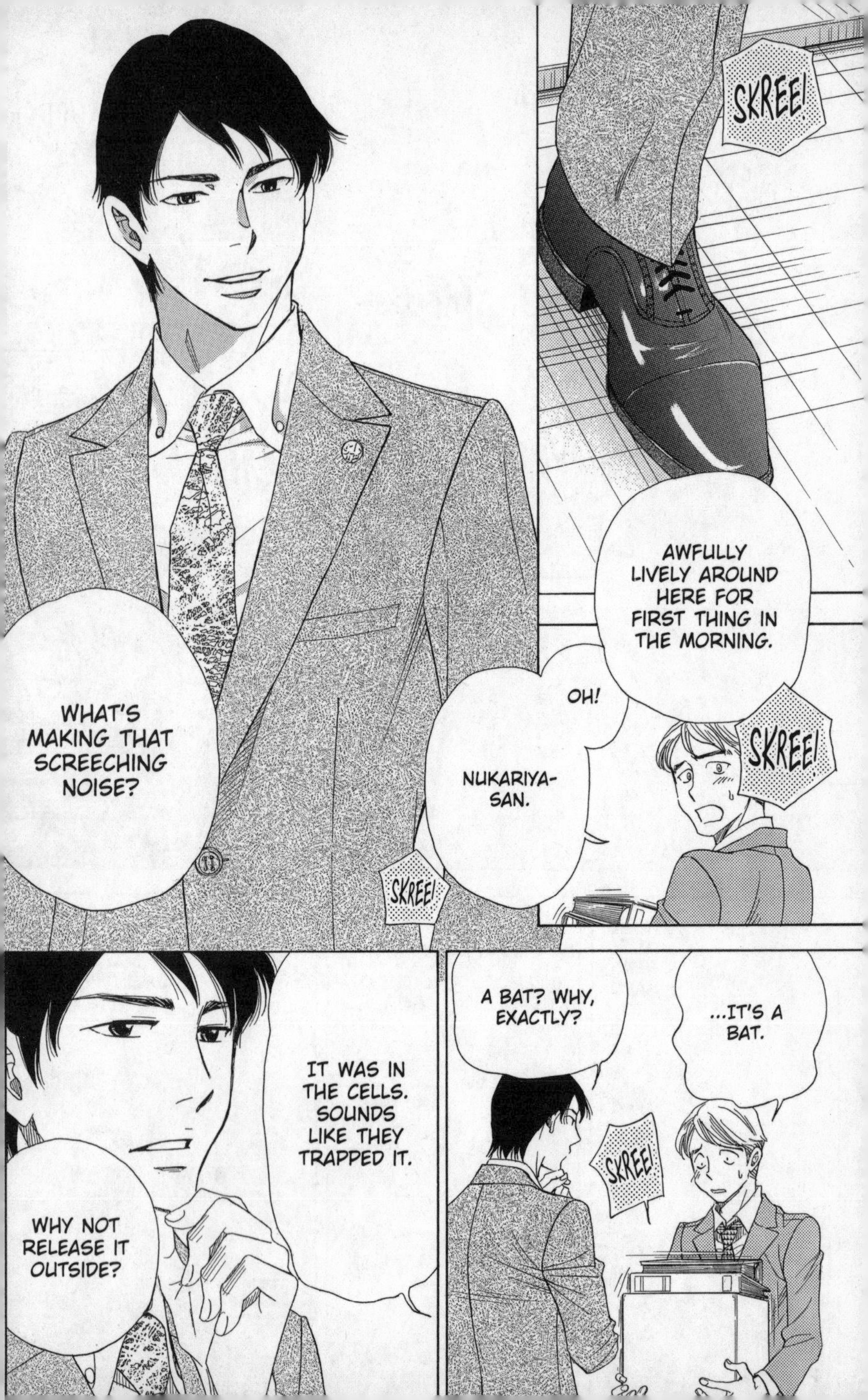
SKREE!
AWFULLY LIVELY AROUND HERE FOR FIRST THING IN THE MORNING.
SKREE!
OH! NUKARIYA-SAN.
WHAT'S MAKING THAT SCREECHING NOISE?
SKREE!
...IT'S A BAT.
A BAT? WHY, EXACTLY?
SKREE!
IT WAS IN THE CELLS. SOUNDS LIKE THEY TRAPPED IT.
WHY NOT RELEASE IT OUTSIDE?

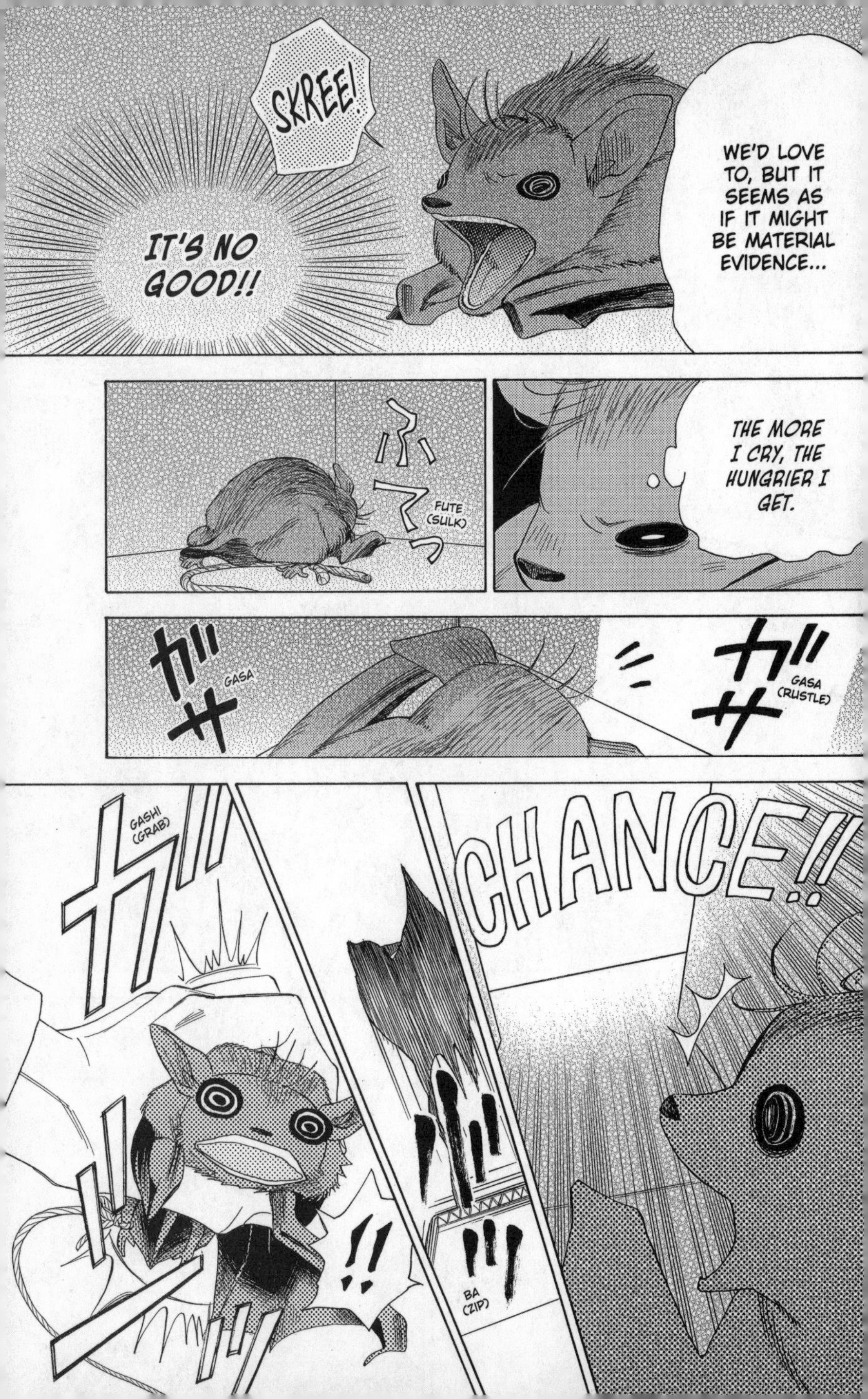
WE'D LOVE TO, BUT IT SEEMS AS IF IT MIGHT BE MATERIAL EVIDENCE...
SKREE!
IT'S NO GOOD!!
THE MORE I CRY, THE HUNGRIER I GET.
ふてっ
FUTE (SULK)
ガサ
GASA (RUSTLE)
ガサ
GASA
CHANCE!!
BA (ZIP)
ガッ
GASHI (GRAB)
!!

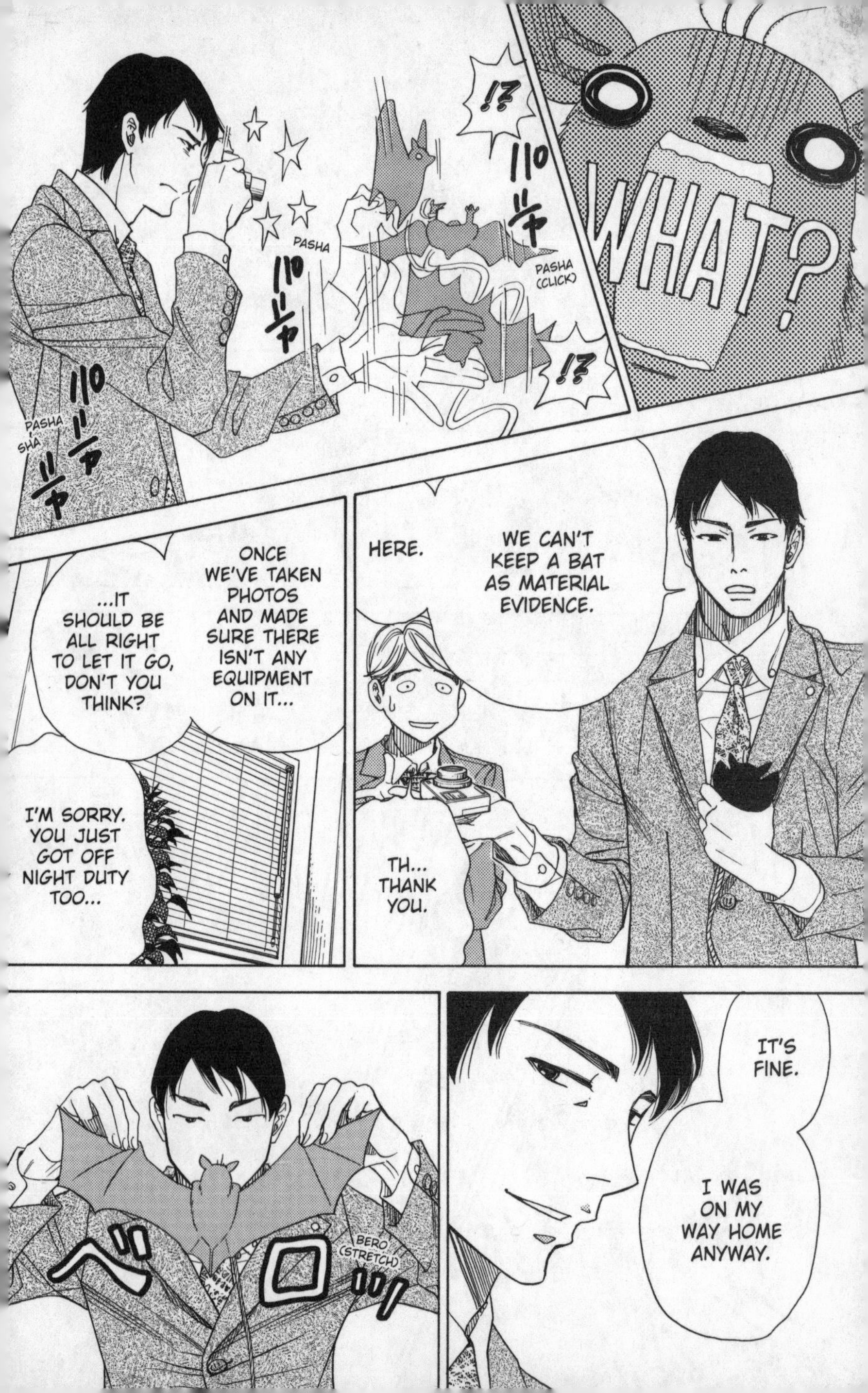
WHAT?
!?
PASHA (CLICK)
!?
PASHA
PASHA SHA
WE CAN'T KEEP A BAT AS MATERIAL EVIDENCE.
HERE.
TH... THANK YOU.
ONCE WE'VE TAKEN PHOTOS AND MADE SURE THERE ISN'T ANY EQUIPMENT ON IT...
...IT SHOULD BE ALL RIGHT TO LET IT GO, DON'T YOU THINK?
I'M SORRY. YOU JUST GOT OFF NIGHT DUTY TOO...
IT'S FINE.
I WAS ON MY WAY HOME ANYWAY.
BERO (STRETCH)

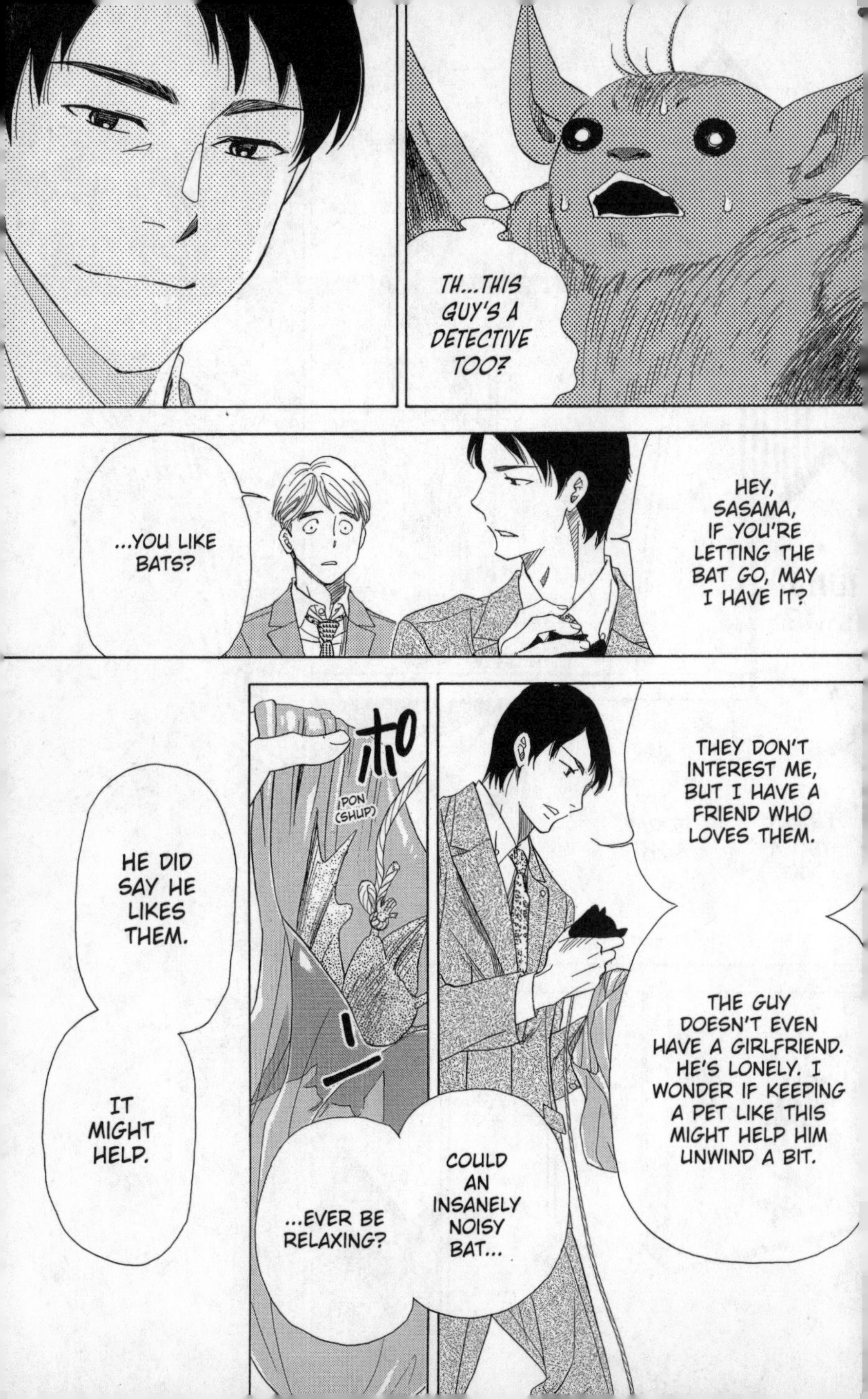
TH...THIS GUY'S A DETECTIVE TOO?
HEY, SASAMA, IF YOU'RE LETTING THE BAT GO, MAY I HAVE IT?
...YOU LIKE BATS?
THEY DON'T INTEREST ME, BUT I HAVE A FRIEND WHO LOVES THEM.
THE GUY DOESN'T EVEN HAVE A GIRLFRIEND. HE'S LONELY. I WONDER IF KEEPING A PET LIKE THIS MIGHT HELP HIM UNWIND A BIT.
COULD AN INSANELY NOISY BAT...
...EVER BE RELAXING?
PON (SHUP)
HE DID SAY HE LIKES THEM.
IT MIGHT HELP.

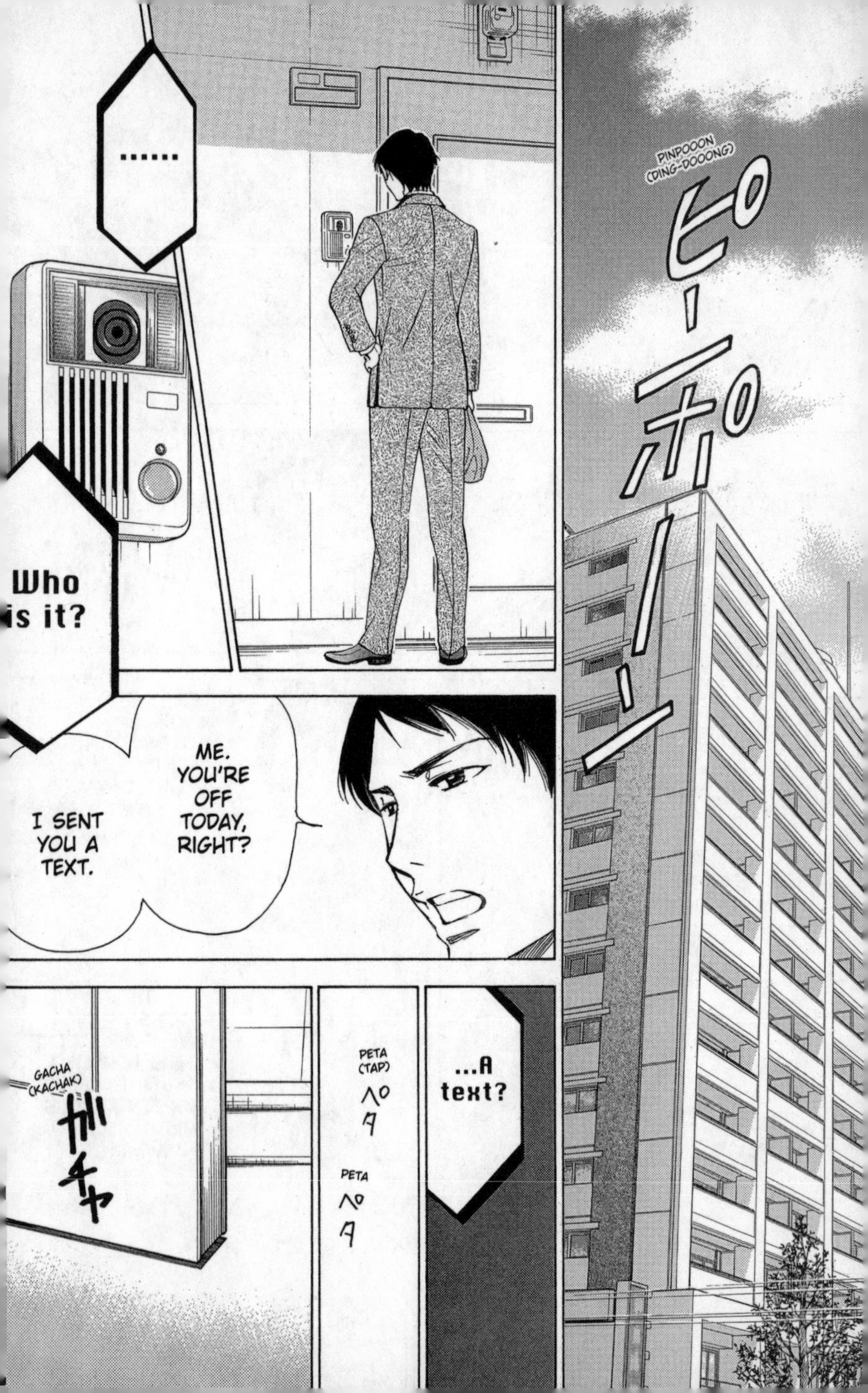

PINPOOON (DING-DOOONG)
......
Who is it?
ME. YOU'RE OFF TODAY, RIGHT?
I SENT YOU A TEXT.
...A text?
PETA (TAP)
ペタ
PETA
ペタ
GACHA (KACHAK)
ガチャ

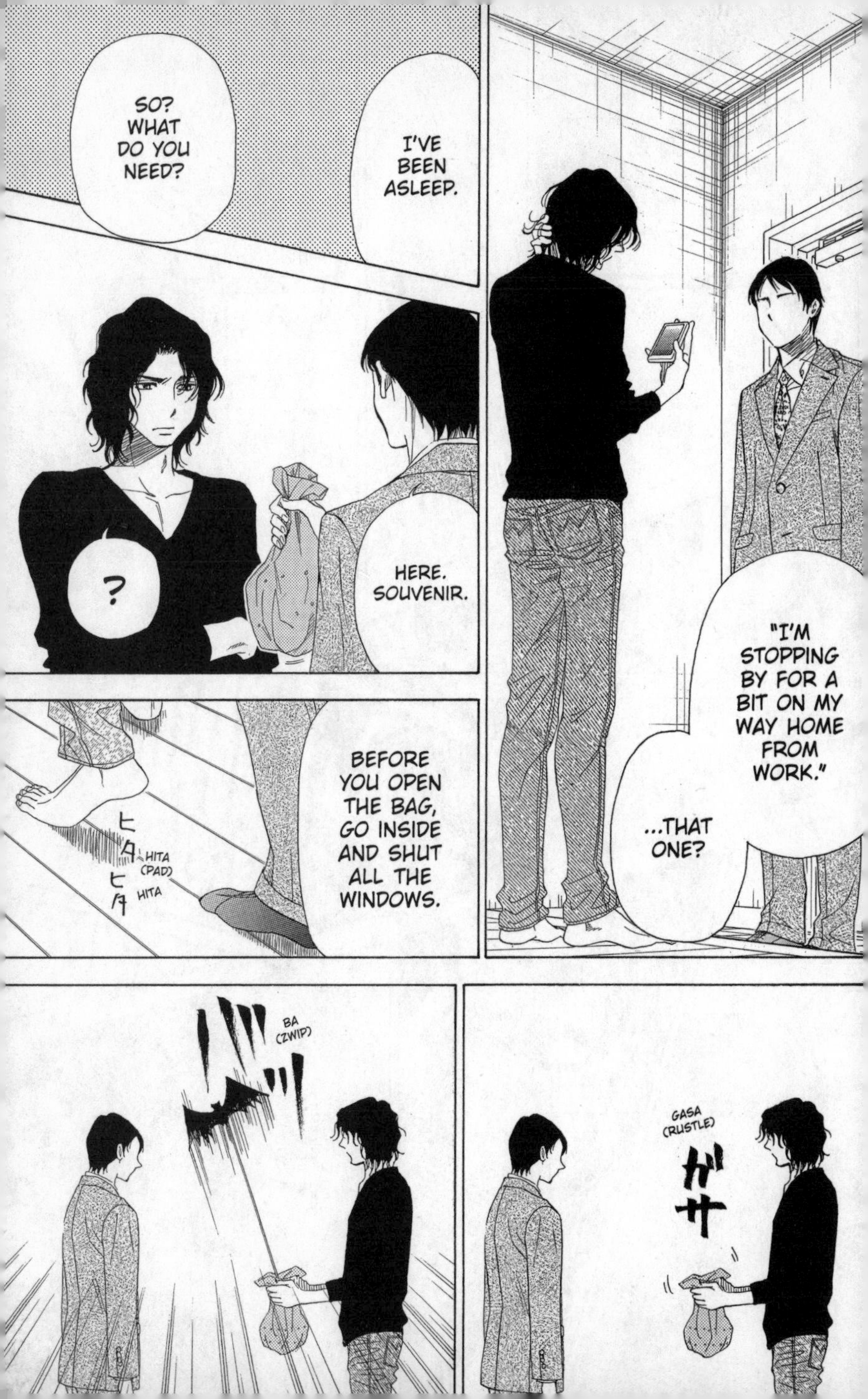
"I'M STOPPING BY FOR A BIT ON MY WAY HOME FROM WORK."
...THAT ONE?
I'VE BEEN ASLEEP.
SO? WHAT DO YOU NEED?
HERE. SOUVENIR.
?
BEFORE YOU OPEN THE BAG, GO INSIDE AND SHUT ALL THE WINDOWS.
ヒタヒタ HITA (PAD) HITA
ガサ GASA (RUSTLE)
バッ BA (ZWIP)

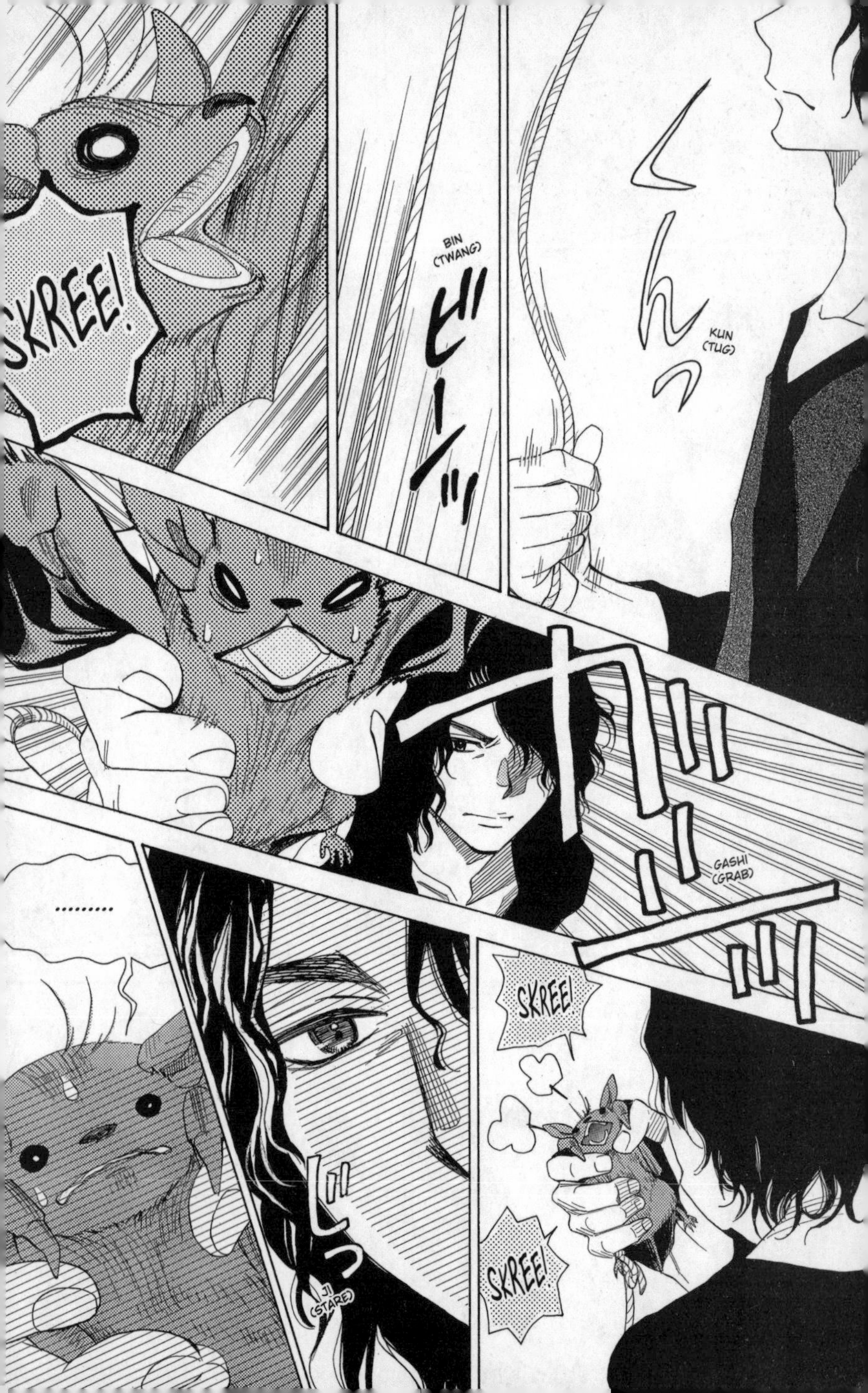
くんっ
KUN (TUG)
ビーンッ
BIN (TWANG)
SKREE!
ガシッ
GASHI (GRAB)
SKREE!
SKREE!
じぃっ
JI (STARE)
....

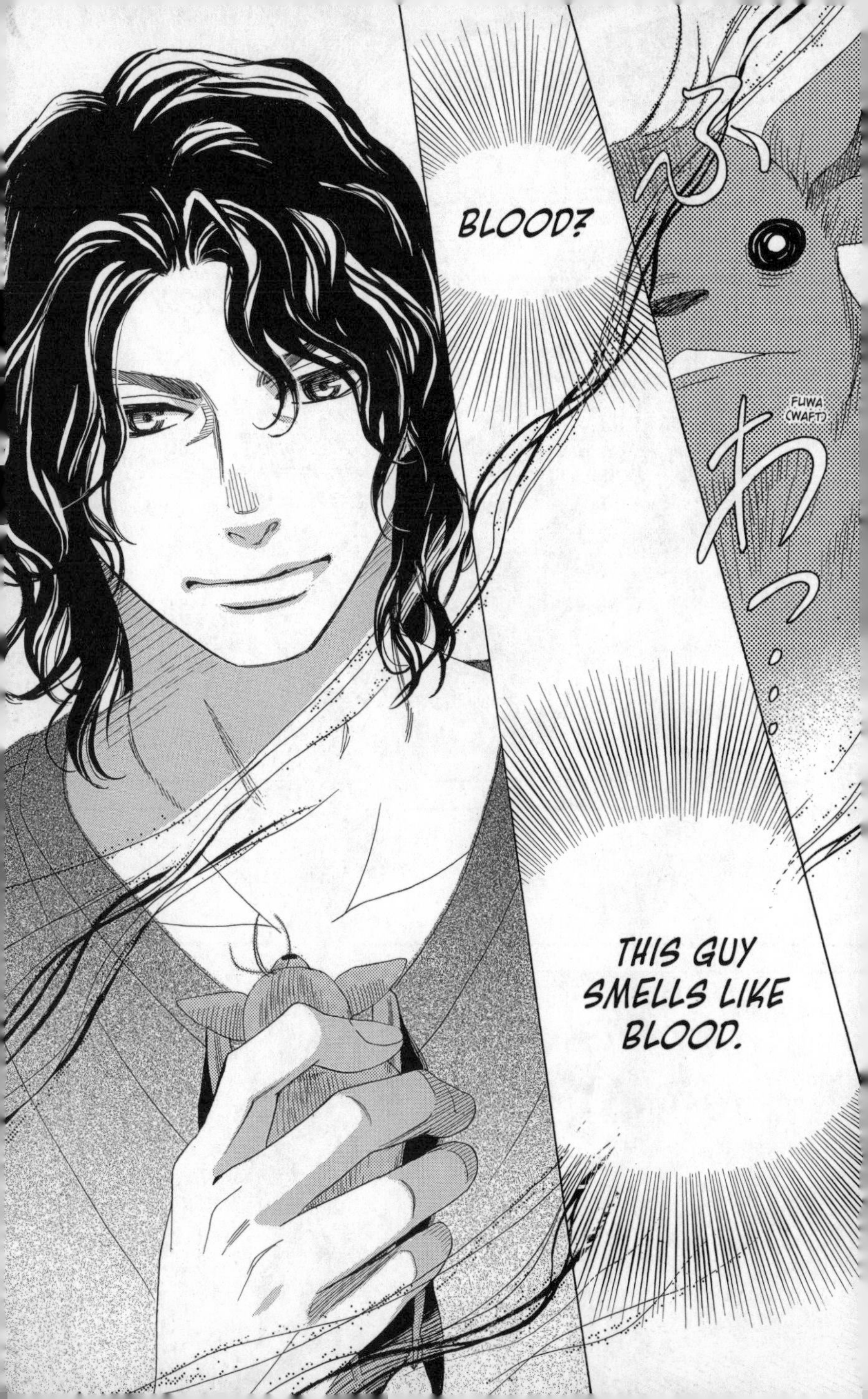
ふわっ…
FUWA (WAFT)
BLOOD?
THIS GUY SMELLS LIKE BLOOD.

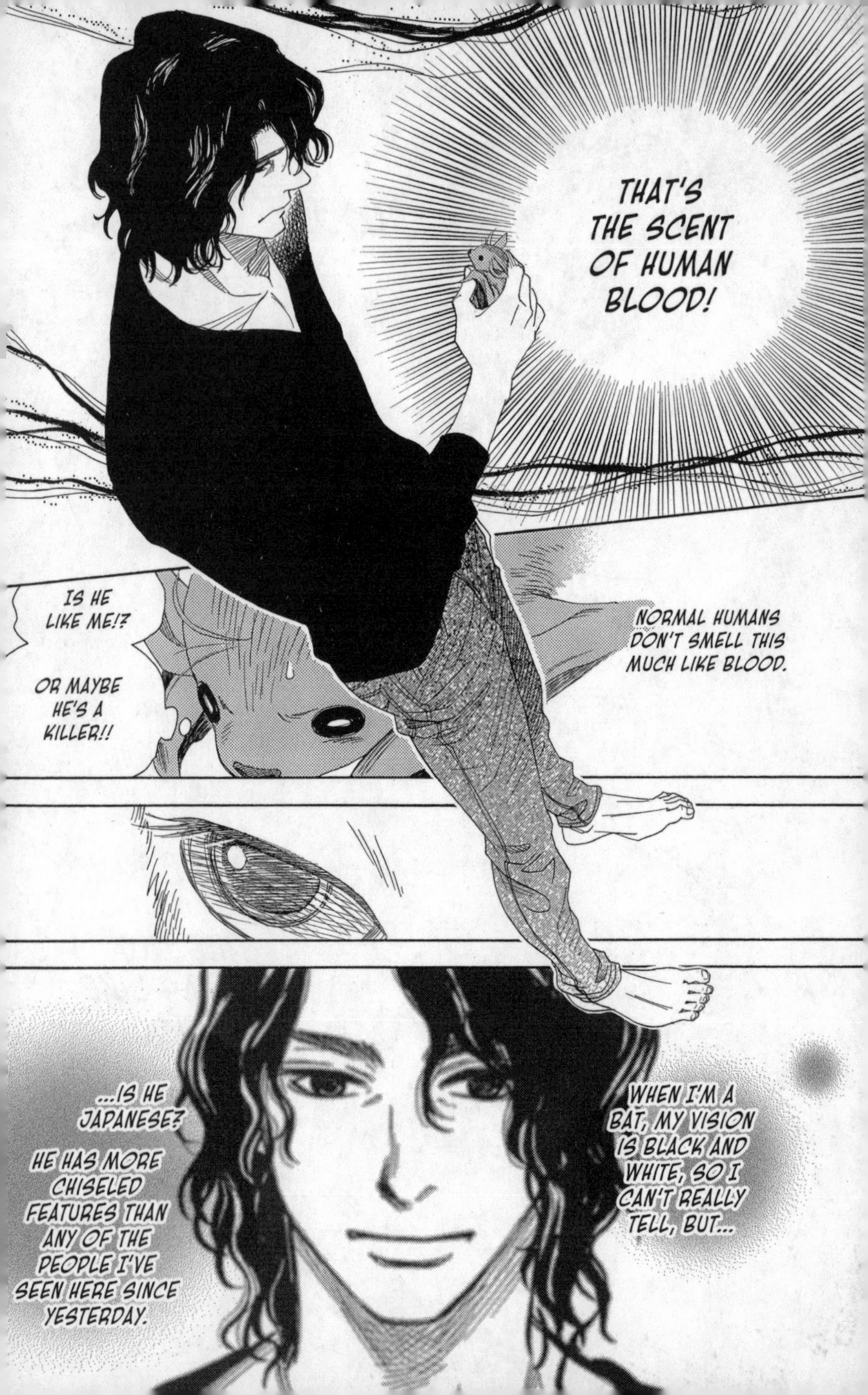

THAT'S THE SCENT OF HUMAN BLOOD!
NORMAL HUMANS DON'T SMELL THIS MUCH LIKE BLOOD.
IS HE LIKE ME!?
OR MAYBE HE'S A KILLER!!
WHEN I'M A BAT, MY VISION IS BLACK AND WHITE, SO I CAN'T REALLY TELL, BUT...
...IS HE JAPANESE?
HE HAS MORE CHISELED FEATURES THAN ANY OF THE PEOPLE I'VE SEEN HERE SINCE YESTERDAY.

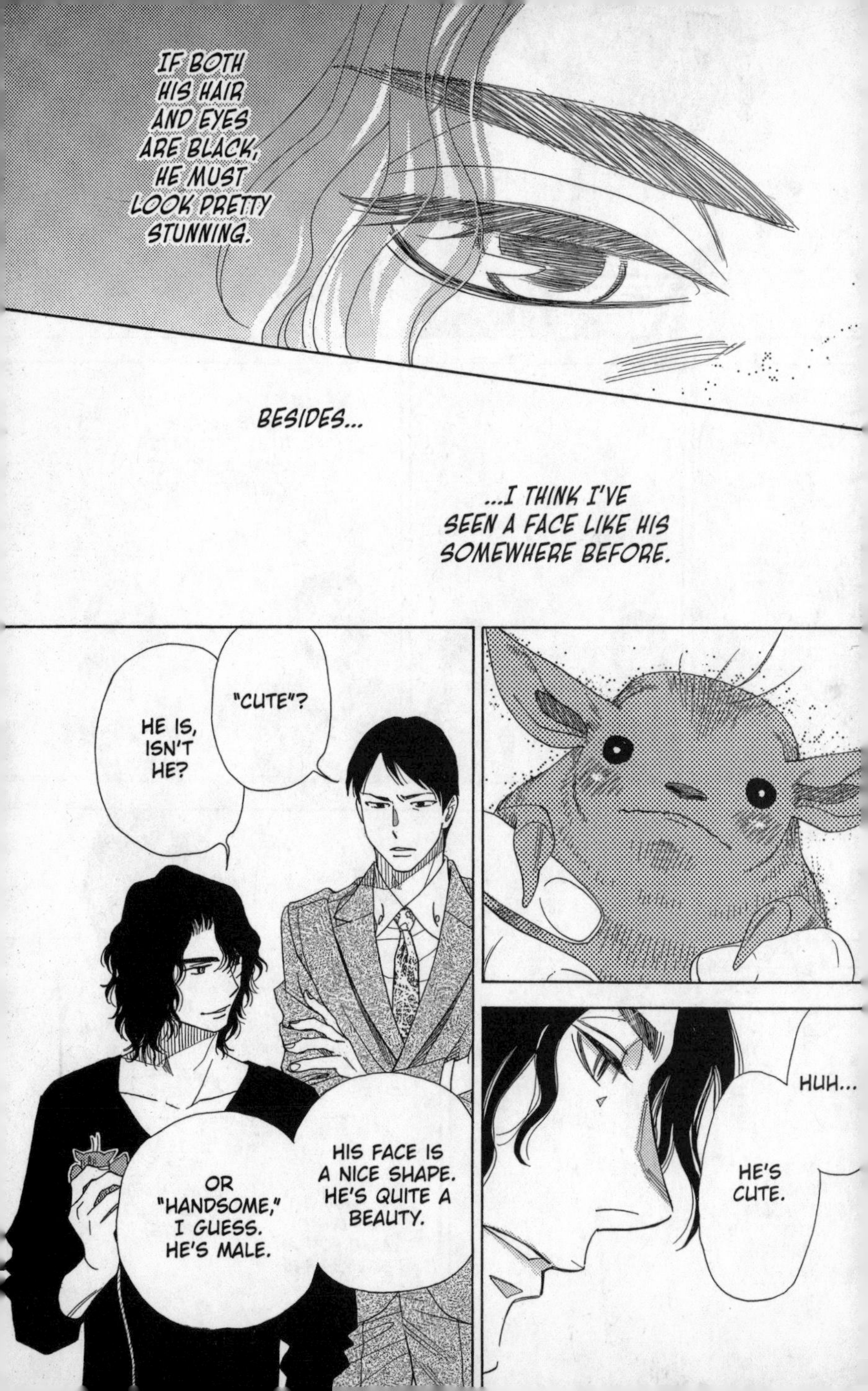

IF BOTH HIS HAIR AND EYES ARE BLACK, HE MUST LOOK PRETTY STUNNING.
BESIDES...
...I THINK I'VE SEEN A FACE LIKE HIS SOMEWHERE BEFORE.
HUH...
HE'S CUTE.
"CUTE"?
HE IS, ISN'T HE?
HIS FACE IS A NICE SHAPE. HE'S QUITE A BEAUTY.
OR "HANDSOME," I GUESS. HE'S MALE.

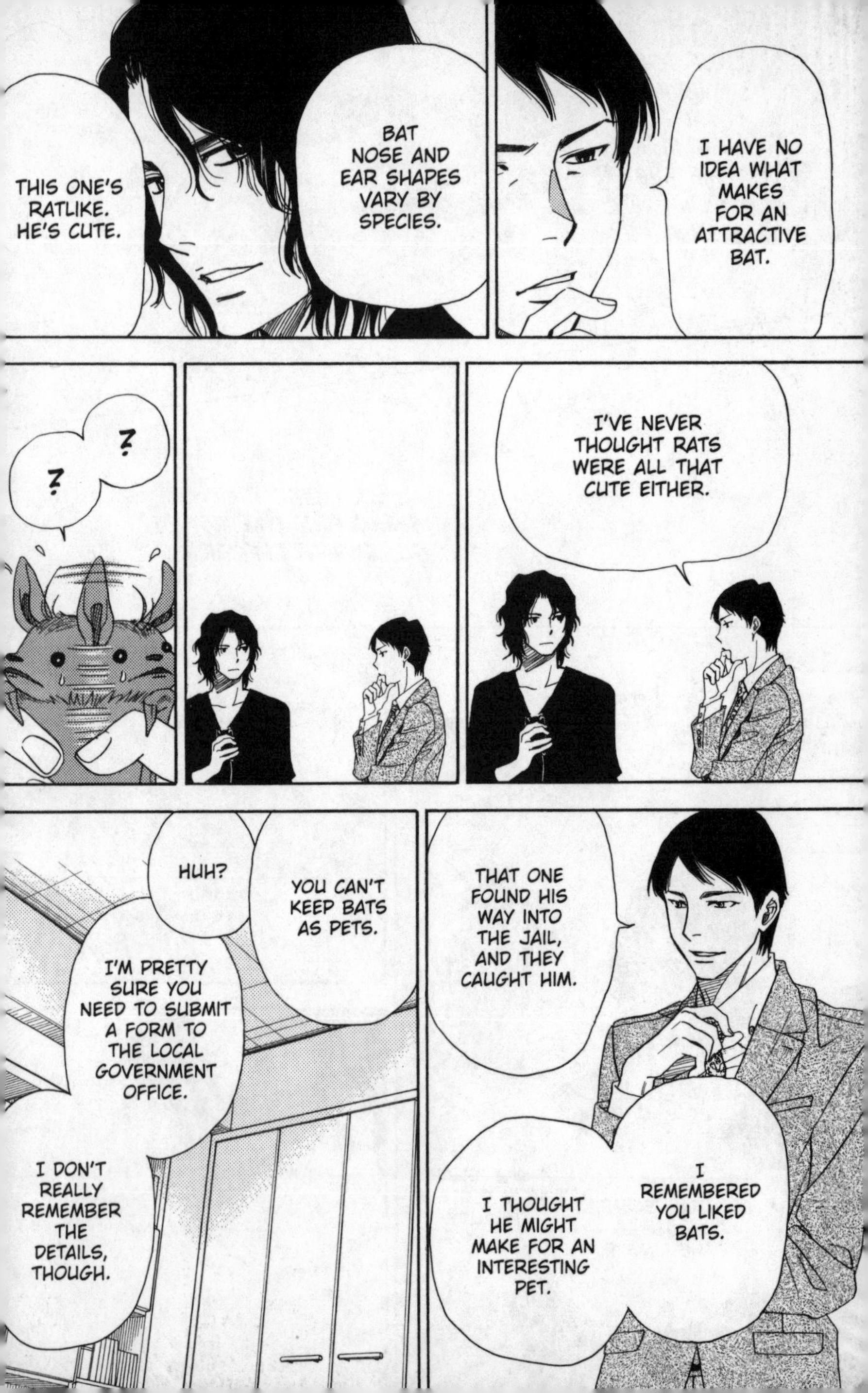
I HAVE NO IDEA WHAT MAKES FOR AN ATTRACTIVE BAT.
BAT NOSE AND EAR SHAPES VARY BY SPECIES.
THIS ONE'S RATLIKE. HE'S CUTE.
I'VE NEVER THOUGHT RATS WERE ALL THAT CUTE EITHER.
? ?
THAT ONE FOUND HIS WAY INTO THE JAIL, AND THEY CAUGHT HIM.
I REMEMBERED YOU LIKED BATS.
I THOUGHT HE MIGHT MAKE FOR AN INTERESTING PET.
YOU CAN'T KEEP BATS AS PETS.
HUH?
I'M PRETTY SURE YOU NEED TO SUBMIT A FORM TO THE LOCAL GOVERNMENT OFFICE.
I DON'T REALLY REMEMBER THE DETAILS, THOUGH.

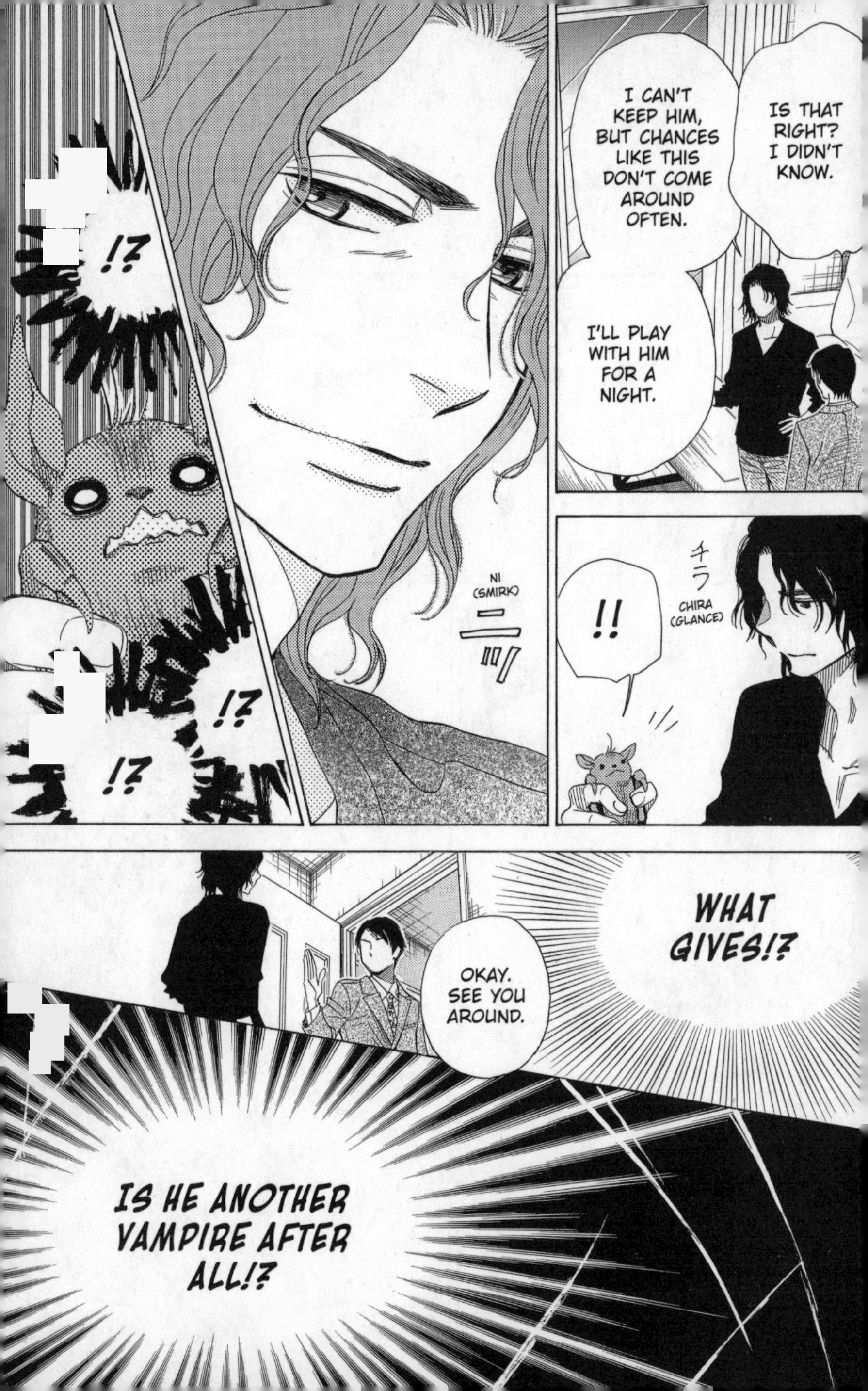
IS THAT RIGHT? I DIDN'T KNOW.
I CAN'T KEEP HIM, BUT CHANCES LIKE THIS DON'T COME AROUND OFTEN.
I'LL PLAY WITH HIM FOR A NIGHT.
チラ
CHIRA (GLANCE)
!!
ニッ
NI (SMIRK)
!?
!?
!?
WHAT GIVES!?
OKAY. SEE YOU AROUND.
IS HE ANOTHER VAMPIRE AFTER ALL!?

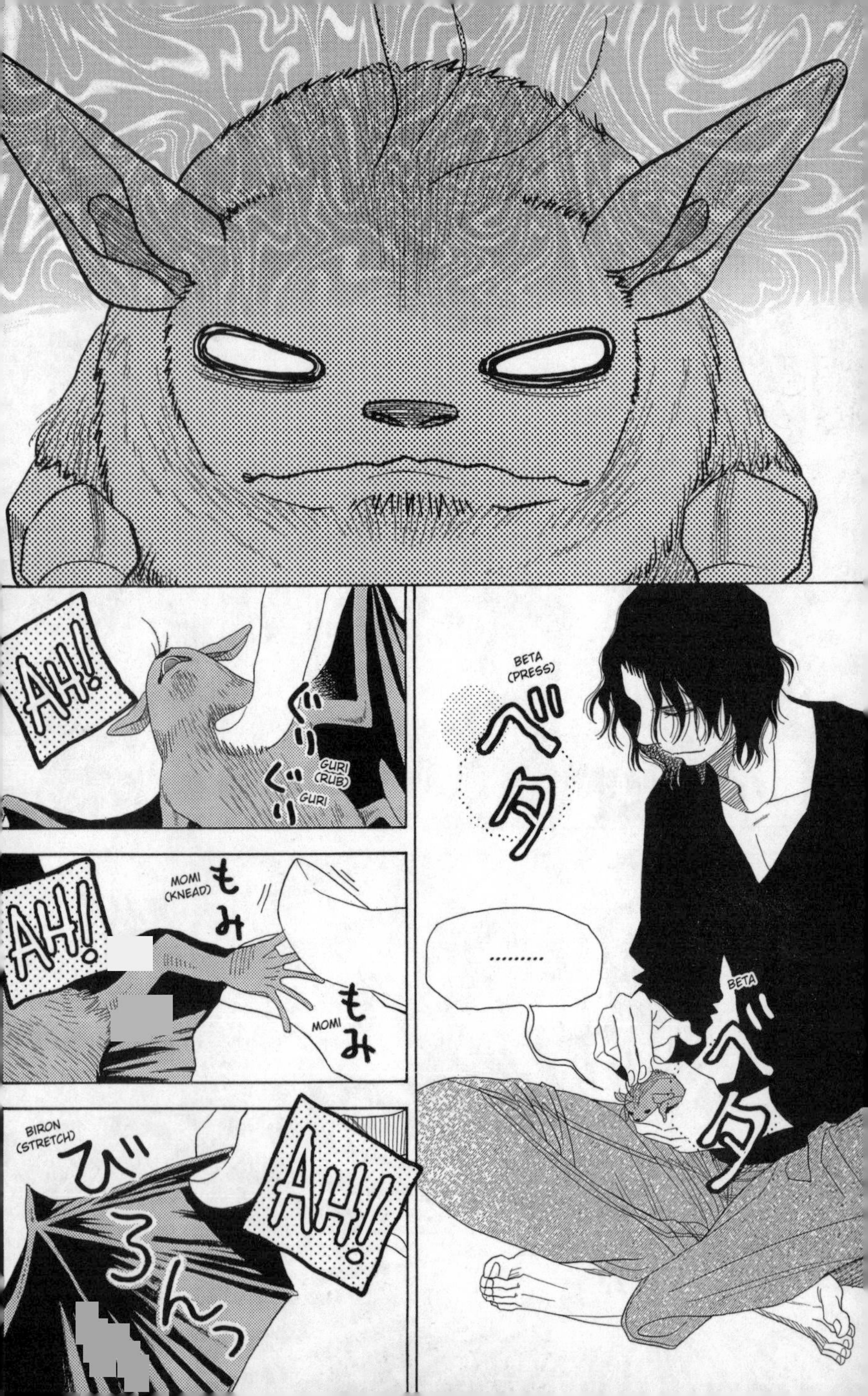
BETA (PRESS)
ベタ
....
BETA
ベタ
AH!
GURI (RUB)
ぐりぐり
GURI
AH!
MOMI (KNEAD)
もみ
MOMI
もみ
BIRON (STRETCH)
びろんっ
AH!

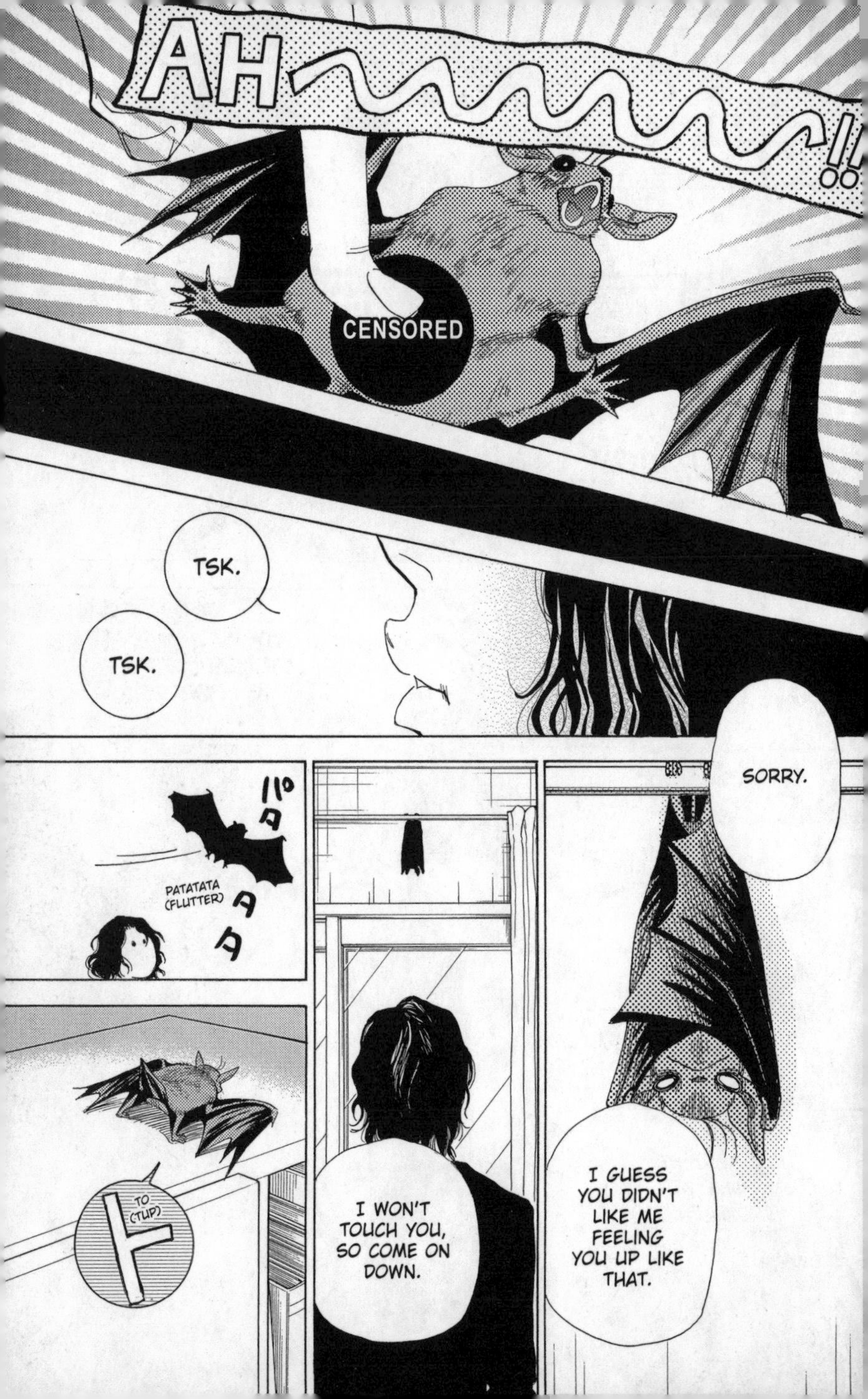
AH~~~!!
CENSORED
TSK.
TSK.
SORRY.
I GUESS YOU DIDN'T LIKE ME FEELING YOU UP LIKE THAT.
I WON'T TOUCH YOU, SO COME ON DOWN.
パタタタ
PATATATA (FLUTTER)
ト
TO (TUP)

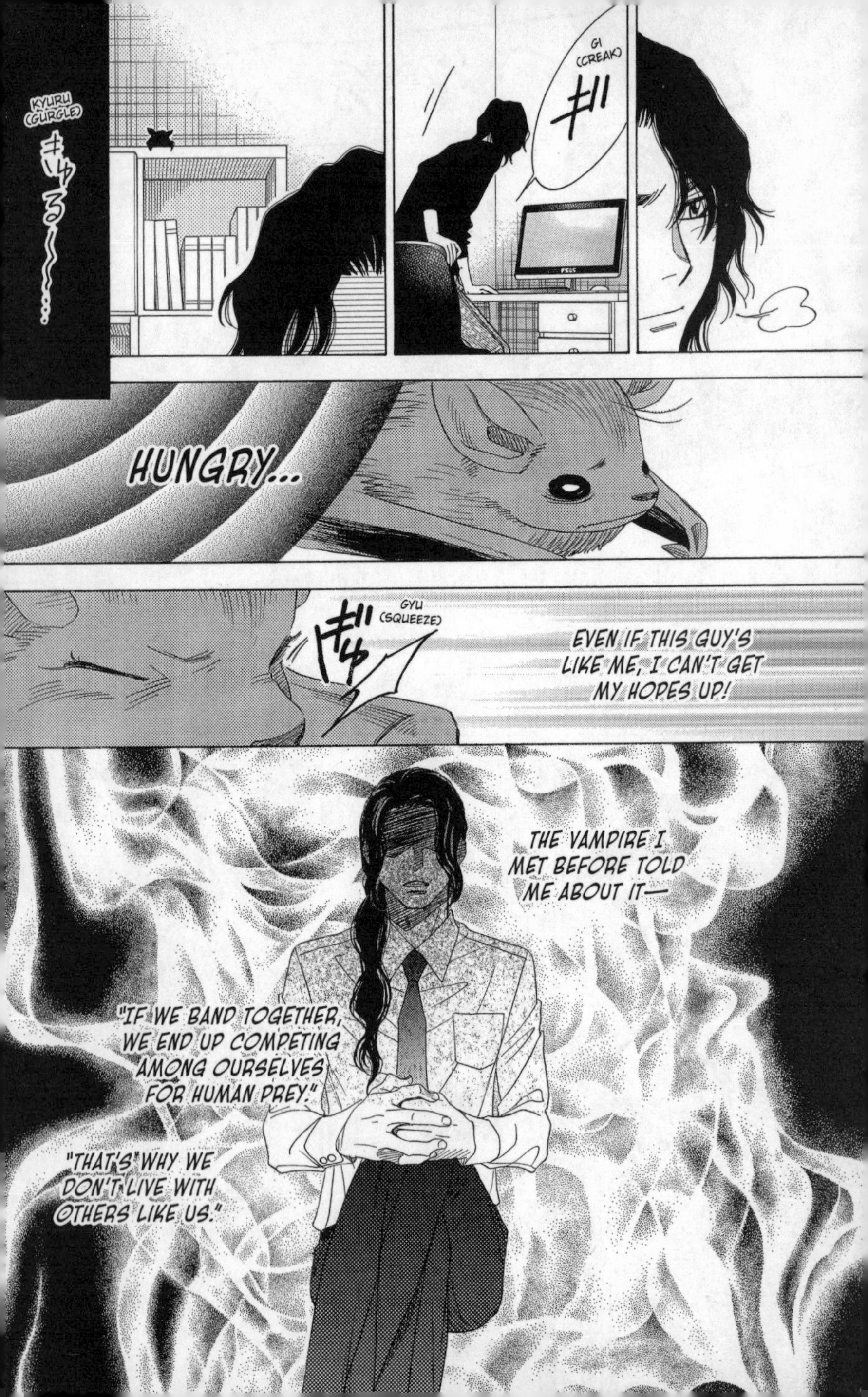
GI (CREAK)
ギ")
KYURU (GURGLE)
きゅる〜〜…
HUNGRY...
GYU (SQUEEZE)
ぎゅ
EVEN IF THIS GUY'S LIKE ME, I CAN'T GET MY HOPES UP!
THE VAMPIRE I MET BEFORE TOLD ME ABOUT IT—
"IF WE BAND TOGETHER, WE END UP COMPETING AMONG OURSELVES FOR HUMAN PREY."
"THAT'S WHY WE DON'T LIVE WITH OTHERS LIKE US."

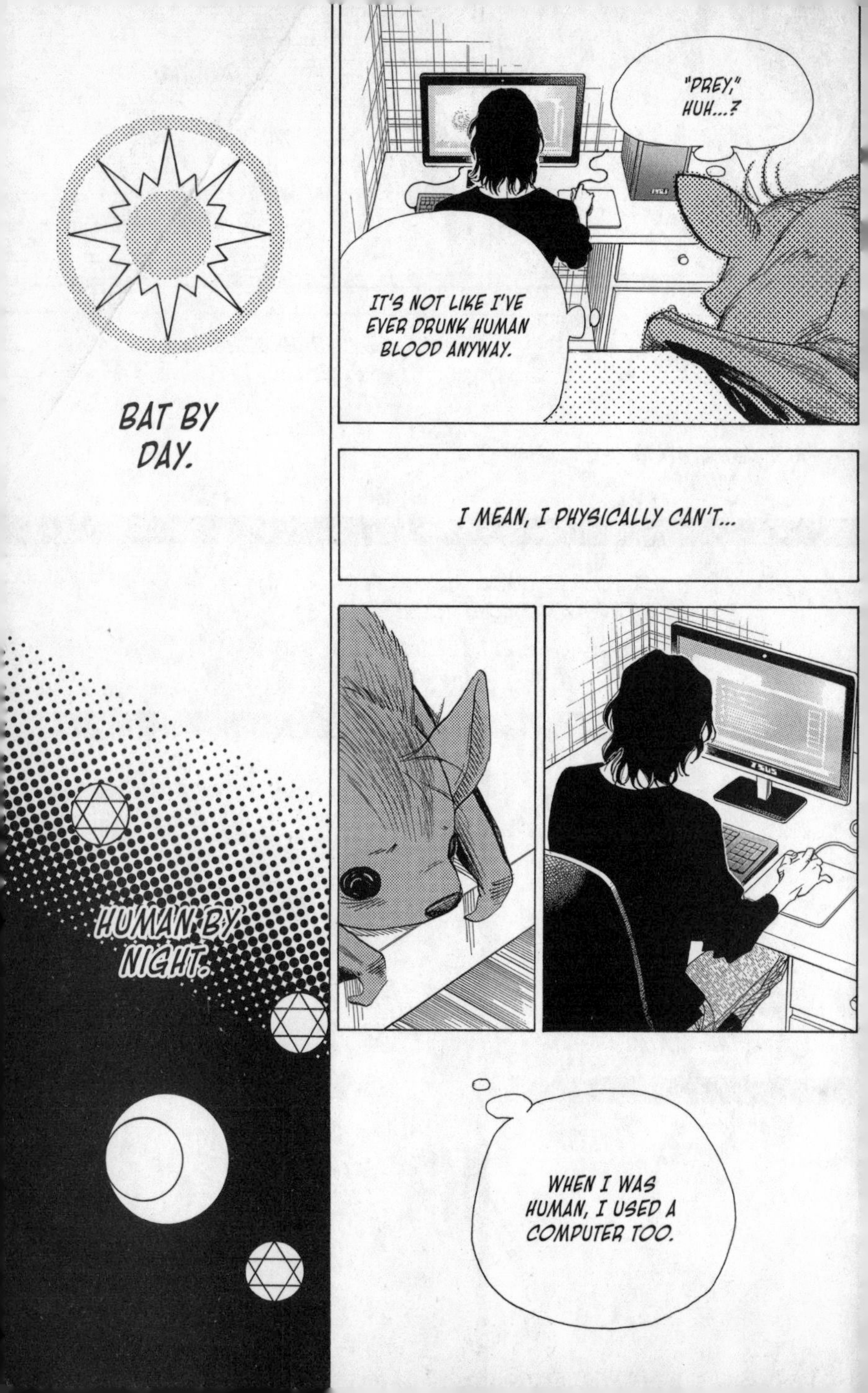
"PREY," HUH...?
IT'S NOT LIKE I'VE EVER DRUNK HUMAN BLOOD ANYWAY.
I MEAN, I PHYSICALLY CAN'T...
WHEN I WAS HUMAN, I USED A COMPUTER TOO.
BAT BY DAY.
HUMAN BY NIGHT.

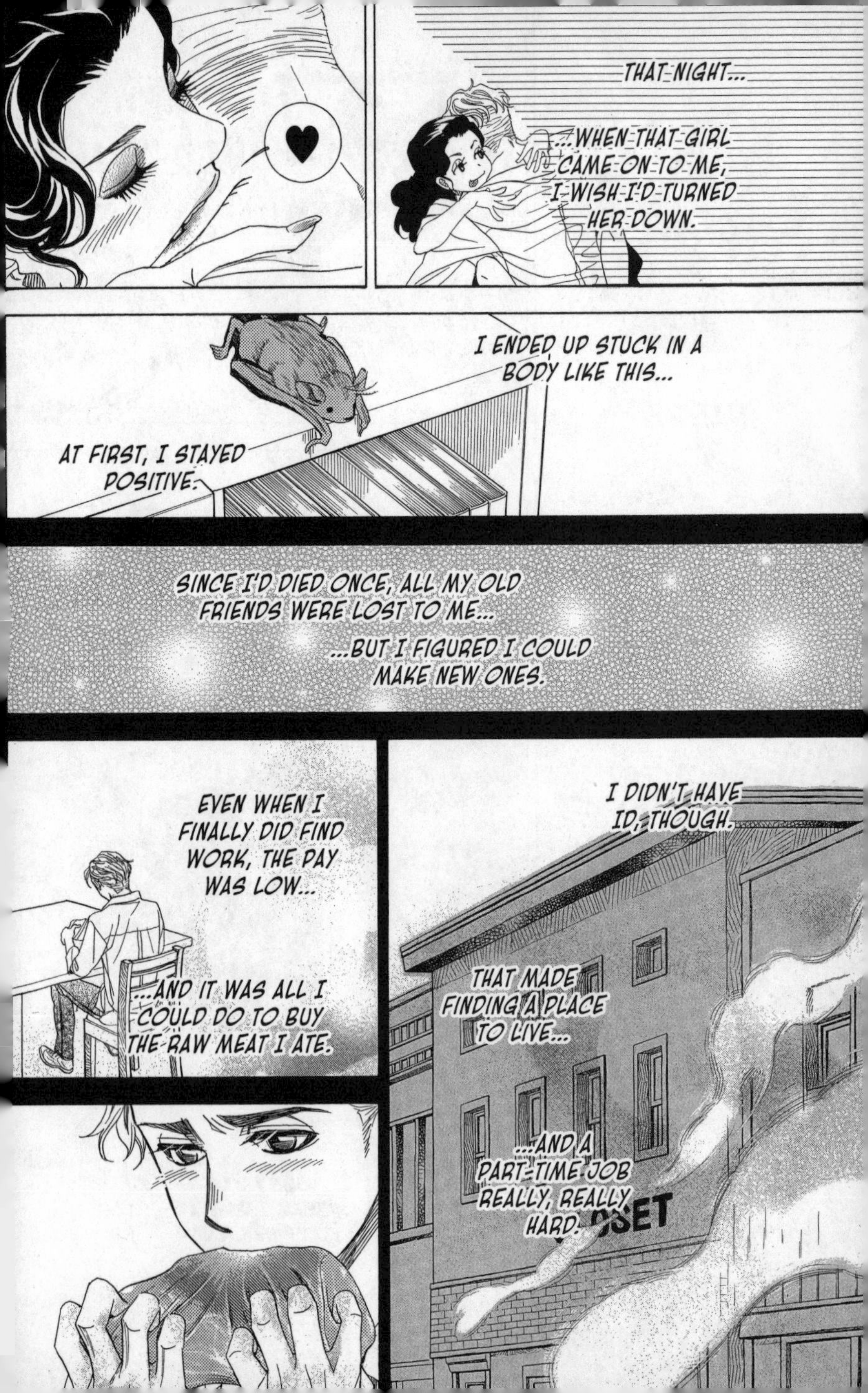
THAT NIGHT...
...WHEN THAT GIRL CAME ON TO ME, I WISH I'D TURNED HER DOWN.
I ENDED UP STUCK IN A BODY LIKE THIS...
AT FIRST, I STAYED POSITIVE.
SINCE I'D DIED ONCE, ALL MY OLD FRIENDS WERE LOST TO ME...
...BUT I FIGURED I COULD MAKE NEW ONES.
I DIDN'T HAVE ID, THOUGH.
THAT MADE FINDING A PLACE TO LIVE...
...AND A PART-TIME JOB REALLY, REALLY HARD.
EVEN WHEN I FINALLY DID FIND WORK, THE PAY WAS LOW...
...AND IT WAS ALL I COULD DO TO BUY THE RAW MEAT I ATE.

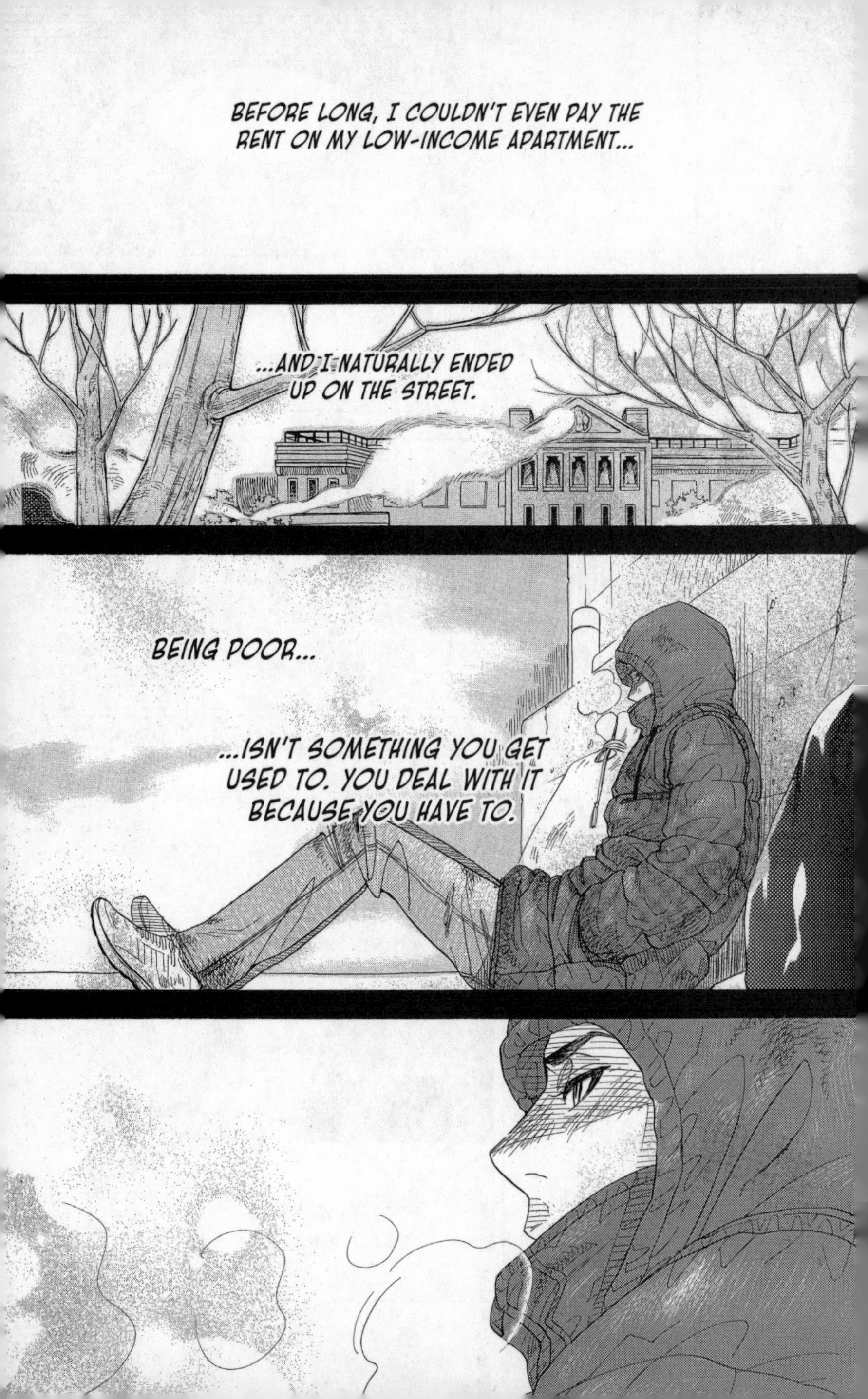
BEFORE LONG, I COULDN'T EVEN PAY THE RENT ON MY LOW-INCOME APARTMENT...
...AND I NATURALLY ENDED UP ON THE STREET.
BEING POOR...
...ISN'T SOMETHING YOU GET USED TO. YOU DEAL WITH IT BECAUSE YOU HAVE TO.

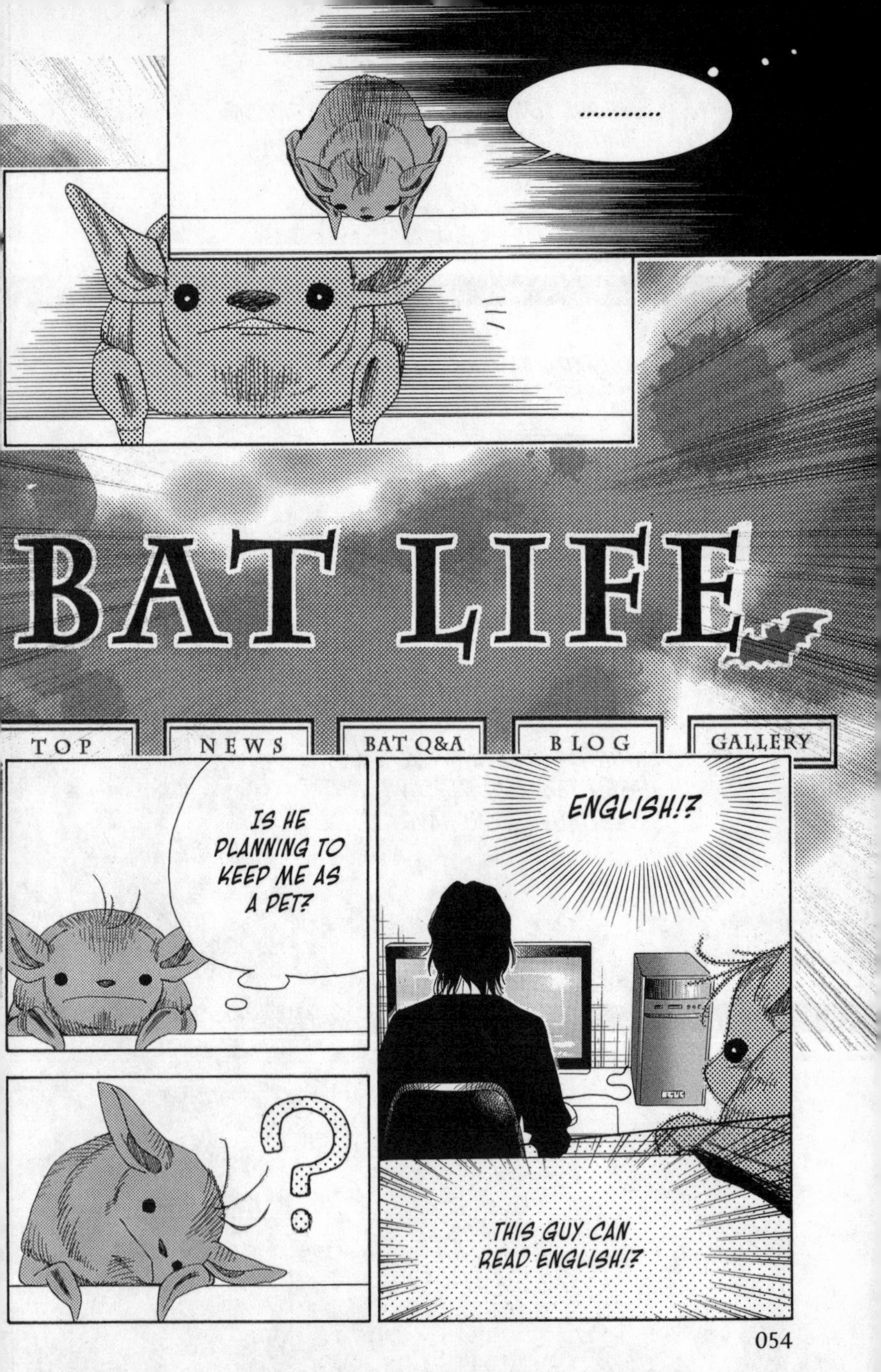
....
BAT LIFE
TOP
NEWS
BAT Q&A
BLOG
GALLERY
ENGLISH!?
THIS GUY CAN READ ENGLISH!?
IS HE PLANNING TO KEEP ME AS A PET?
?

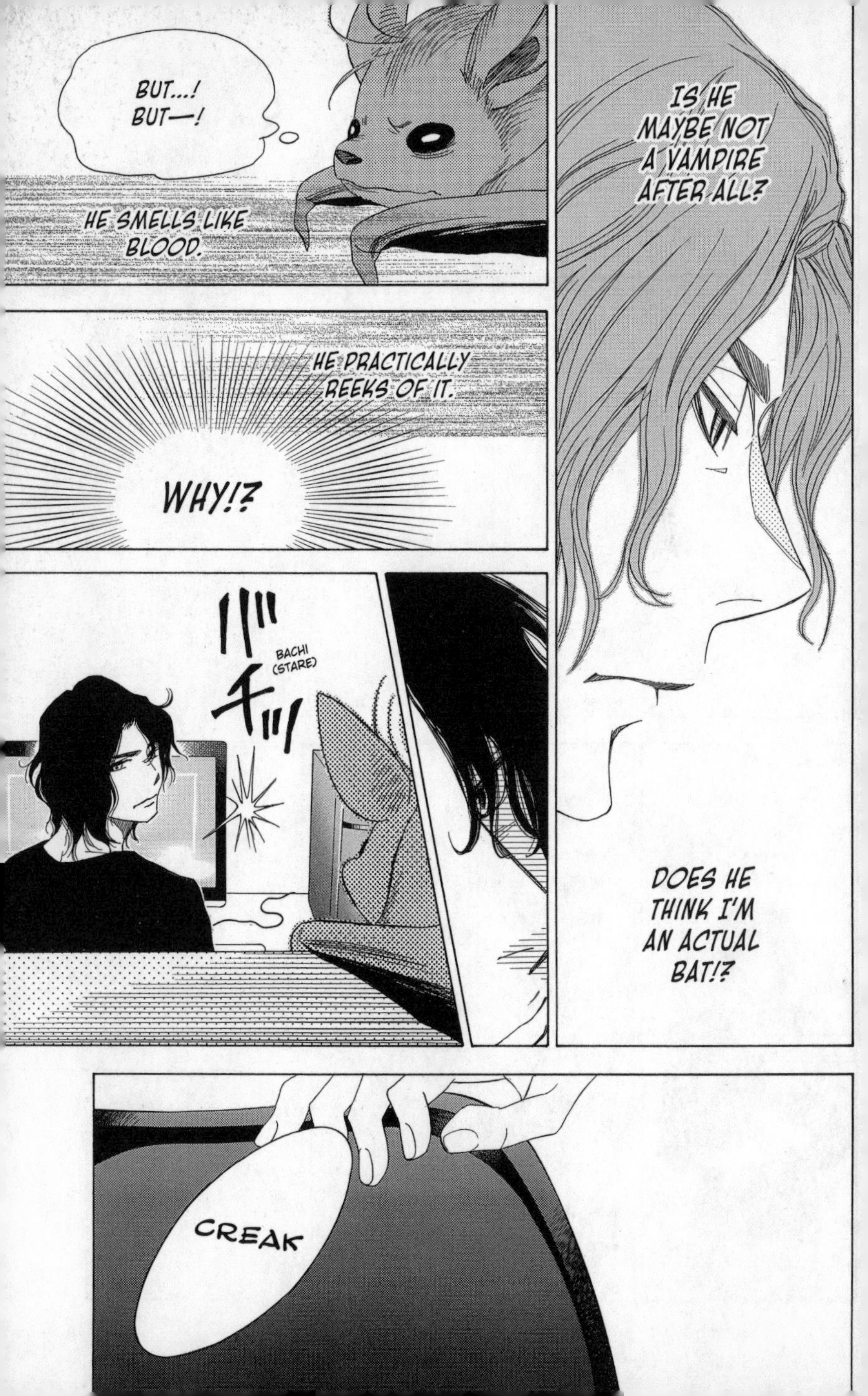
IS HE MAYBE NOT A VAMPIRE AFTER ALL?
DOES HE THINK I'M AN ACTUAL BAT!?
BUT...! BUT—!
HE SMELLS LIKE BLOOD.
HE PRACTICALLY REEKS OF IT.
WHY!?
バチッ
BACHI (STARE)
CREAK

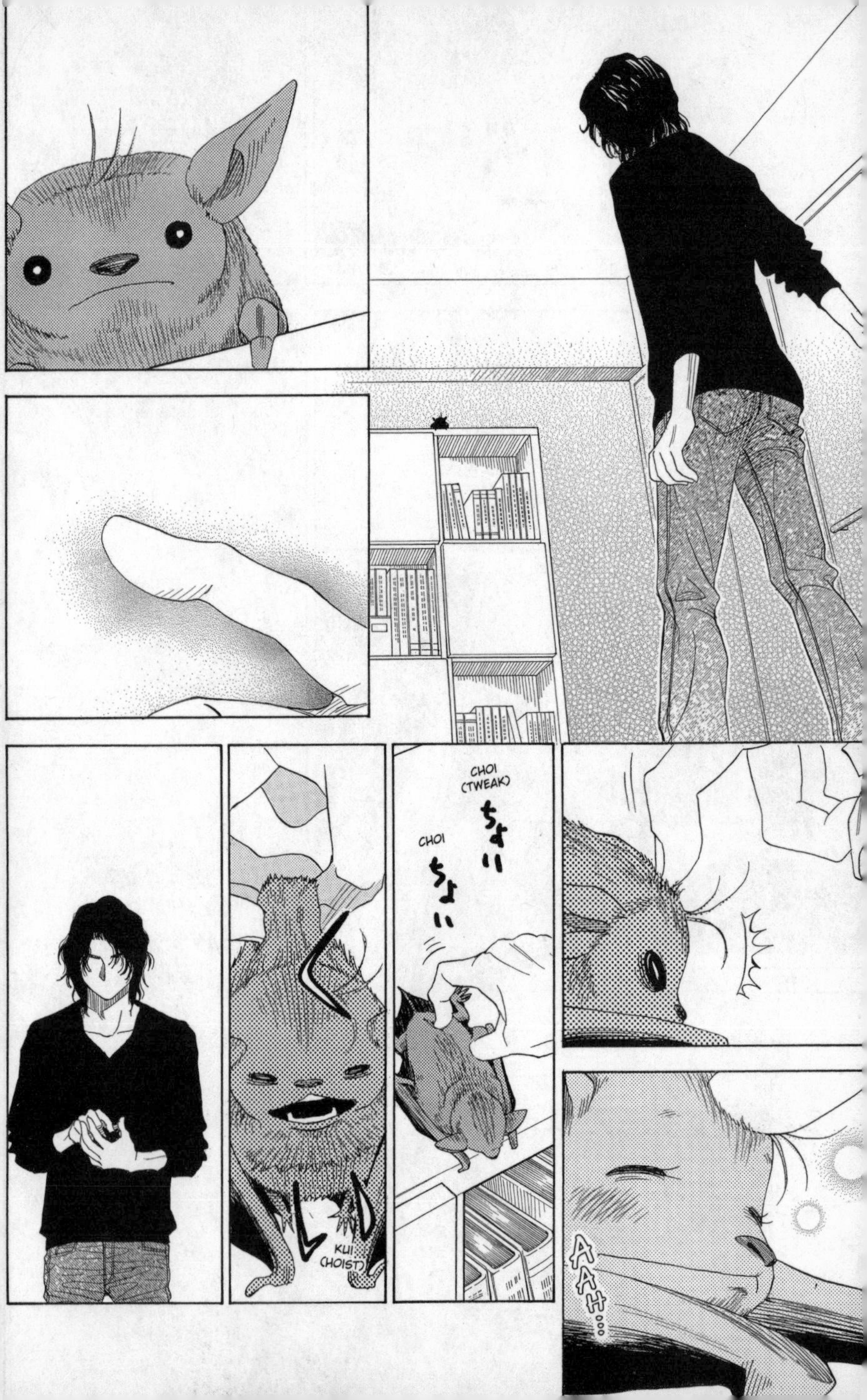

AAH...
CHOI (TWEAK)
ちょい
CHOI
ちょい
KUI (HOIST)

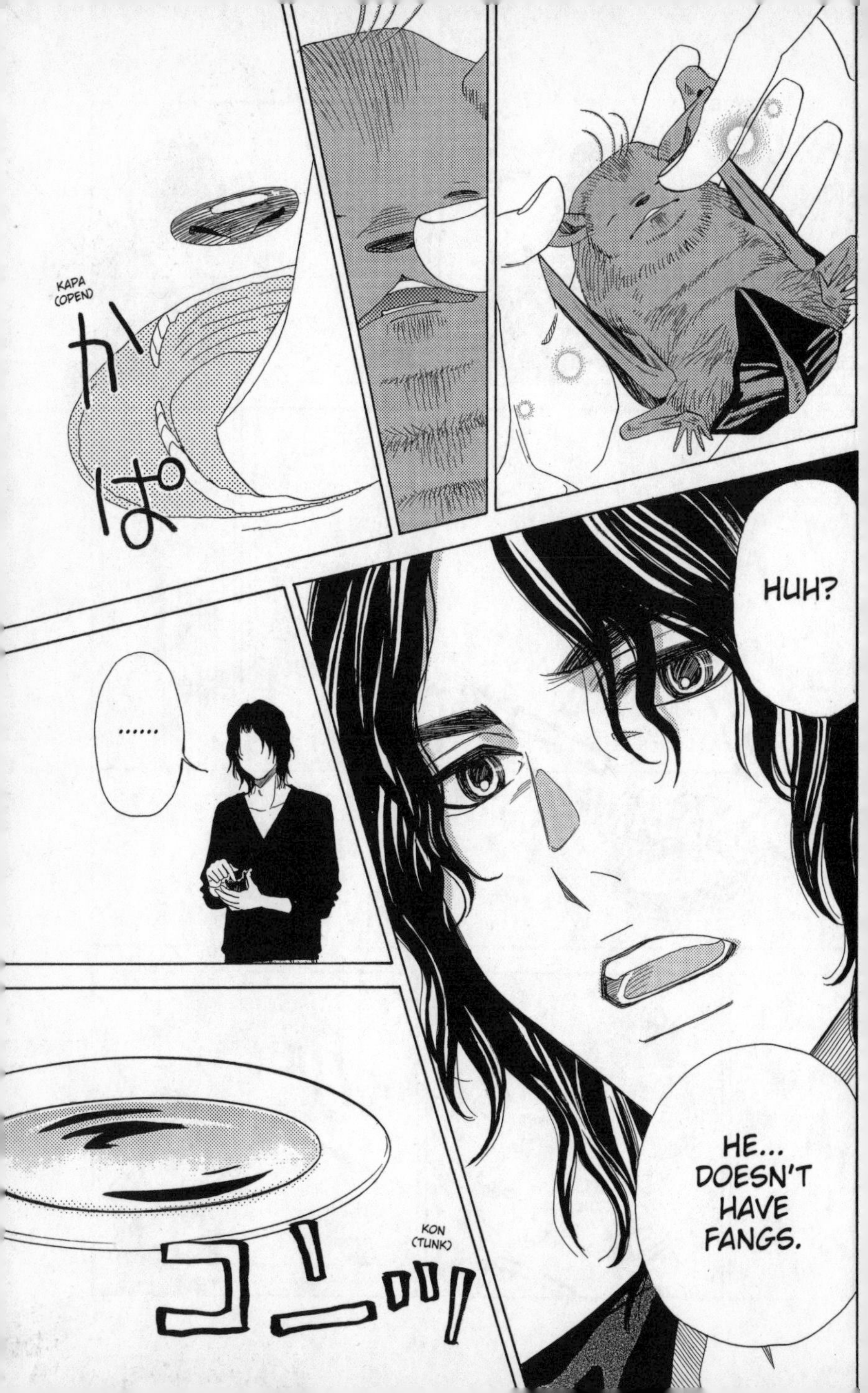
KAPA (OPEN)
かぱ
HUH?
HE... DOESN'T HAVE FANGS.
......
KON (TUNK)
コーッ

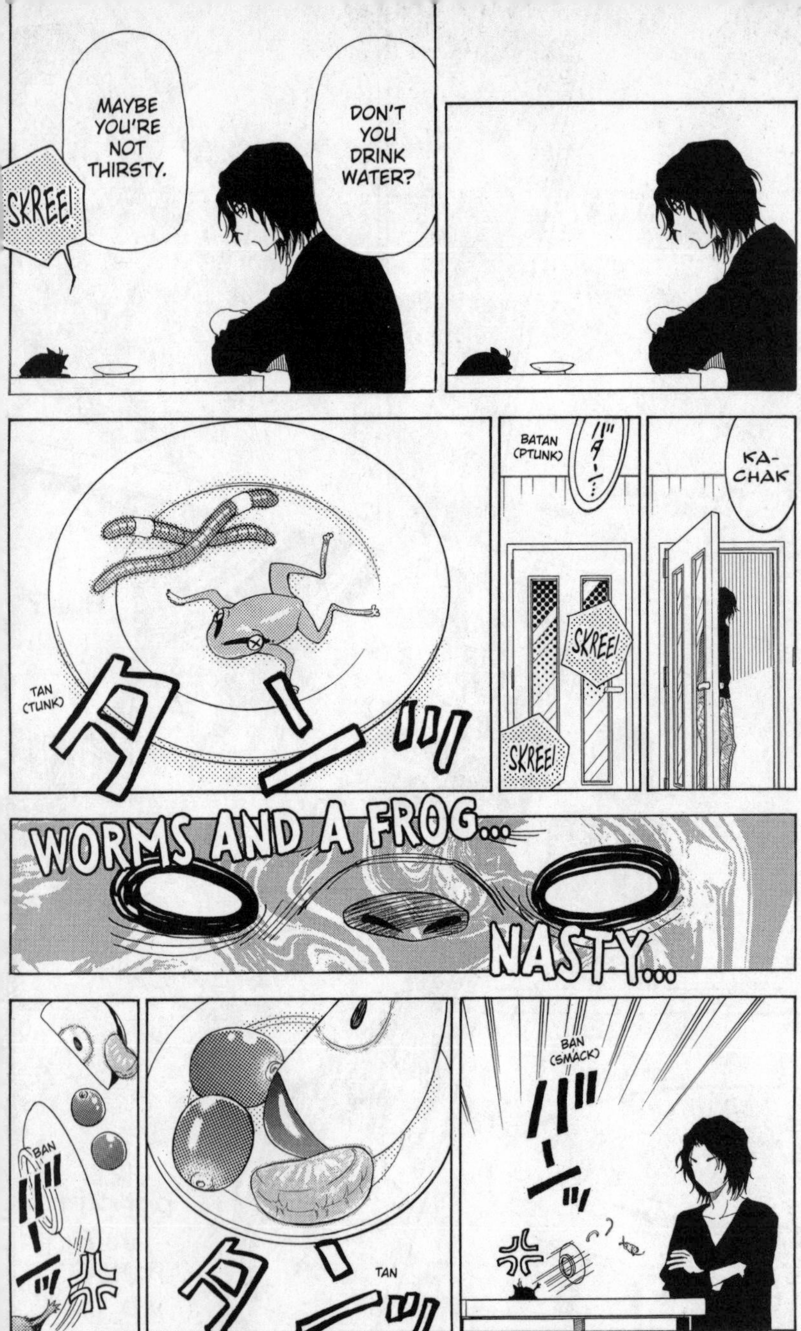
DON'T YOU DRINK WATER?
MAYBE YOU'RE NOT THIRSTY.
SKREE!
KA-CHAK
BATAN (PTUNK)
SKREE!
SKREE!
TAN (TUNK)
WORMS AND A FROG...
NASTY...
BAN (SMACK)
TAN
BAN

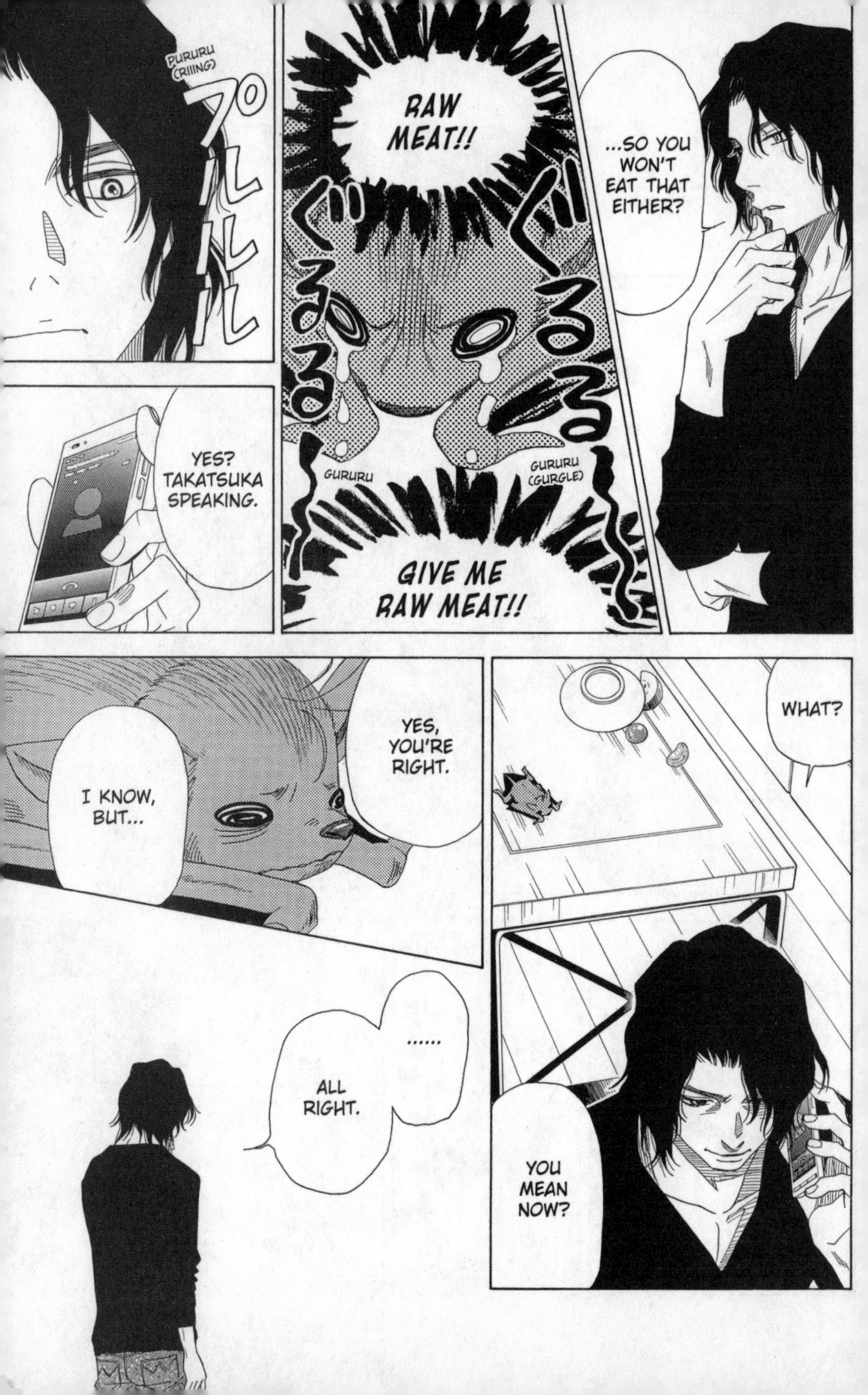
...SO YOU WON'T EAT THAT EITHER?
RAW MEAT!!
ぐるるる
ぐるるる
GURURU (GURGLE)
GURURU
GIVE ME RAW MEAT!!
PURURU (RIIING)
プルルル
YES? TAKATSUKA SPEAKING.
WHAT?
YES, YOU'RE RIGHT.
I KNOW, BUT...
YOU MEAN NOW?
......
ALL RIGHT.

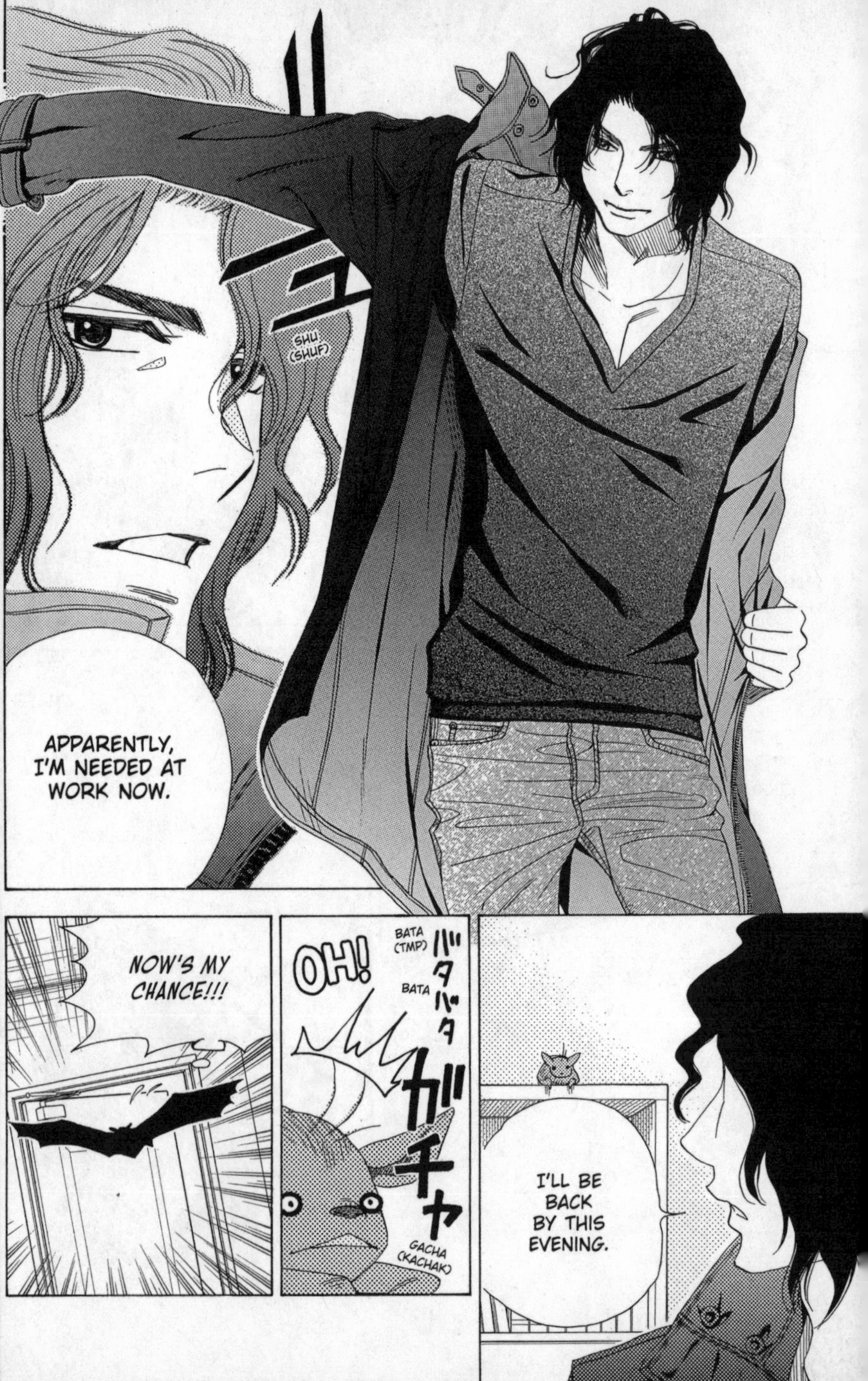
SHU (SHUF)
APPARENTLY, I'M NEEDED AT WORK NOW.
I'LL BE BACK BY THIS EVENING.
OH!
バタバタ
BATA (TMP) BATA
ガチャ
GACHA (KACHAK)
NOW'S MY CHANCE!!!

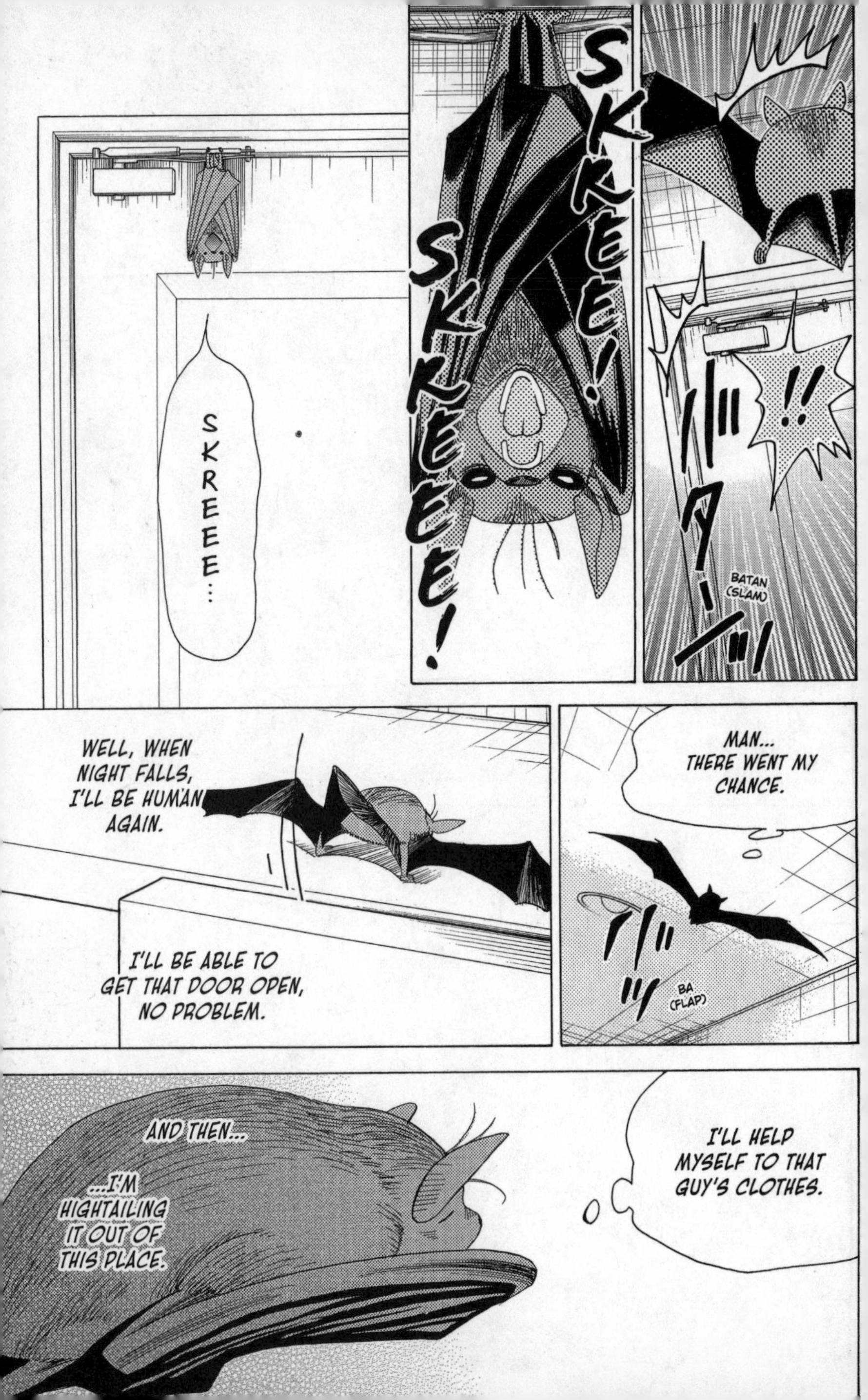
!!
BATAN (SLAM)
SKREE!
SKREEE!
SKREEE...
MAN... THERE WENT MY CHANCE.
BA (FLAP)
WELL, WHEN NIGHT FALLS, I'LL BE HUMAN AGAIN.
I'LL BE ABLE TO GET THAT DOOR OPEN, NO PROBLEM.
I'LL HELP MYSELF TO THAT GUY'S CLOTHES.
AND THEN...
...I'M HIGHTAILING IT OUT OF THIS PLACE.

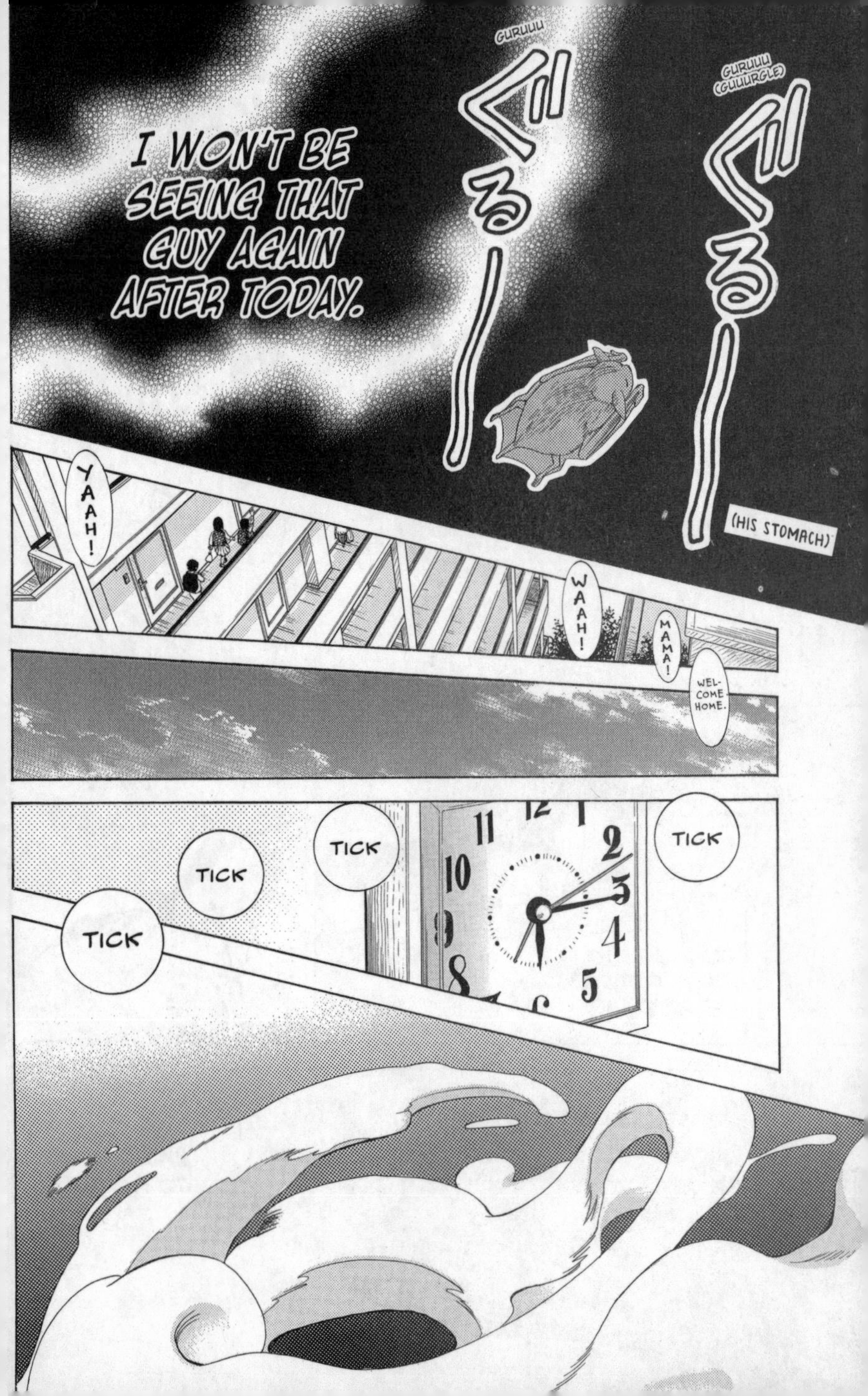
GURUUU (GUUURGLE)
ぐるー
GURUUU
ぐるー
(HIS STOMACH)
I WON'T BE SEEING THAT GUY AGAIN AFTER TODAY.
WEL-COME HOME.
MAMA!
WAAAH!
YAAAH!
TICK
TICK
TICK
TICK

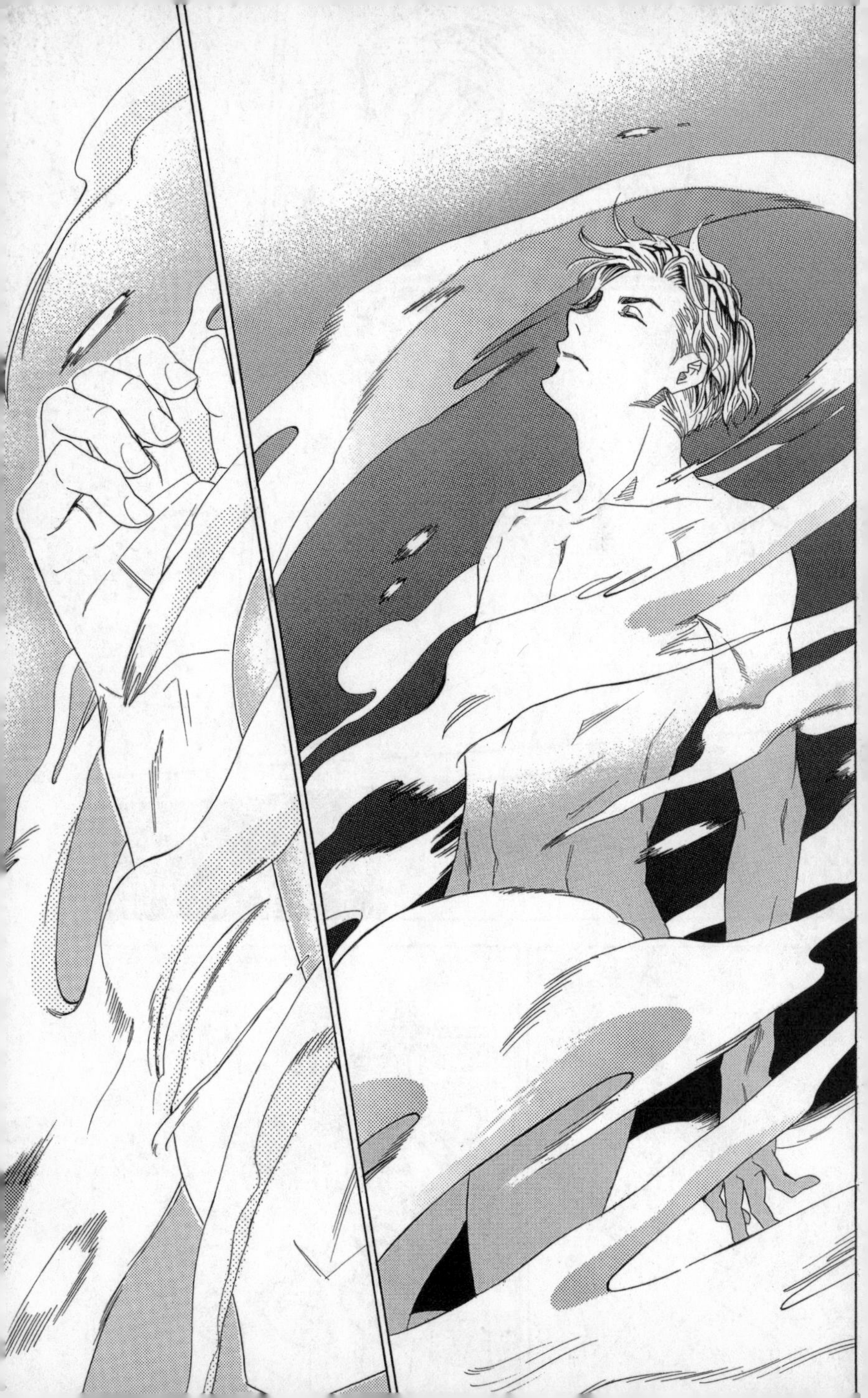

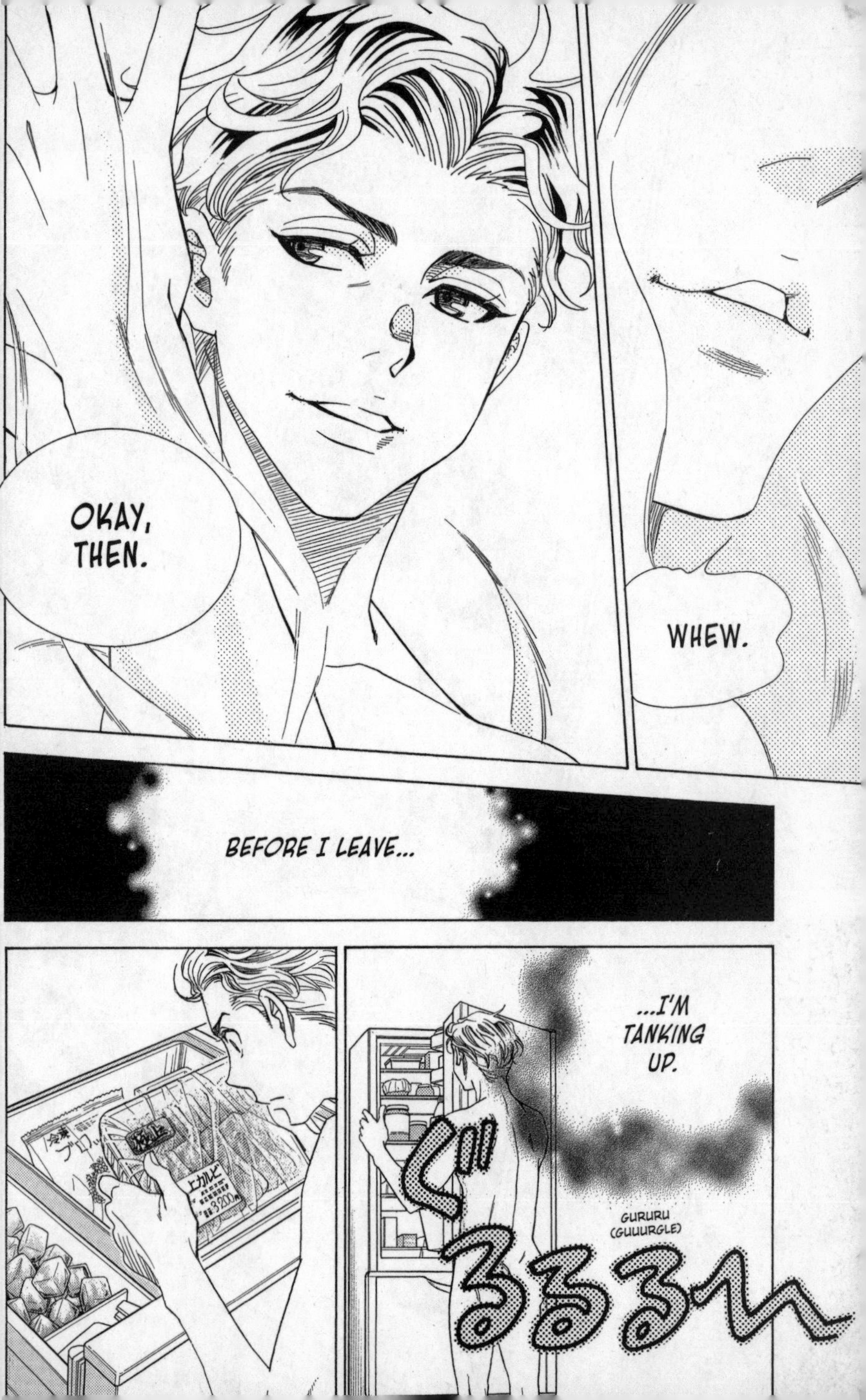
WHEW.
OKAY, THEN.
BEFORE I LEAVE...
...I'M TANKING UP.
ぐるるるん
GURURU (GUUURGLE)

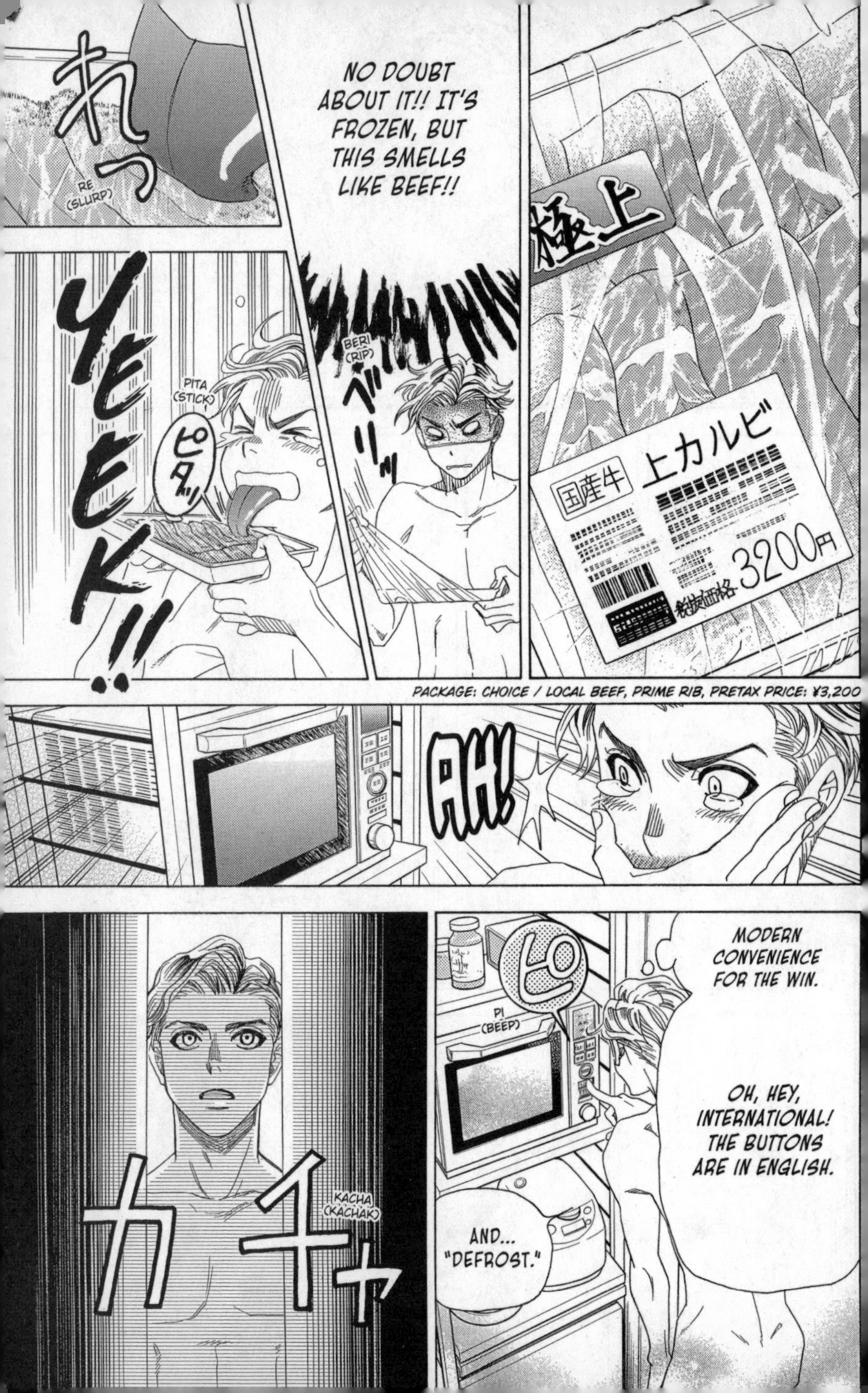
極上
国産牛 上カルビ
税抜価格 3200円
PACKAGE: CHOICE / LOCAL BEEF, PRIME RIB, PRETAX PRICE: ¥3,200
NO DOUBT ABOUT IT!! IT'S FROZEN, BUT THIS SMELLS LIKE BEEF!!
ベリッ
BERI (RIP)
れっ
RE (SLURP)
YEEEK!!
ピタッ
PITA (STICK)
AH!
MODERN CONVENIENCE FOR THE WIN.
OH, HEY, INTERNATIONAL! THE BUTTONS ARE IN ENGLISH.
ピ
PI (BEEP)
AND... "DEFROST."
カイャ
KACHA (KACHAK)

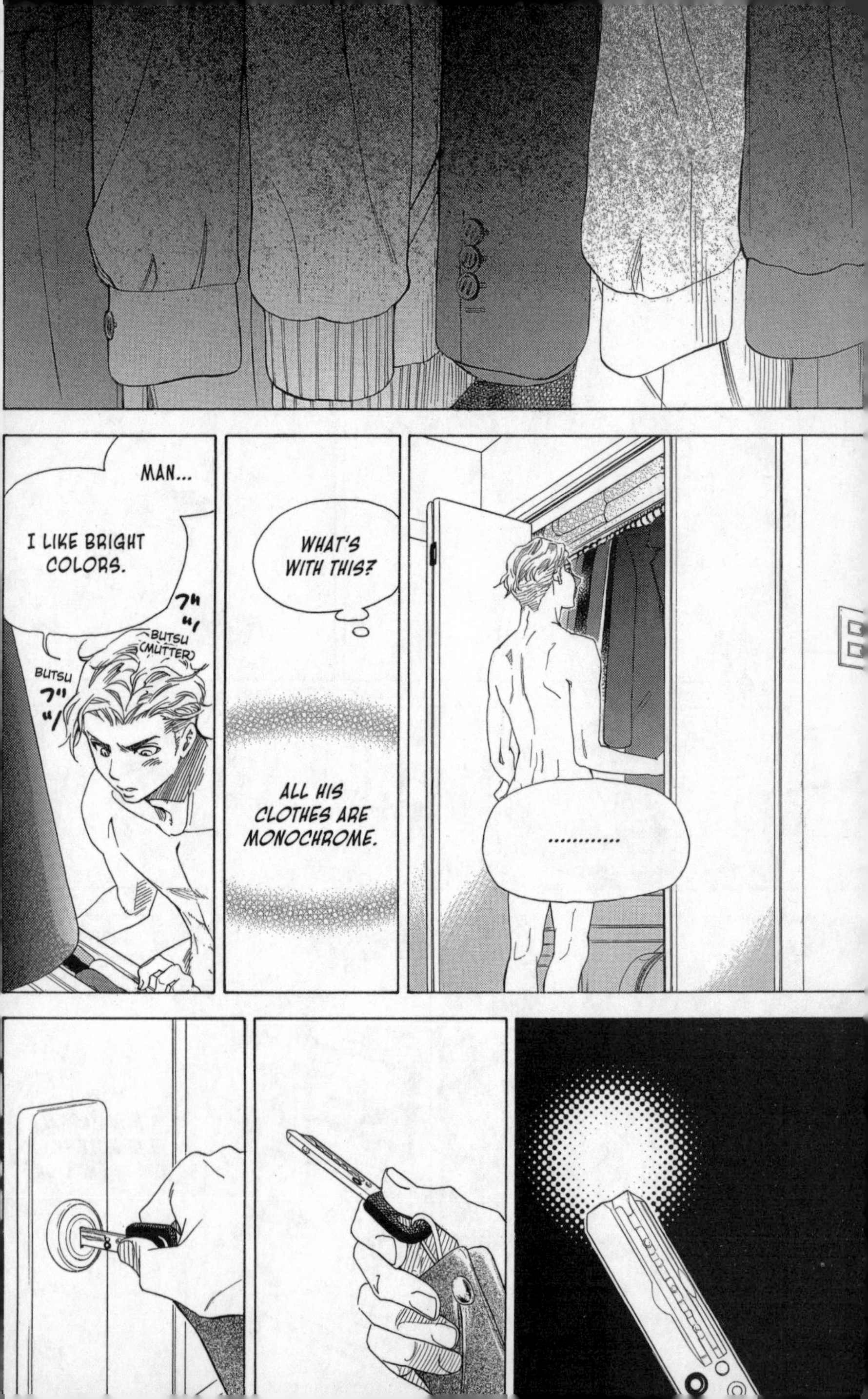
....
WHAT'S WITH THIS?
ALL HIS CLOTHES ARE MONOCHROME.
MAN...
I LIKE BRIGHT COLORS.
BUTSU (MUTTER)
BUTSU

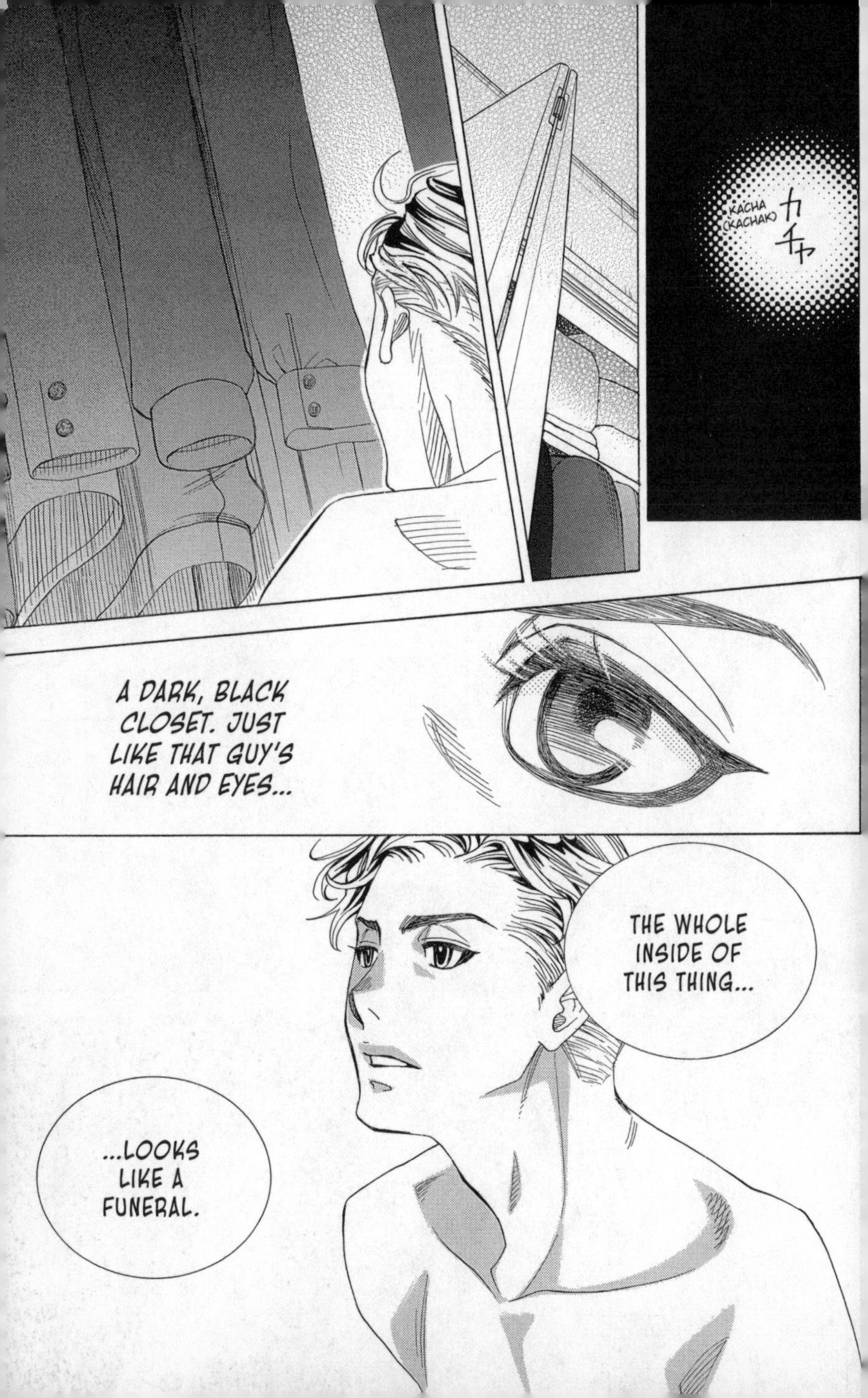
KACHA (KACHAK)
カチャ
A DARK, BLACK CLOSET. JUST LIKE THAT GUY'S HAIR AND EYES...
THE WHOLE INSIDE OF THIS THING...
...LOOKS LIKE A FUNERAL.

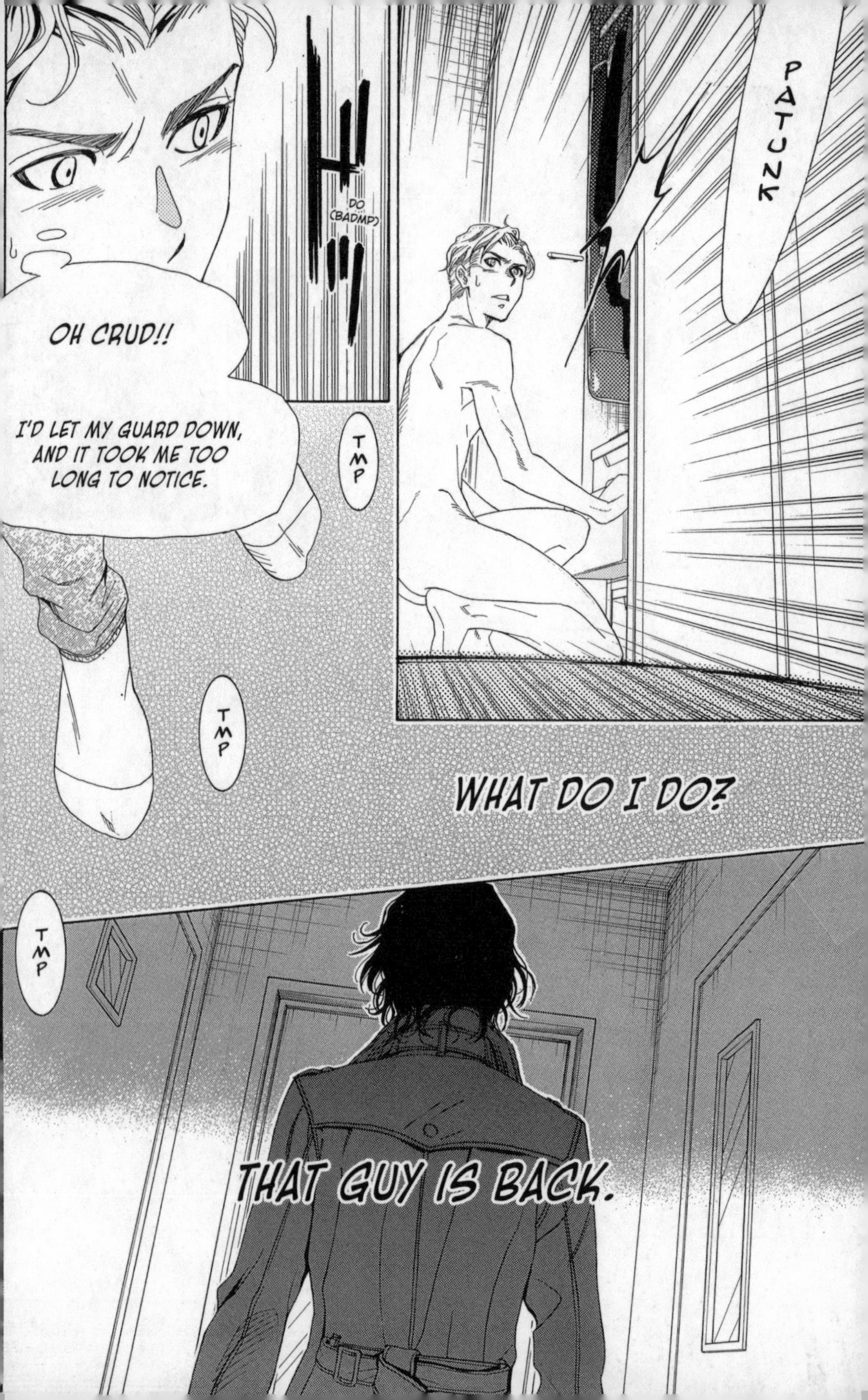
PATUNK
DO (BADMP)
OH CRUD!!
I'D LET MY GUARD DOWN, AND IT TOOK ME TOO LONG TO NOTICE.
TMP
TMP
WHAT DO I DO?
TMP
THAT GUY IS BACK.

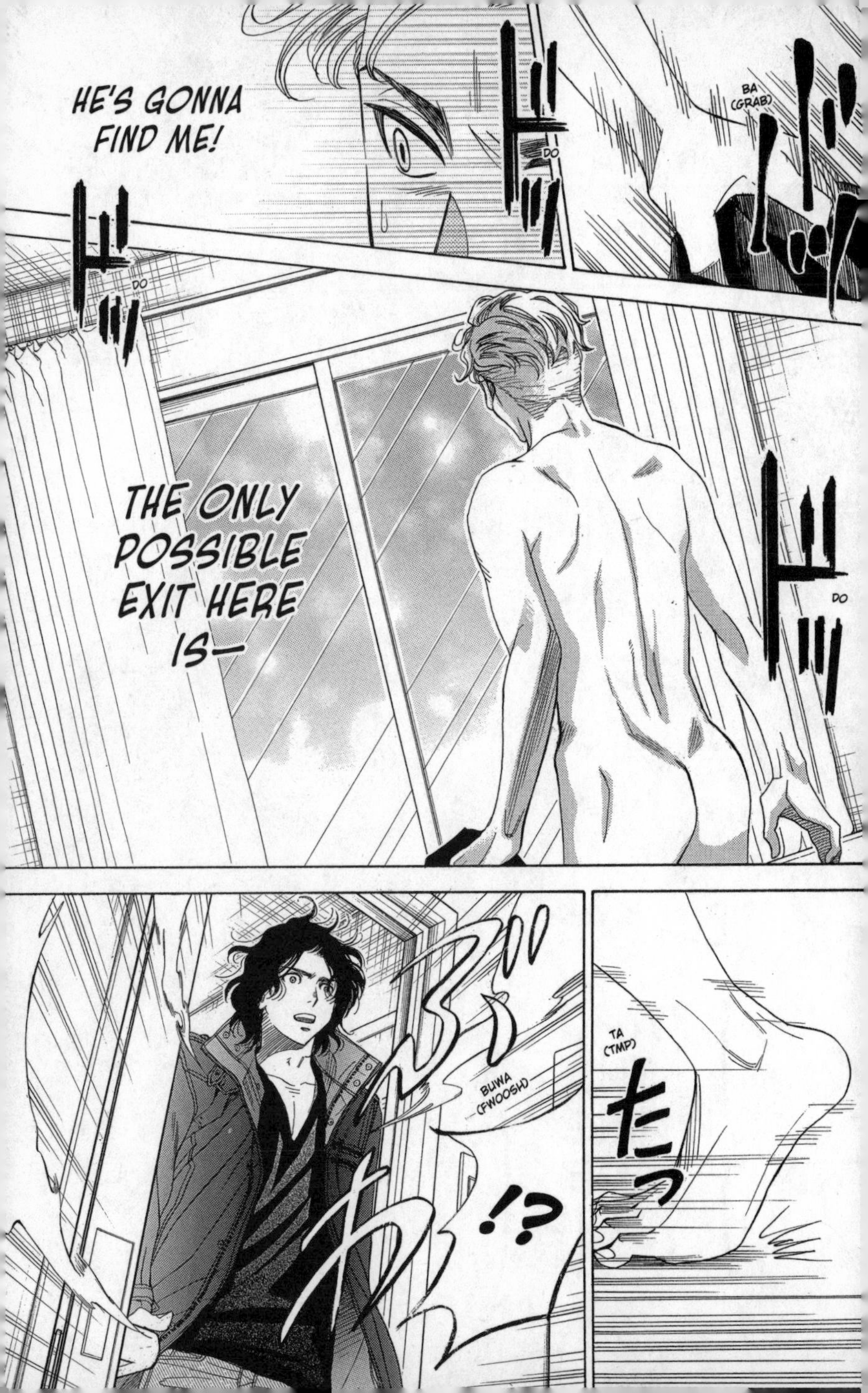
BA (GRAB)
DO
HE'S GONNA FIND ME!
DO
THE ONLY POSSIBLE EXIT HERE IS—
DO
TA (TMP)
BUWA (FWOOSH)
!?

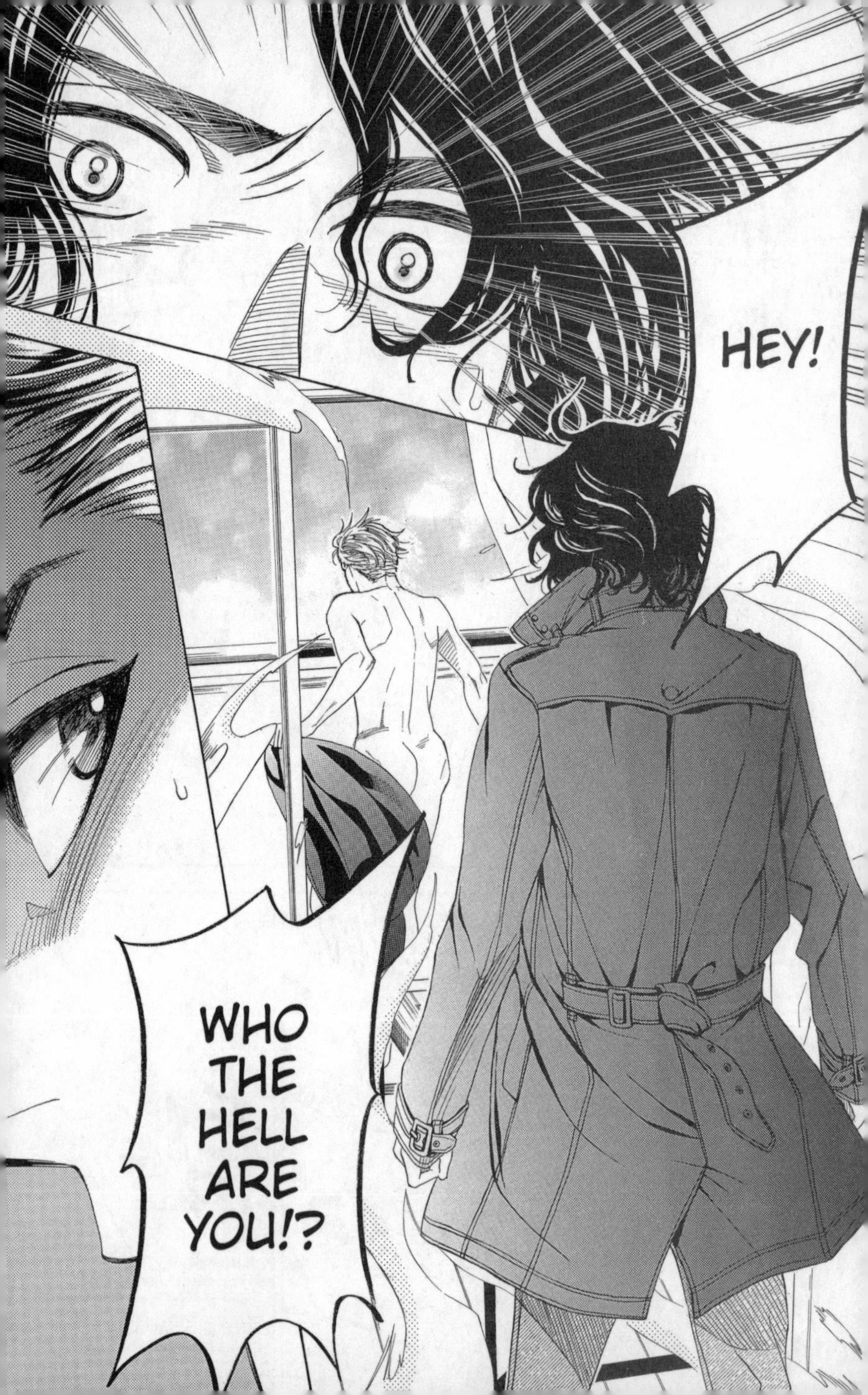
HEY!
WHO THE HELL ARE YOU!?

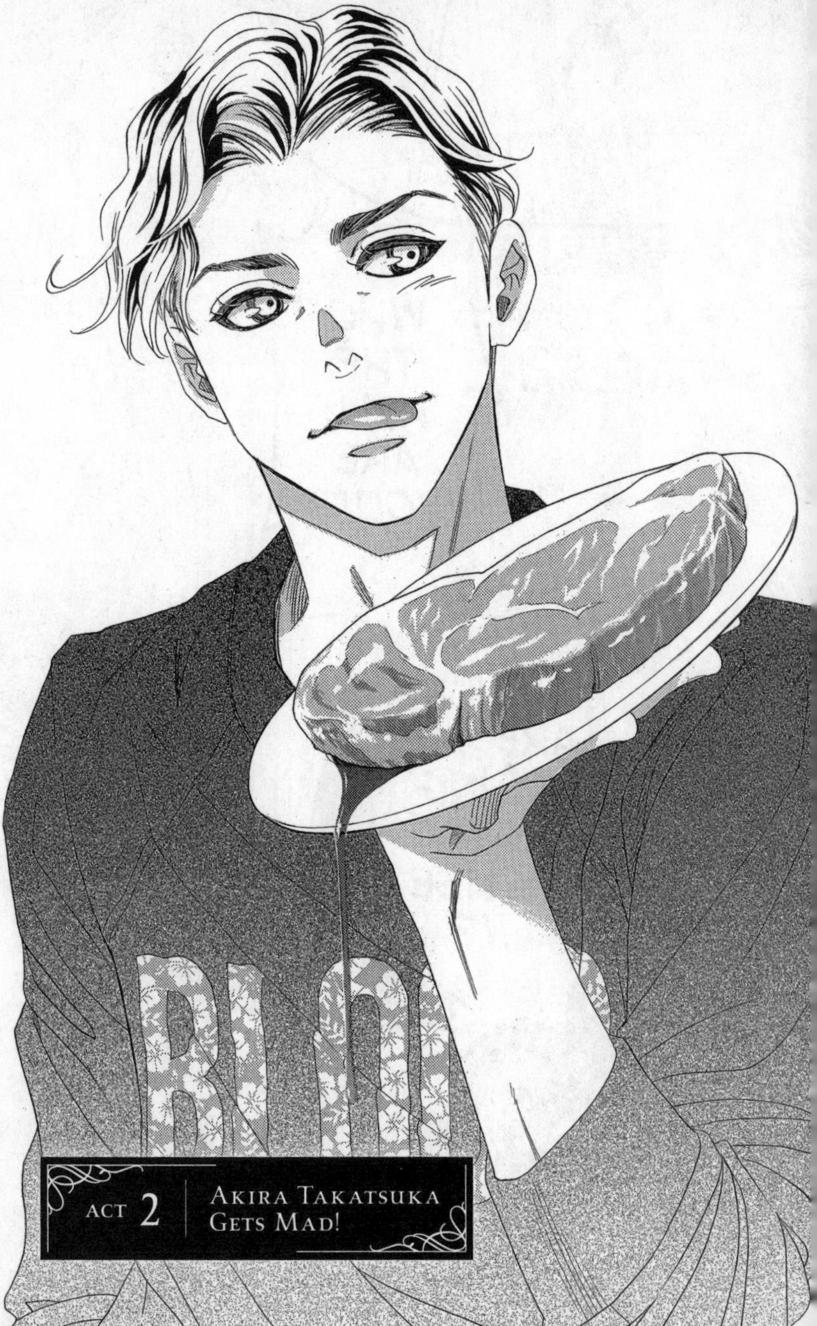

ACT 2 | Akira Takatsuka Gets Mad!

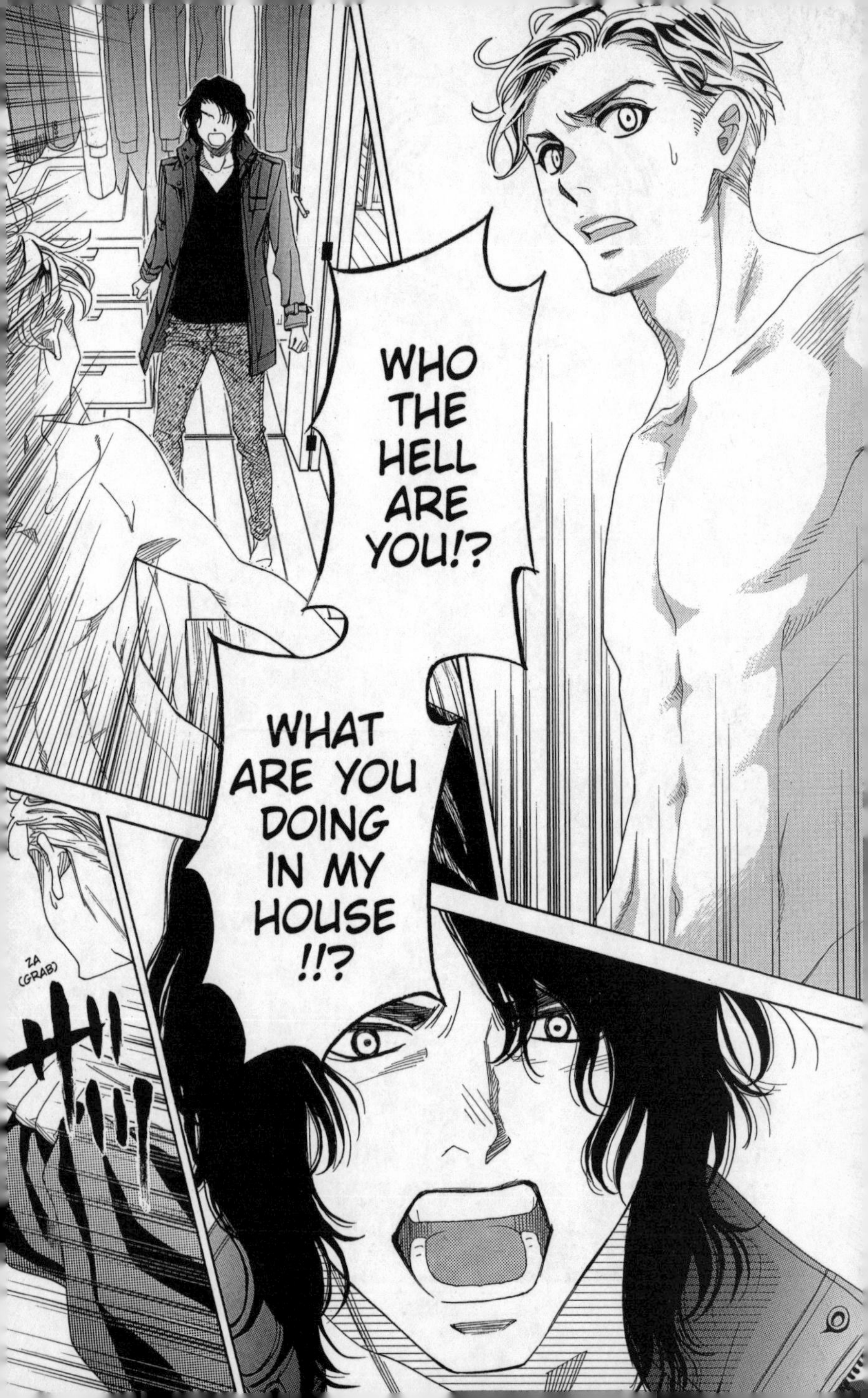
WHO THE HELL ARE YOU!?
WHAT ARE YOU DOING IN MY HOUSE !!?
ZA (GRAB)

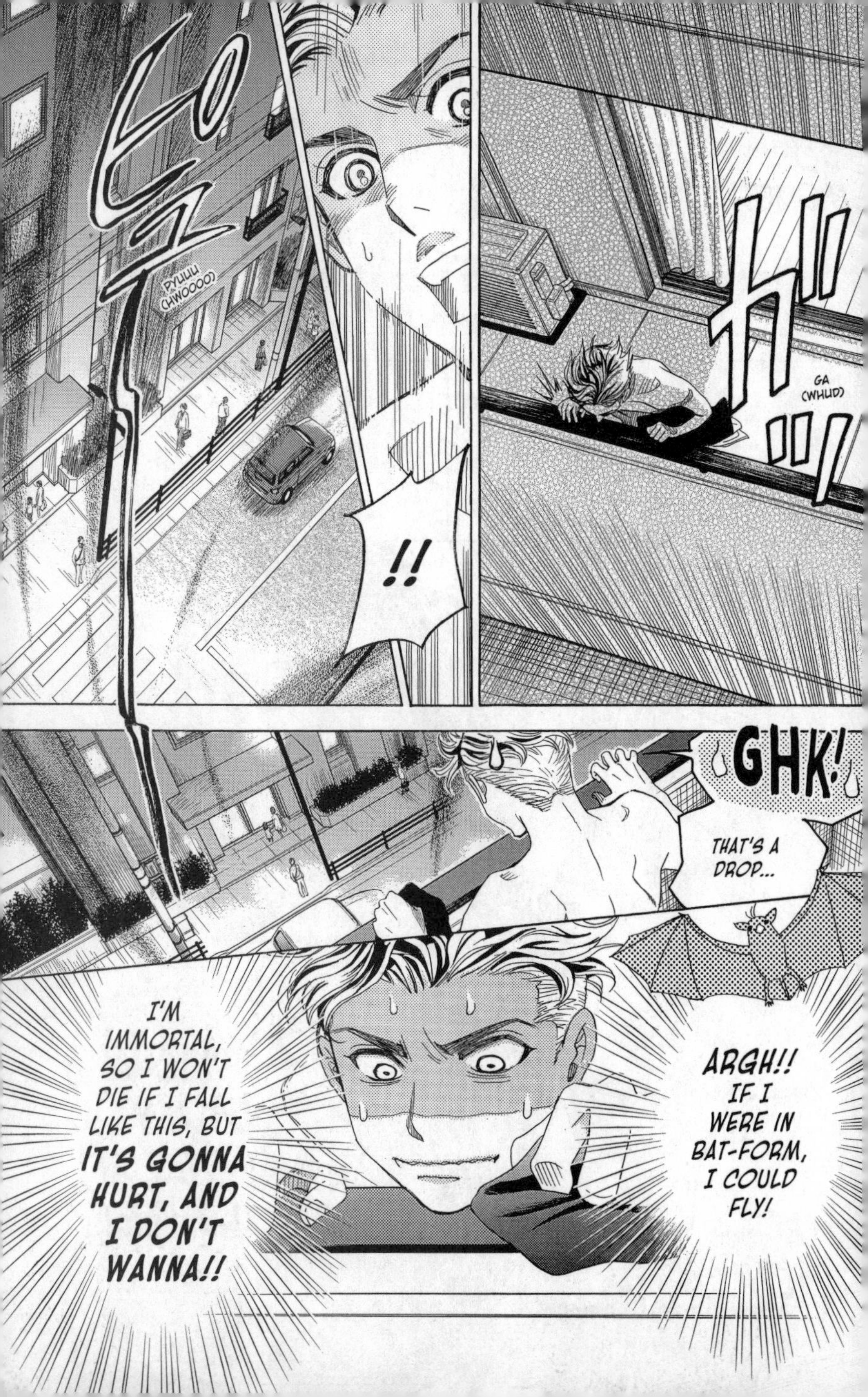
GA
(WHUD)
!!
PYUUU
(WHOOOO)
GHK!
THAT'S A DROP...
ARGH!! IF I WERE IN BAT-FORM, I COULD FLY!
I'M IMMORTAL, SO I WON'T DIE IF I FALL LIKE THIS, BUT IT'S GONNA HURT, AND I DON'T WANNA!!

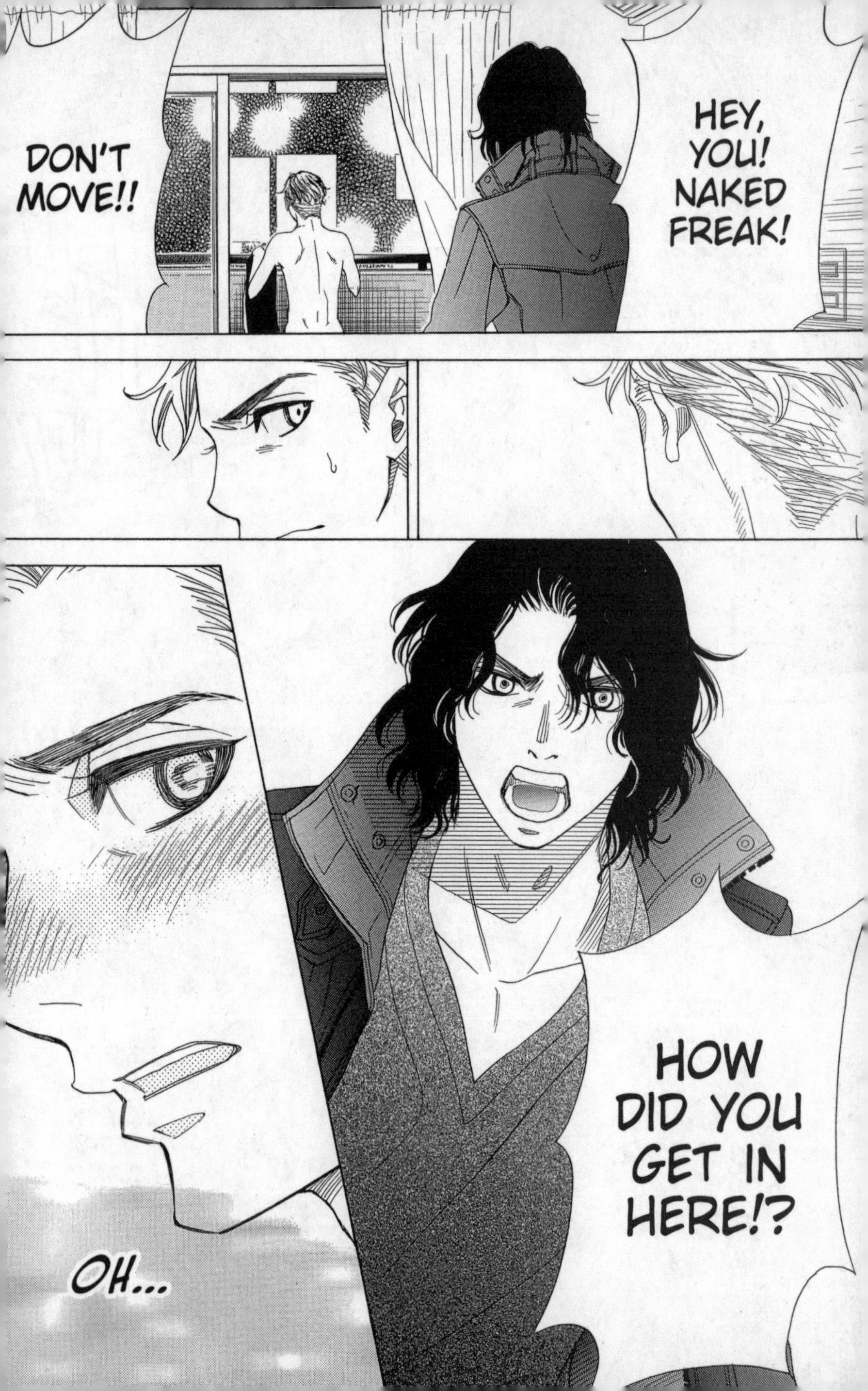
HEY, YOU! NAKED FREAK!
DON'T MOVE!!
HOW DID YOU GET IN HERE!?
OH...

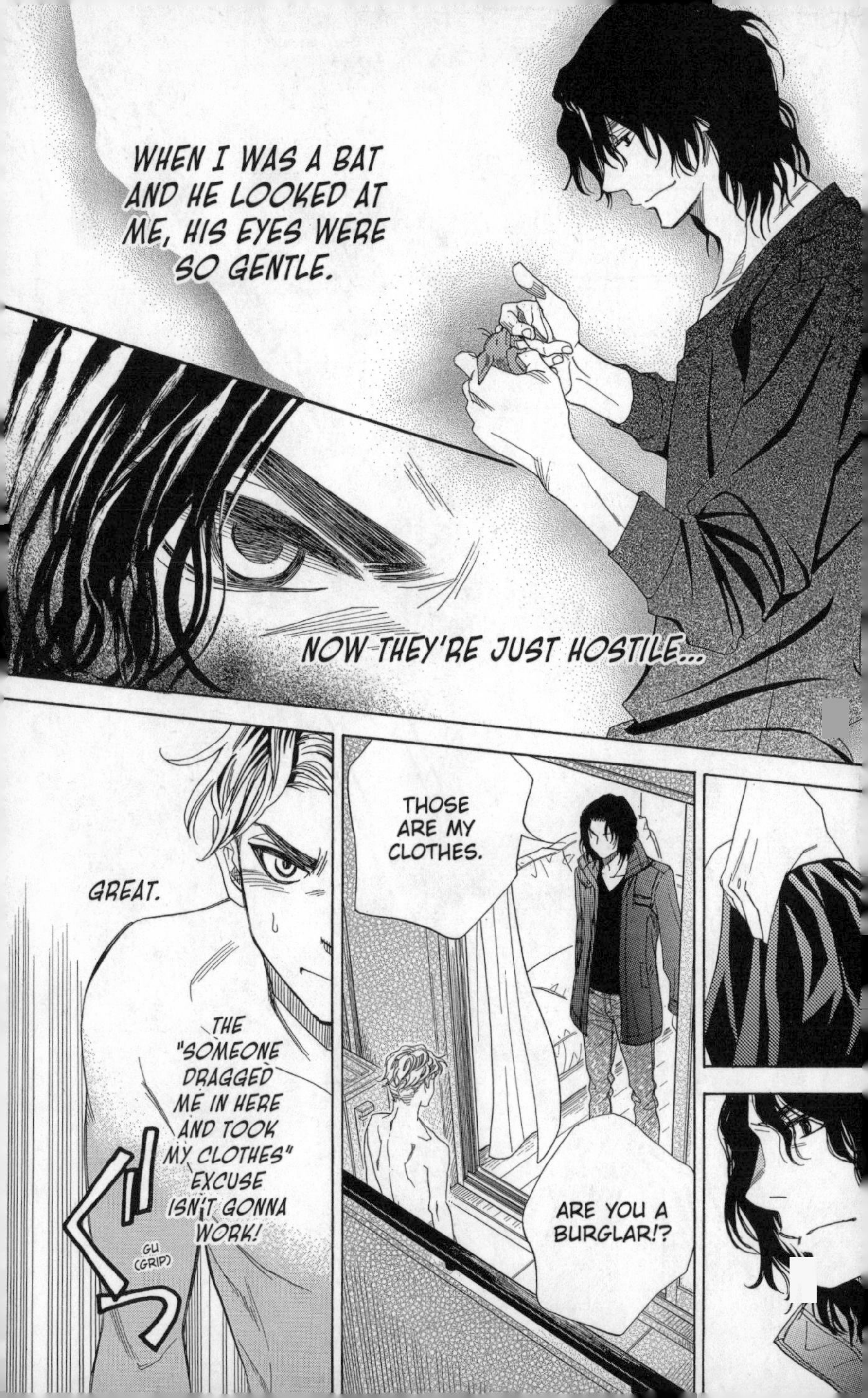
WHEN I WAS A BAT AND HE LOOKED AT ME, HIS EYES WERE SO GENTLE.
NOW THEY'RE JUST HOSTILE...
THOSE ARE MY CLOTHES.
ARE YOU A BURGLAR!?
GREAT.
THE "SOMEONE DRAGGED ME IN HERE AND TOOK MY CLOTHES" EXCUSE ISN'T GONNA WORK!
GU (GRIP)

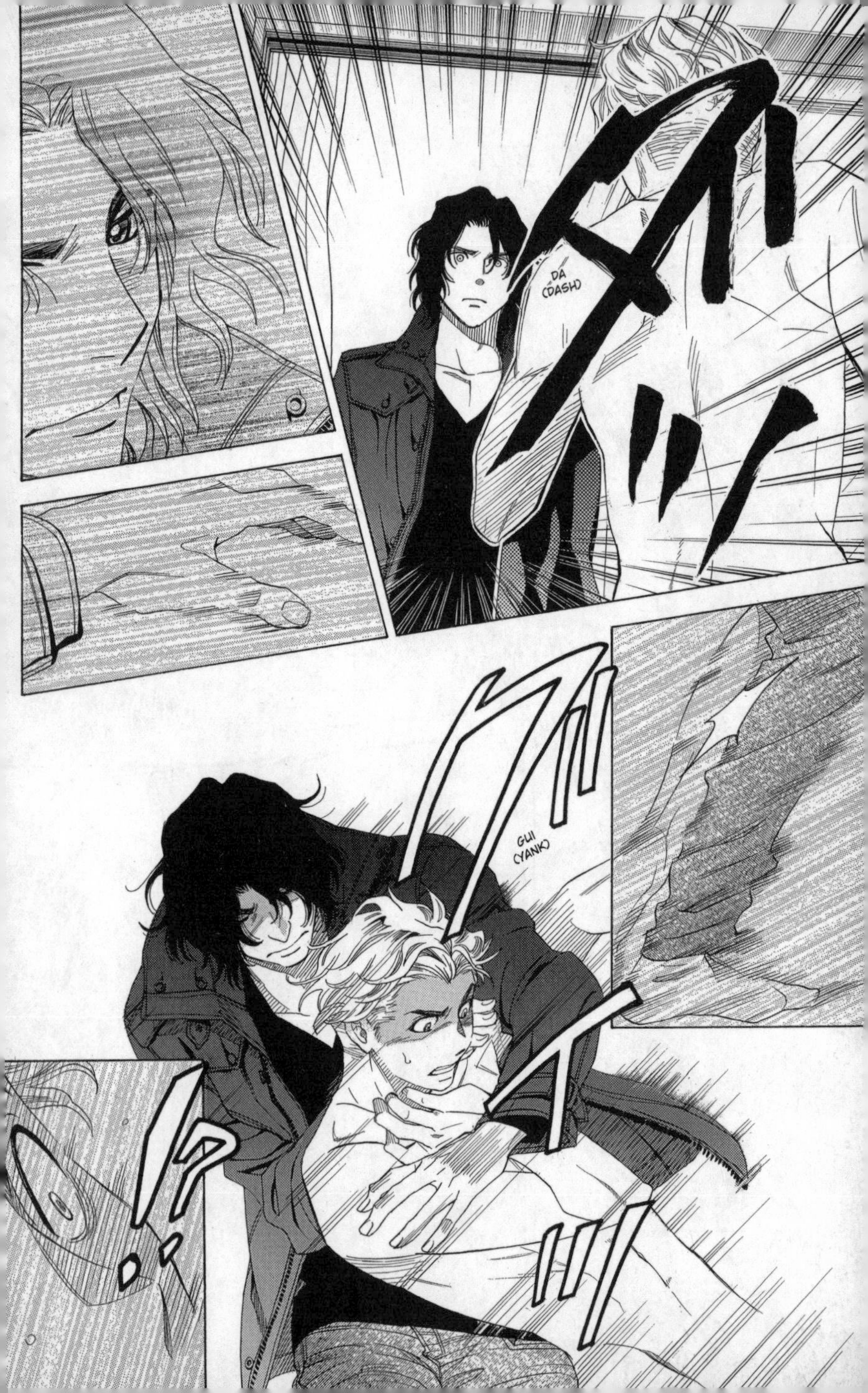
DA
(DASH)
GUI
(YANK)
!?

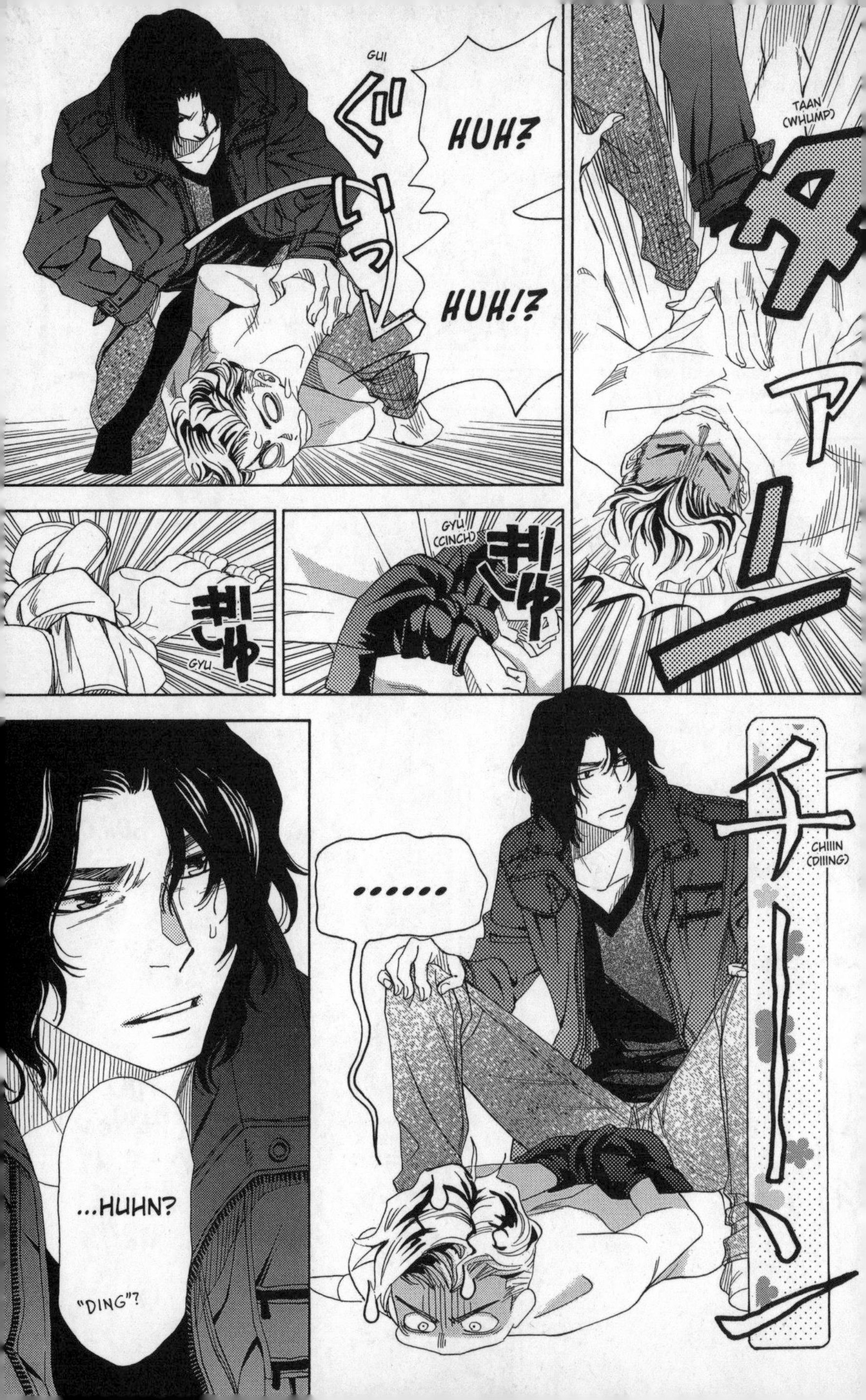
TAAN (WHUMP)
GUI
HUH?
HUH!?
GYU (CINCH)
GYU
CHIIIN (DIIING)
......
...HUHN?
"DING"?

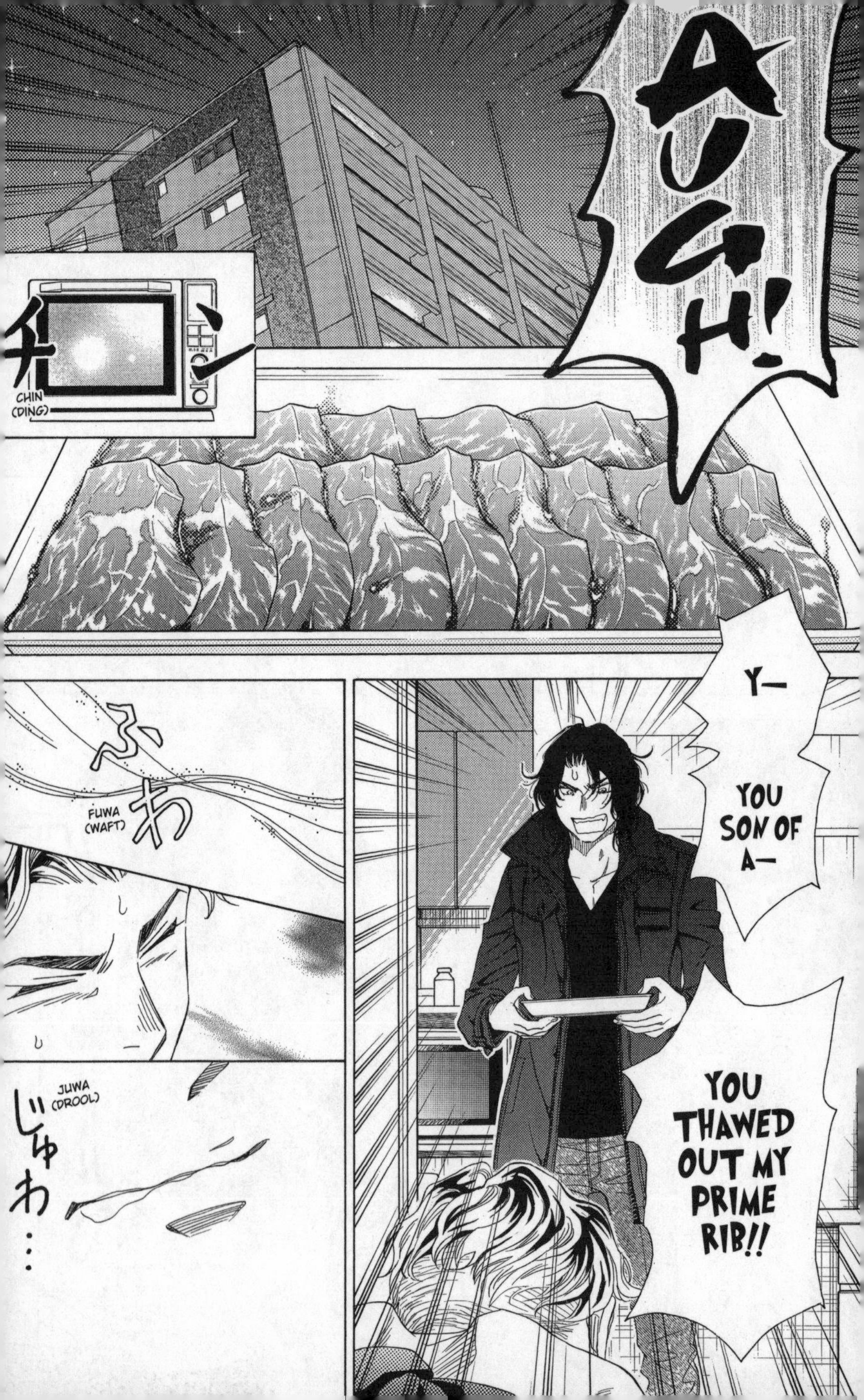
AUGH!
チン
CHIN (DING)
Y—
YOU SON OF A—
YOU THAWED OUT MY PRIME RIB!!
ふわ
FUWA (WAFT)
じゅわ…
JUWA (DROOL)

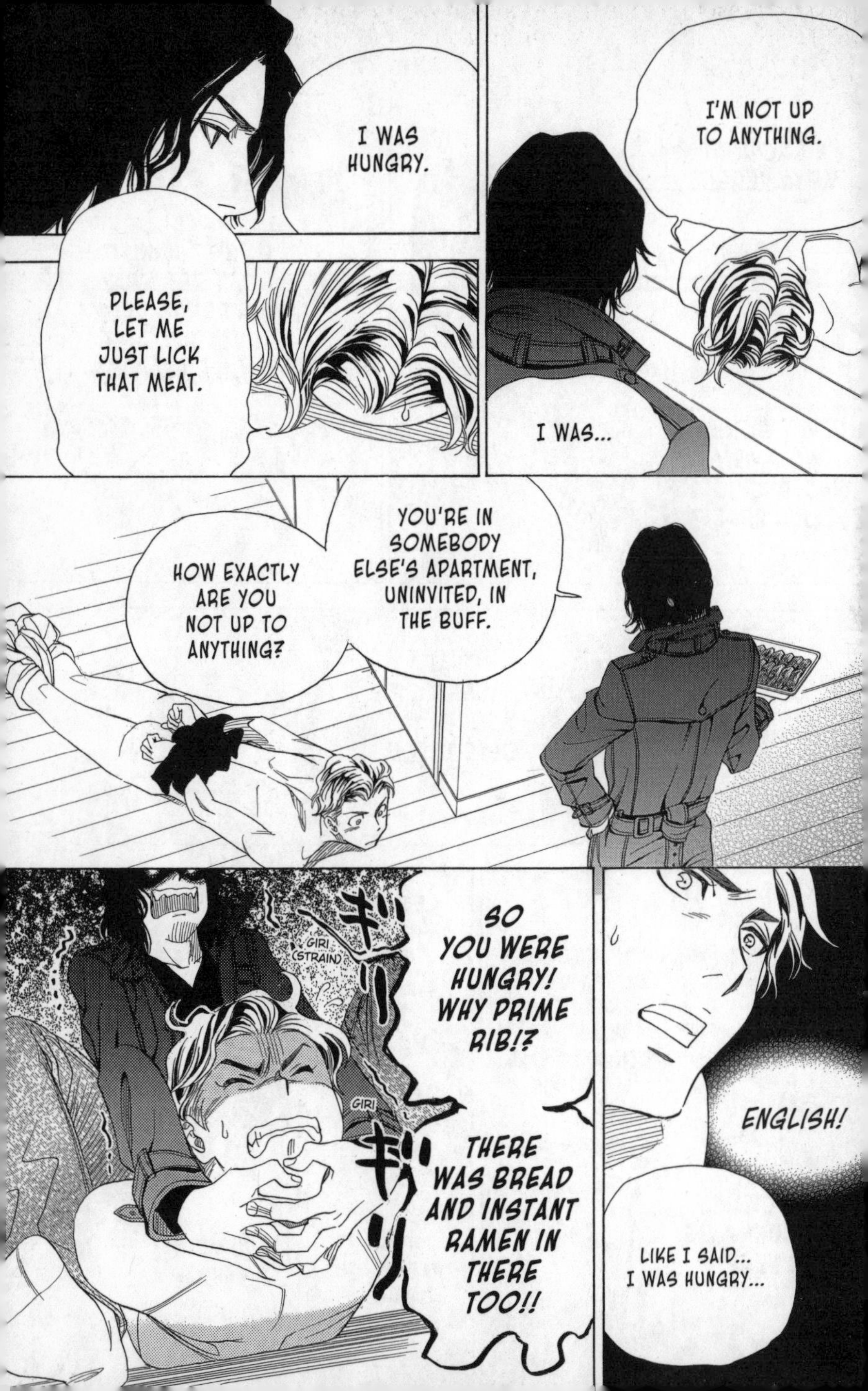
I'M NOT UP TO ANYTHING.
I WAS...
I WAS HUNGRY.
PLEASE, LET ME JUST LICK THAT MEAT.
YOU'RE IN SOMEBODY ELSE'S APARTMENT, UNINVITED, IN THE BUFF.
HOW EXACTLY ARE YOU NOT UP TO ANYTHING?
ENGLISH!
LIKE I SAID... I WAS HUNGRY...
SO YOU WERE HUNGRY! WHY PRIME RIB!?
GIRI (STRAIN)
GIRI
THERE WAS BREAD AND INSTANT RAMEN IN THERE TOO!!

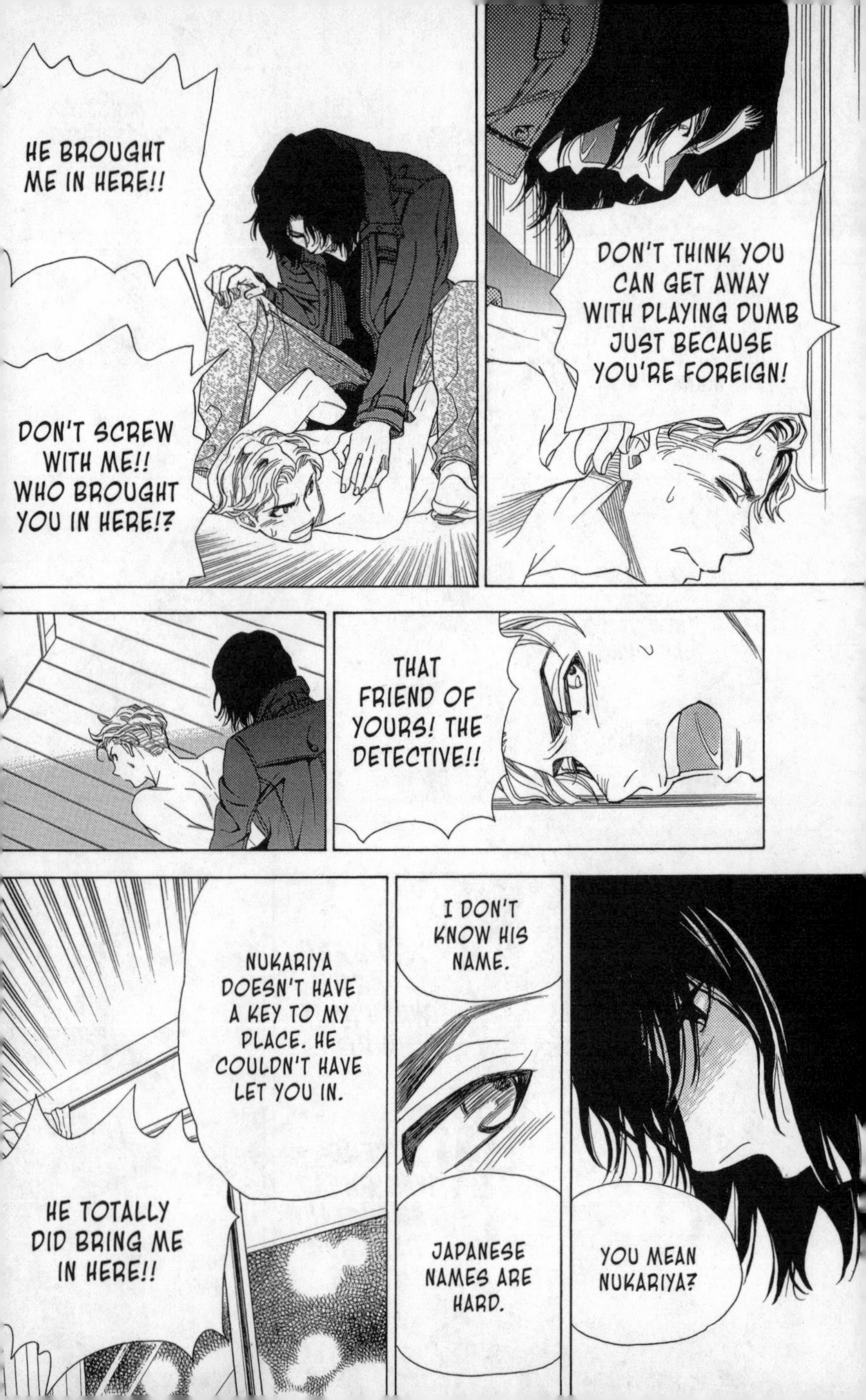
DON'T THINK YOU CAN GET AWAY WITH PLAYING DUMB JUST BECAUSE YOU'RE FOREIGN!
HE BROUGHT ME IN HERE!!
DON'T SCREW WITH ME!! WHO BROUGHT YOU IN HERE!?
THAT FRIEND OF YOURS! THE DETECTIVE!!
YOU MEAN NUKARIYA?
I DON'T KNOW HIS NAME.
JAPANESE NAMES ARE HARD.
NUKARIYA DOESN'T HAVE A KEY TO MY PLACE. HE COULDN'T HAVE LET YOU IN.
HE TOTALLY DID BRING ME IN HERE!!

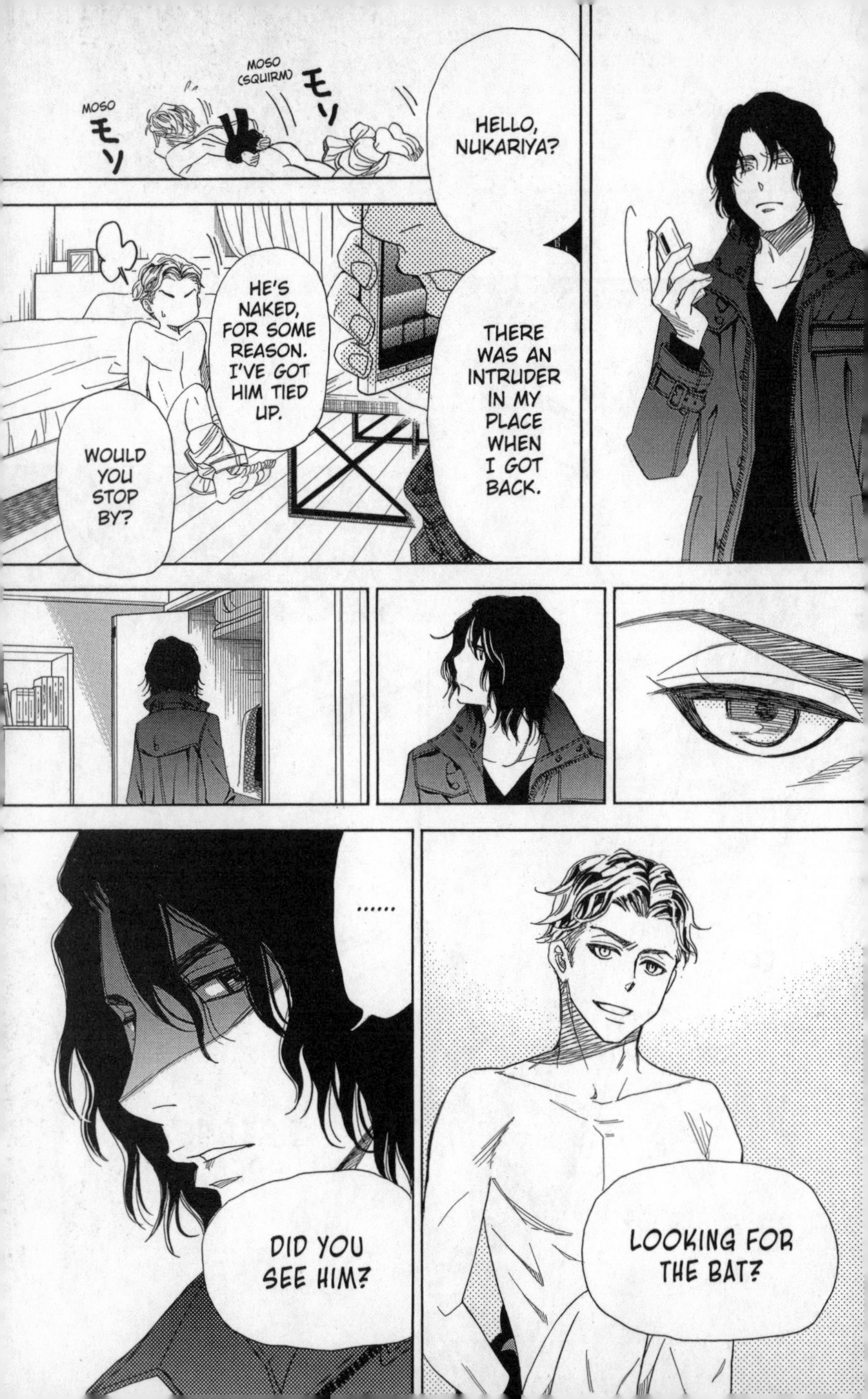
HELLO, NUKARIYA?
THERE WAS AN INTRUDER IN MY PLACE WHEN I GOT BACK.
MOSO (SQUIRM) モソ
MOSO モソ
HE'S NAKED, FOR SOME REASON. I'VE GOT HIM TIED UP.
WOULD YOU STOP BY?
LOOKING FOR THE BAT?
......
DID YOU SEE HIM?

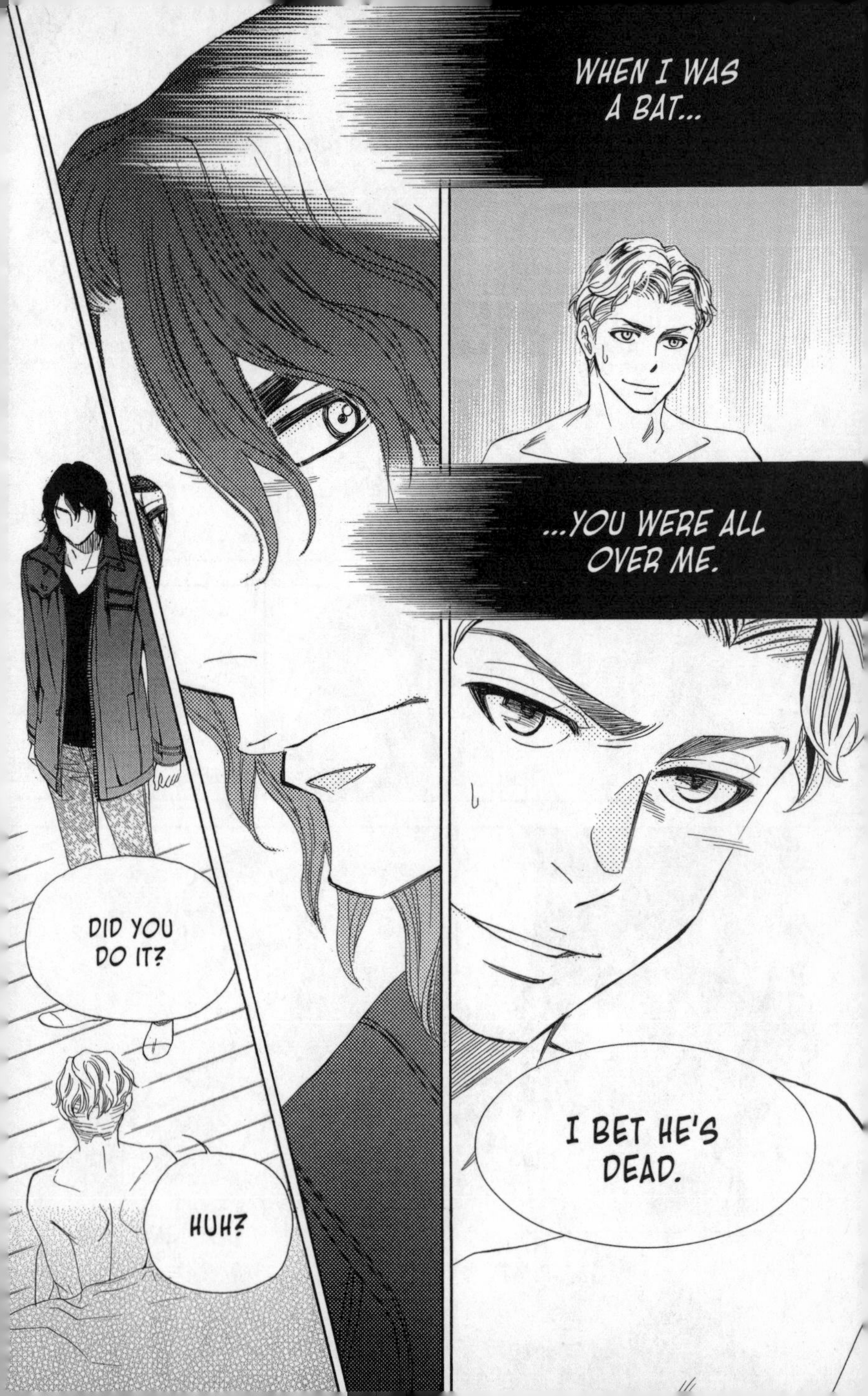
WHEN I WAS A BAT...
...YOU WERE ALL OVER ME.
I BET HE'S DEAD.
DID YOU DO IT?
HUH?

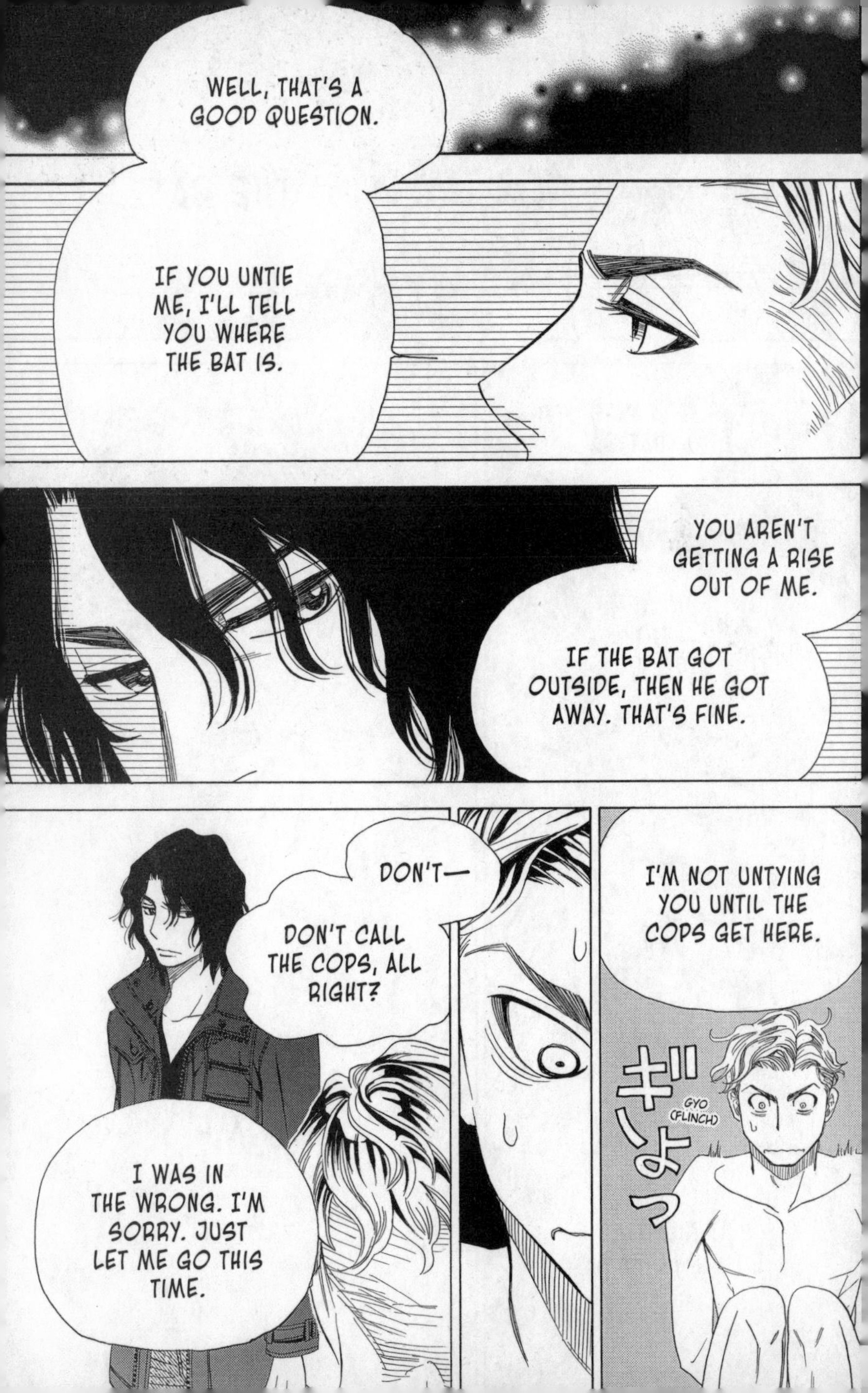
WELL, THAT'S A GOOD QUESTION.
IF YOU UNTIE ME, I'LL TELL YOU WHERE THE BAT IS.
YOU AREN'T GETTING A RISE OUT OF ME.
IF THE BAT GOT OUTSIDE, THEN HE GOT AWAY. THAT'S FINE.
I'M NOT UNTYING YOU UNTIL THE COPS GET HERE.
ぎょっ
GYO (FLINCH)
DON'T—
DON'T CALL THE COPS, ALL RIGHT?
I WAS IN THE WRONG. I'M SORRY. JUST LET ME GO THIS TIME.

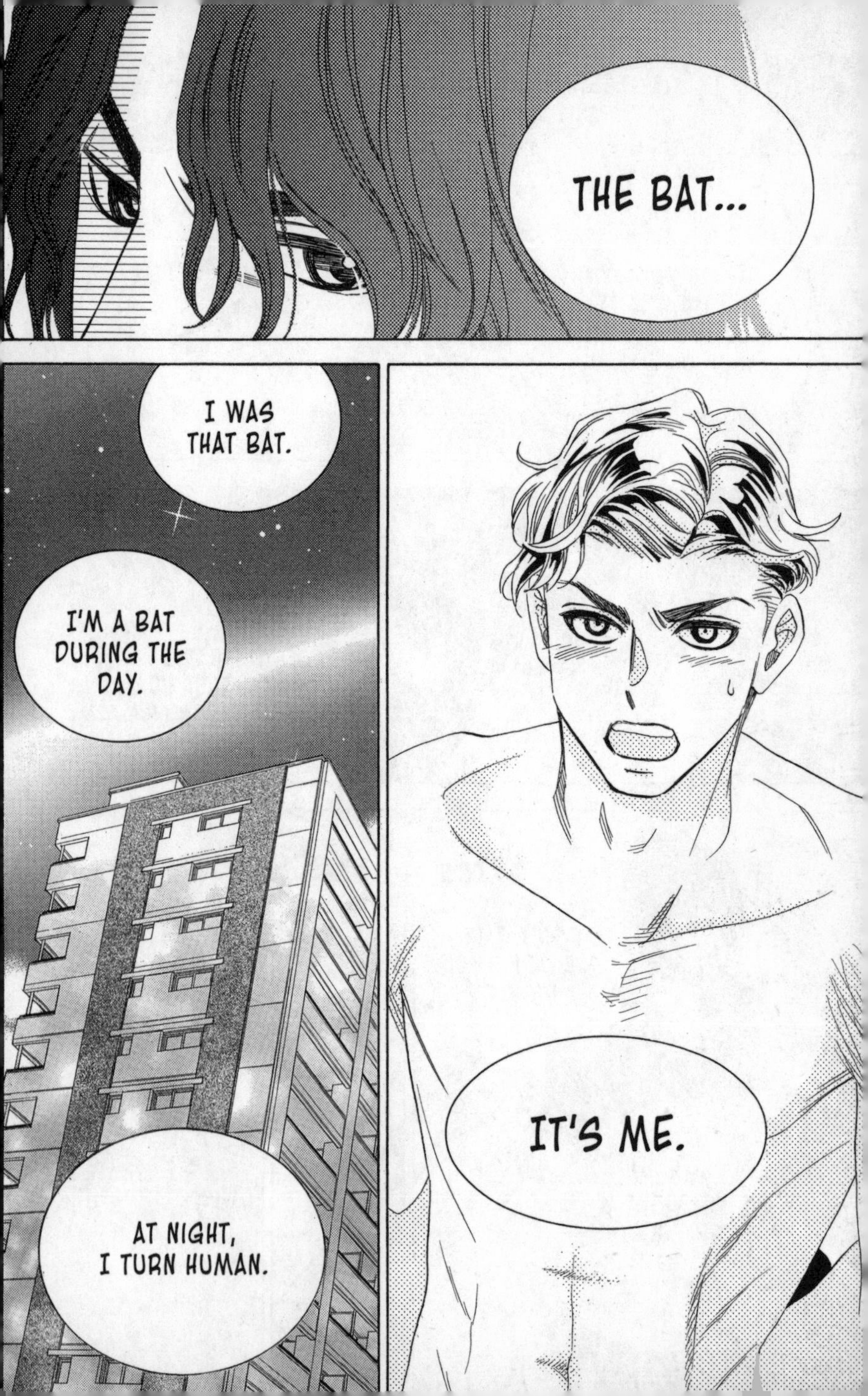
THE BAT...
IT'S ME.
I WAS THAT BAT.
I'M A BAT DURING THE DAY.
AT NIGHT, I TURN HUMAN.

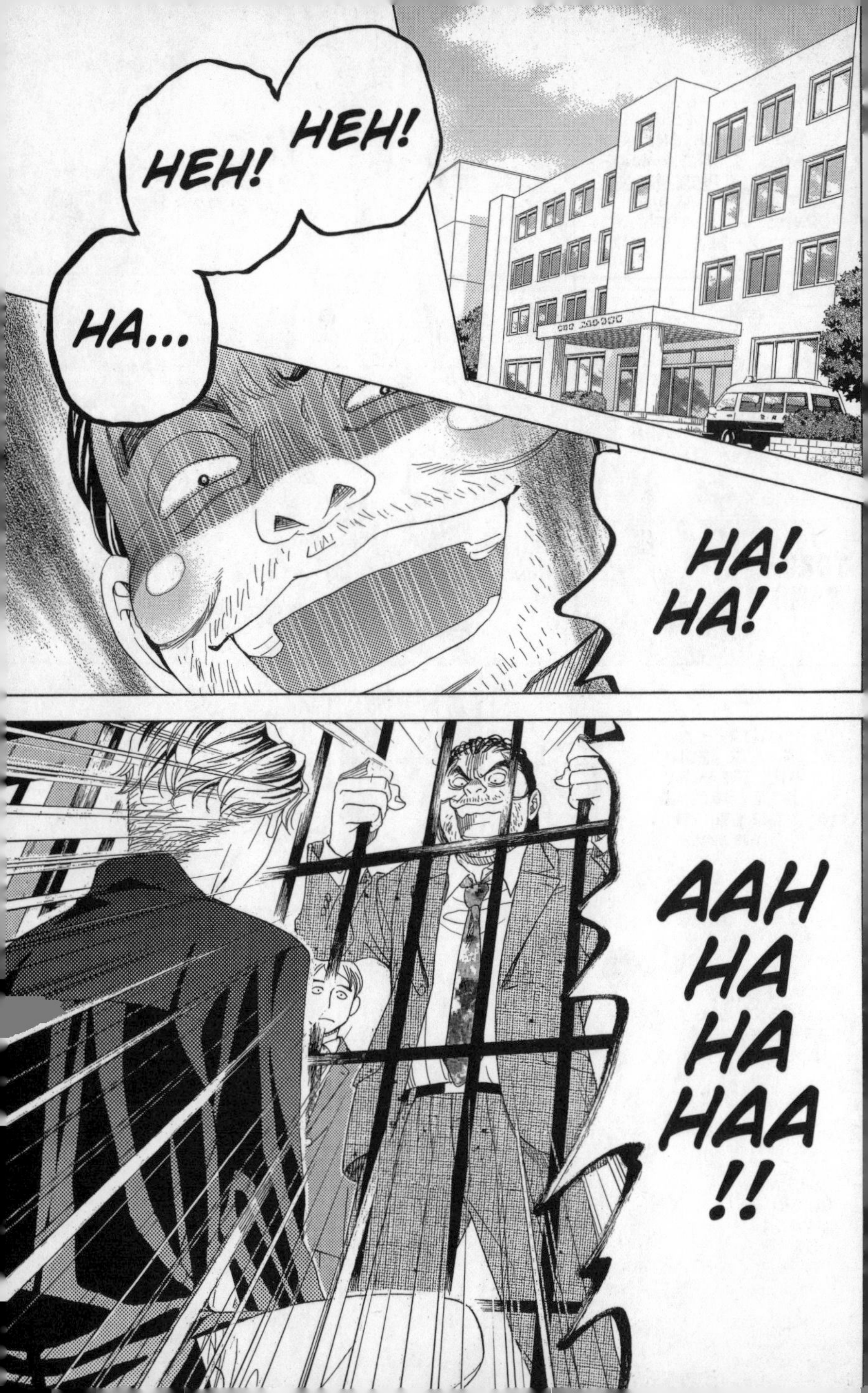
HEH! HEH! HA...
HA! HA!
AAH HA HA HAA!!

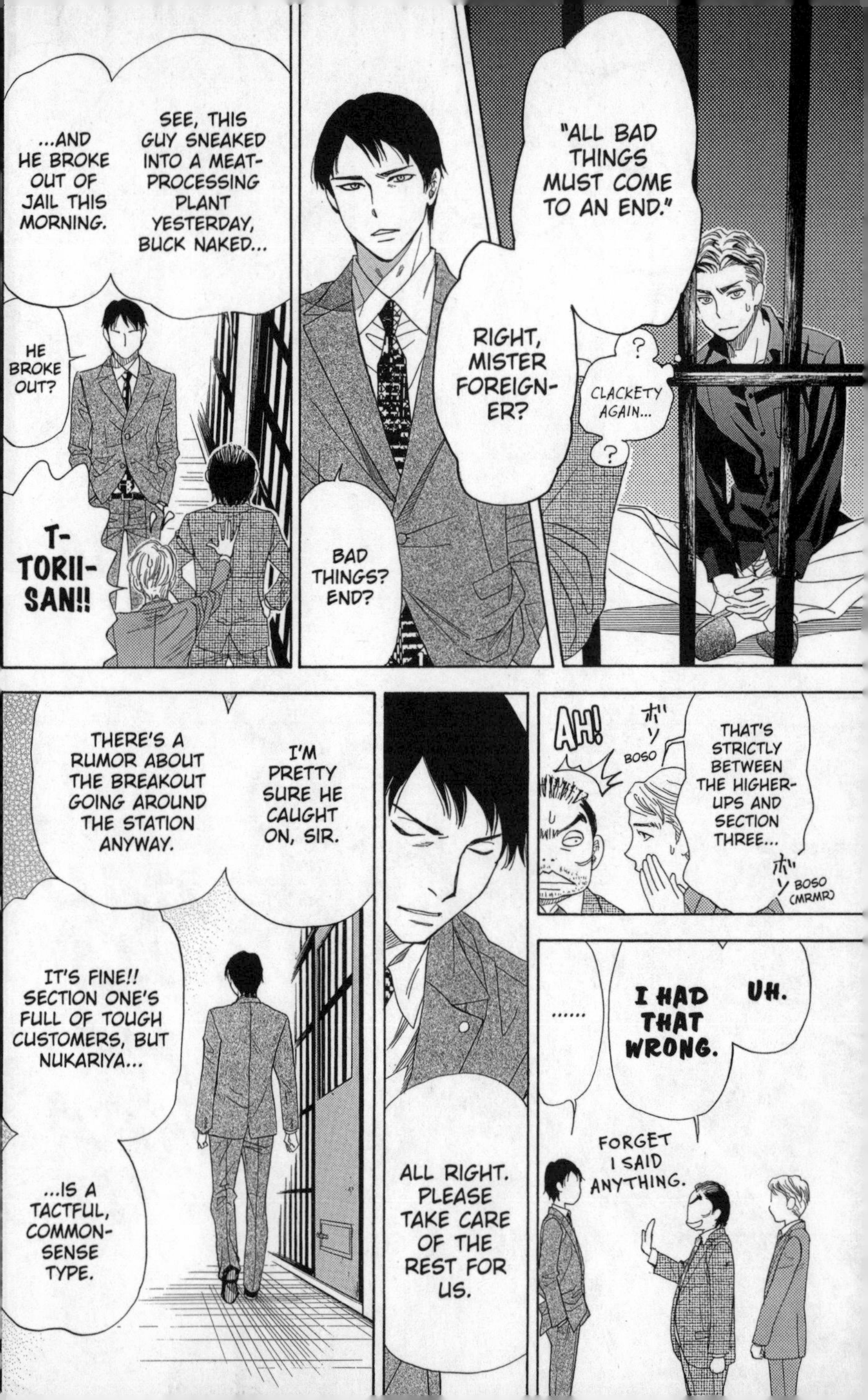
"ALL BAD THINGS MUST COME TO AN END."
RIGHT, MISTER FOREIGNER?
?
CLACKETY AGAIN...
?
BAD THINGS? END?
SEE, THIS GUY SNEAKED INTO A MEAT-PROCESSING PLANT YESTERDAY, BUCK NAKED...
...AND HE BROKE OUT OF JAIL THIS MORNING.
HE BROKE OUT?
T-TORII-SAN!!
THAT'S STRICTLY BETWEEN THE HIGHER-UPS AND SECTION THREE...
ボソ BOSO
AH!
ボソ BOSO (MRMR)
UH.
I HAD THAT WRONG.
......
FORGET I SAID ANYTHING.
I'M PRETTY SURE HE CAUGHT ON, SIR.
THERE'S A RUMOR ABOUT THE BREAKOUT GOING AROUND THE STATION ANYWAY.
ALL RIGHT. PLEASE TAKE CARE OF THE REST FOR US.
IT'S FINE!! SECTION ONE'S FULL OF TOUGH CUSTOMERS, BUT NUKARIYA...
...IS A TACTFUL, COMMONSENSE TYPE.

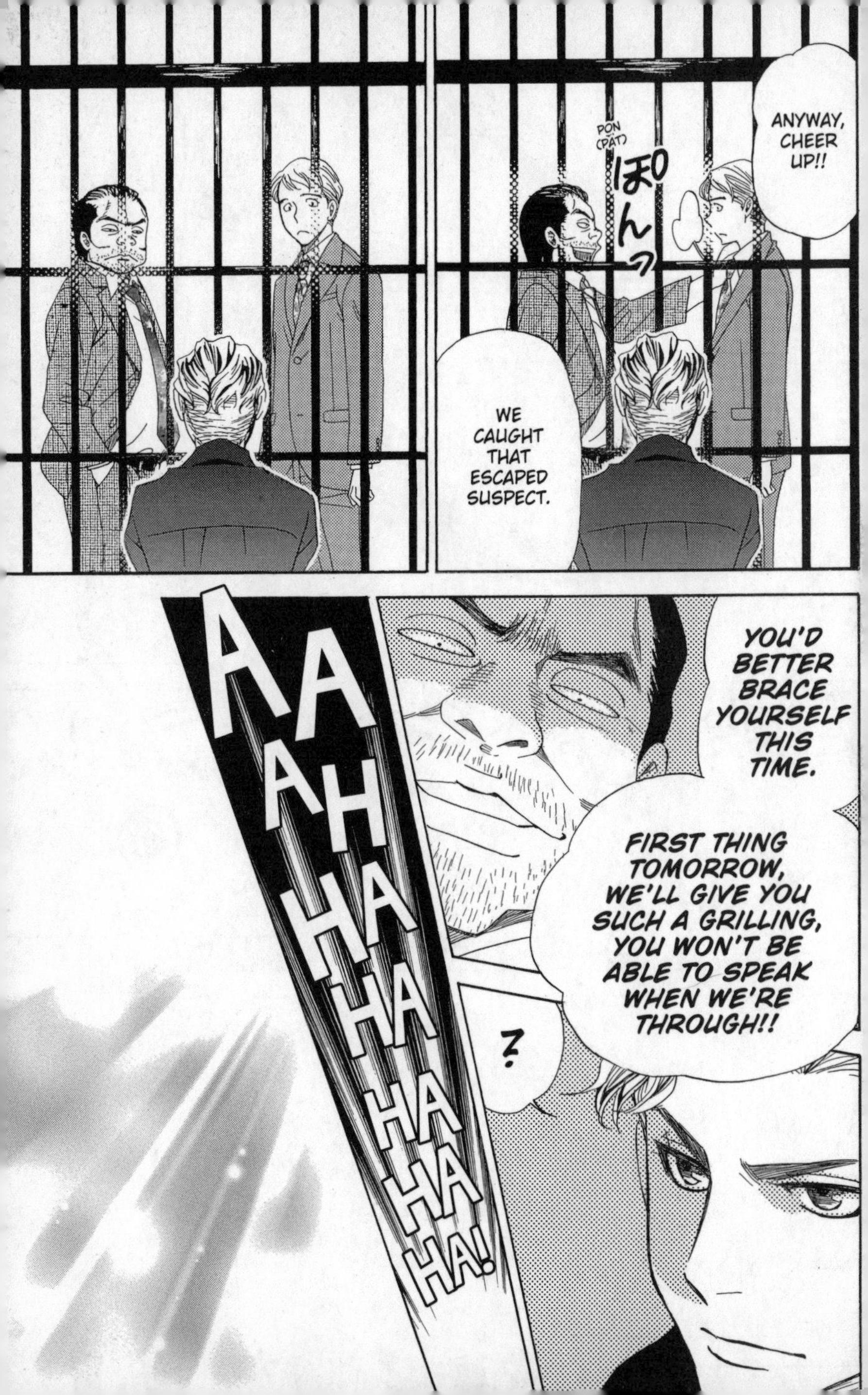
ANYWAY, CHEER UP!!
PON (PAT)
ぽんっ
WE CAUGHT THAT ESCAPED SUSPECT.
YOU'D BETTER BRACE YOURSELF THIS TIME.
FIRST THING TOMORROW, WE'LL GIVE YOU SUCH A GRILLING, YOU WON'T BE ABLE TO SPEAK WHEN WE'RE THROUGH!!
?
AAAHAHAHAHAHAHAHA!

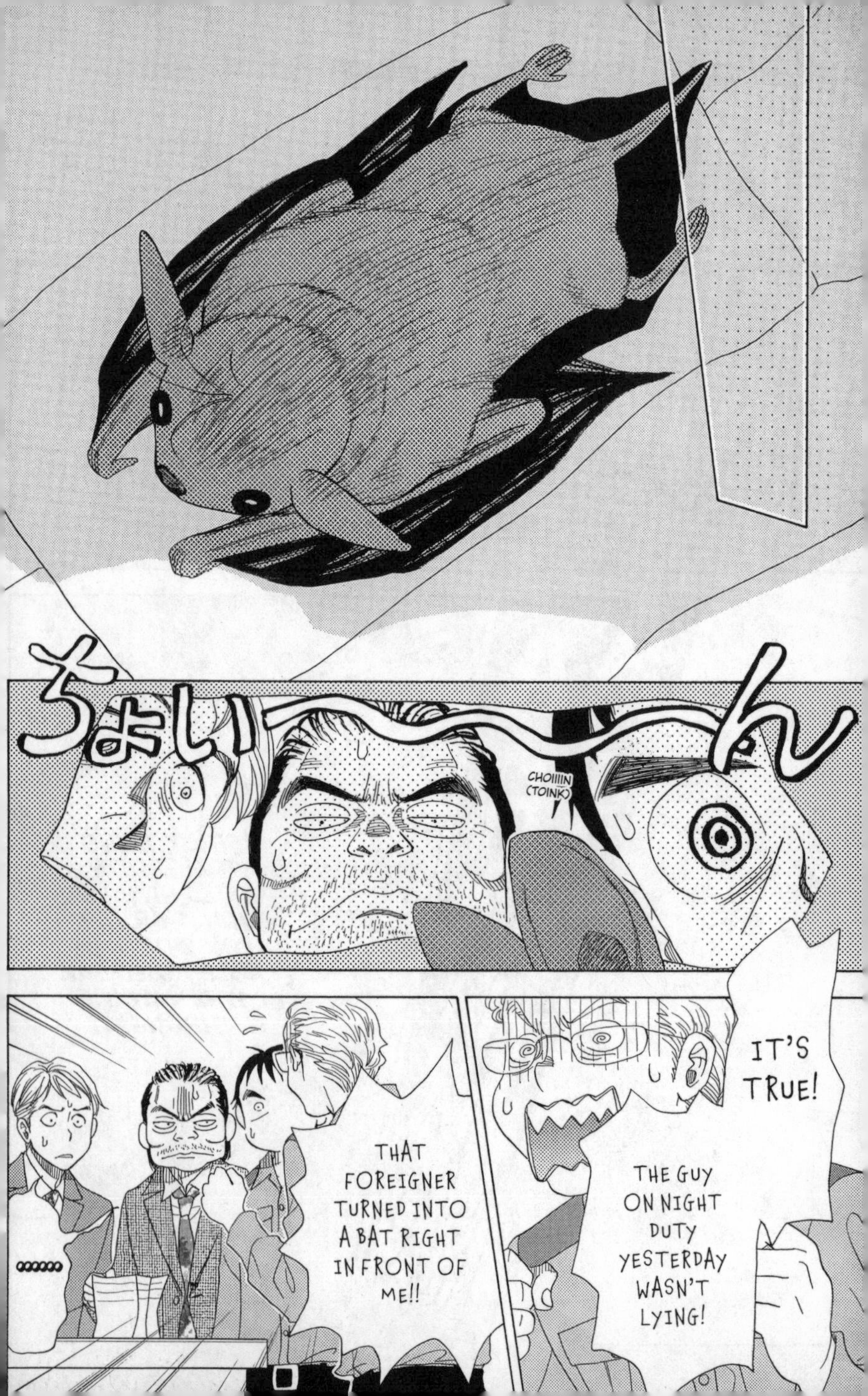
ちょい～～ん
CHOIIIIN (TOINK)
IT'S TRUE!
THE GUY ON NIGHT DUTY YESTERDAY WASN'T LYING!
THAT FOREIGNER TURNED INTO A BAT RIGHT IN FRONT OF ME!!
......

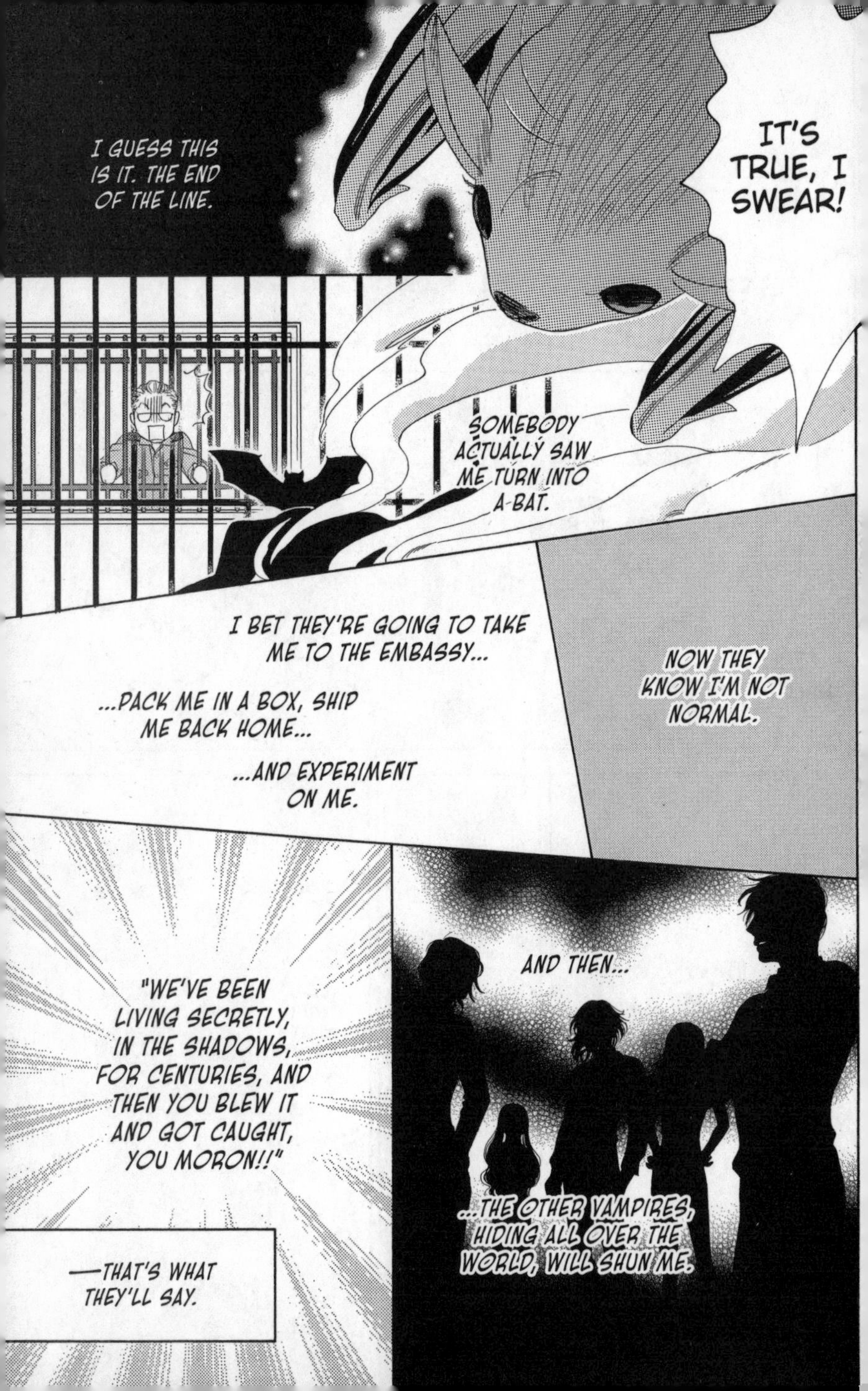
IT'S TRUE, I SWEAR!
I GUESS THIS IS IT. THE END OF THE LINE.
SOMEBODY ACTUALLY SAW ME TURN INTO A-BAT.
NOW THEY KNOW I'M NOT NORMAL.
I BET THEY'RE GOING TO TAKE ME TO THE EMBASSY...
...PACK ME IN A BOX, SHIP ME BACK HOME...
...AND EXPERIMENT ON ME.
AND THEN...
...THE OTHER VAMPIRES, HIDING ALL OVER THE WORLD, WILL SHUN ME.
"WE'VE BEEN LIVING SECRETLY, IN THE SHADOWS, FOR CENTURIES, AND THEN YOU BLEW IT AND GOT CAUGHT, YOU MORON!!"
—THAT'S WHAT THEY'LL SAY.

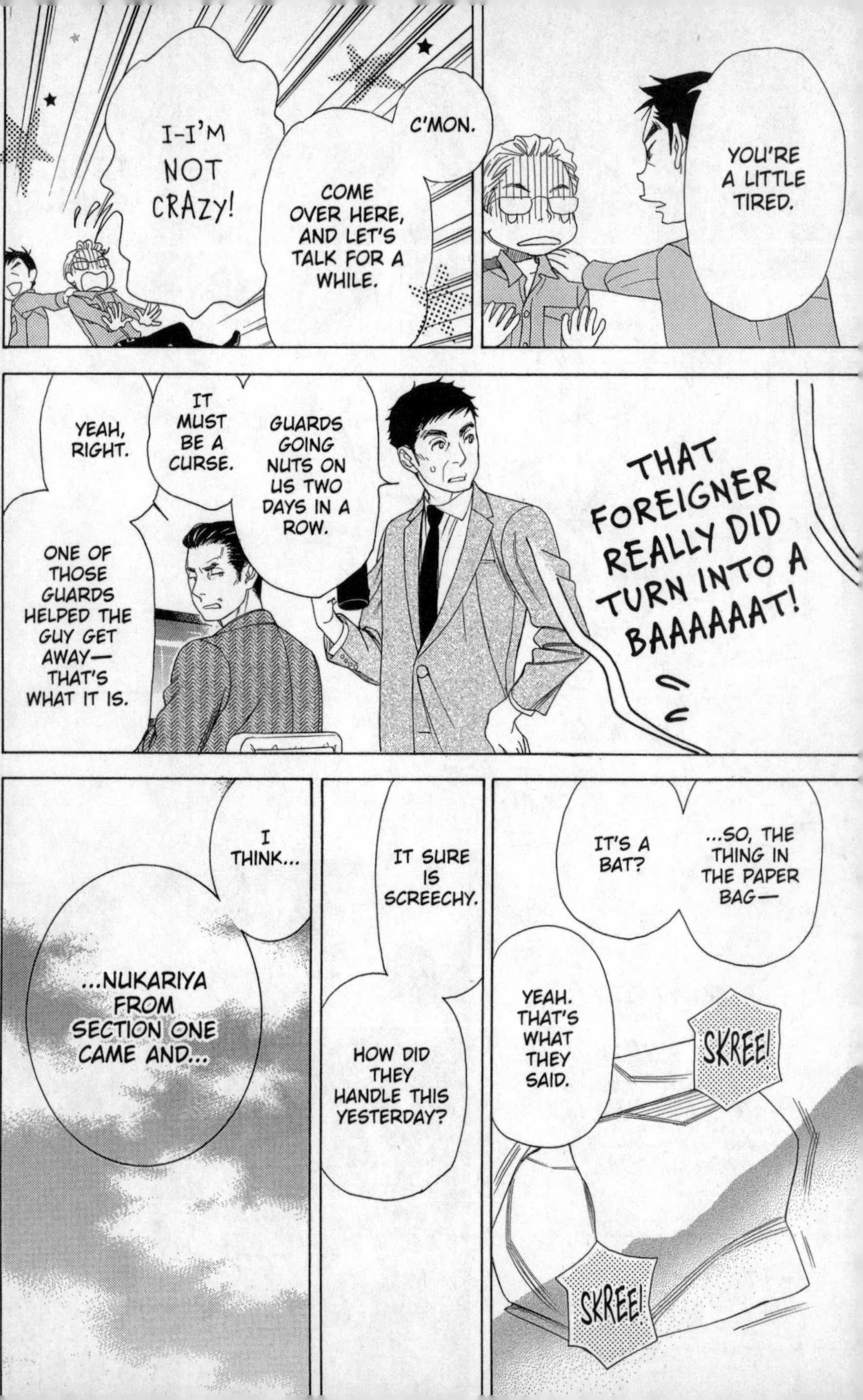
YOU'RE A LITTLE TIRED.
C'MON.
COME OVER HERE, AND LET'S TALK FOR A WHILE.
I-I'M NOT CRAZY!
THAT FOREIGNER REALLY DID TURN INTO A BAAAAAAT!
GUARDS GOING NUTS ON US TWO DAYS IN A ROW.
IT MUST BE A CURSE.
YEAH, RIGHT.
ONE OF THOSE GUARDS HELPED THE GUY GET AWAY—THAT'S WHAT IT IS.
...SO, THE THING IN THE PAPER BAG—
IT'S A BAT?
SKREE!
YEAH. THAT'S WHAT THEY SAID.
SKREE!
IT SURE IS SCREECHY.
HOW DID THEY HANDLE THIS YESTERDAY?
I THINK...
...NUKARIYA FROM SECTION ONE CAME AND...

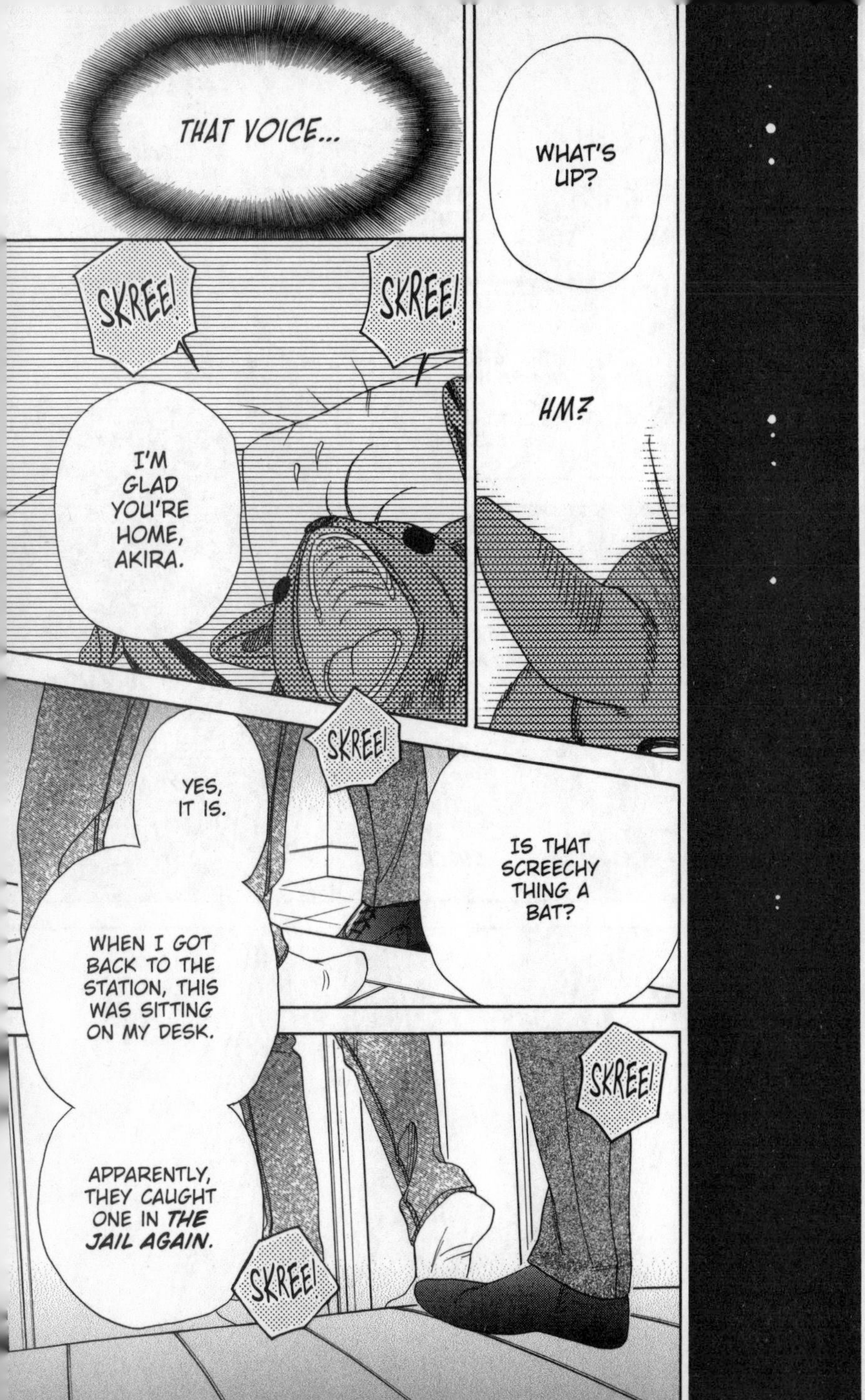
WHAT'S UP?
HM?
THAT VOICE...
SKREE!
SKREE!
I'M GLAD YOU'RE HOME, AKIRA.
IS THAT SCREECHY THING A BAT?
SKREE!
YES, IT IS.
WHEN I GOT BACK TO THE STATION, THIS WAS SITTING ON MY DESK.
SKREE!
APPARENTLY, THEY CAUGHT ONE IN THE JAIL AGAIN.
SKREE!

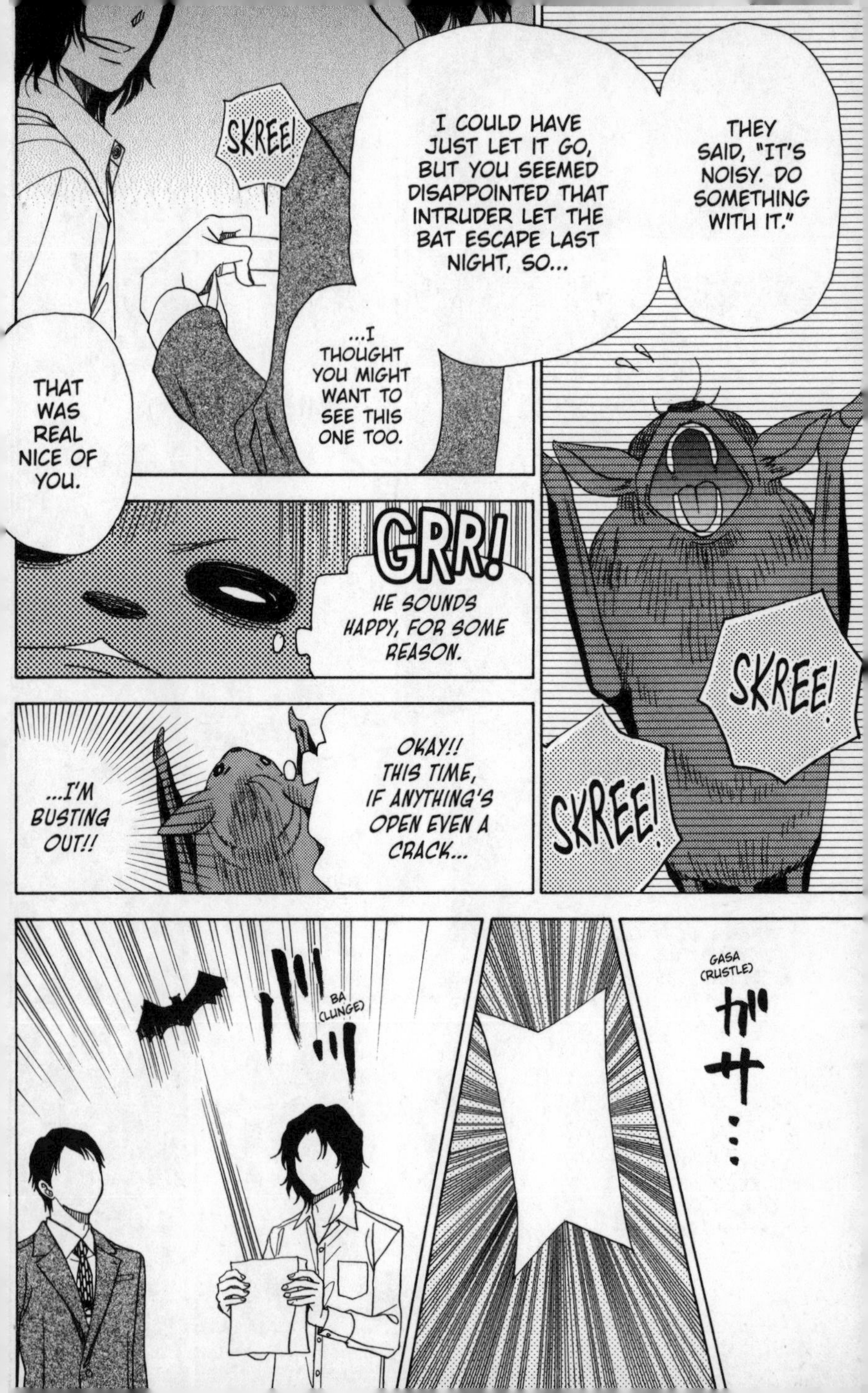
THEY SAID, "IT'S NOISY. DO SOMETHING WITH IT."
SKREE!
SKREE!
SKREE!
I COULD HAVE JUST LET IT GO, BUT YOU SEEMED DISAPPOINTED THAT INTRUDER LET THE BAT ESCAPE LAST NIGHT, SO...
...I THOUGHT YOU MIGHT WANT TO SEE THIS ONE TOO.
THAT WAS REAL NICE OF YOU.
GRR!
HE SOUNDS HAPPY, FOR SOME REASON.
OKAY!! THIS TIME, IF ANYTHING'S OPEN EVEN A CRACK...
...I'M BUSTING OUT!!
GASA (RUSTLE)
ガサ…
BA (LUNGE)
バッ

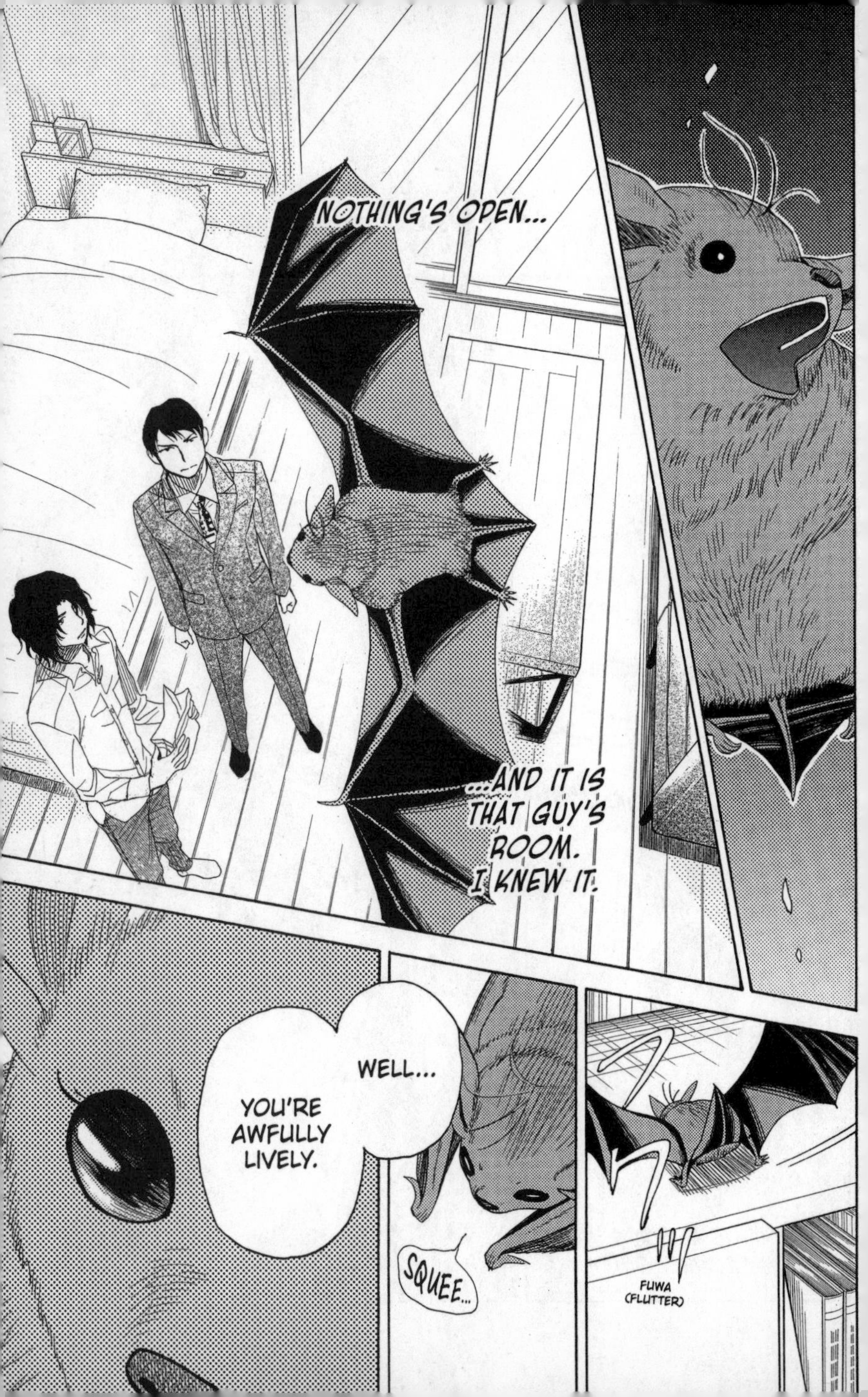
NOTHING'S OPEN...
...AND IT IS THAT GUY'S ROOM. I KNEW IT.
FUWA (FLUTTER)
SQUEE...
WELL...
YOU'RE AWFULLY LIVELY.

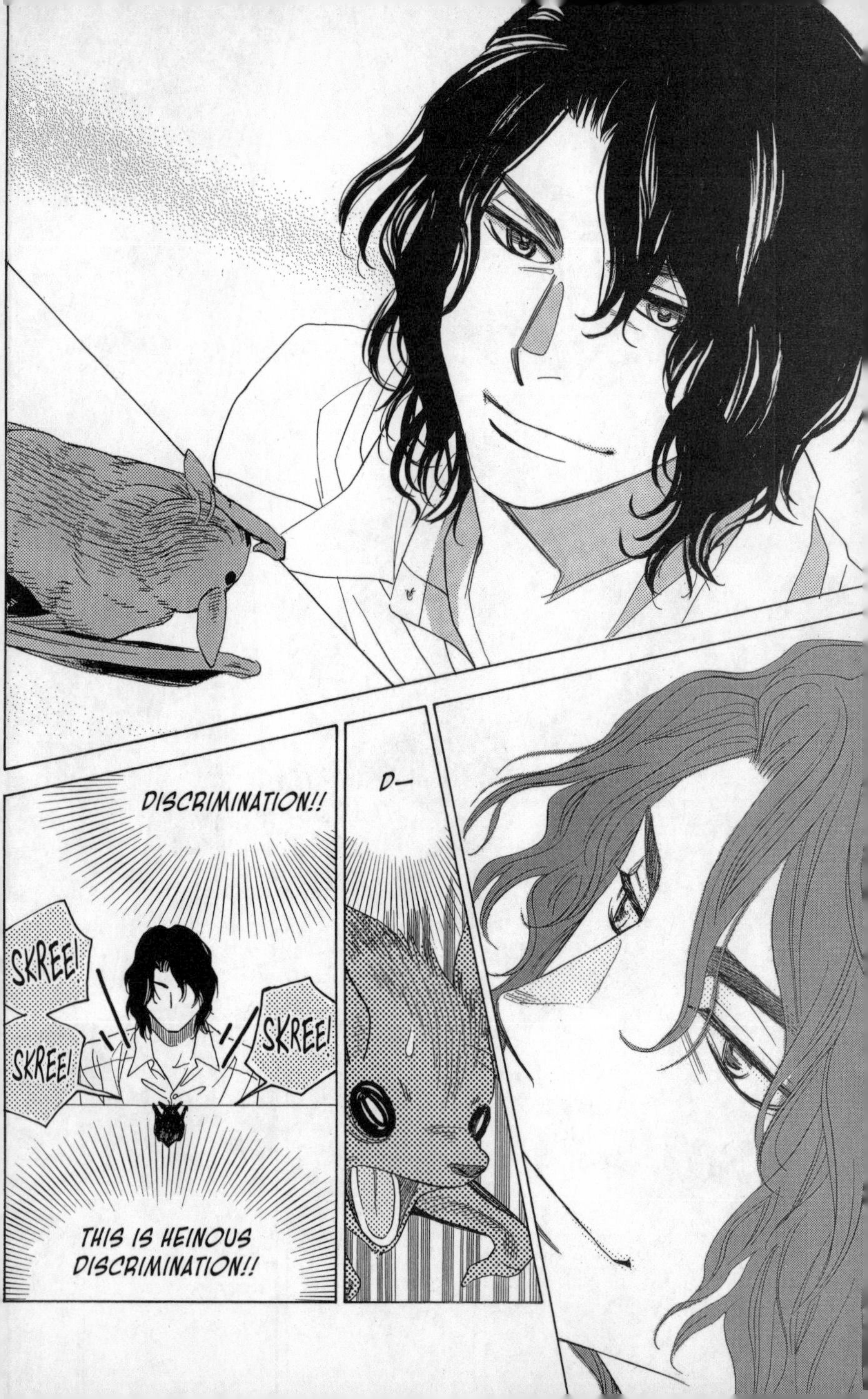
D—
DISCRIMINATION!!
SKREE!
SKREE!
SKREE!
THIS IS HEINOUS DISCRIMINATION!!

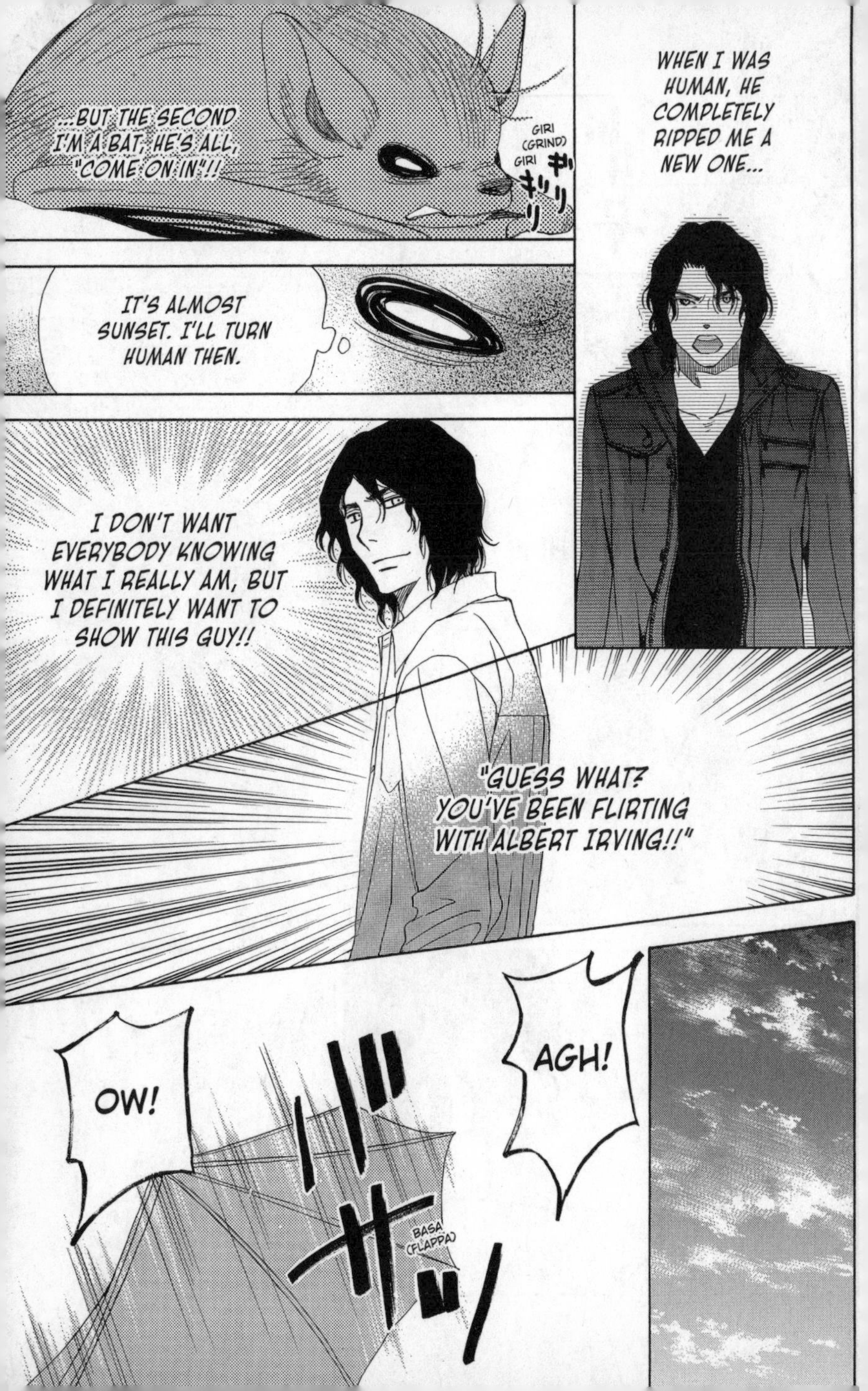
WHEN I WAS HUMAN, HE COMPLETELY RIPPED ME A NEW ONE...
...BUT THE SECOND I'M A BAT, HE'S ALL, "COME ON IN"!!
GIRI (GRIND) GIRI
IT'S ALMOST SUNSET. I'LL TURN HUMAN THEN.
I DON'T WANT EVERYBODY KNOWING WHAT I REALLY AM, BUT I DEFINITELY WANT TO SHOW THIS GUY!!
"GUESS WHAT? YOU'VE BEEN FLIRTING WITH ALBERT IRVING!!"
AGH!
BASA (FLAPPA)
OW!

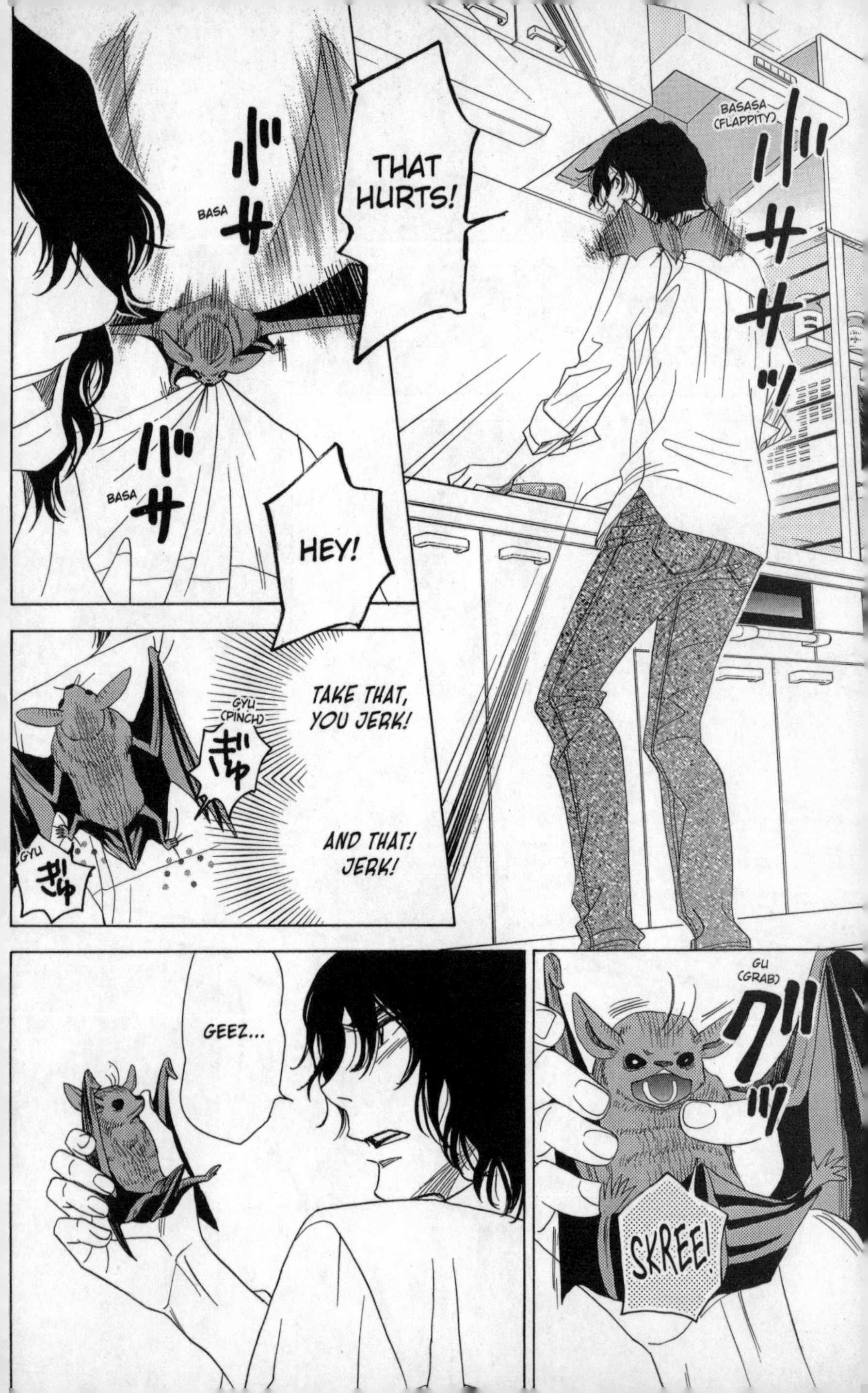
BASASA (FLAPPITY)
THAT HURTS!
BASA
BASA
HEY!
TAKE THAT, YOU JERK!
GYU (PINCH)
AND THAT! JERK!
GYU
GU (GRAB)
SKREE!
GEEZ...

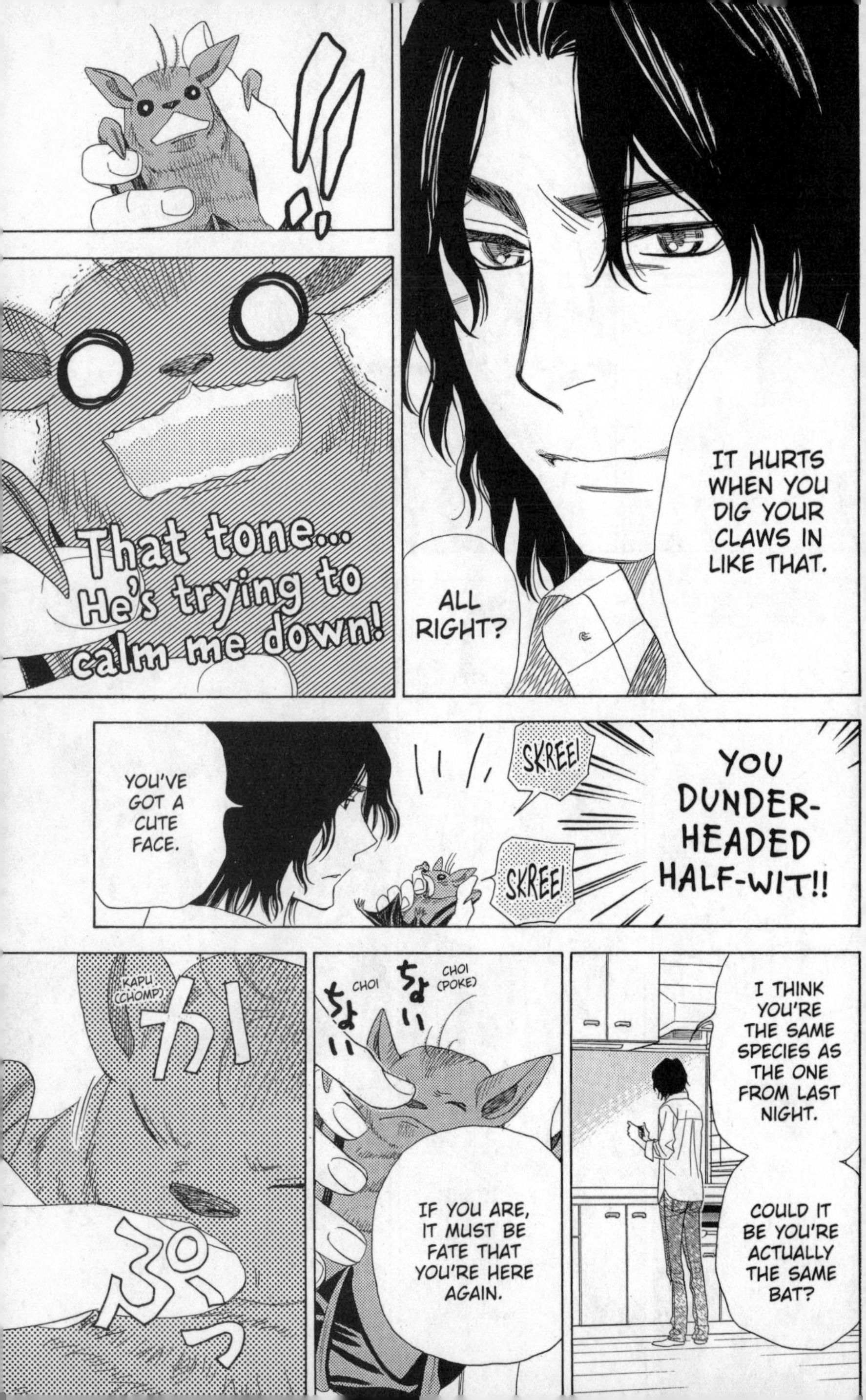
IT HURTS WHEN YOU DIG YOUR CLAWS IN LIKE THAT.
ALL RIGHT?
That tone... He's trying to calm me down!
YOU DUNDER-HEADED HALF-WIT!!
SKREE!
SKREE!
YOU'VE GOT A CUTE FACE.
I THINK YOU'RE THE SAME SPECIES AS THE ONE FROM LAST NIGHT.
COULD IT BE YOU'RE ACTUALLY THE SAME BAT?
ちょい
CHOI (POKE)
ちょい
CHOI
IF YOU ARE, IT MUST BE FATE THAT YOU'RE HERE AGAIN.
かぷっ
KAPU (CHOMP)

BATA
(FLAP)

BIKU
(FLINCH)

BATA

!?

WHAT?
ARE YOU
HUNGRY?

ギギギ
GIGIGI
(GRIND)

LOOK!

SKREE!

SKREE!

LOOK
AT ME!!

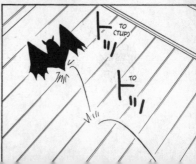

ト
(TO
(TUP)

ト
TO

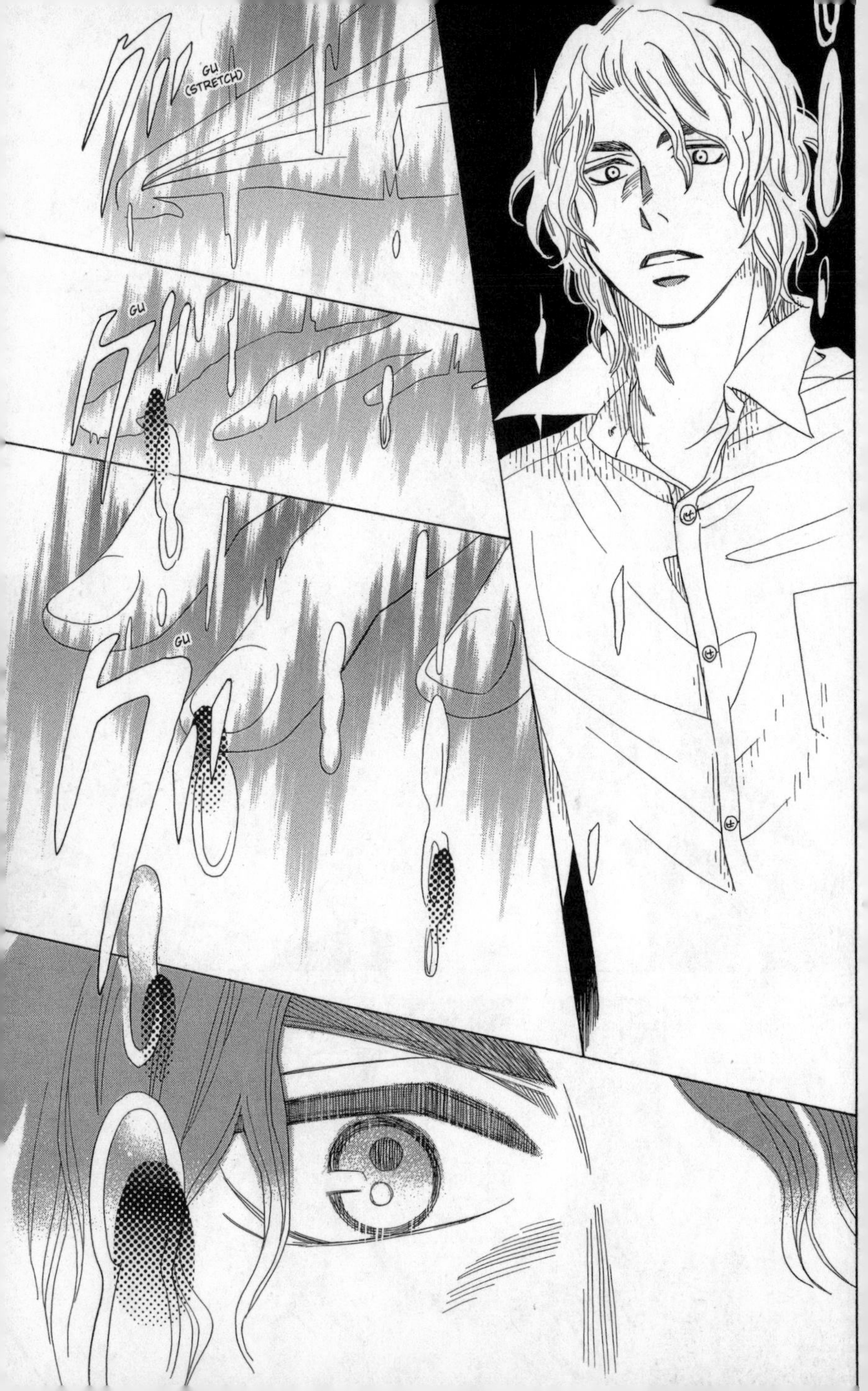
GU
(STRETCH)
GU
GU

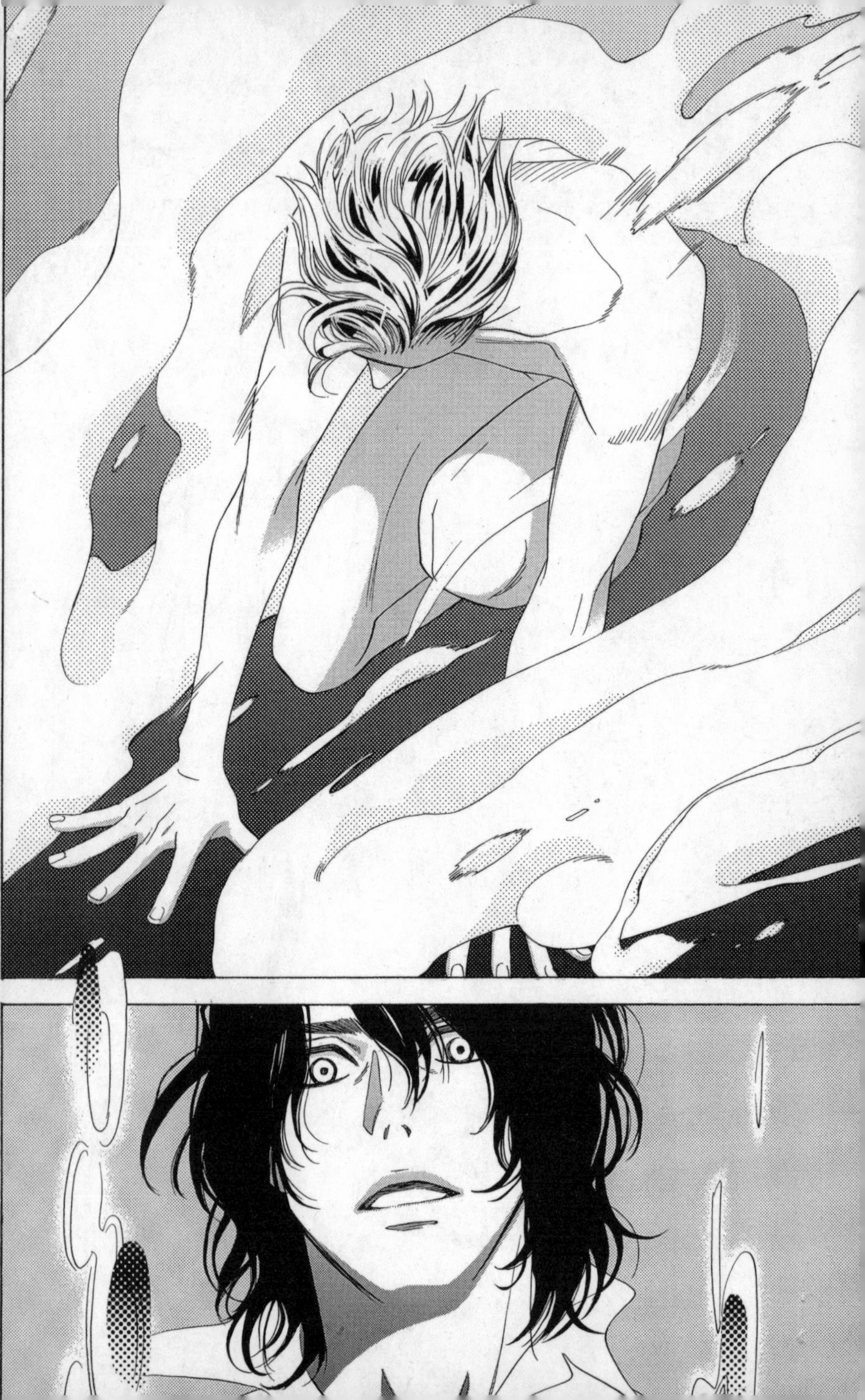

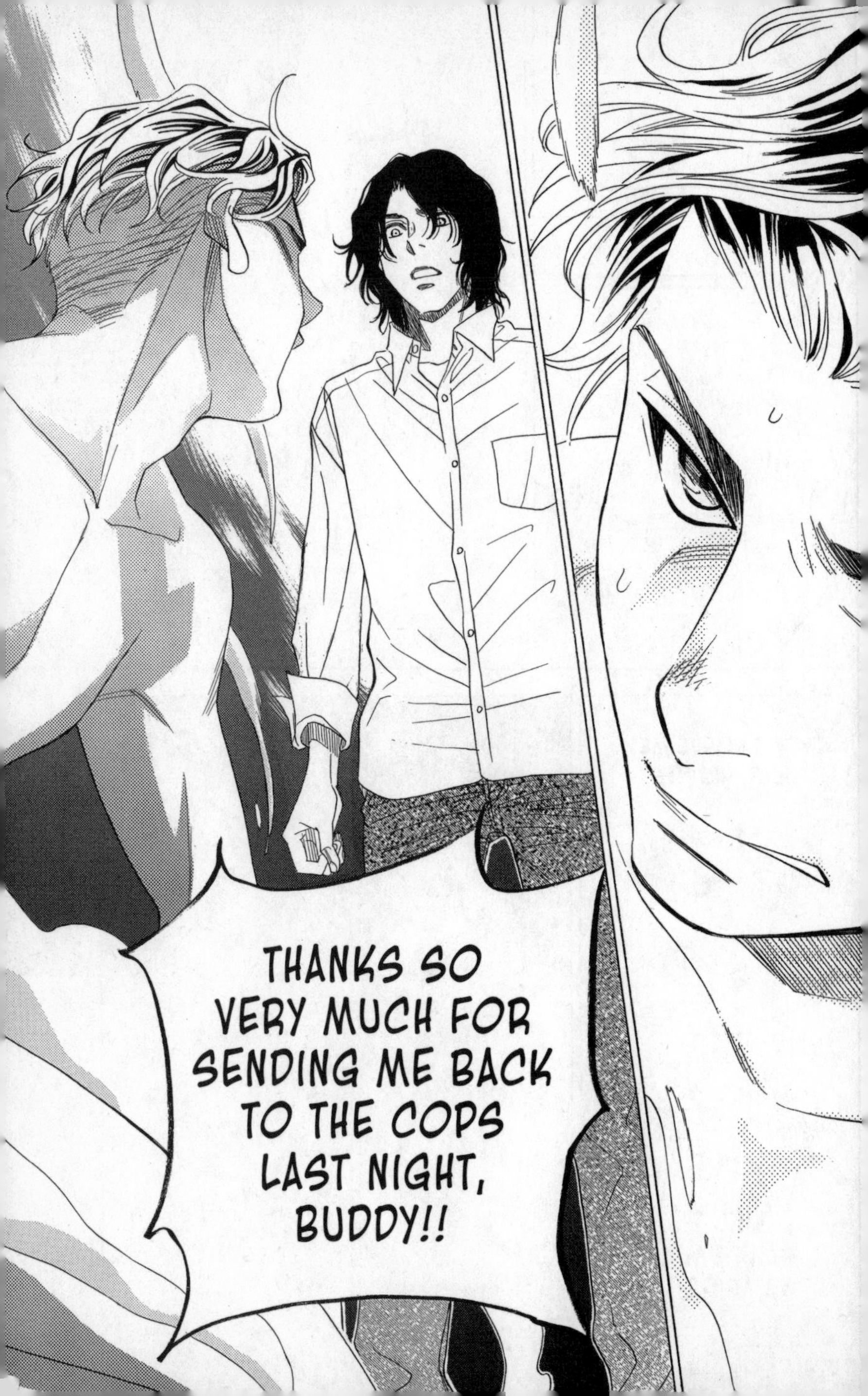
THANKS SO VERY MUCH FOR SENDING ME BACK TO THE COPS LAST NIGHT, BUDDY!!

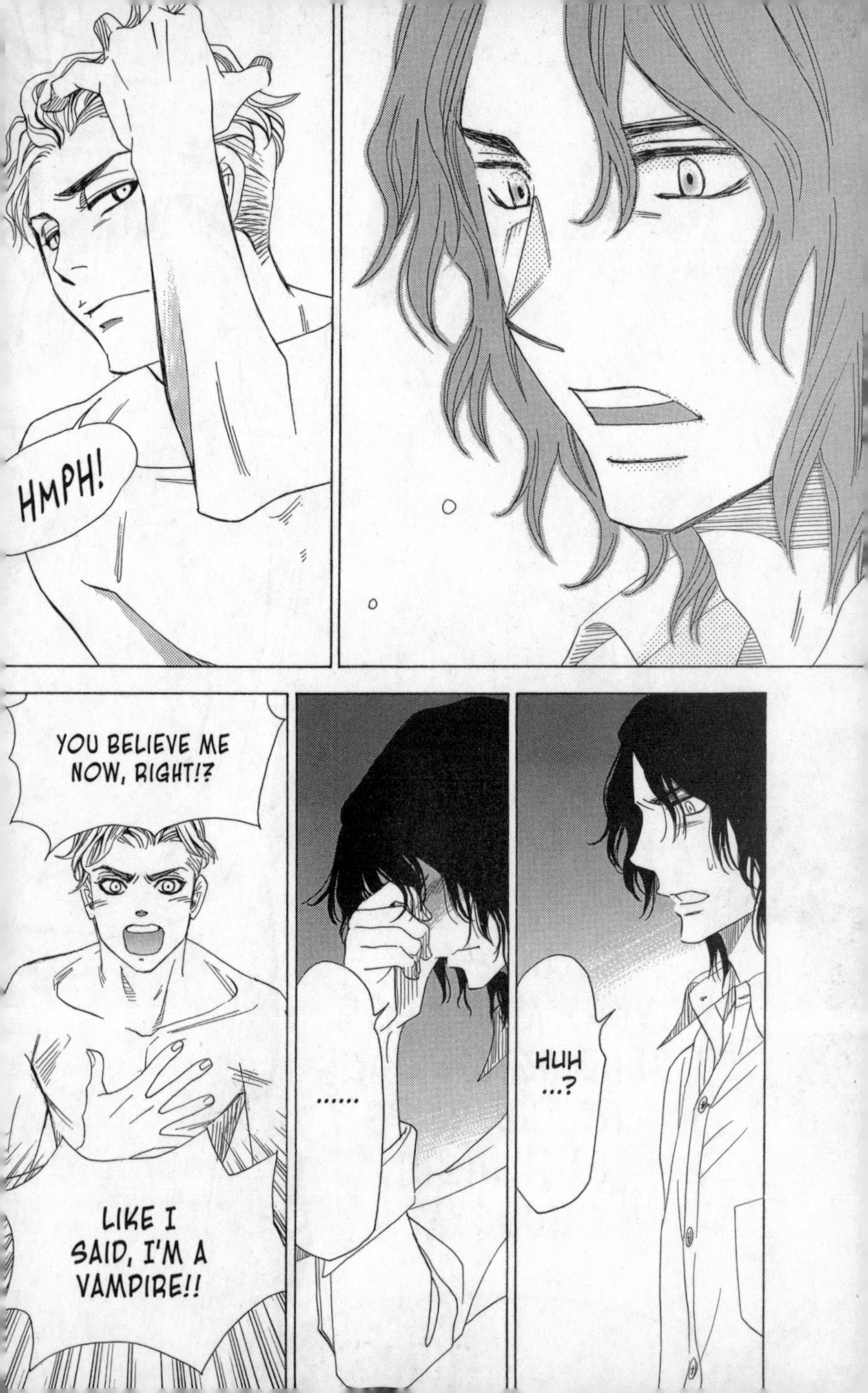
HMPH!
HUH ...?
......
YOU BELIEVE ME NOW, RIGHT!?
LIKE I SAID, I'M A VAMPIRE!!

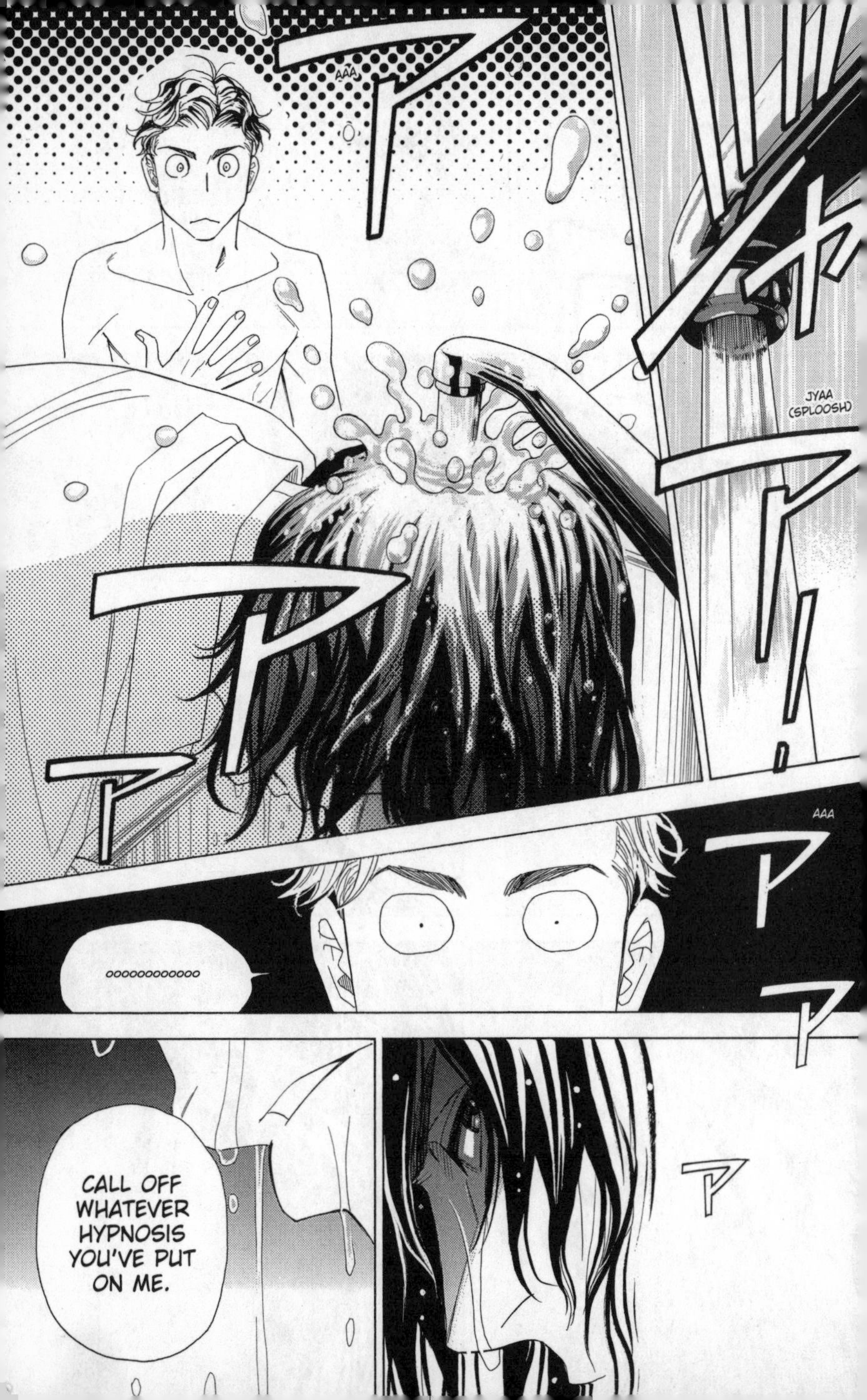
AAA
JYAA
(SPLOOSH)
AAA
oooooooooooo
CALL OFF WHATEVER HYPNOSIS YOU'VE PUT ON ME.

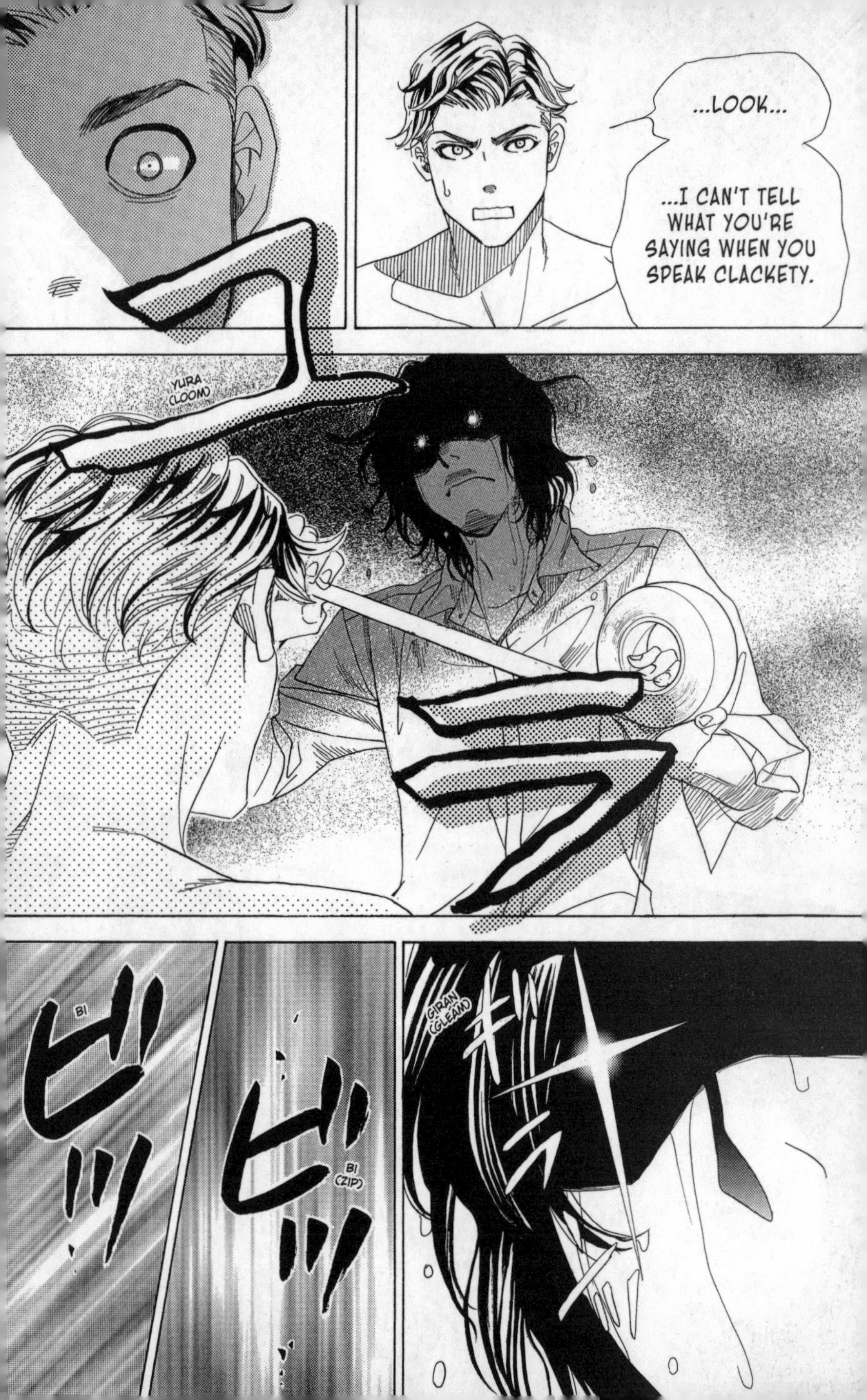
...LOOK...
...I CAN'T TELL WHAT YOU'RE SAYING WHEN YOU SPEAK CLACKETY.
YURA (LOOM)
GIRAN (GLEAM)
BI (ZIP)
BI

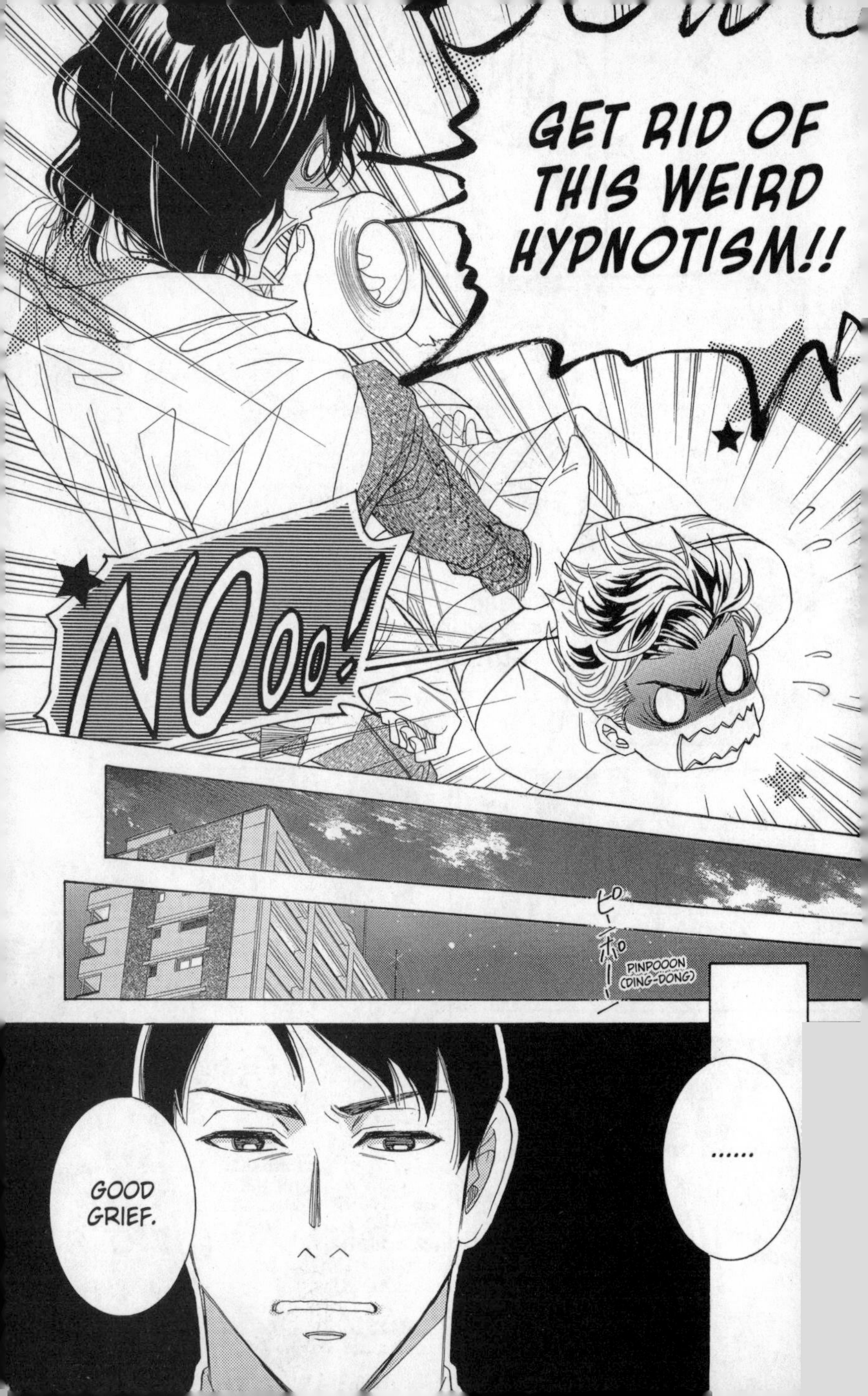
GET RID OF THIS WEIRD HYPNOTISM!!
NOOoo!
PINPOOON (DING-DONG)
......
GOOD GRIEF.

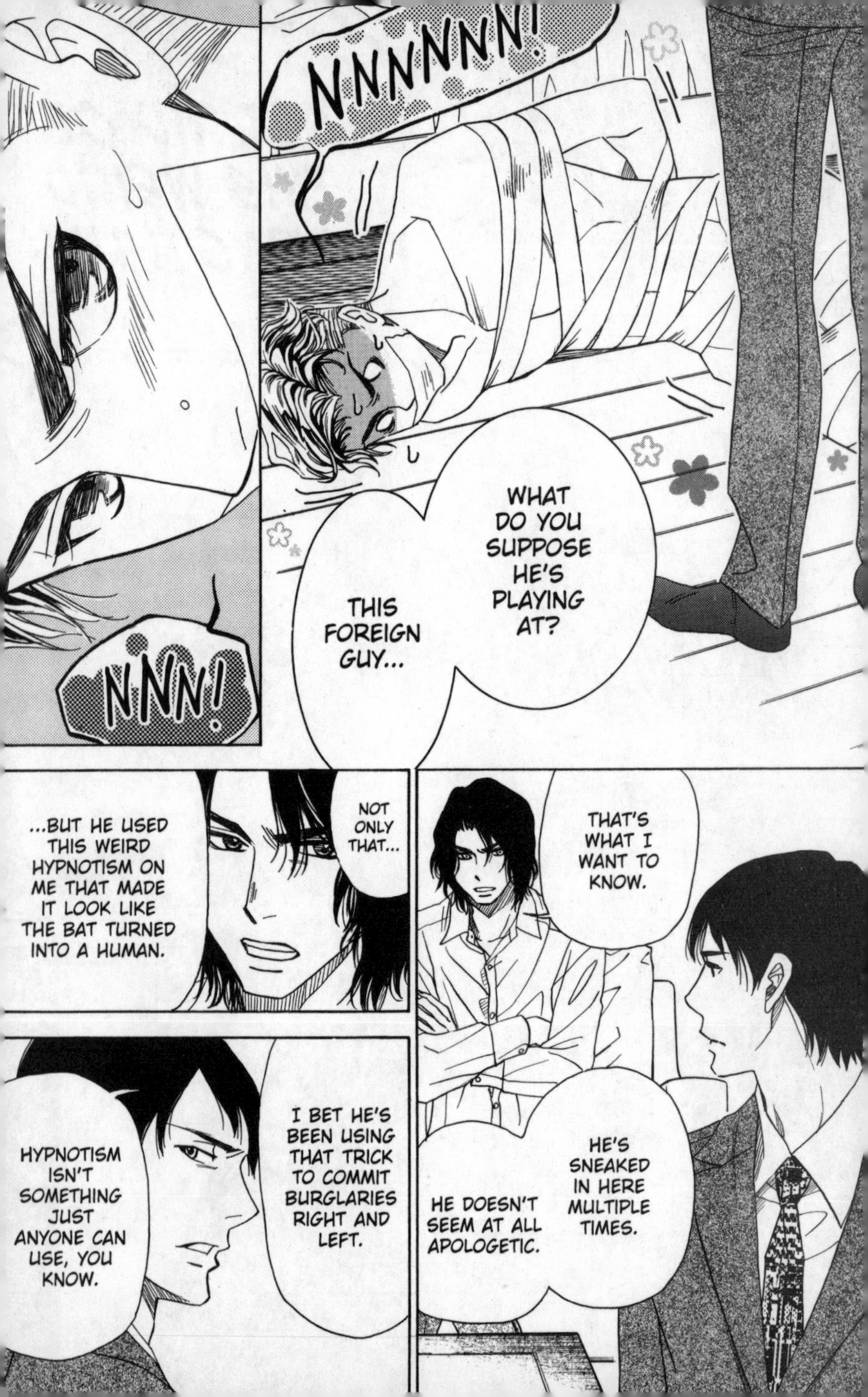
NNNNNN!
WHAT DO YOU SUPPOSE HE'S PLAYING AT?
THIS FOREIGN GUY...
NNN!
THAT'S WHAT I WANT TO KNOW.
HE'S SNEAKED IN HERE MULTIPLE TIMES.
HE DOESN'T SEEM AT ALL APOLOGETIC.
NOT ONLY THAT...
...BUT HE USED THIS WEIRD HYPNOTISM ON ME THAT MADE IT LOOK LIKE THE BAT TURNED INTO A HUMAN.
I BET HE'S BEEN USING THAT TRICK TO COMMIT BURGLARIES RIGHT AND LEFT.
HYPNOTISM ISN'T SOMETHING JUST ANYONE CAN USE, YOU KNOW.

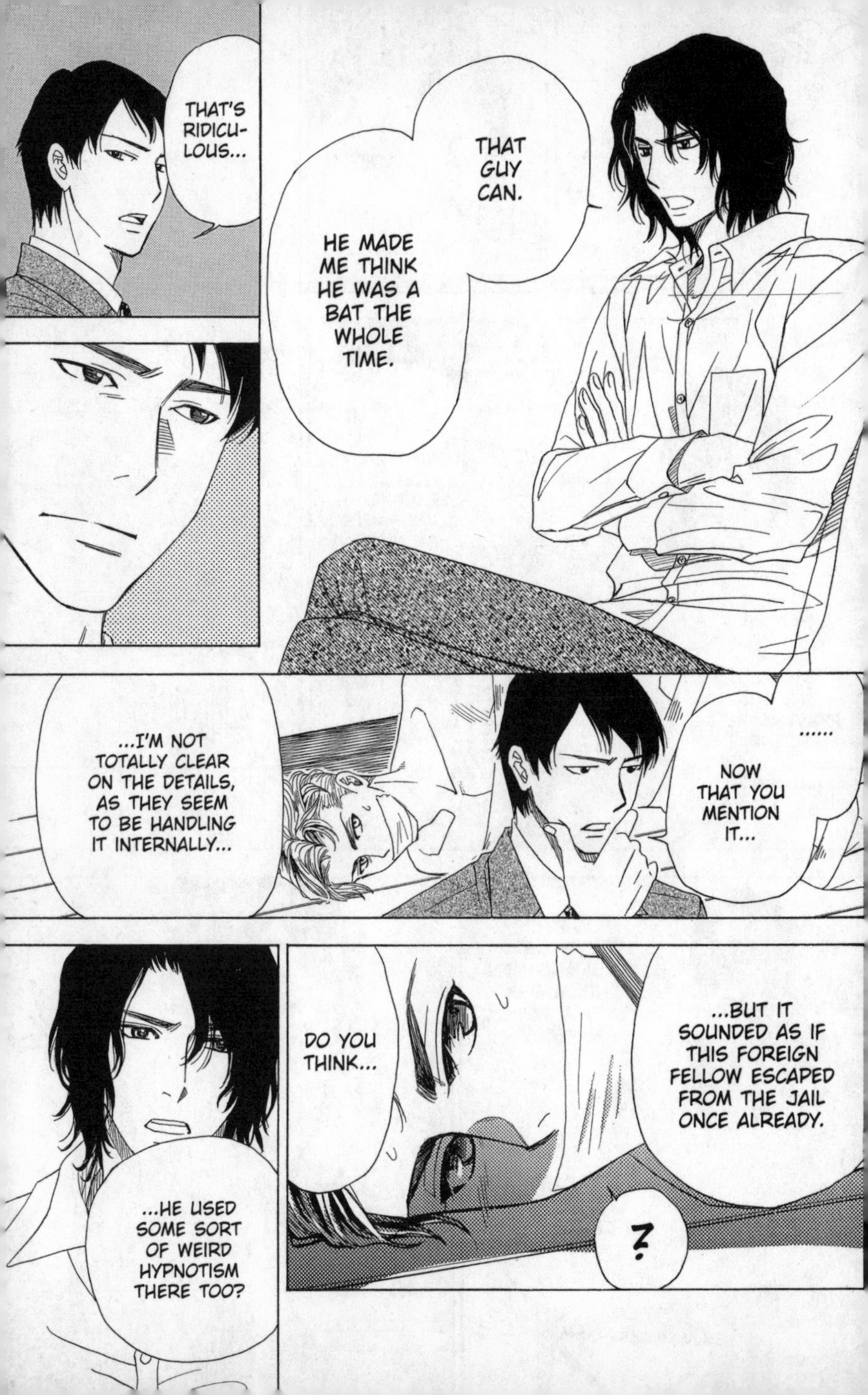
THAT GUY CAN.
HE MADE ME THINK HE WAS A BAT THE WHOLE TIME.
THAT'S RIDICU-LOUS...
......
NOW THAT YOU MENTION IT...
...I'M NOT TOTALLY CLEAR ON THE DETAILS, AS THEY SEEM TO BE HANDLING IT INTERNALLY...
...BUT IT SOUNDED AS IF THIS FOREIGN FELLOW ESCAPED FROM THE JAIL ONCE ALREADY.
DO YOU THINK...
?
...HE USED SOME SORT OF WEIRD HYPNOTISM THERE TOO?

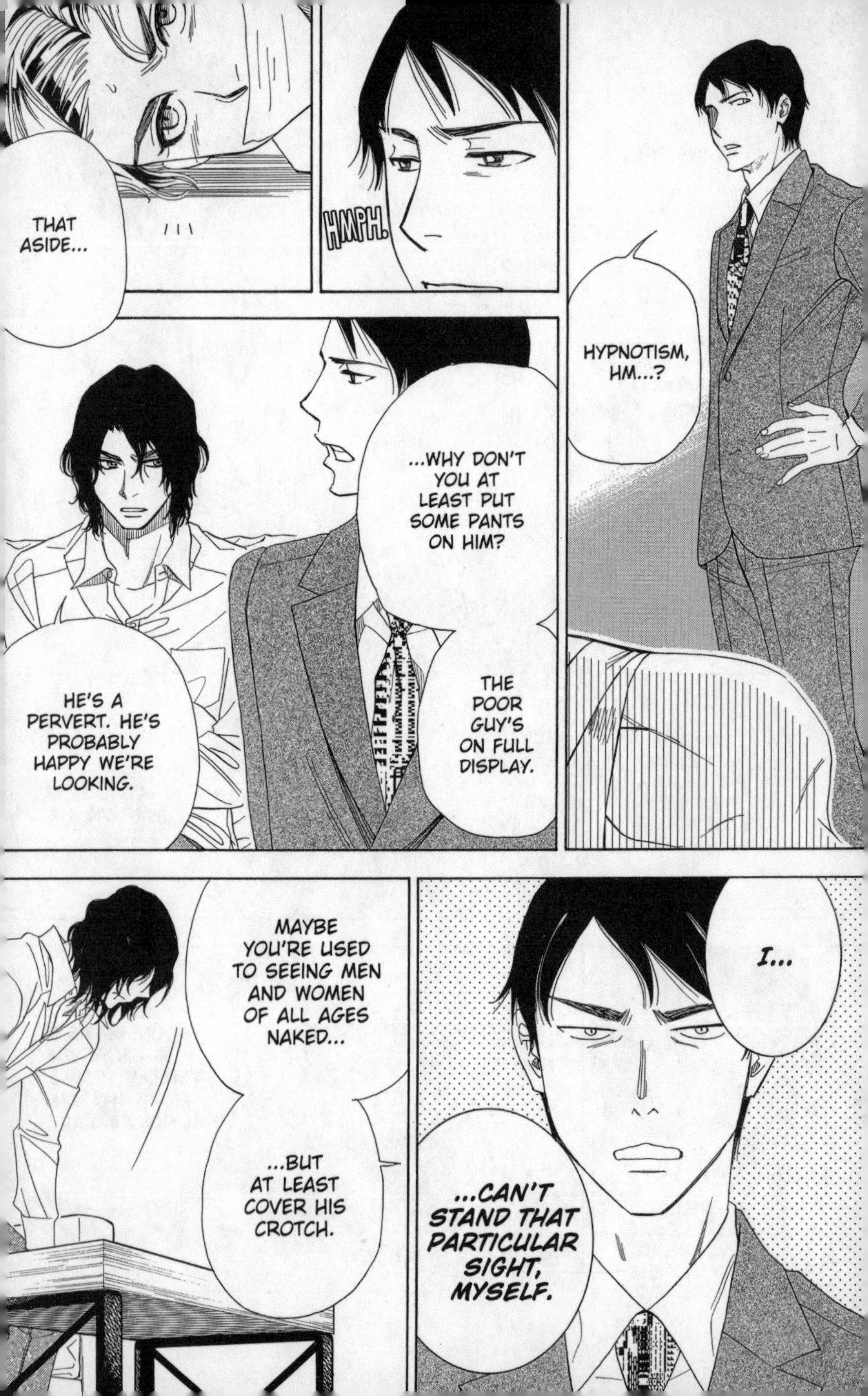
HYPNOTISM, HM...?
HMPH.
THAT ASIDE...
...WHY DON'T YOU AT LEAST PUT SOME PANTS ON HIM?
THE POOR GUY'S ON FULL DISPLAY.
HE'S A PERVERT. HE'S PROBABLY HAPPY WE'RE LOOKING.
I...
...CAN'T STAND THAT PARTICULAR SIGHT, MYSELF.
MAYBE YOU'RE USED TO SEEING MEN AND WOMEN OF ALL AGES NAKED...
...BUT AT LEAST COVER HIS CROTCH.

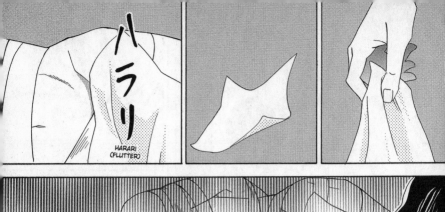

ハラリ
HARARI (FLUTTER)
THAT'LL DO IT.
NO, IT WON'T.
SOMEHOW, THAT LOOKS EVEN MORE INDECENT.
ブル
BURU
BESIDES, THIS ROOM IS CHILLY.
RGH!
THIS IS HUMILIATING!
ブル
BURU (TREMBLE)
LOOK—HE'S SHAKING. PUT A BLANKET OVER HIM OR SOMETHING.
カチャ
KACHA (KACHAK)

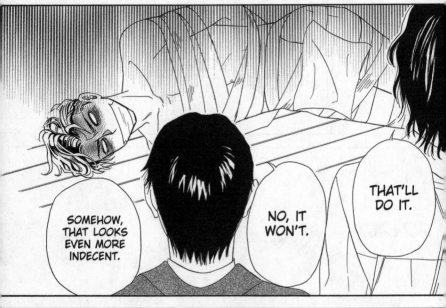

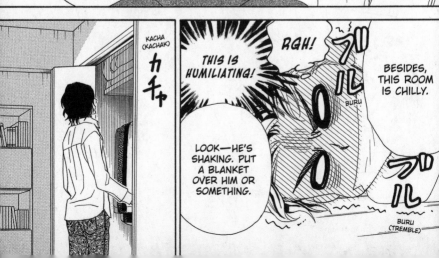

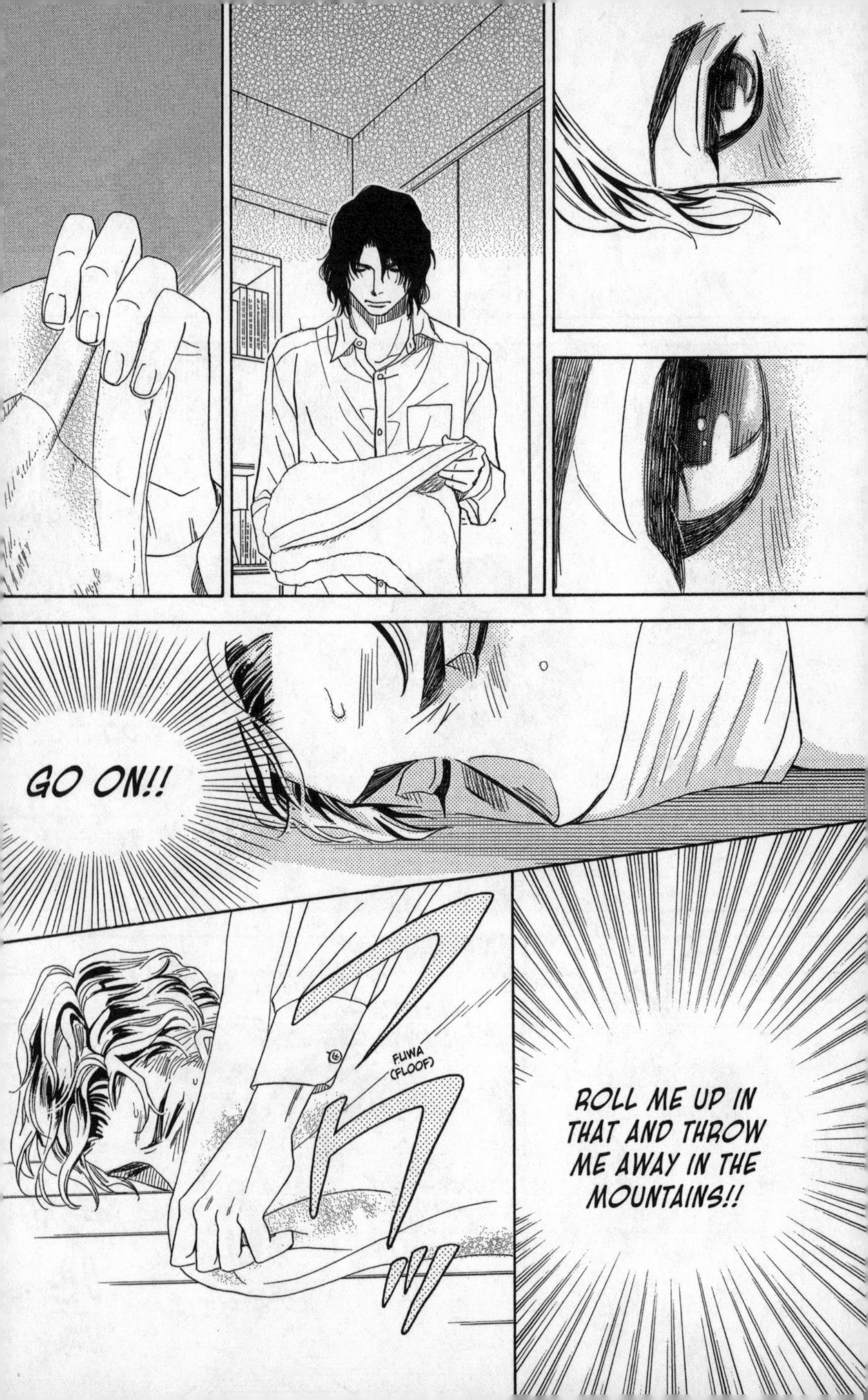
GO ON!!
ROLL ME UP IN THAT AND THROW ME AWAY IN THE MOUNTAINS!!
FUWA (FLOOF)

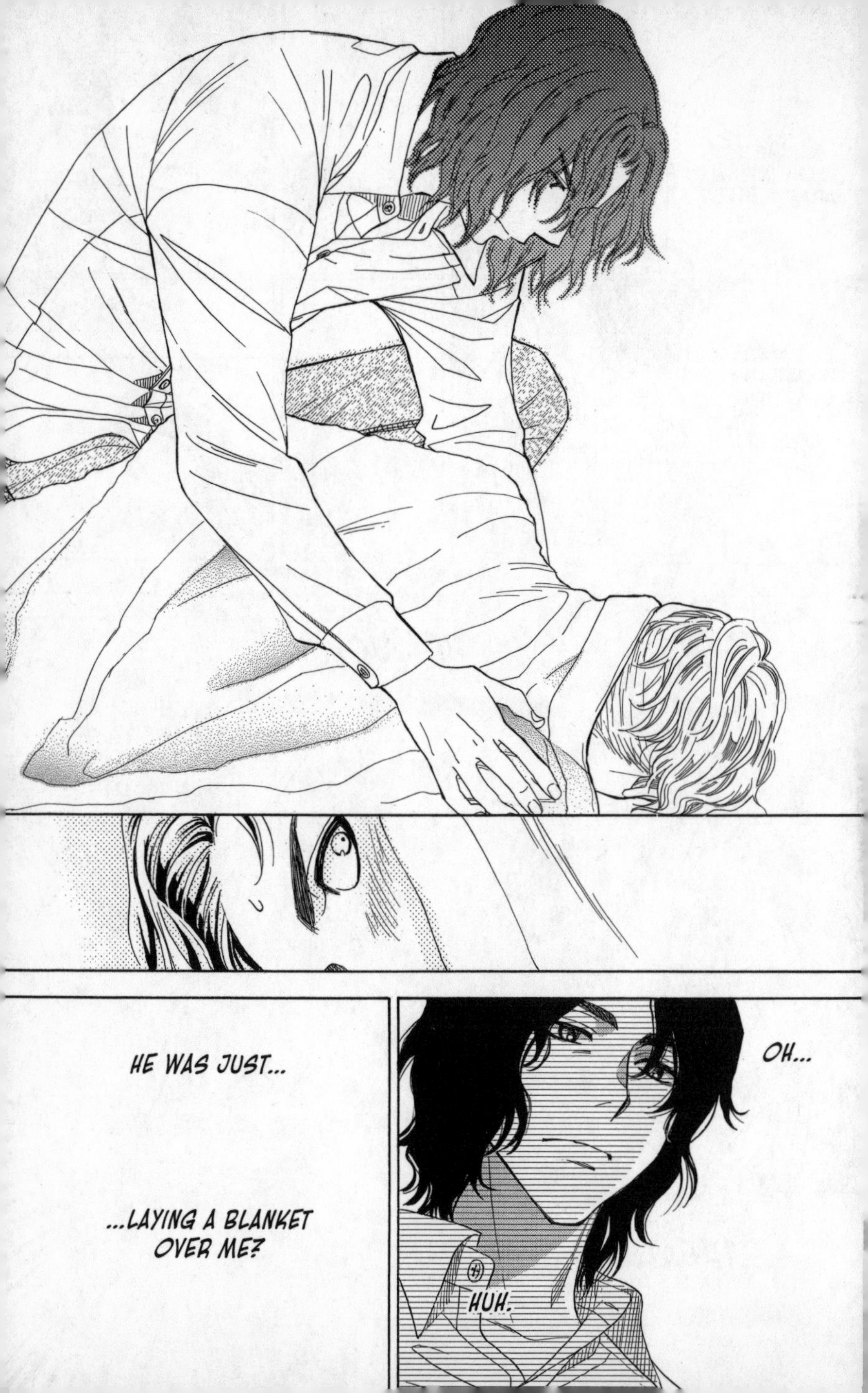
OH...
HUH.
HE WAS JUST...
...LAYING A BLANKET OVER ME?

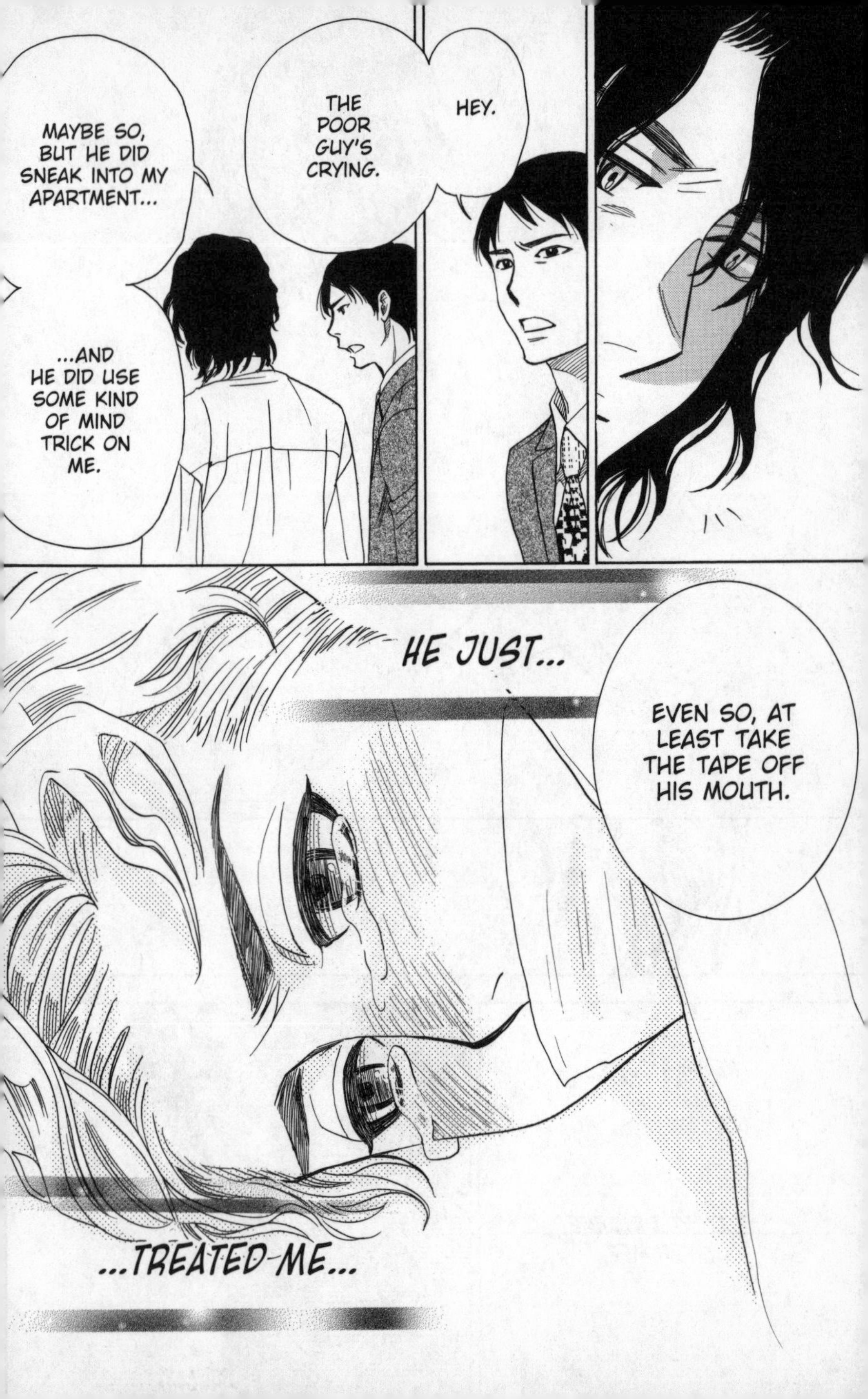
HEY.
THE POOR GUY'S CRYING.
MAYBE SO, BUT HE DID SNEAK INTO MY APARTMENT...
...AND HE DID USE SOME KIND OF MIND TRICK ON ME.
EVEN SO, AT LEAST TAKE THE TAPE OFF HIS MOUTH.
HE JUST...
...TREATED ME...

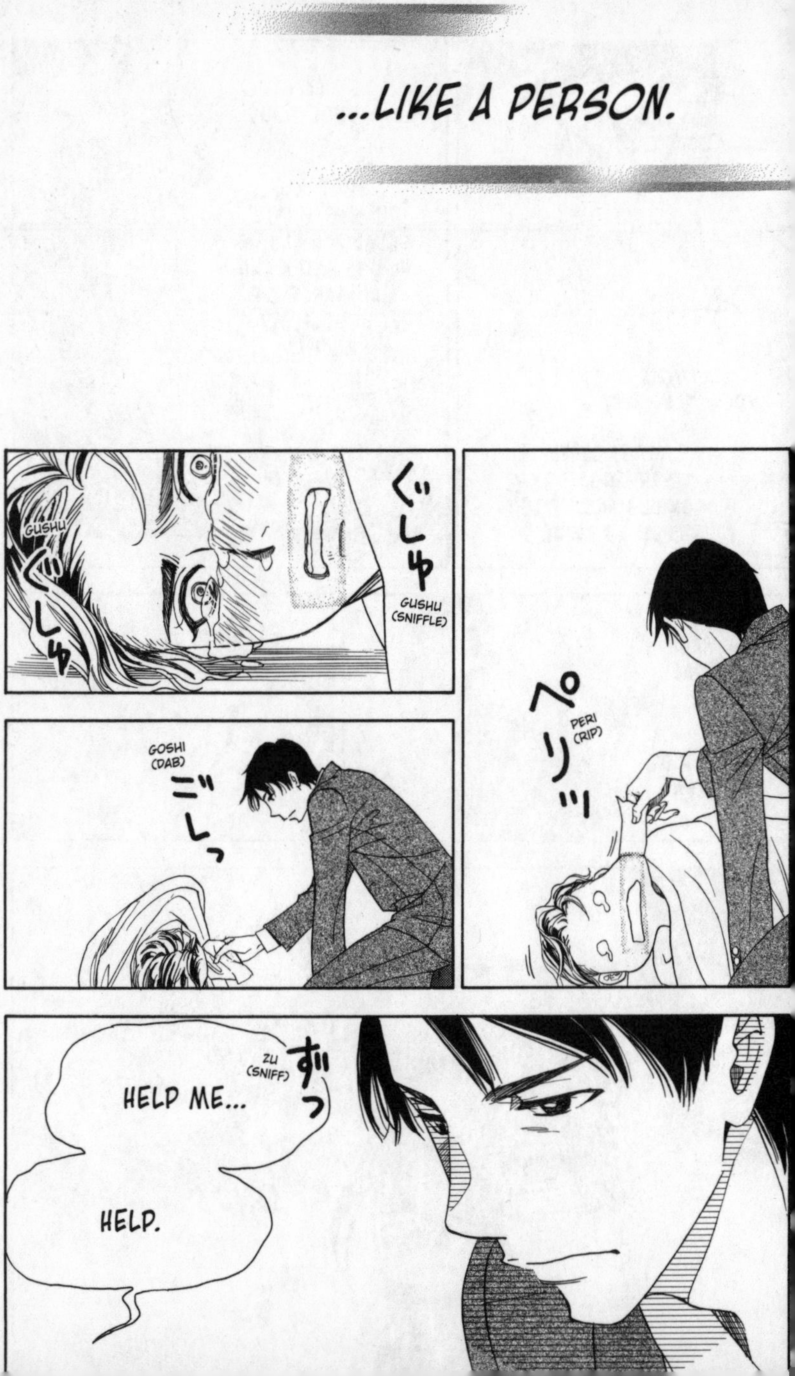
...LIKE A PERSON.
ペリッ
PERI (RIP)
ぐしゅ
GUSHU (SNIFFLE)
GUSHU
ぐしゅ
GOSHI (DAB)
ごしっ
ずっ
ZU (SNIFF)
HELP ME...
HELP.

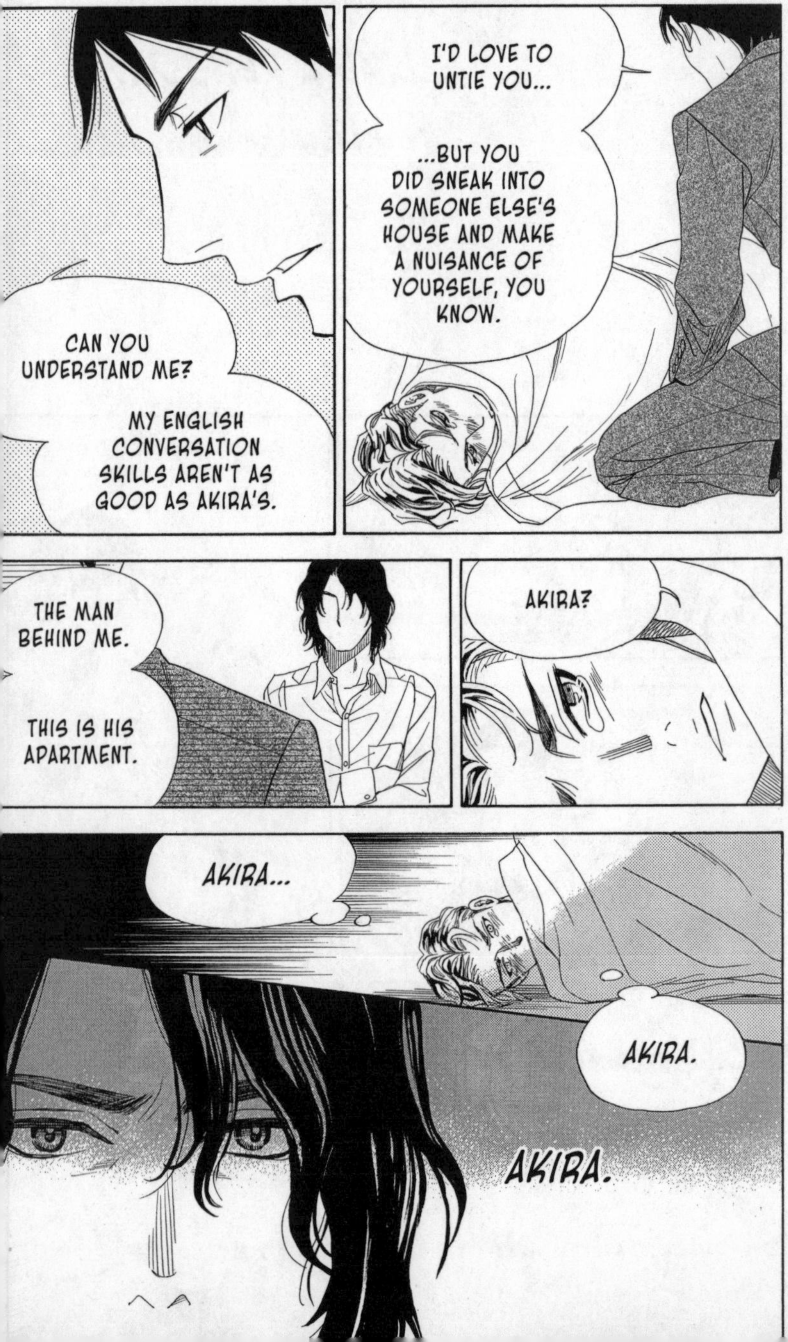
I'D LOVE TO UNTIE YOU...
...BUT YOU DID SNEAK INTO SOMEONE ELSE'S HOUSE AND MAKE A NUISANCE OF YOURSELF, YOU KNOW.
CAN YOU UNDERSTAND ME?
MY ENGLISH CONVERSATION SKILLS AREN'T AS GOOD AS AKIRA'S.
AKIRA?
THE MAN BEHIND ME.
THIS IS HIS APARTMENT.
AKIRA...
AKIRA.
AKIRA.

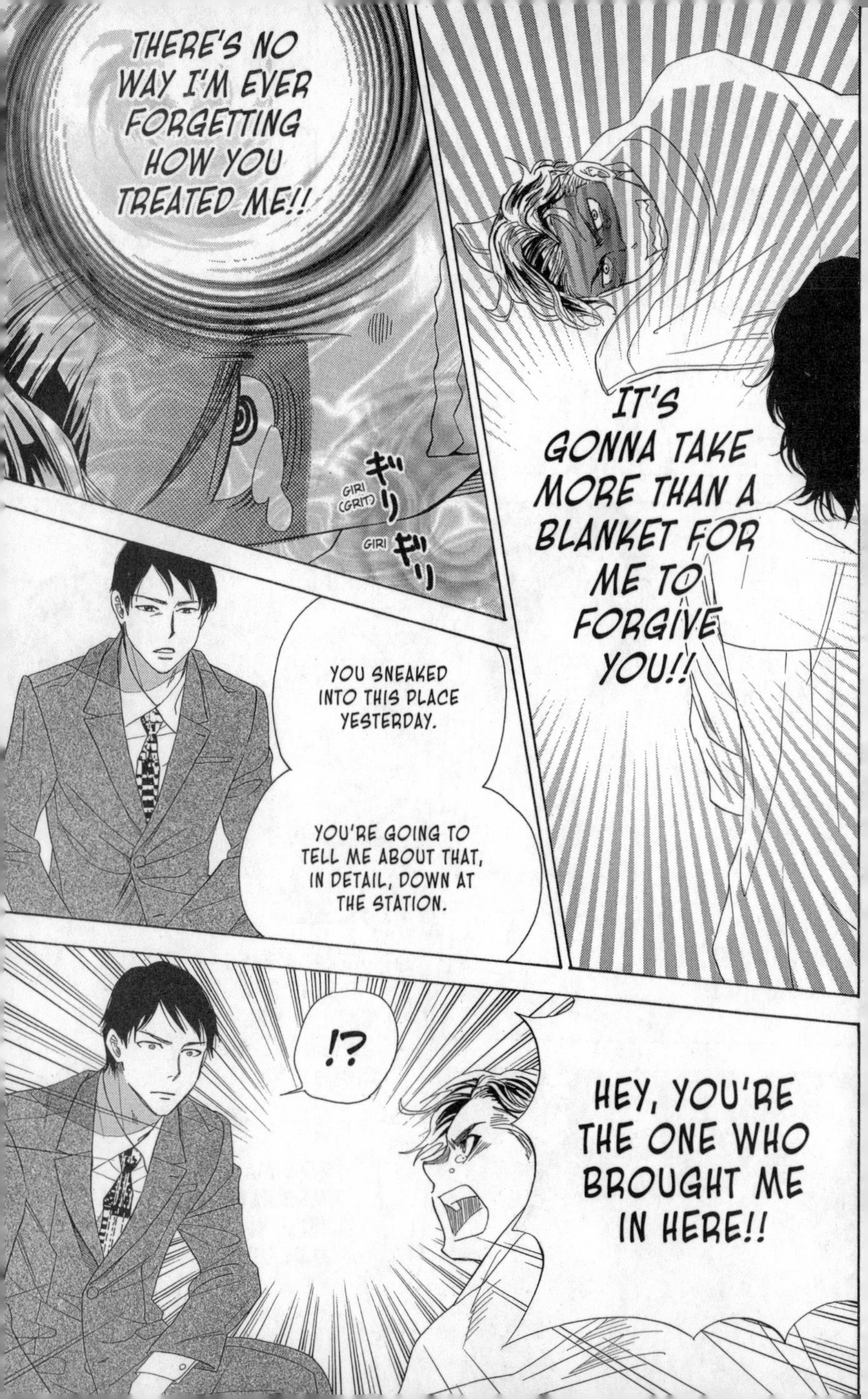
IT'S GONNA TAKE MORE THAN A BLANKET FOR ME TO FORGIVE YOU!!
THERE'S NO WAY I'M EVER FORGETTING HOW YOU TREATED ME!!
ギリ
GIRI (GRIT)
ギリ
GIRI
YOU SNEAKED INTO THIS PLACE YESTERDAY.
YOU'RE GOING TO TELL ME ABOUT THAT, IN DETAIL, DOWN AT THE STATION.
HEY, YOU'RE THE ONE WHO BROUGHT ME IN HERE!!
!?

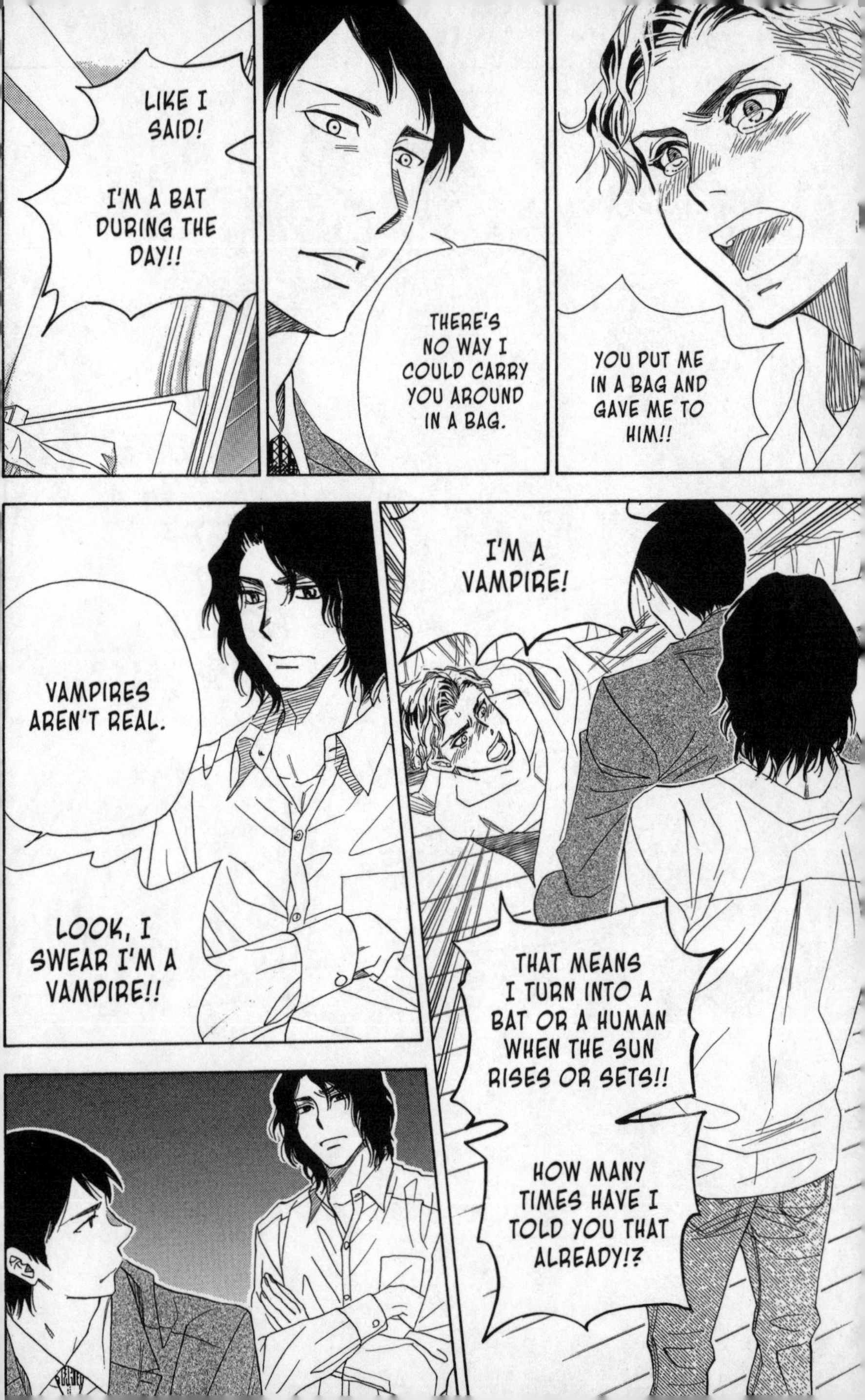
YOU PUT ME IN A BAG AND GAVE ME TO HIM!!
THERE'S NO WAY I COULD CARRY YOU AROUND IN A BAG.
LIKE I SAID!
I'M A BAT DURING THE DAY!!
I'M A VAMPIRE!
THAT MEANS I TURN INTO A BAT OR A HUMAN WHEN THE SUN RISES OR SETS!!
HOW MANY TIMES HAVE I TOLD YOU THAT ALREADY!?
VAMPIRES AREN'T REAL.
LOOK, I SWEAR I'M A VAMPIRE!!

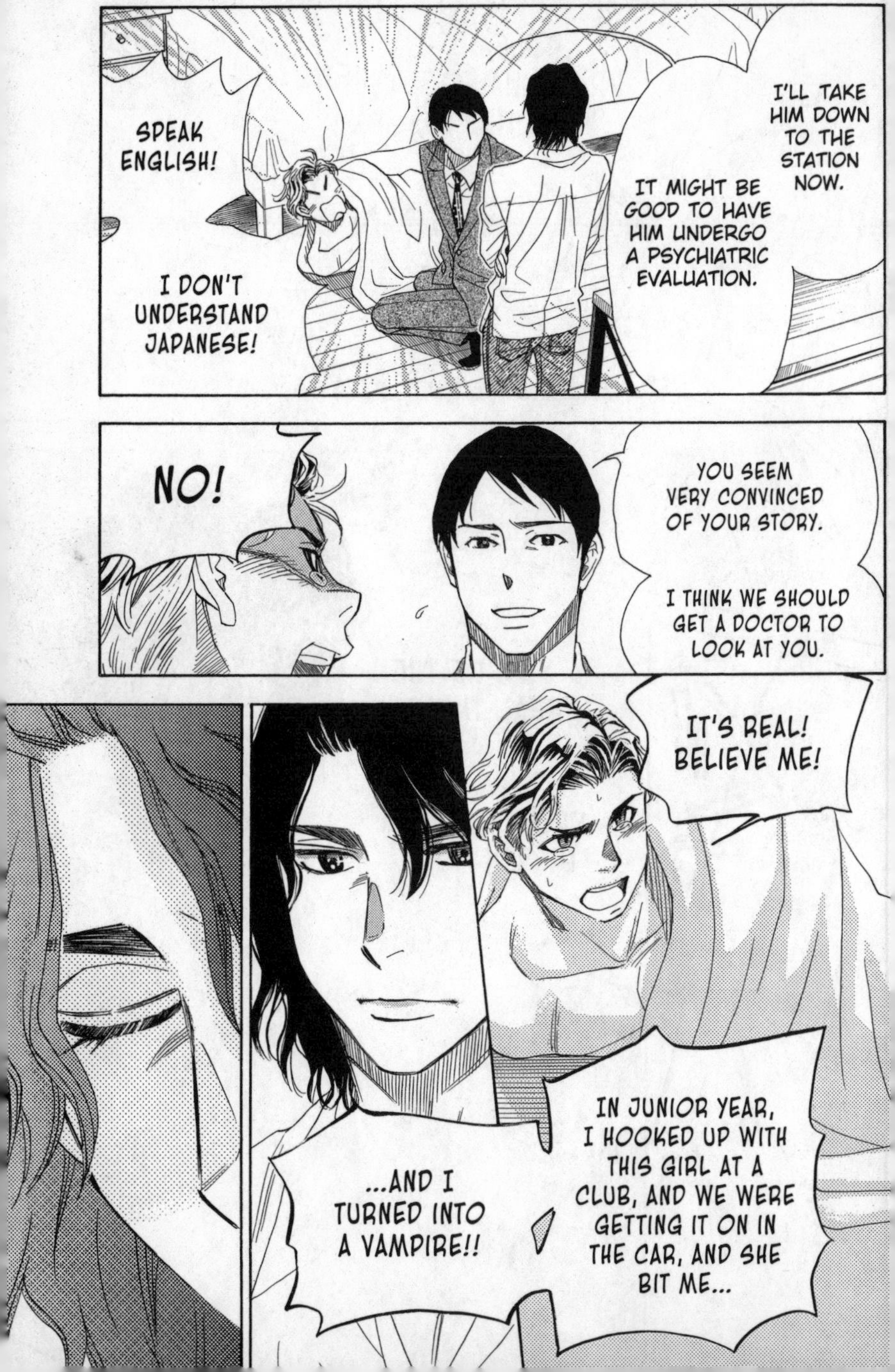
I'LL TAKE HIM DOWN TO THE STATION NOW.
IT MIGHT BE GOOD TO HAVE HIM UNDERGO A PSYCHIATRIC EVALUATION.
SPEAK ENGLISH!
I DON'T UNDERSTAND JAPANESE!
YOU SEEM VERY CONVINCED OF YOUR STORY.
I THINK WE SHOULD GET A DOCTOR TO LOOK AT YOU.
NO!
IT'S REAL! BELIEVE ME!
IN JUNIOR YEAR, I HOOKED UP WITH THIS GIRL AT A CLUB, AND WE WERE GETTING IT ON IN THE CAR, AND SHE BIT ME...
...AND I TURNED INTO A VAMPIRE!!

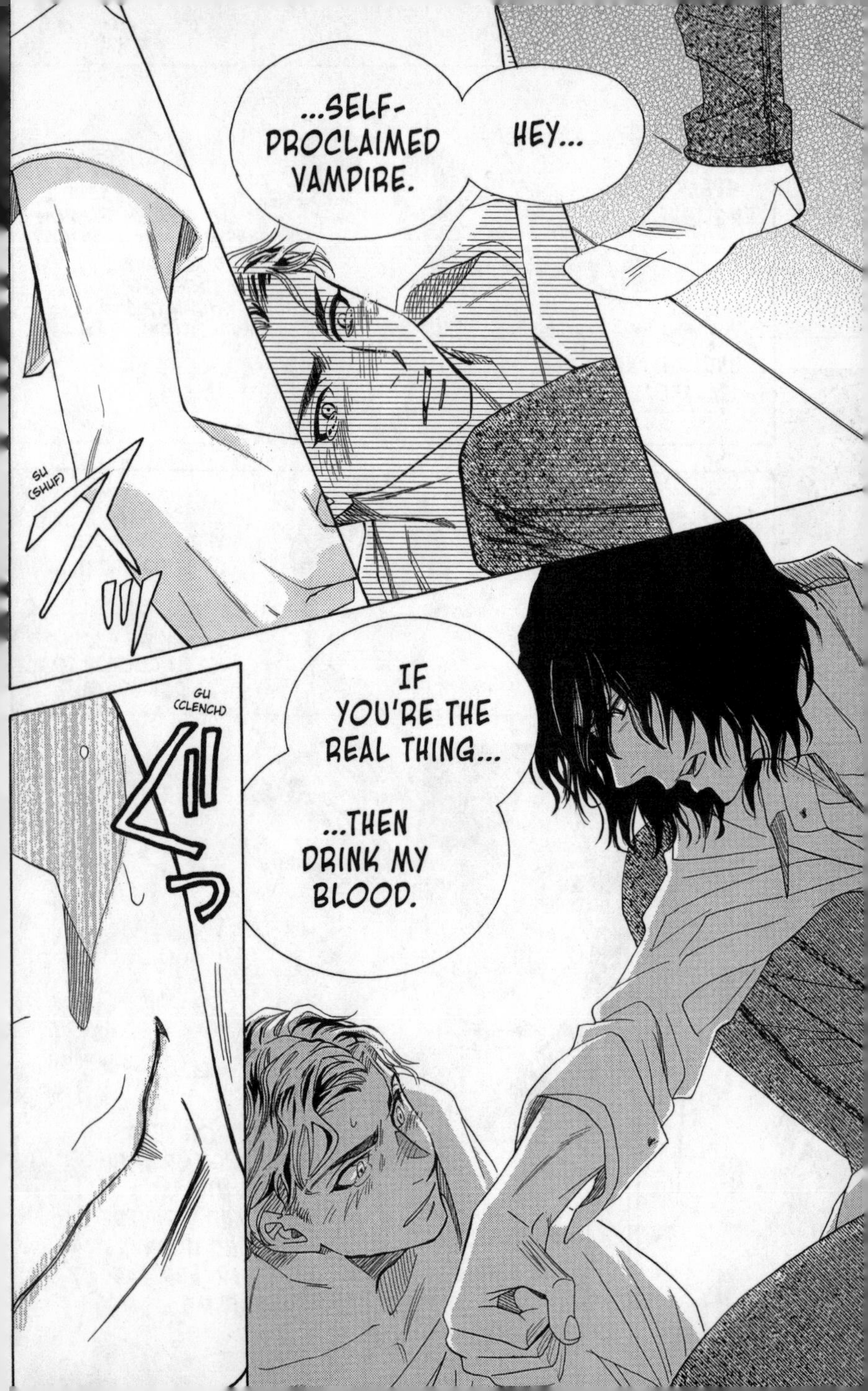
HEY...
...SELF-PROCLAIMED VAMPIRE.
SU (SHUF)
IF YOU'RE THE REAL THING...
...THEN DRINK MY BLOOD.
GU (CLENCH)

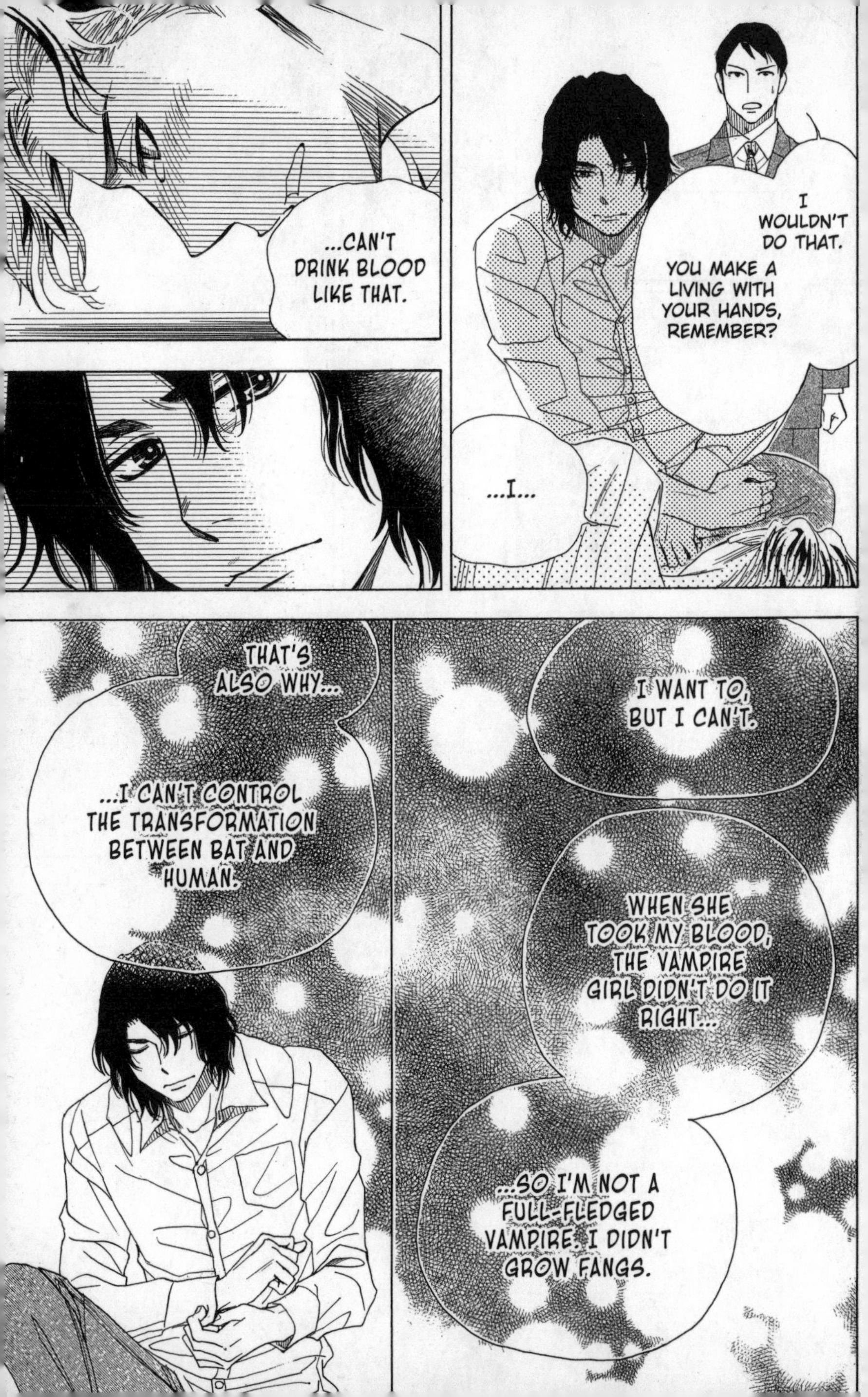
I WOULDN'T DO THAT.
YOU MAKE A LIVING WITH YOUR HANDS, REMEMBER?
...I...
...CAN'T DRINK BLOOD LIKE THAT.
I WANT TO, BUT I CAN'T.
WHEN SHE TOOK MY BLOOD, THE VAMPIRE GIRL DIDN'T DO IT RIGHT...
...SO I'M NOT A FULL-FLEDGED VAMPIRE. I DIDN'T GROW FANGS.
THAT'S ALSO WHY...
...I CAN'T CONTROL THE TRANSFORMATION BETWEEN BAT AND HUMAN.

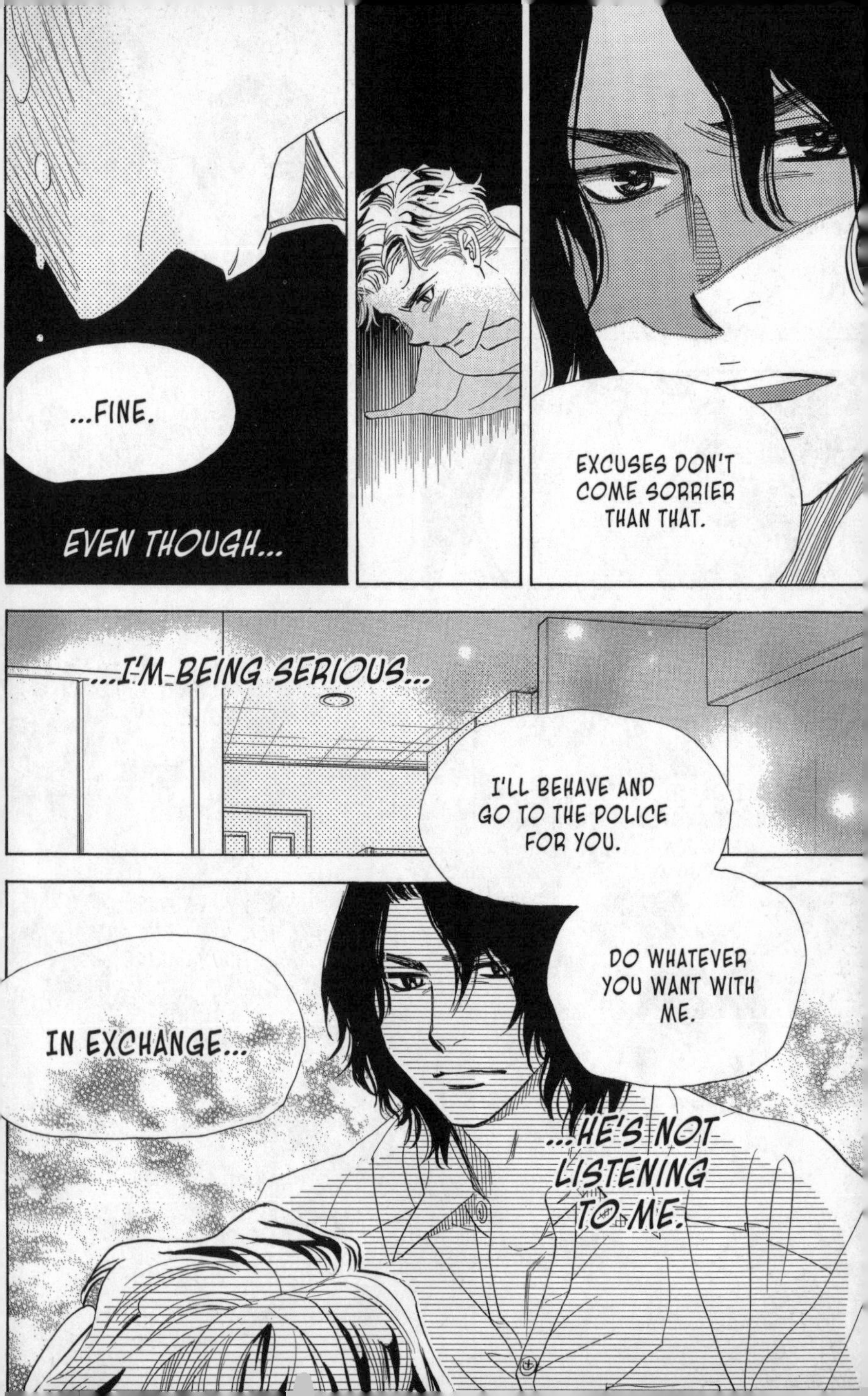
EXCUSES DON'T COME SORRIER THAN THAT.
...FINE.
EVEN THOUGH...
...I'M BEING SERIOUS...
I'LL BEHAVE AND GO TO THE POLICE FOR YOU.
DO WHATEVER YOU WANT WITH ME.
IN EXCHANGE...
...HE'S NOT LISTENING TO ME.

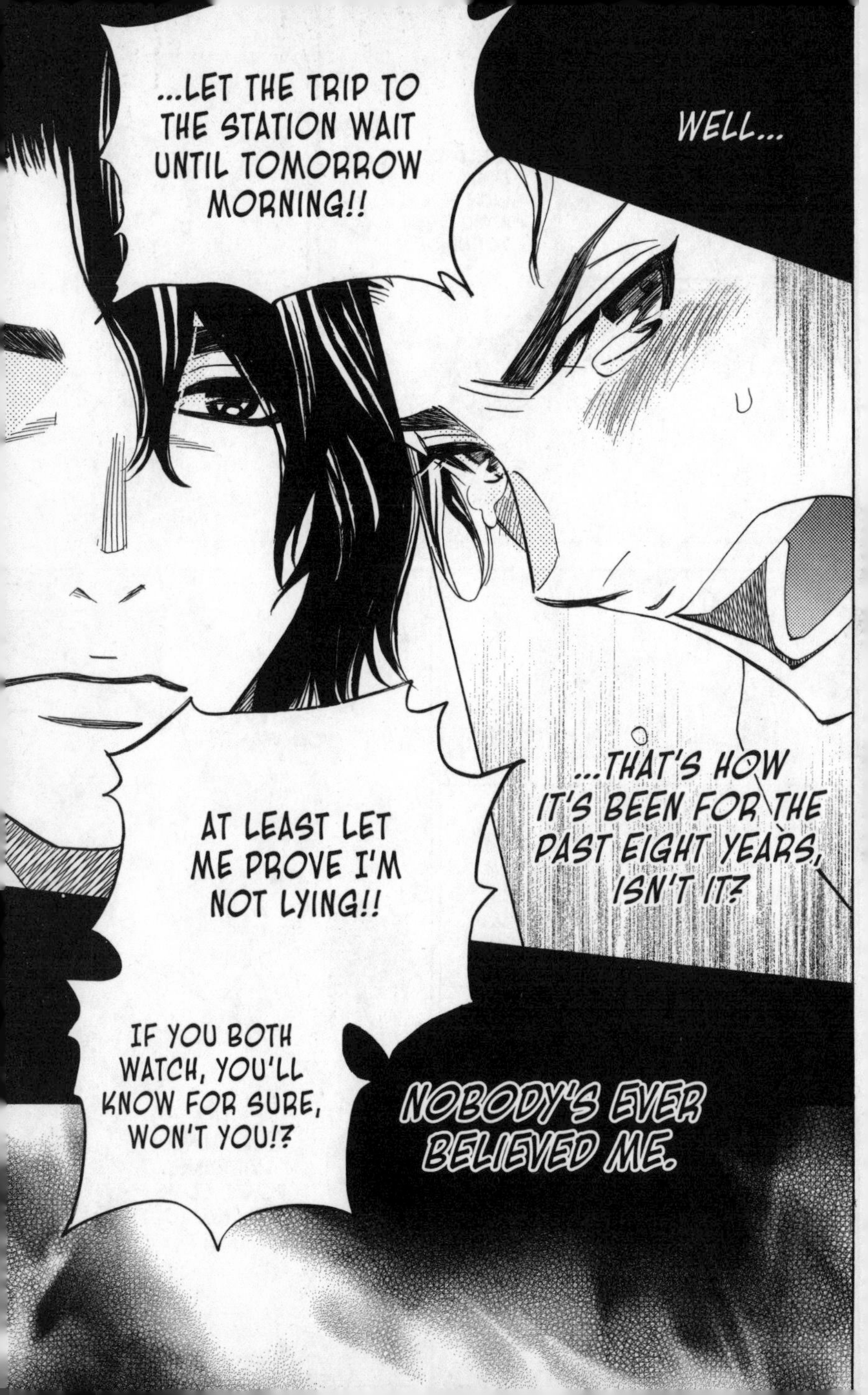
WELL...
...LET THE TRIP TO THE STATION WAIT UNTIL TOMORROW MORNING!!
...THAT'S HOW IT'S BEEN FOR THE PAST EIGHT YEARS, ISN'T IT?
AT LEAST LET ME PROVE I'M NOT LYING!!
NOBODY'S EVER BELIEVED ME.
IF YOU BOTH WATCH, YOU'LL KNOW FOR SURE, WON'T YOU!?

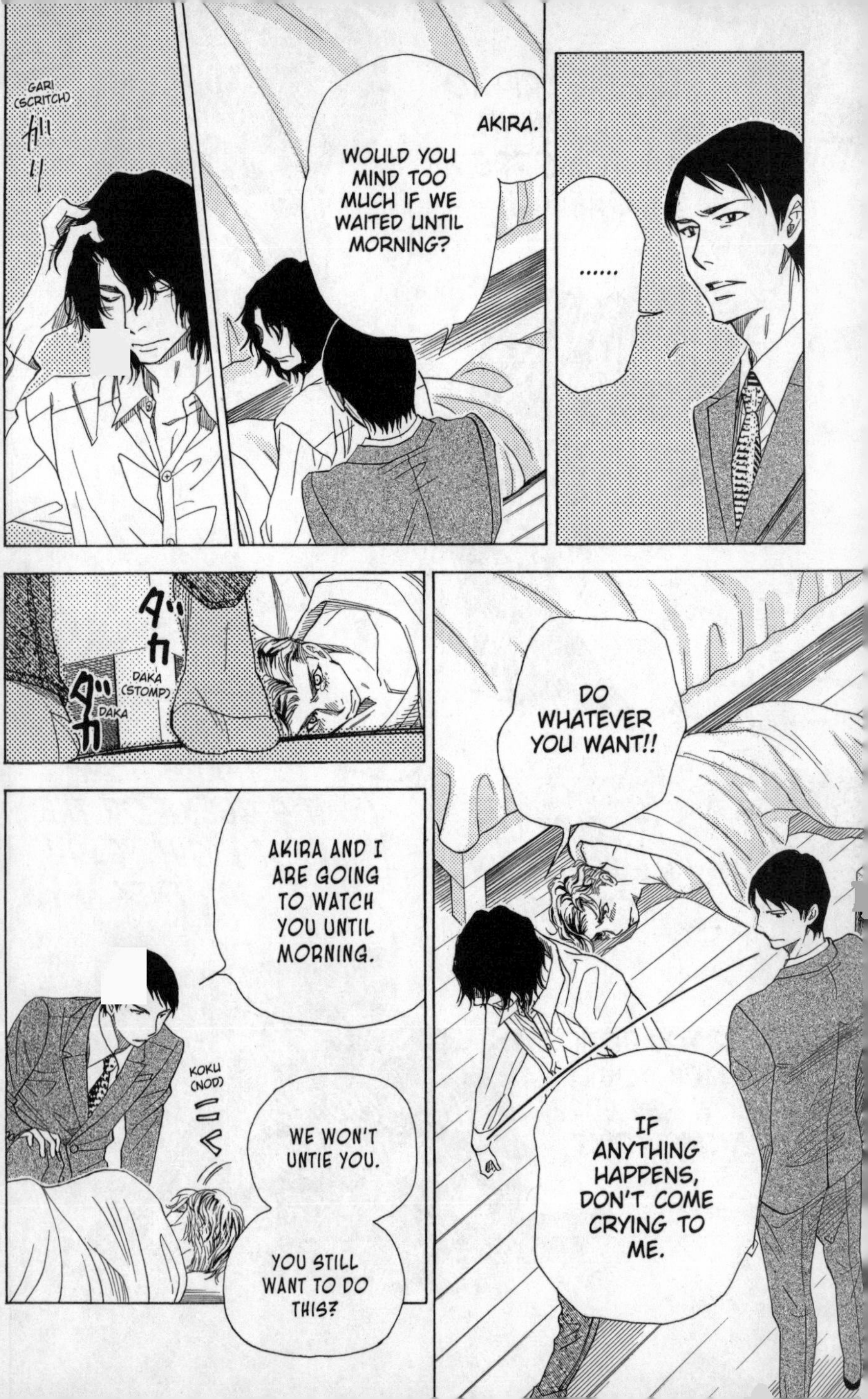
......
AKIRA.
WOULD YOU MIND TOO MUCH IF WE WAITED UNTIL MORNING?
ガリ
GARI (SCRITCH)
DO WHATEVER YOU WANT!!
IF ANYTHING HAPPENS, DON'T COME CRYING TO ME.
ダカ
DAKA (STOMP)
ダカ
DAKA
AKIRA AND I ARE GOING TO WATCH YOU UNTIL MORNING.
WE WON'T UNTIE YOU.
YOU STILL WANT TO DO THIS?
KOKU (NOD)

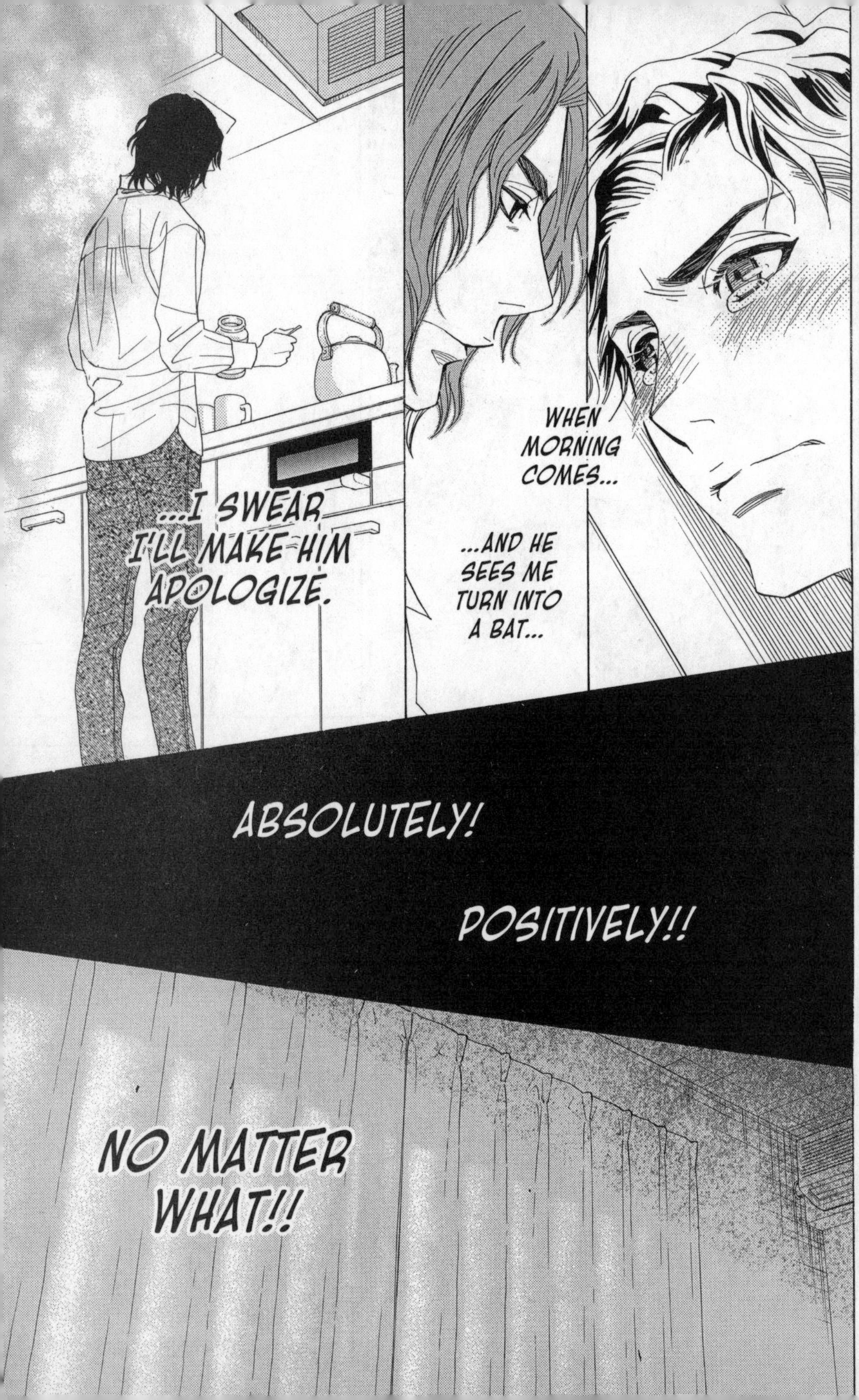
WHEN MORNING COMES...
...AND HE SEES ME TURN INTO A BAT...
...I SWEAR I'LL MAKE HIM APOLOGIZE.
ABSOLUTELY!
POSITIVELY!!
NO MATTER WHAT!!

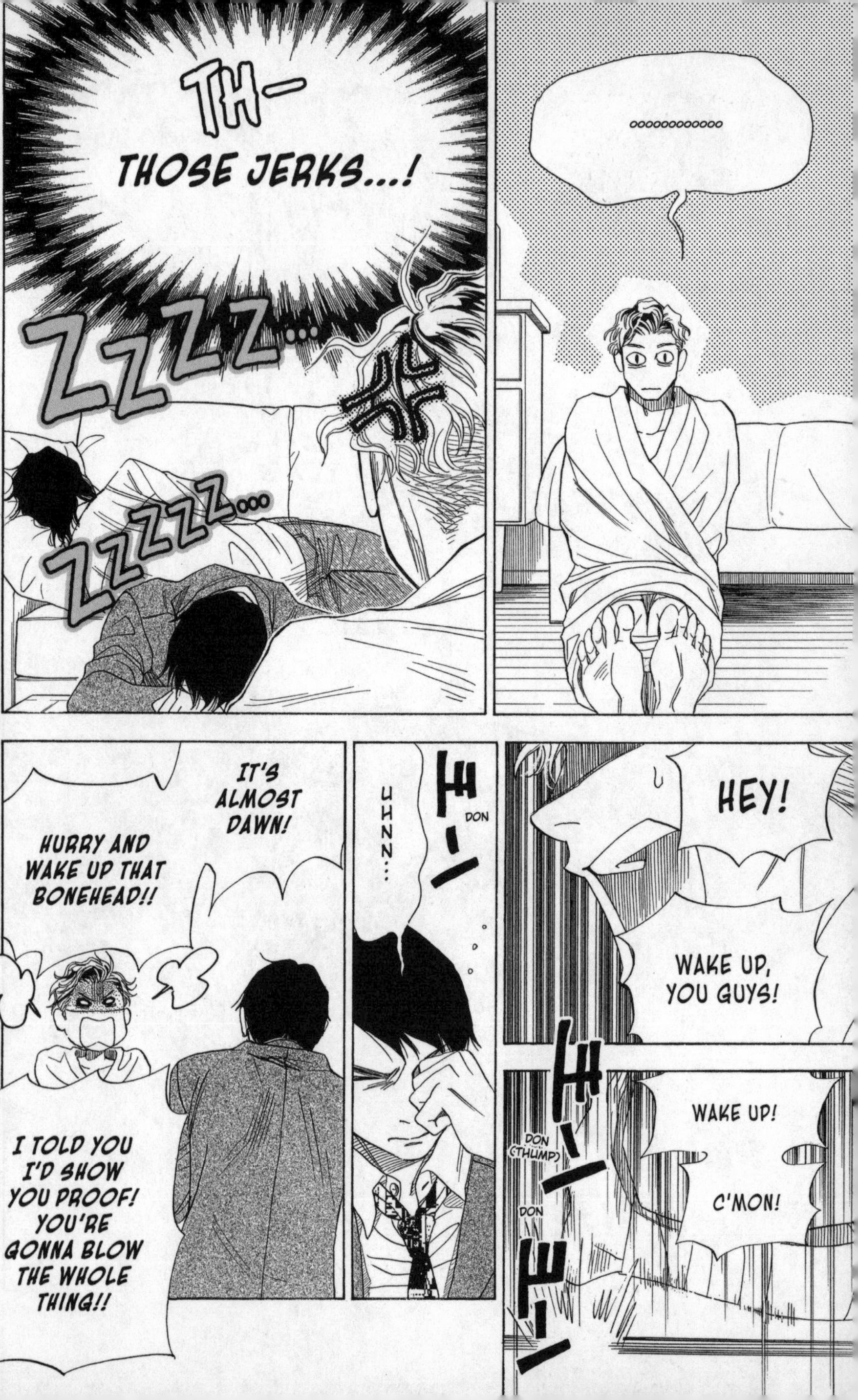

....
TH-
THOSE JERKS...!
ZZZZZ...
ZZZZZZ...
HEY!
WAKE UP, YOU GUYS!
DON (THUMP)
WAKE UP!
C'MON!
DON
DON
UHNN...
IT'S ALMOST DAWN!
HURRY AND WAKE UP THAT BONEHEAD!!
I TOLD YOU I'D SHOW YOU PROOF! YOU'RE GONNA BLOW THE WHOLE THING!!

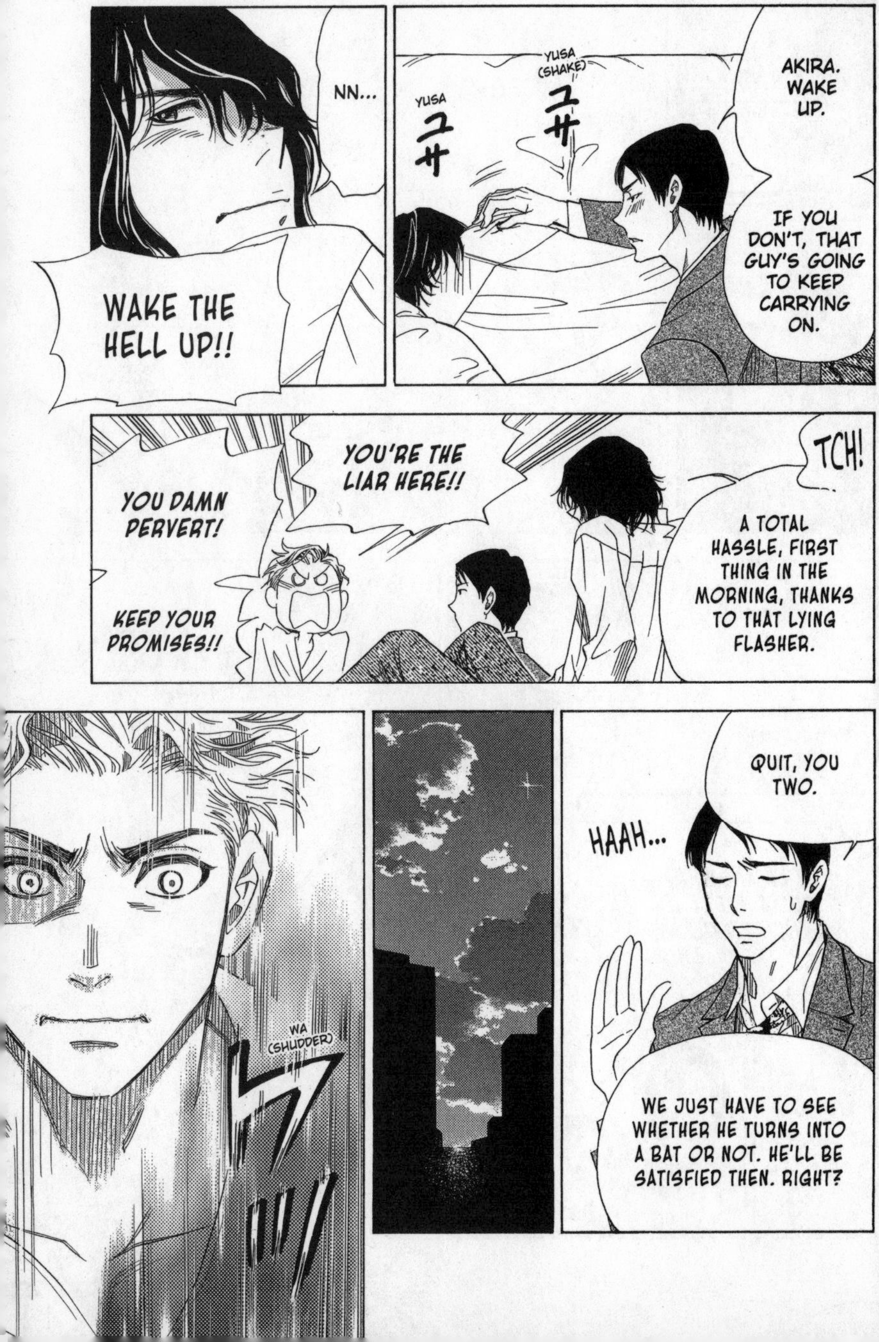
YUSA (SHAKE)
ユサ
YUSA
ユサ
AKIRA. WAKE UP.
IF YOU DON'T, THAT GUY'S GOING TO KEEP CARRYING ON.
NN...
WAKE THE HELL UP!!
TCH!
A TOTAL HASSLE, FIRST THING IN THE MORNING, THANKS TO THAT LYING FLASHER.
YOU'RE THE LIAR HERE!!
YOU DAMN PERVERT!
KEEP YOUR PROMISES!!
QUIT, YOU TWO.
HAAH...
WE JUST HAVE TO SEE WHETHER HE TURNS INTO A BAT OR NOT. HE'LL BE SATISFIED THEN. RIGHT?
WA (SHUDDER)

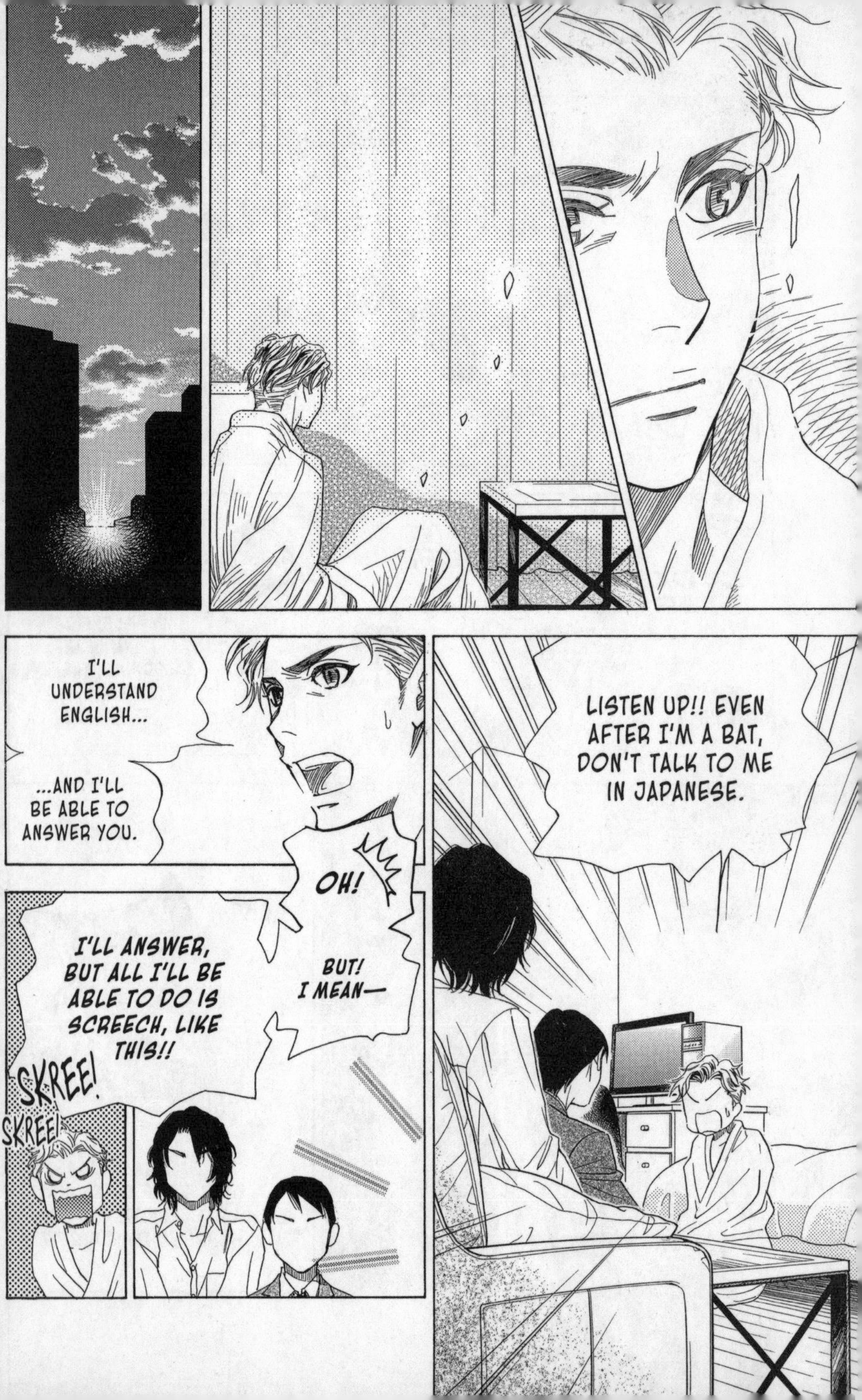
LISTEN UP!! EVEN AFTER I'M A BAT, DON'T TALK TO ME IN JAPANESE.
I'LL UNDERSTAND ENGLISH...
...AND I'LL BE ABLE TO ANSWER YOU.
OH!
BUT! I MEAN—
I'LL ANSWER, BUT ALL I'LL BE ABLE TO DO IS SCREECH, LIKE THIS!!
SKREE!
SKREE!

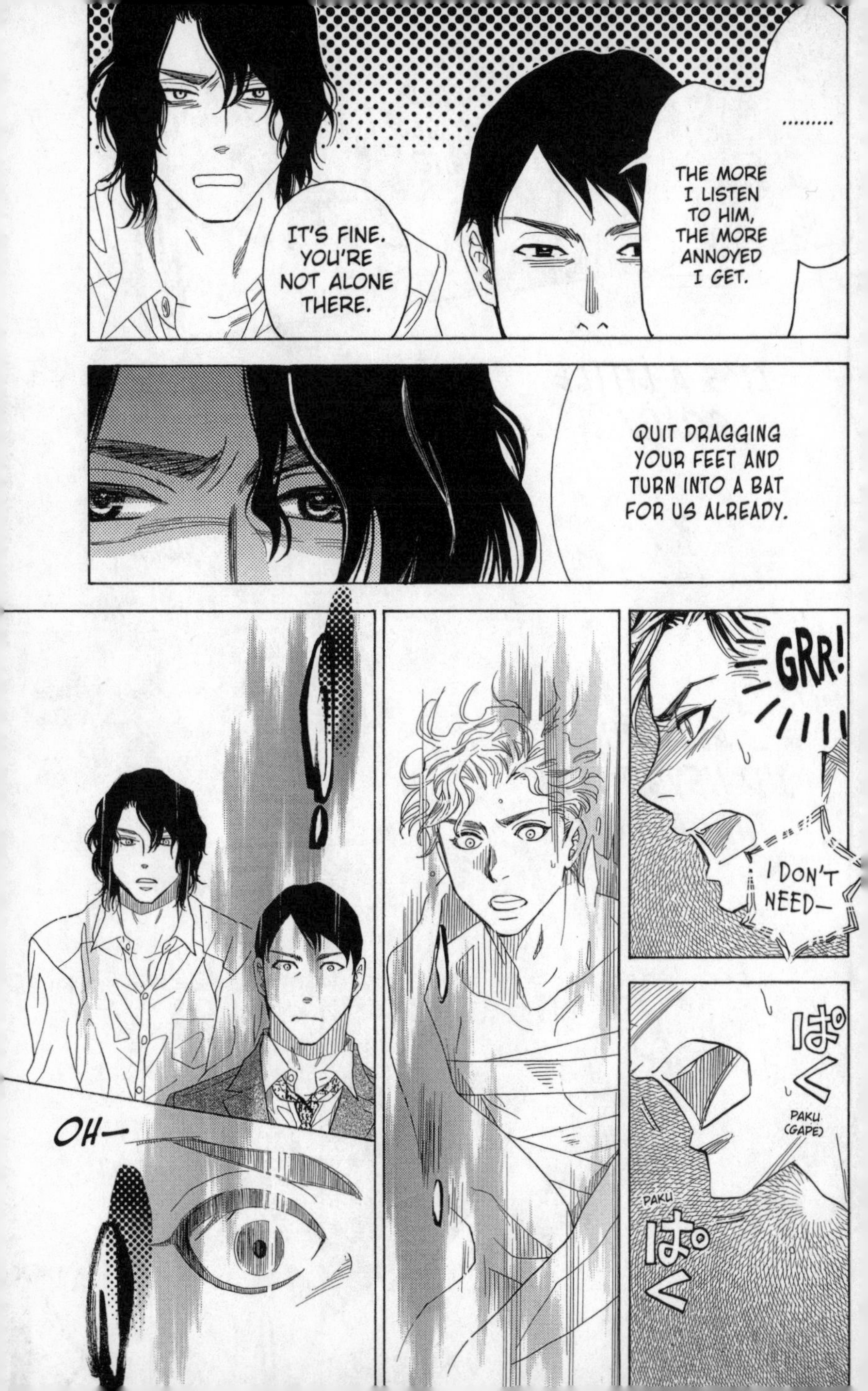

....
THE MORE I LISTEN TO HIM, THE MORE ANNOYED I GET.
IT'S FINE. YOU'RE NOT ALONE THERE.
QUIT DRAGGING YOUR FEET AND TURN INTO A BAT FOR US ALREADY.
GRR!
I DON'T NEED—
ぱく
PAKU (GAPE)
PAKU
ぱく
OH—

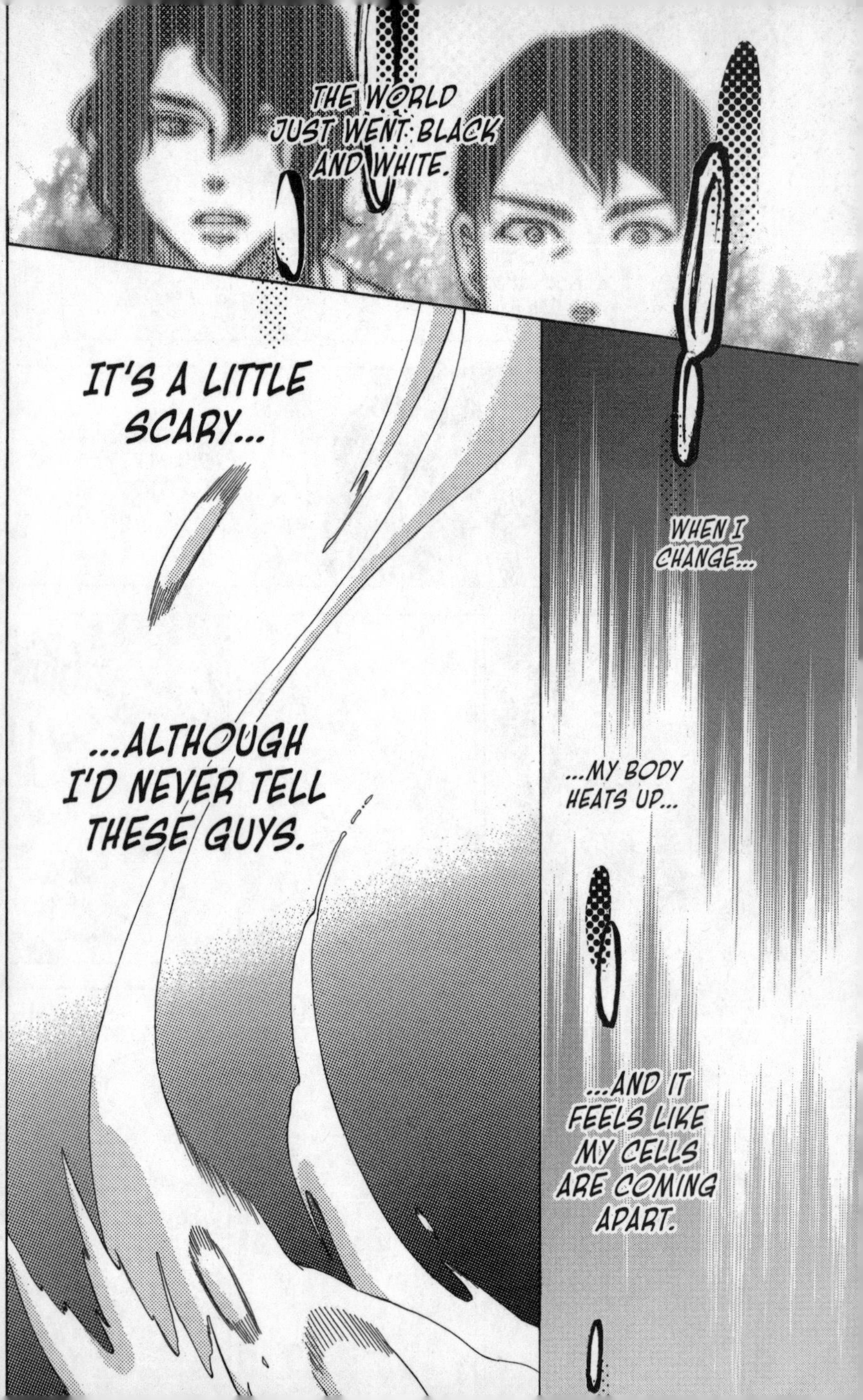
THE WORLD JUST WENT BLACK AND WHITE.
WHEN I CHANGE...
...MY BODY HEATS UP...
...AND IT FEELS LIKE MY CELLS ARE COMING APART.
IT'S A LITTLE SCARY...
...ALTHOUGH I'D NEVER TELL THESE GUYS.

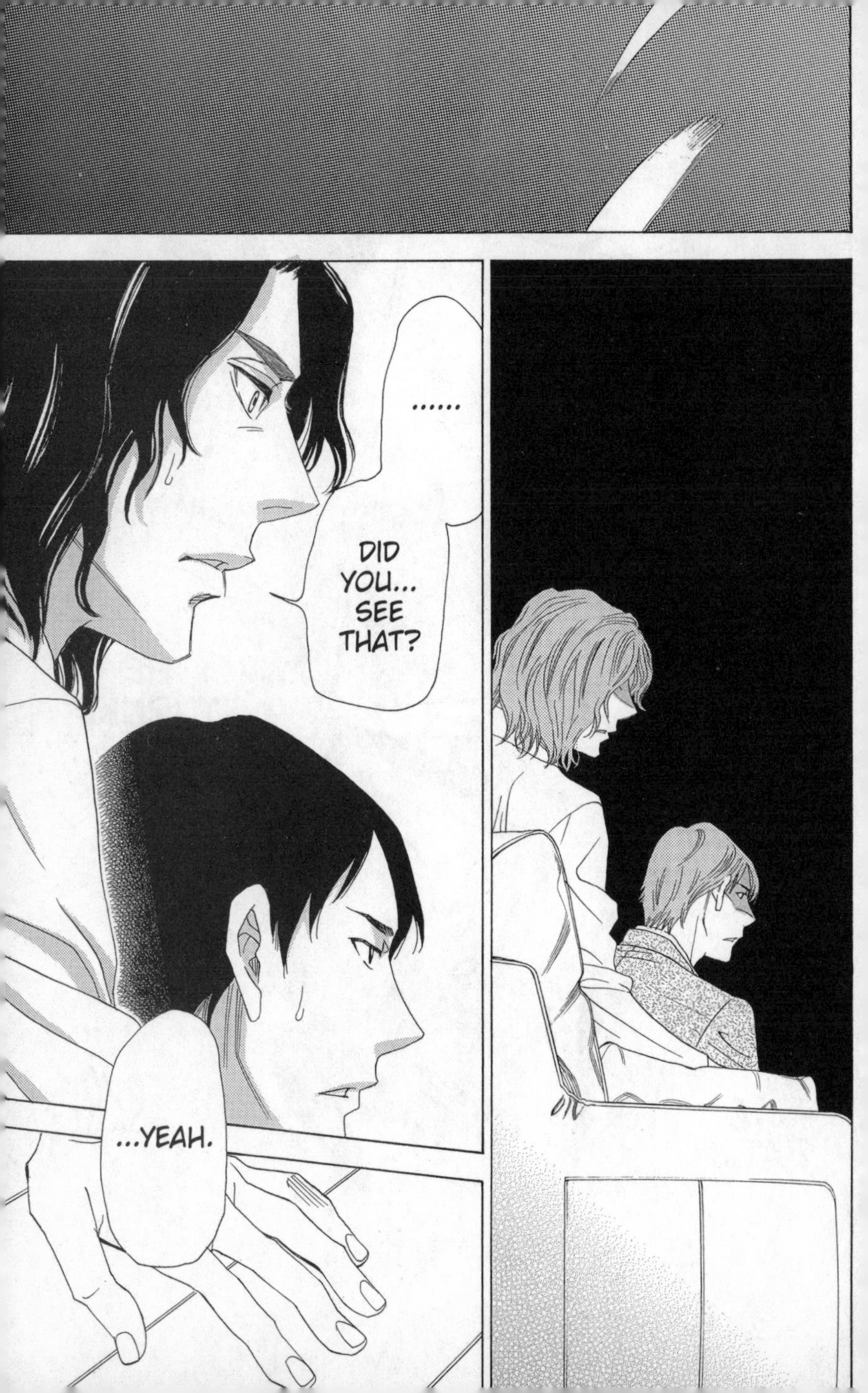
......
DID YOU... SEE THAT?
...YEAH.

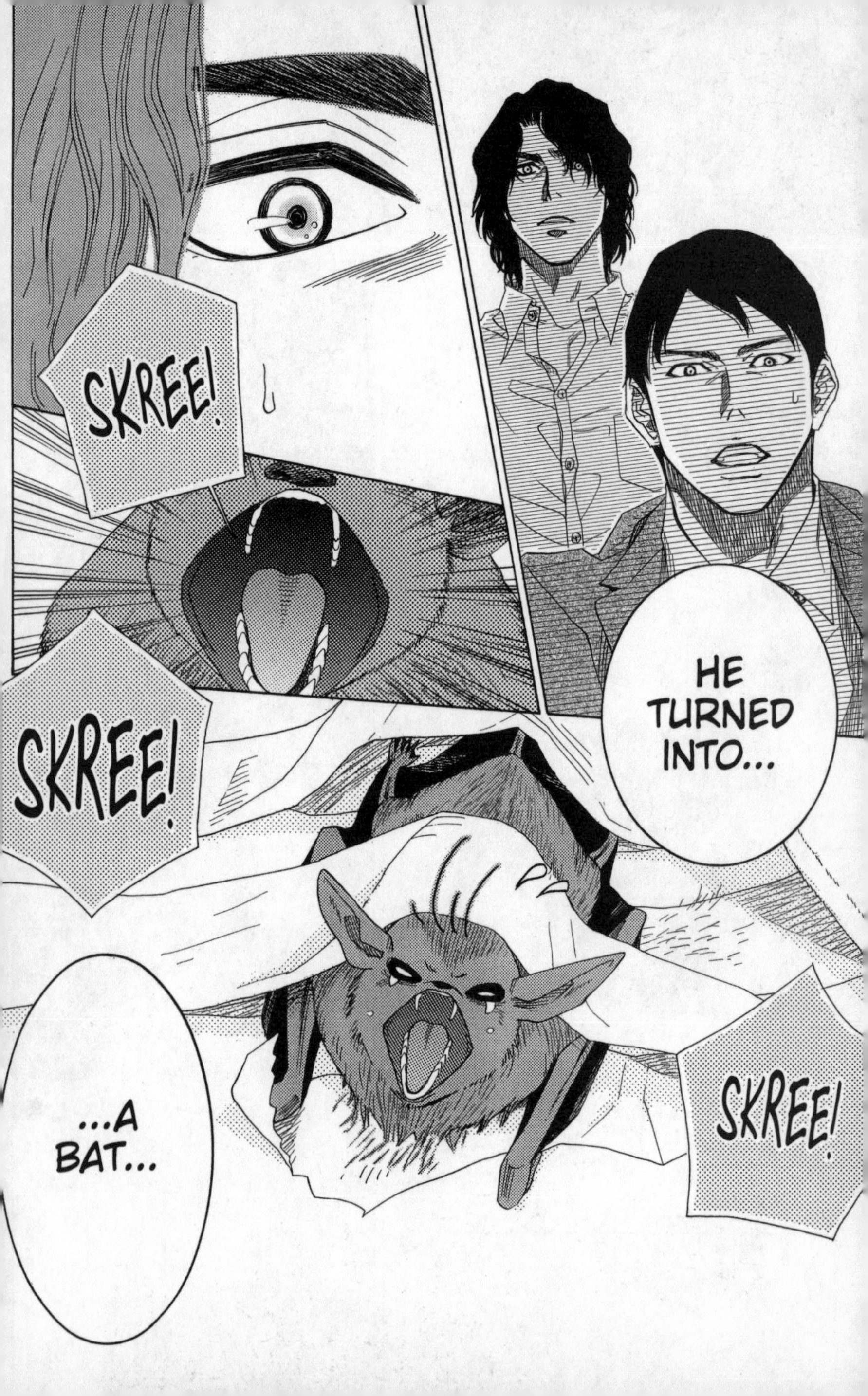
HE TURNED INTO...
SKREE!
SKREE!
SKREE!
...A BAT...

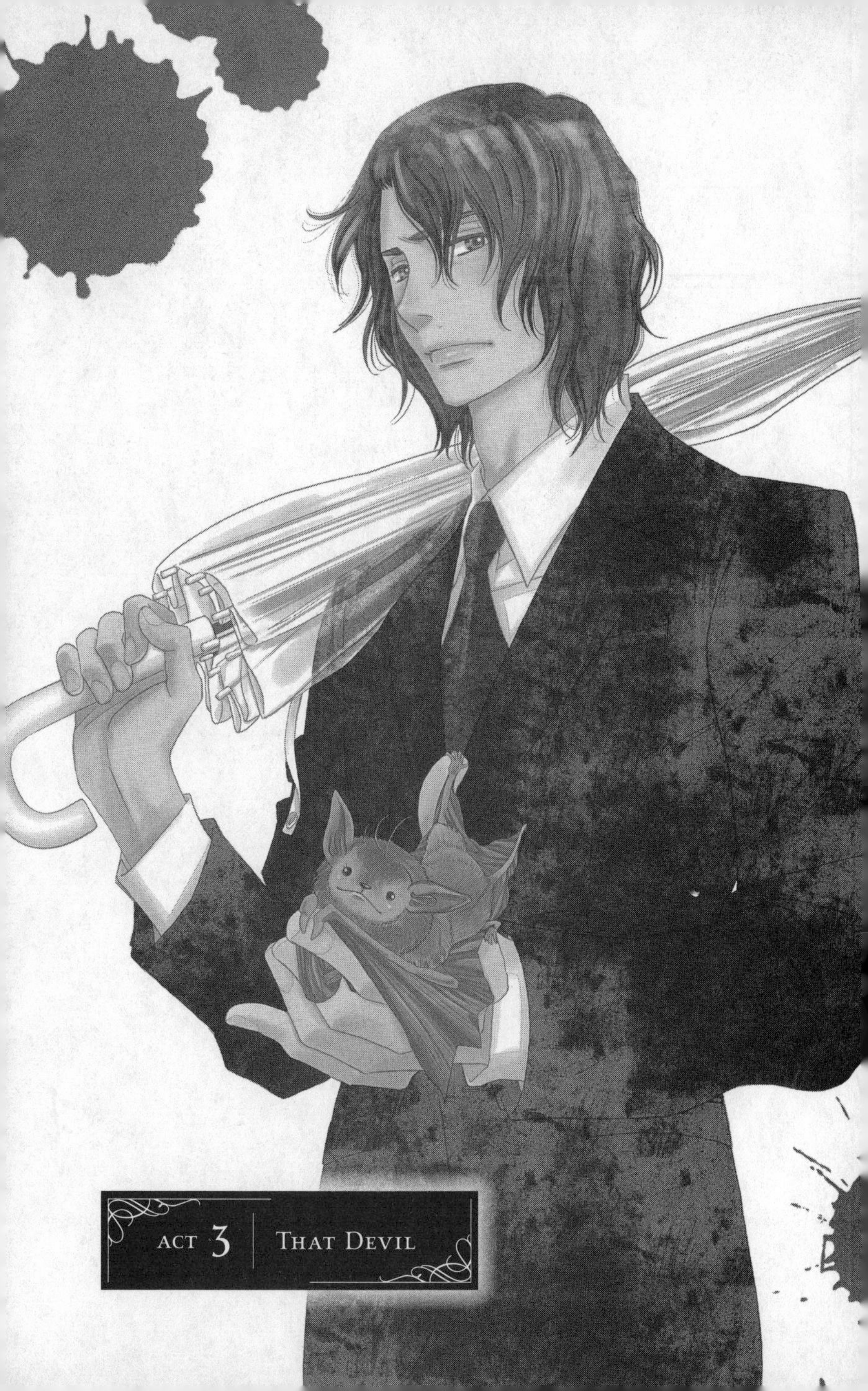
ACT 3
That Devil

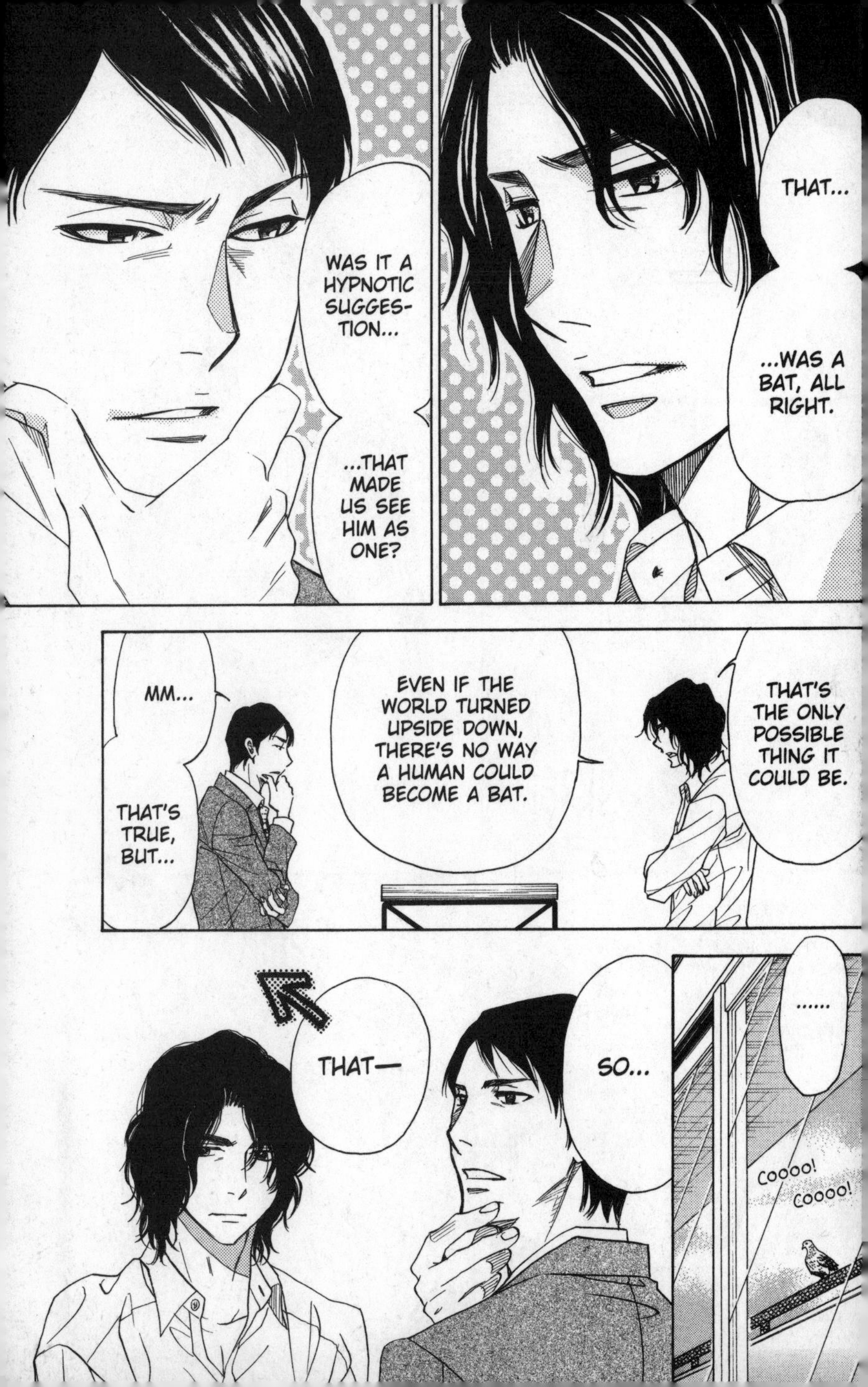
THAT...
...WAS A BAT, ALL RIGHT.
WAS IT A HYPNOTIC SUGGES-TION...
...THAT MADE US SEE HIM AS ONE?
THAT'S THE ONLY POSSIBLE THING IT COULD BE.
EVEN IF THE WORLD TURNED UPSIDE DOWN, THERE'S NO WAY A HUMAN COULD BECOME A BAT.
MM...
THAT'S TRUE, BUT...
......
COOOO!
COOOO!
SO...
THAT—

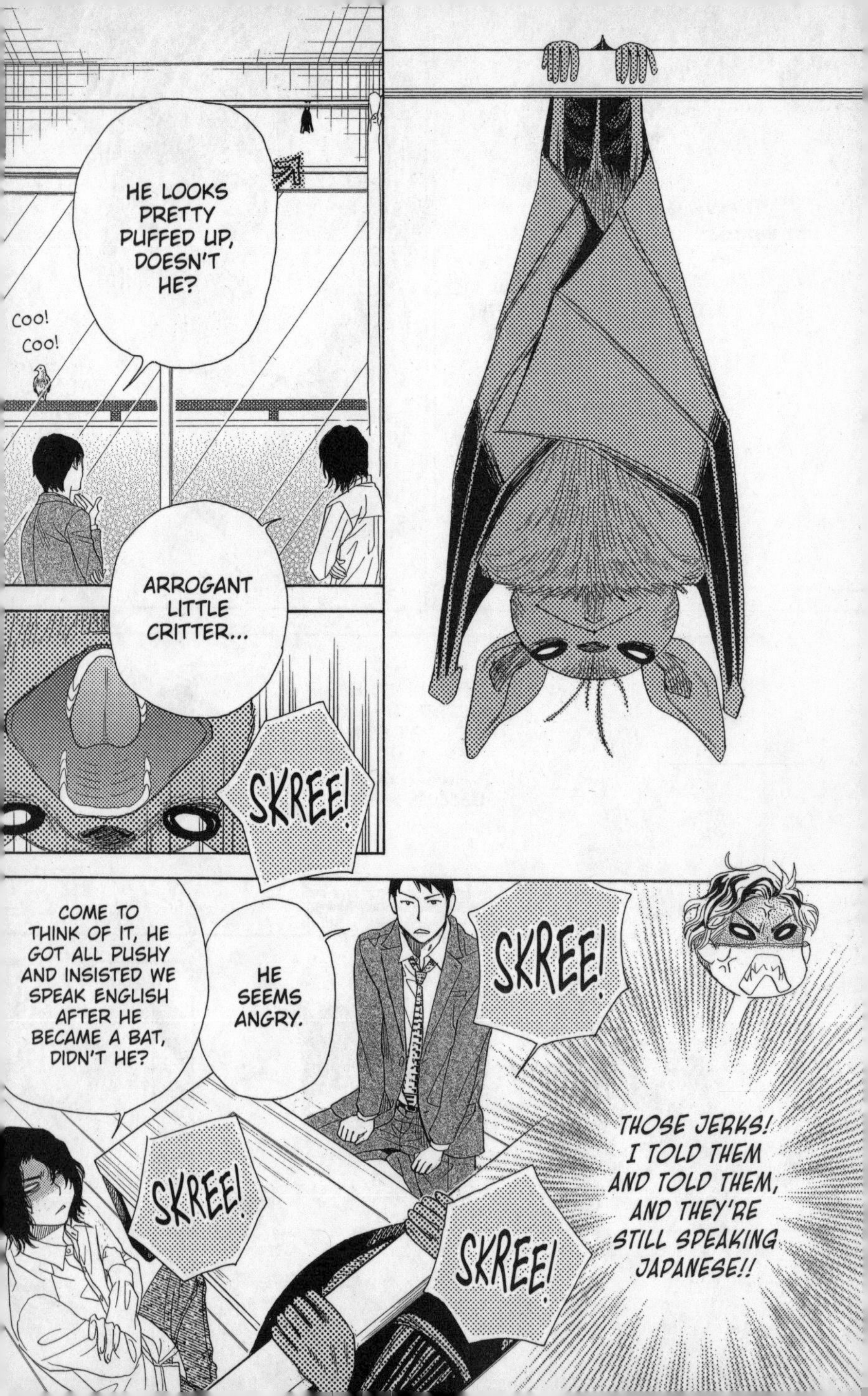
HE LOOKS PRETTY PUFFED UP, DOESN'T HE?
COO! COO!
ARROGANT LITTLE CRITTER...
SKREE!
SKREE!
HE SEEMS ANGRY.
COME TO THINK OF IT, HE GOT ALL PUSHY AND INSISTED WE SPEAK ENGLISH AFTER HE BECAME A BAT, DIDN'T HE?
THOSE JERKS! I TOLD THEM AND TOLD THEM, AND THEY'RE STILL SPEAKING JAPANESE!!
SKREE!
SKREE!

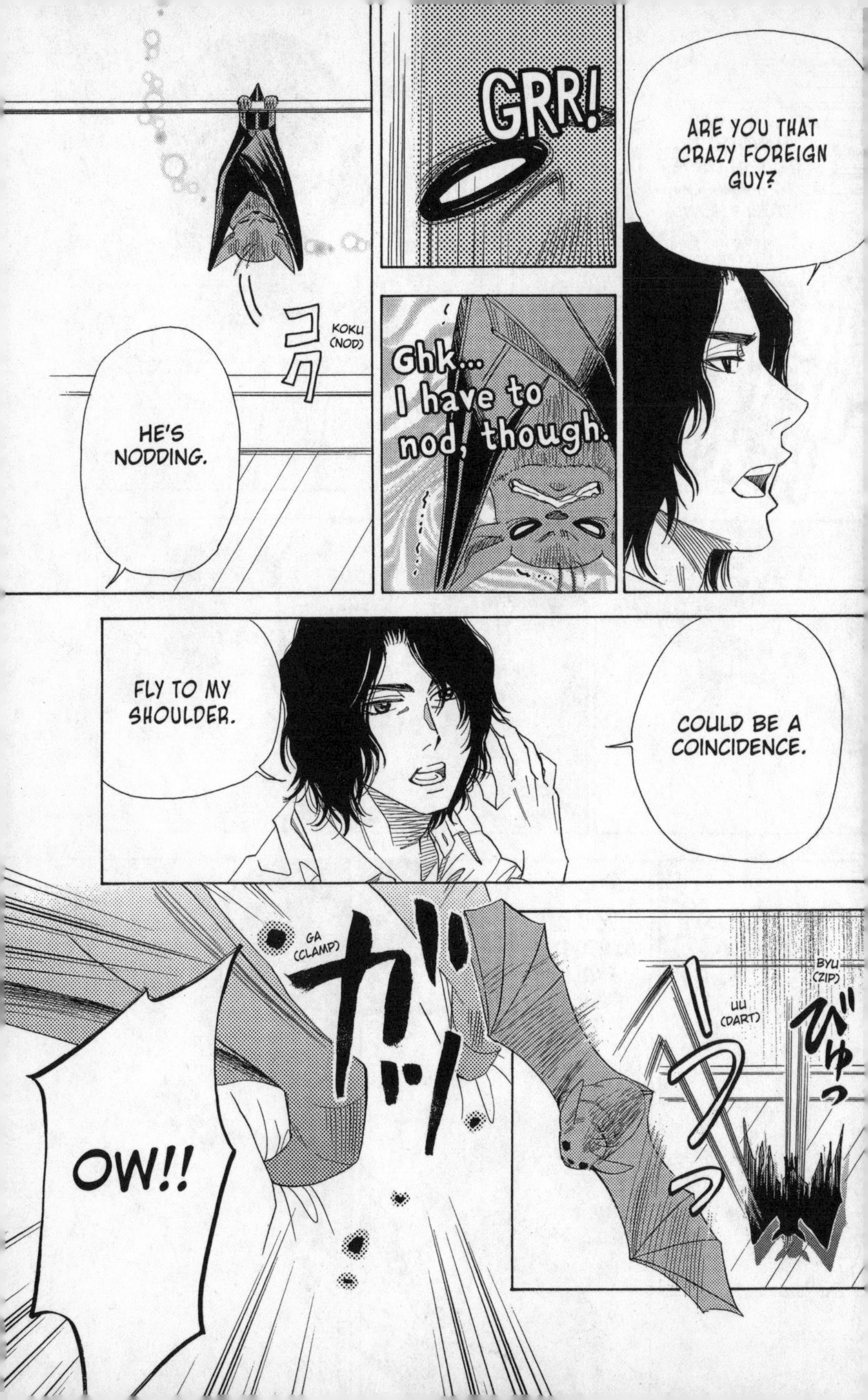
ARE YOU THAT CRAZY FOREIGN GUY?
GRR!
Ghk... I have to nod, though.
KOKU (NOD)
HE'S NODDING.
COULD BE A COINCIDENCE.
FLY TO MY SHOULDER.
BYU (ZIP)
UU (DART)
GA (CLAMP)
OW!!

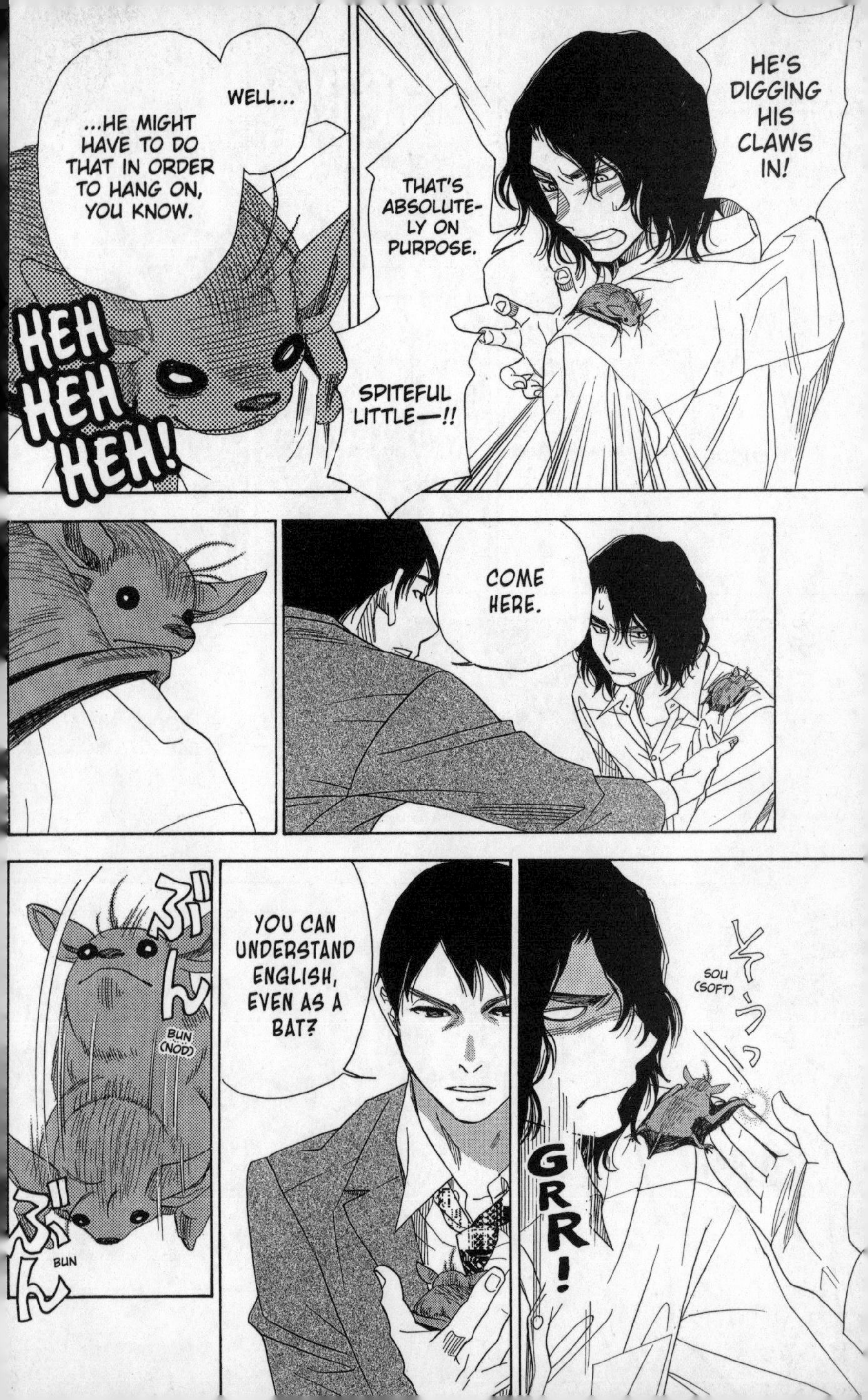
HE'S DIGGING HIS CLAWS IN!
THAT'S ABSOLUTE-LY ON PURPOSE.
SPITEFUL LITTLE—!!
WELL...
...HE MIGHT HAVE TO DO THAT IN ORDER TO HANG ON, YOU KNOW.
HEH HEH HEH!
COME HERE.
そうっ
SOU (SOFT)
GRR!
YOU CAN UNDERSTAND ENGLISH, EVEN AS A BAT?
ぶん
BUN (NOD)
ぶん
BUN

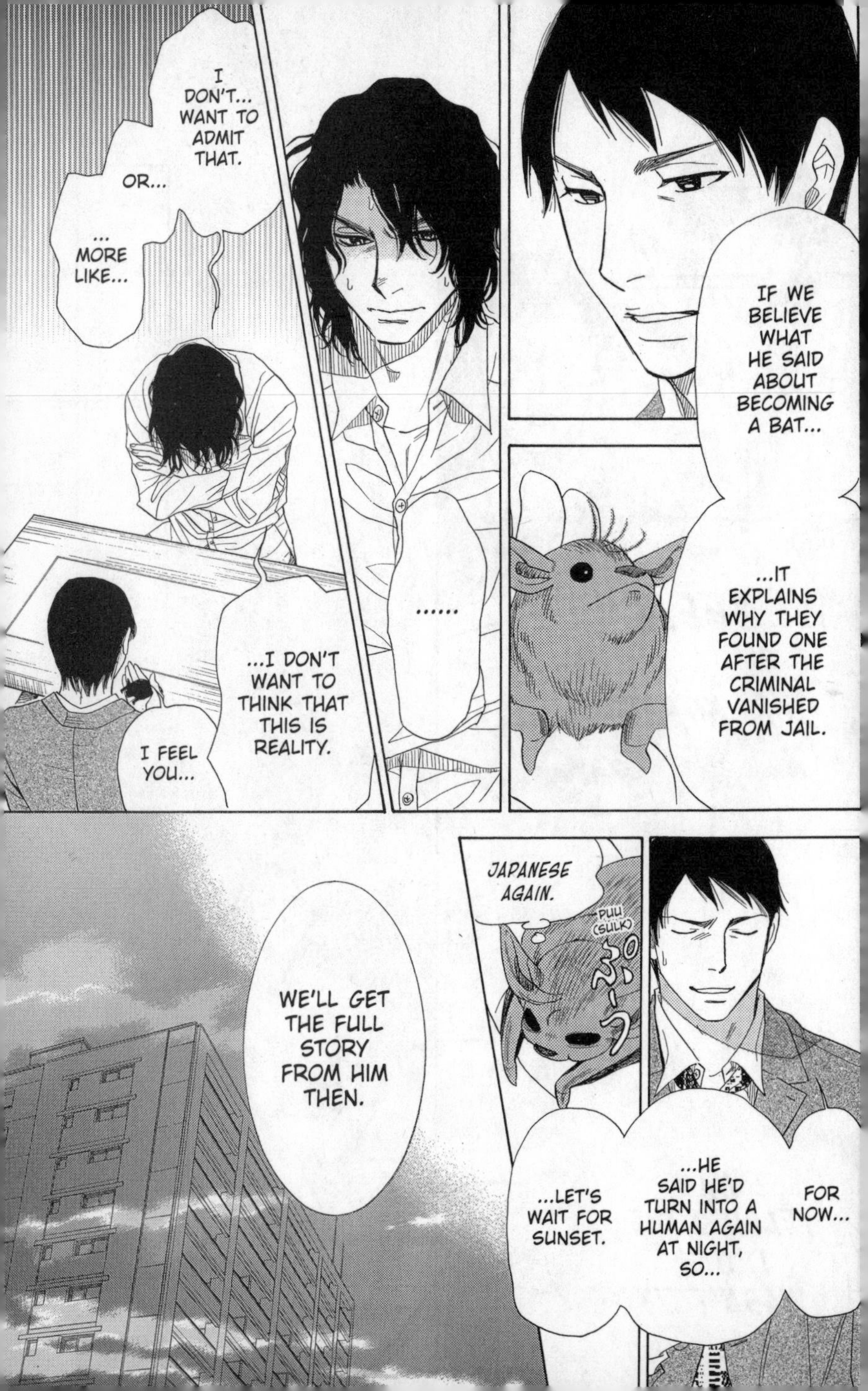
IF WE BELIEVE WHAT HE SAID ABOUT BECOMING A BAT...
...IT EXPLAINS WHY THEY FOUND ONE AFTER THE CRIMINAL VANISHED FROM JAIL.
......
I DON'T... WANT TO ADMIT THAT.
OR...
... MORE LIKE...
...I DON'T WANT TO THINK THAT THIS IS REALITY.
I FEEL YOU...
FOR NOW...
...HE SAID HE'D TURN INTO A HUMAN AGAIN AT NIGHT, SO...
...LET'S WAIT FOR SUNSET.
JAPANESE AGAIN.
PUU (SULK)
WE'LL GET THE FULL STORY FROM HIM THEN.

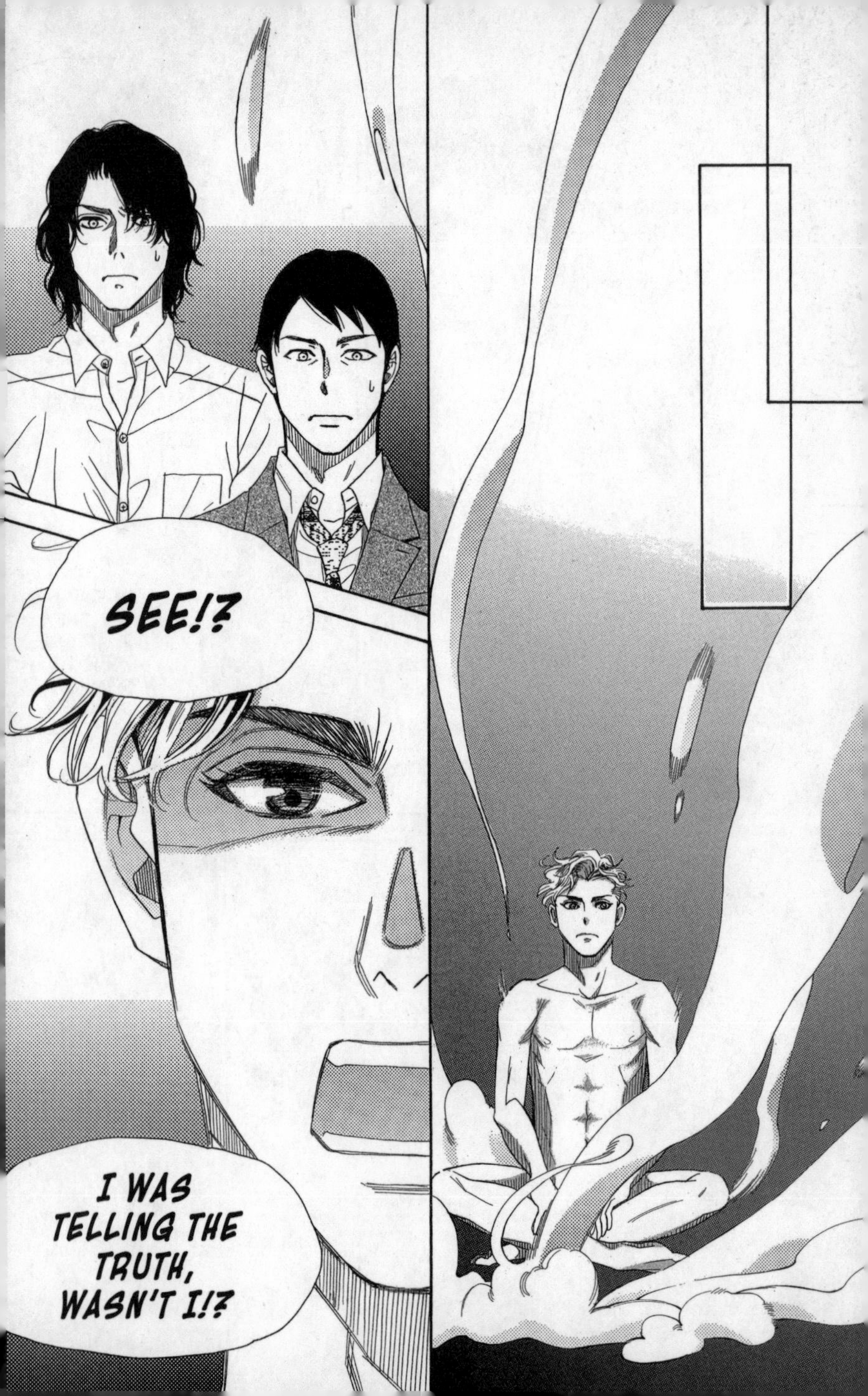
SEE!?
I WAS TELLING THE TRUTH, WASN'T I!?

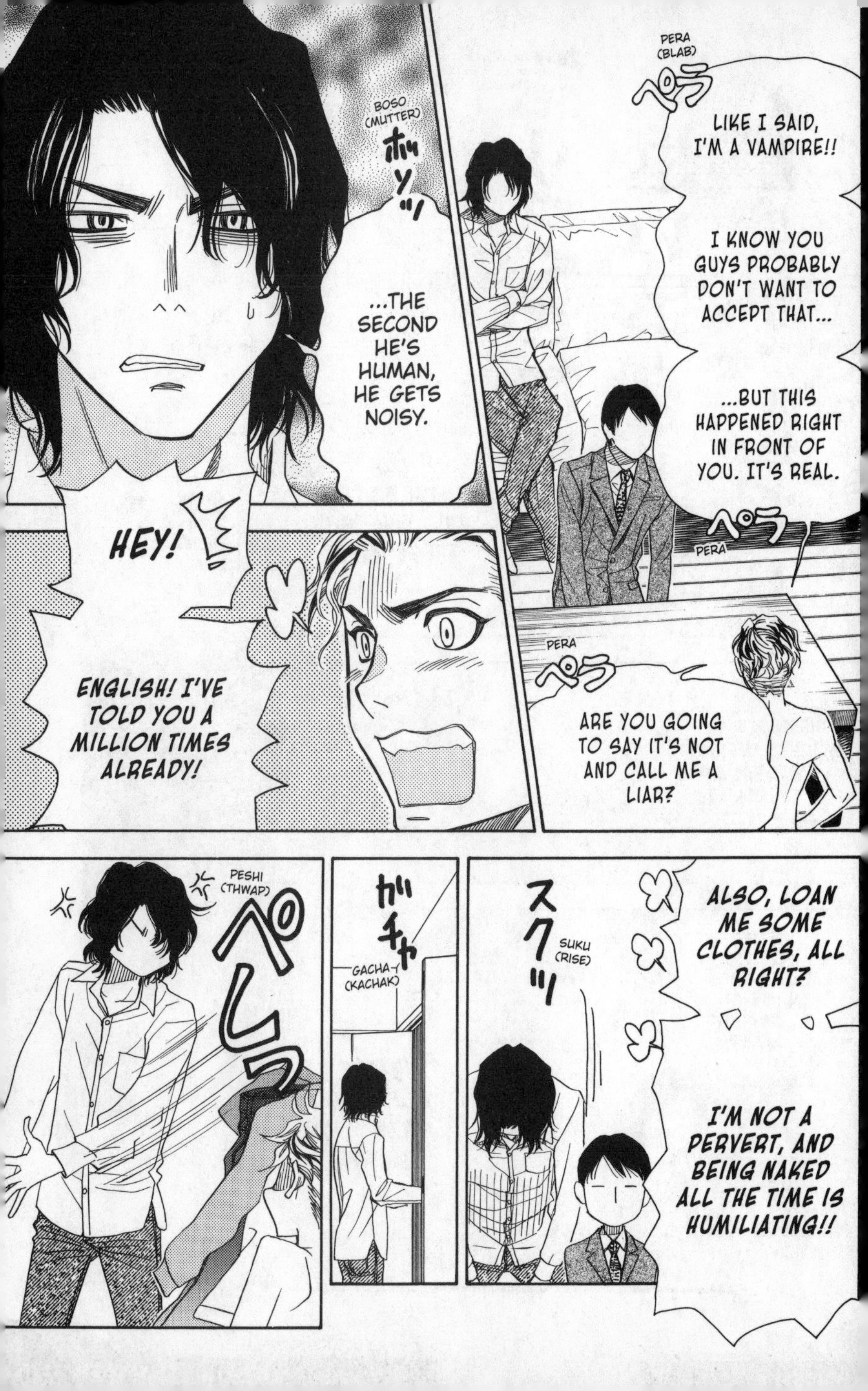
PERA
(BLAB)
ペラ
LIKE I SAID, I'M A VAMPIRE!!
I KNOW YOU GUYS PROBABLY DON'T WANT TO ACCEPT THAT...
...BUT THIS HAPPENED RIGHT IN FRONT OF YOU. IT'S REAL.
ペラ
PERA
PERA
ペラ
ARE YOU GOING TO SAY IT'S NOT AND CALL ME A LIAR?
BOSO
(MUTTER)
ボソッ
...THE SECOND HE'S HUMAN, HE GETS NOISY.
HEY!
ENGLISH! I'VE TOLD YOU A MILLION TIMES ALREADY!
スクッ
SUKU
(RISE)
ALSO, LOAN ME SOME CLOTHES, ALL RIGHT?
I'M NOT A PERVERT, AND BEING NAKED ALL THE TIME IS HUMILIATING!!
ガチャ
GACHA
(KACHAK)
PESHI
(THWAP)
ぺしっ

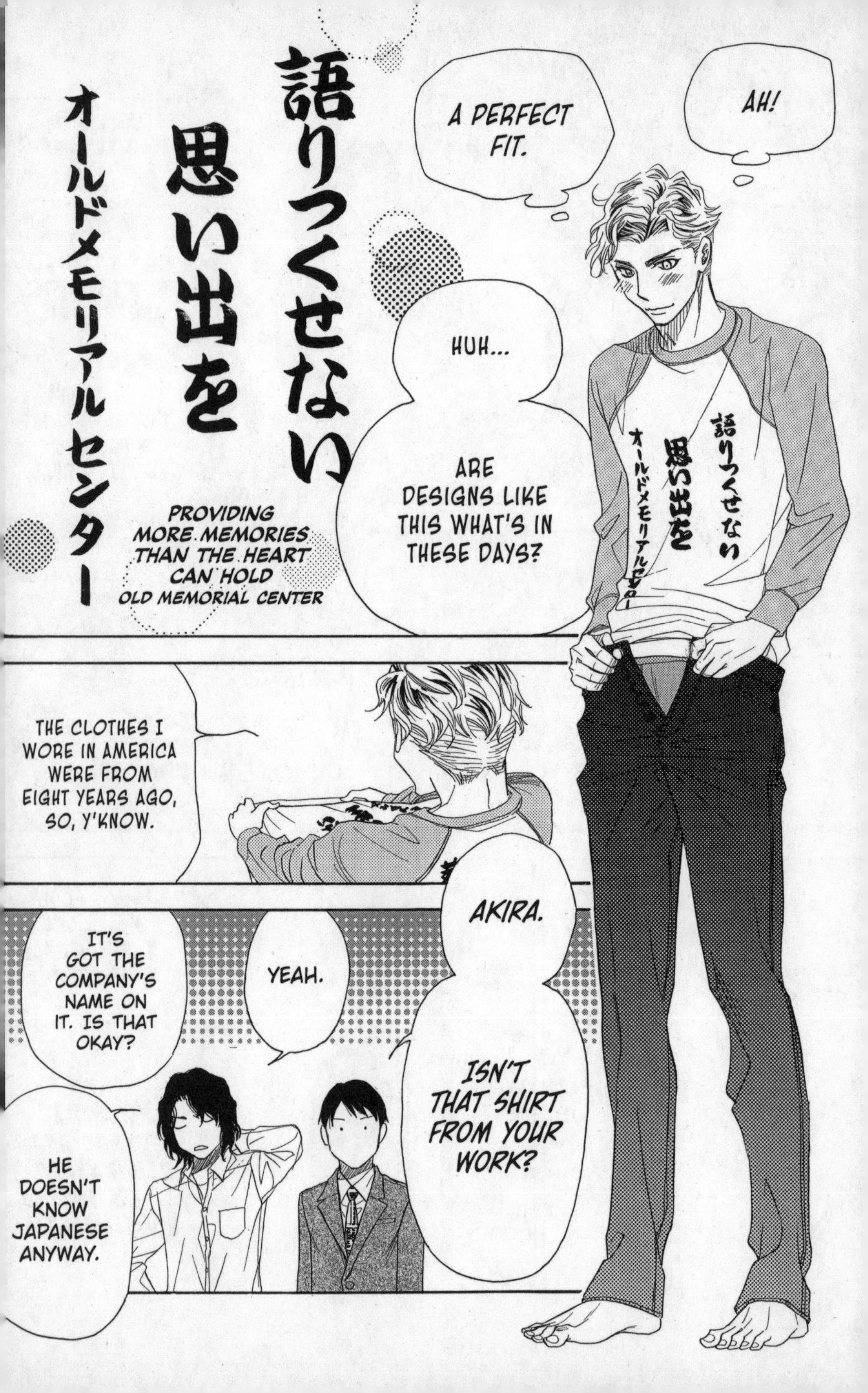
AH!
A PERFECT FIT.
HUH... ARE DESIGNS LIKE THIS WHAT'S IN THESE DAYS?
語りつくせない思い出を
オールドメモリアルセンター
PROVIDING MORE MEMORIES THAN THE HEART CAN HOLD
OLD MEMORIAL CENTER
THE CLOTHES I WORE IN AMERICA WERE FROM EIGHT YEARS AGO, SO, Y'KNOW.
AKIRA. ISN'T THAT SHIRT FROM YOUR WORK?
YEAH.
IT'S GOT THE COMPANY'S NAME ON IT. IS THAT OKAY?
HE DOESN'T KNOW JAPANESE ANYWAY.

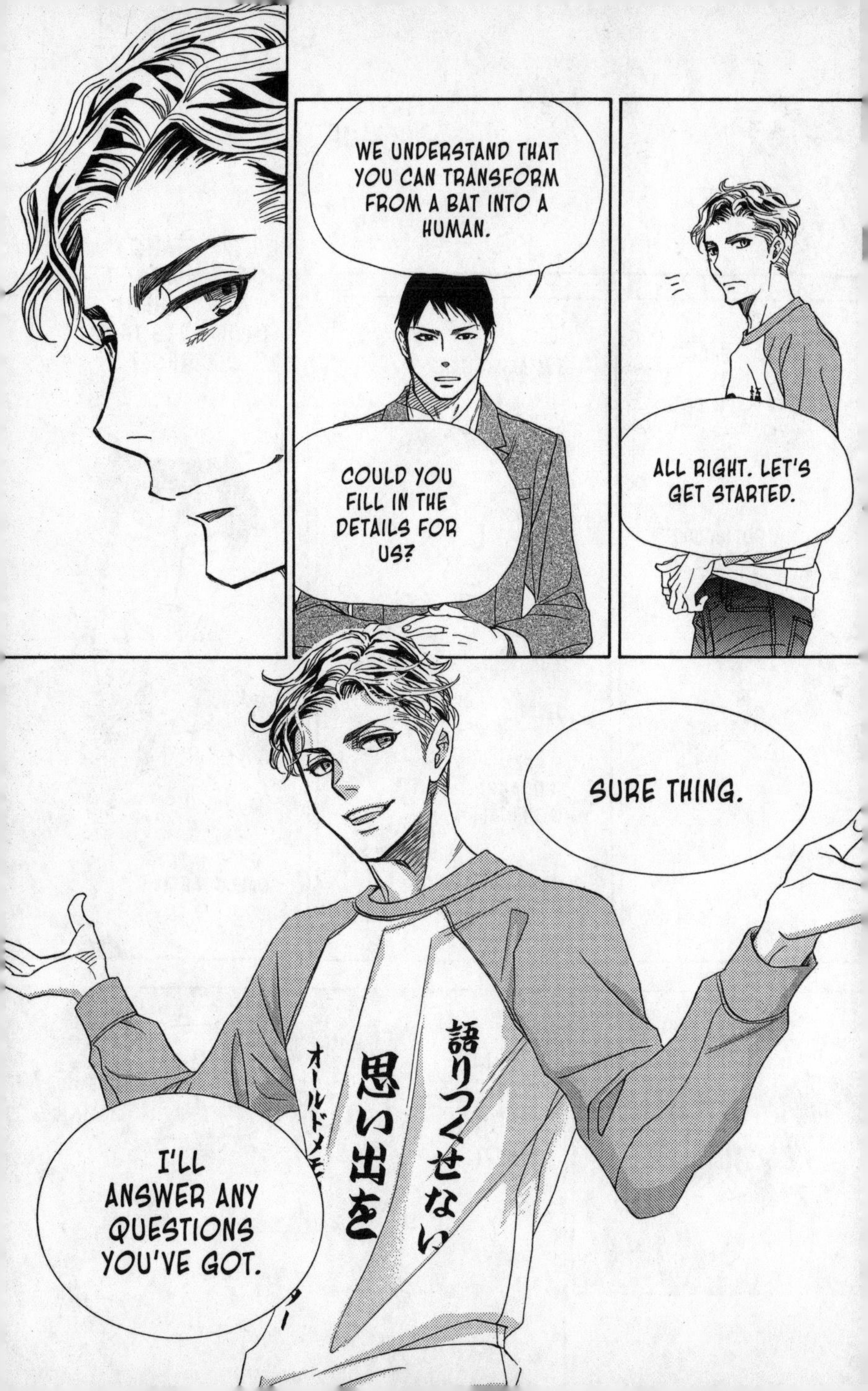
ALL RIGHT. LET'S GET STARTED.
WE UNDERSTAND THAT YOU CAN TRANSFORM FROM A BAT INTO A HUMAN.
COULD YOU FILL IN THE DETAILS FOR US?
SURE THING.
I'LL ANSWER ANY QUESTIONS YOU'VE GOT.
語りつくせない
思い出を

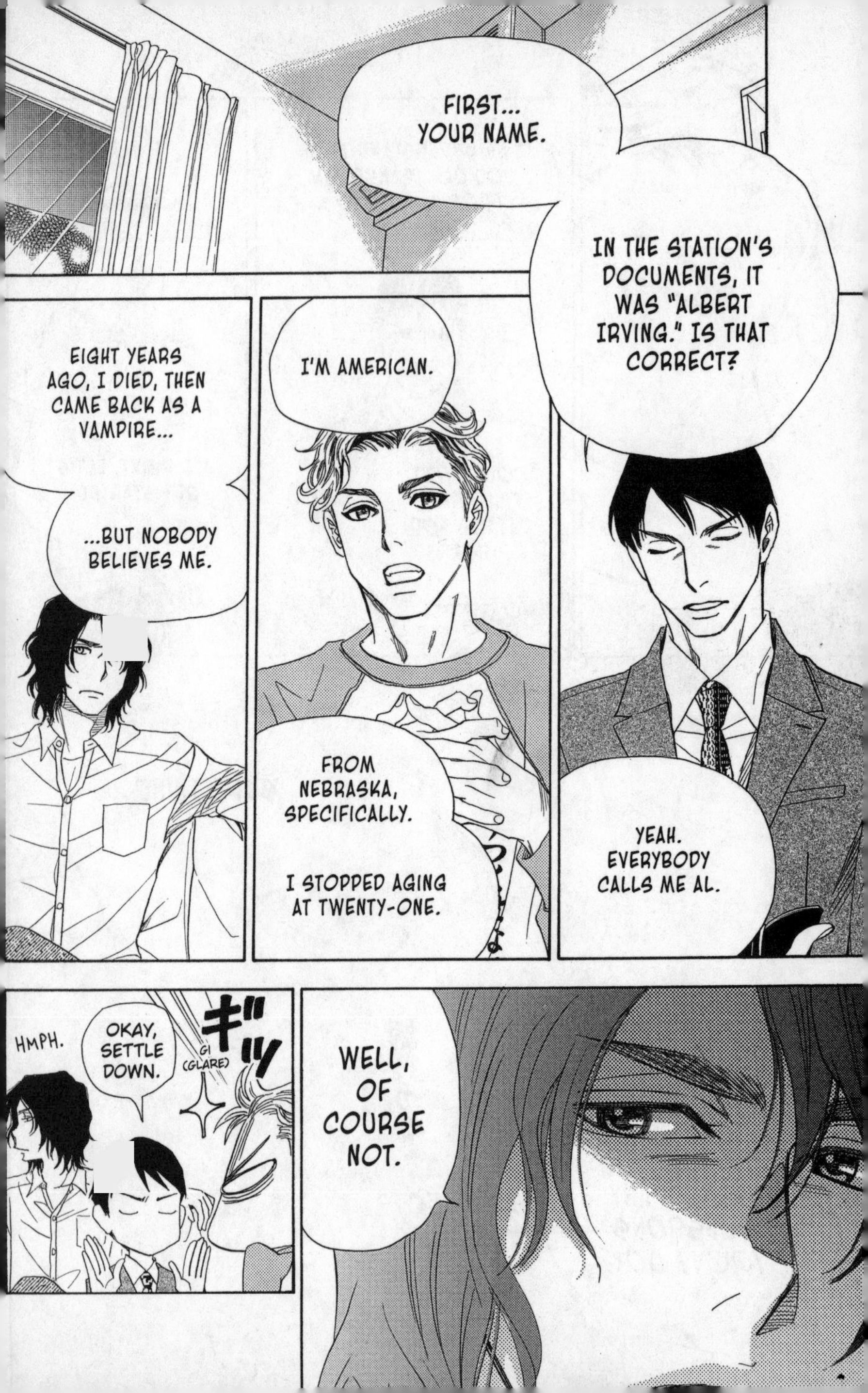
FIRST... YOUR NAME.
IN THE STATION'S DOCUMENTS, IT WAS "ALBERT IRVING." IS THAT CORRECT?
YEAH. EVERYBODY CALLS ME AL.
I'M AMERICAN.
FROM NEBRASKA, SPECIFICALLY.
I STOPPED AGING AT TWENTY-ONE.
EIGHT YEARS AGO, I DIED, THEN CAME BACK AS A VAMPIRE...
...BUT NOBODY BELIEVES ME.
WELL, OF COURSE NOT.
ギッ
GI (GLARE)
OKAY, SETTLE DOWN.
HMPH.

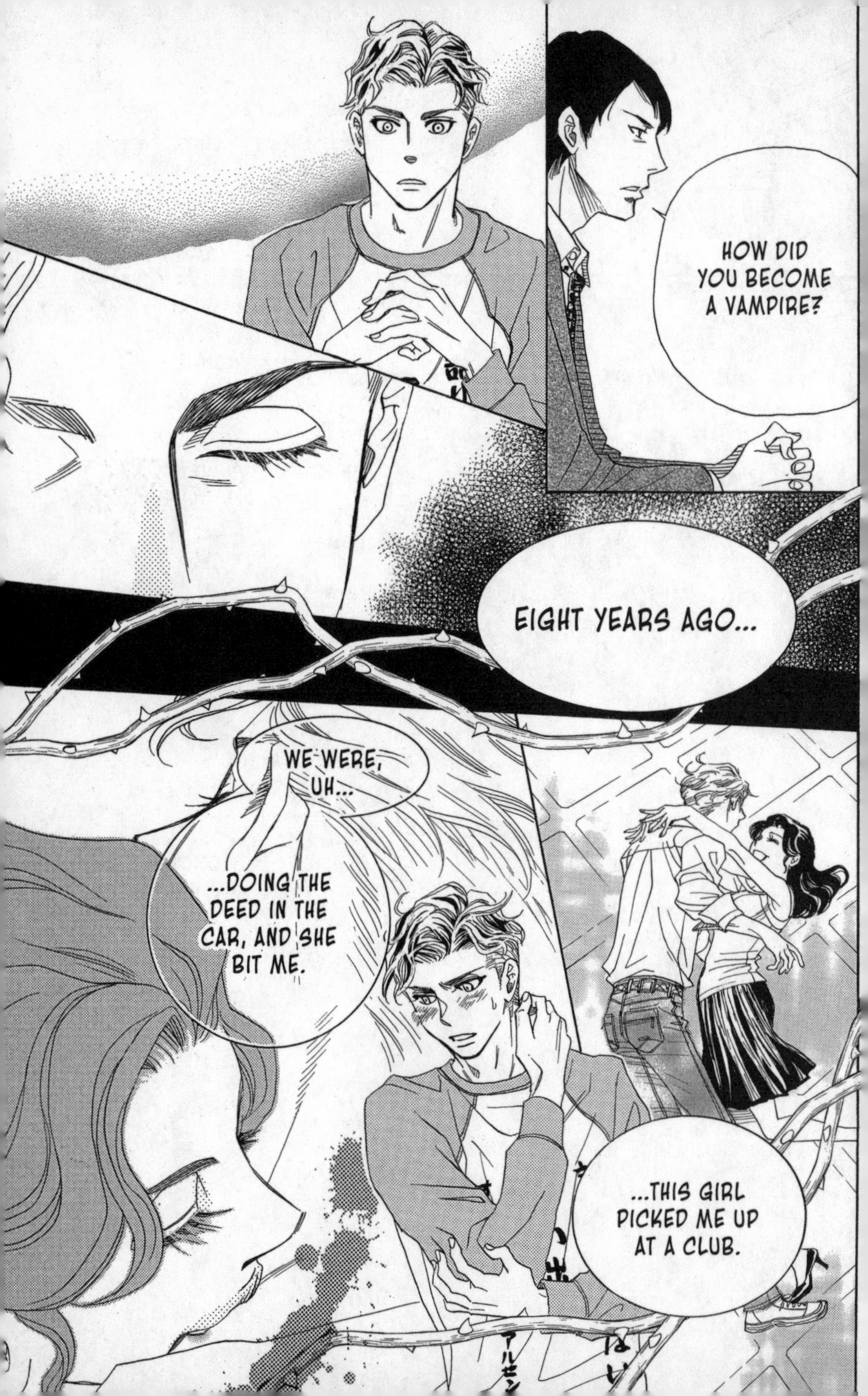
HOW DID YOU BECOME A VAMPIRE?
EIGHT YEARS AGO...
...THIS GIRL PICKED ME UP AT A CLUB.
WE WERE, UH...
...DOING THE DEED IN THE CAR, AND SHE BIT ME.

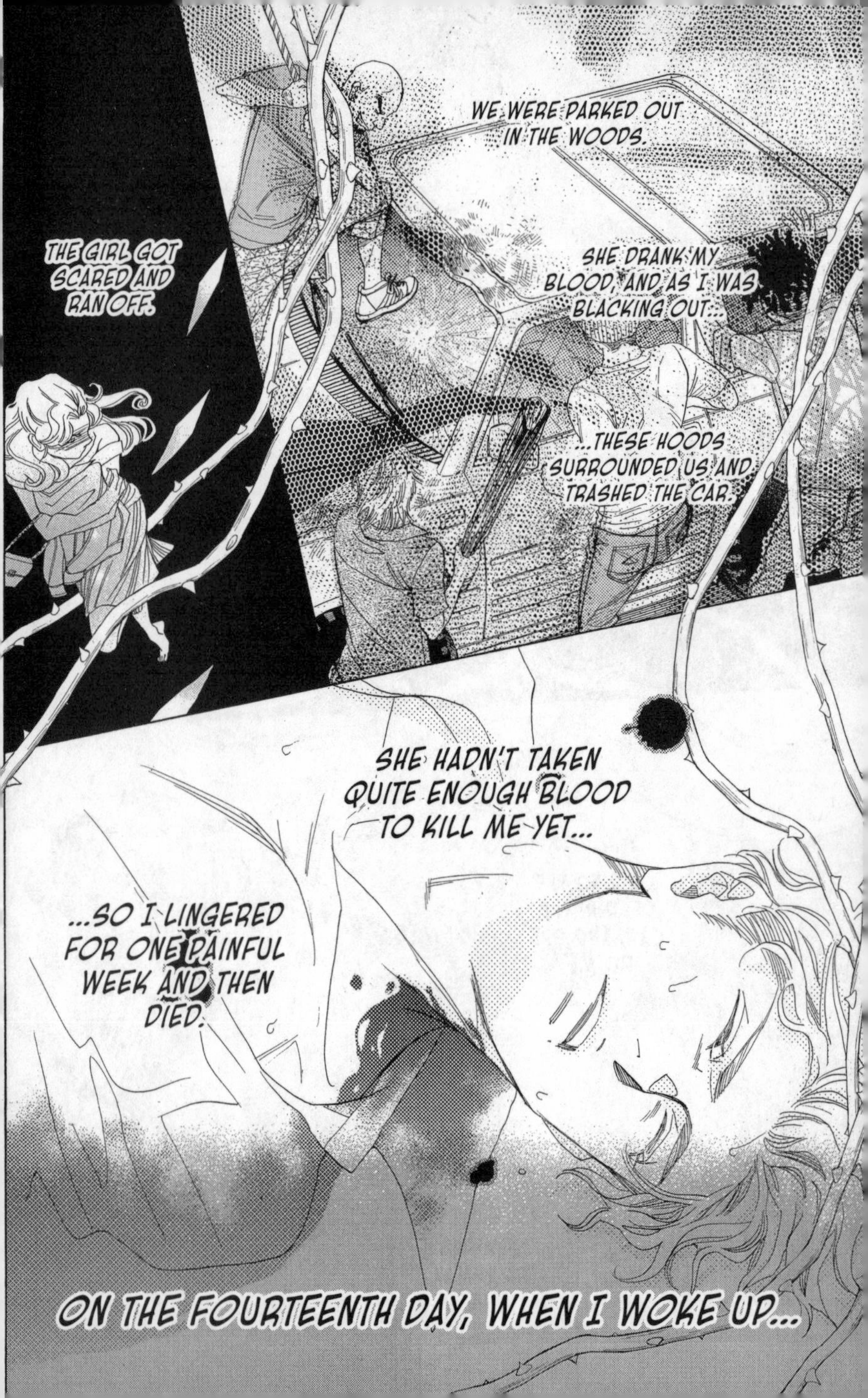
WE WERE PARKED OUT IN THE WOODS.
SHE DRANK MY BLOOD, AND AS I WAS BLACKING OUT...
...THESE HOODS SURROUNDED US AND TRASHED THE CAR.
THE GIRL GOT SCARED AND RAN OFF.
SHE HADN'T TAKEN QUITE ENOUGH BLOOD TO KILL ME YET...
...SO I LINGERED FOR ONE PAINFUL WEEK AND THEN DIED.
ON THE FOURTEENTH DAY, WHEN I WOKE UP...

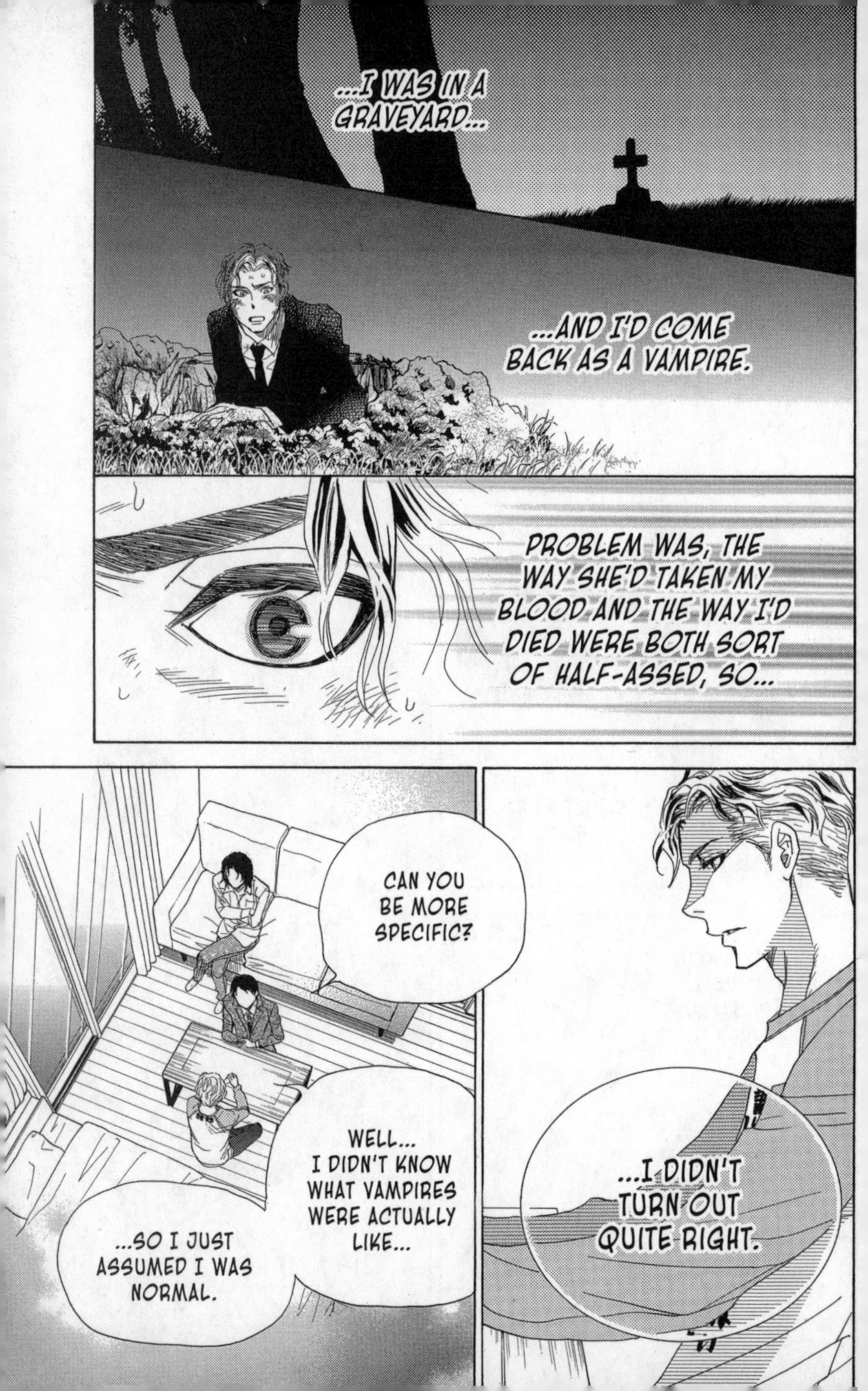
...I WAS IN A GRAVEYARD...
...AND I'D COME BACK AS A VAMPIRE.
PROBLEM WAS, THE WAY SHE'D TAKEN MY BLOOD AND THE WAY I'D DIED WERE BOTH SORT OF HALF-ASSED, SO...
...I DIDN'T TURN OUT QUITE RIGHT.
CAN YOU BE MORE SPECIFIC?
WELL... I DIDN'T KNOW WHAT VAMPIRES WERE ACTUALLY LIKE...
...SO I JUST ASSUMED I WAS NORMAL.

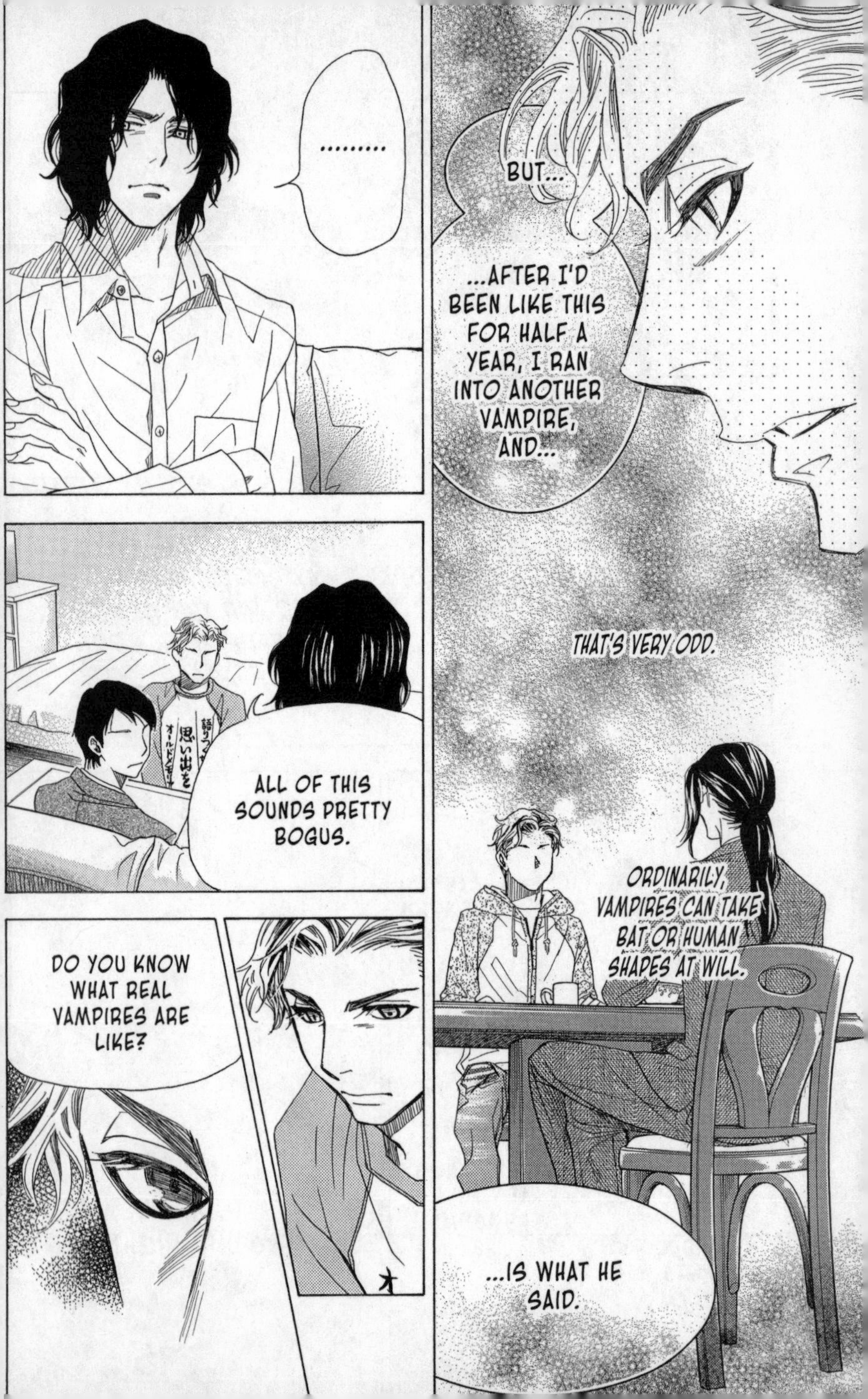
BUT...
...AFTER I'D BEEN LIKE THIS FOR HALF A YEAR, I RAN INTO ANOTHER VAMPIRE, AND...
THAT'S VERY ODD.
ORDINARILY, VAMPIRES CAN TAKE BAT OR HUMAN SHAPES AT WILL.
...IS WHAT HE SAID.
....
ALL OF THIS SOUNDS PRETTY BOGUS.
DO YOU KNOW WHAT REAL VAMPIRES ARE LIKE?

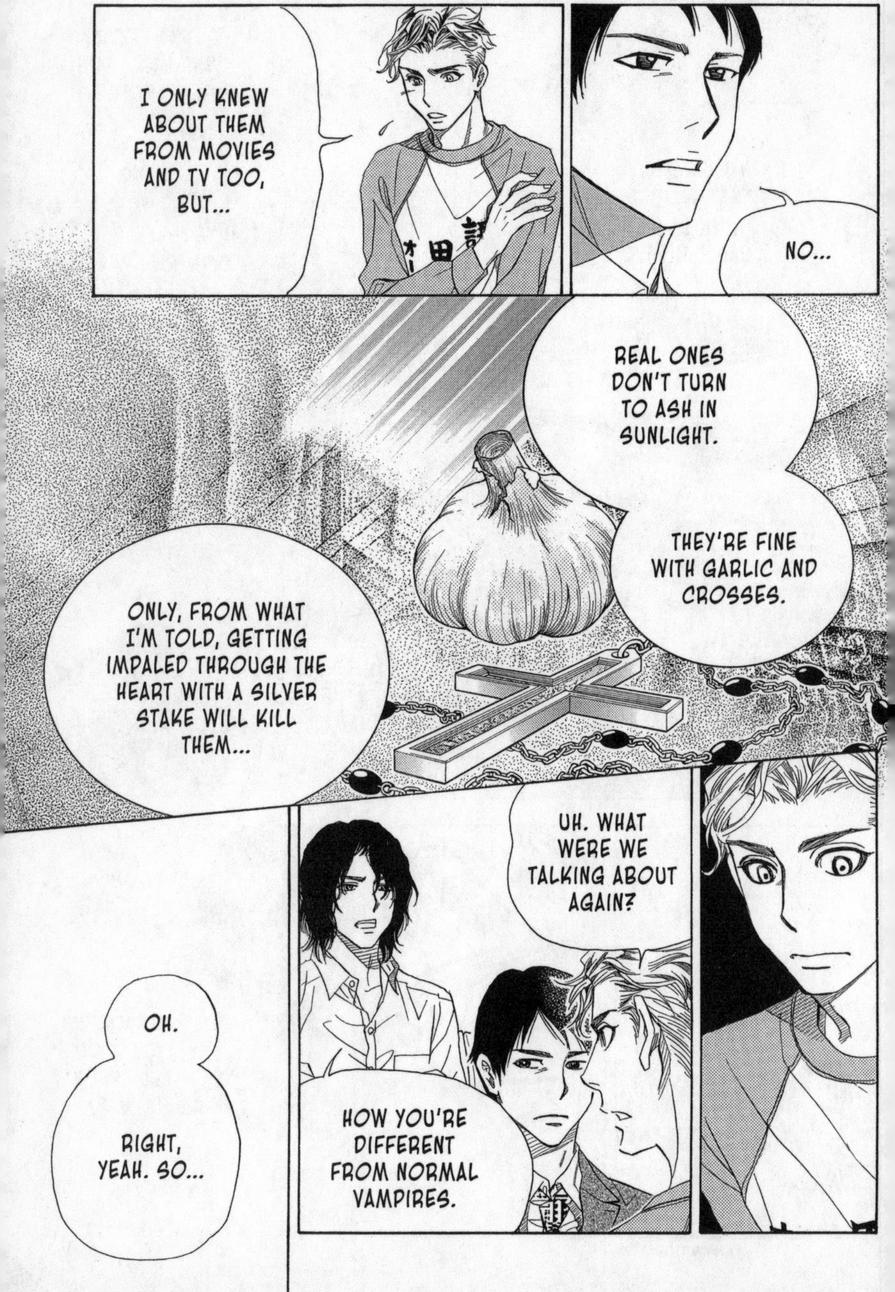
NO...
I ONLY KNEW ABOUT THEM FROM MOVIES AND TV TOO, BUT...
REAL ONES DON'T TURN TO ASH IN SUNLIGHT.
THEY'RE FINE WITH GARLIC AND CROSSES.
ONLY, FROM WHAT I'M TOLD, GETTING IMPALED THROUGH THE HEART WITH A SILVER STAKE WILL KILL THEM...
UH. WHAT WERE WE TALKING ABOUT AGAIN?
HOW YOU'RE DIFFERENT FROM NORMAL VAMPIRES.
OH.
RIGHT, YEAH. SO...

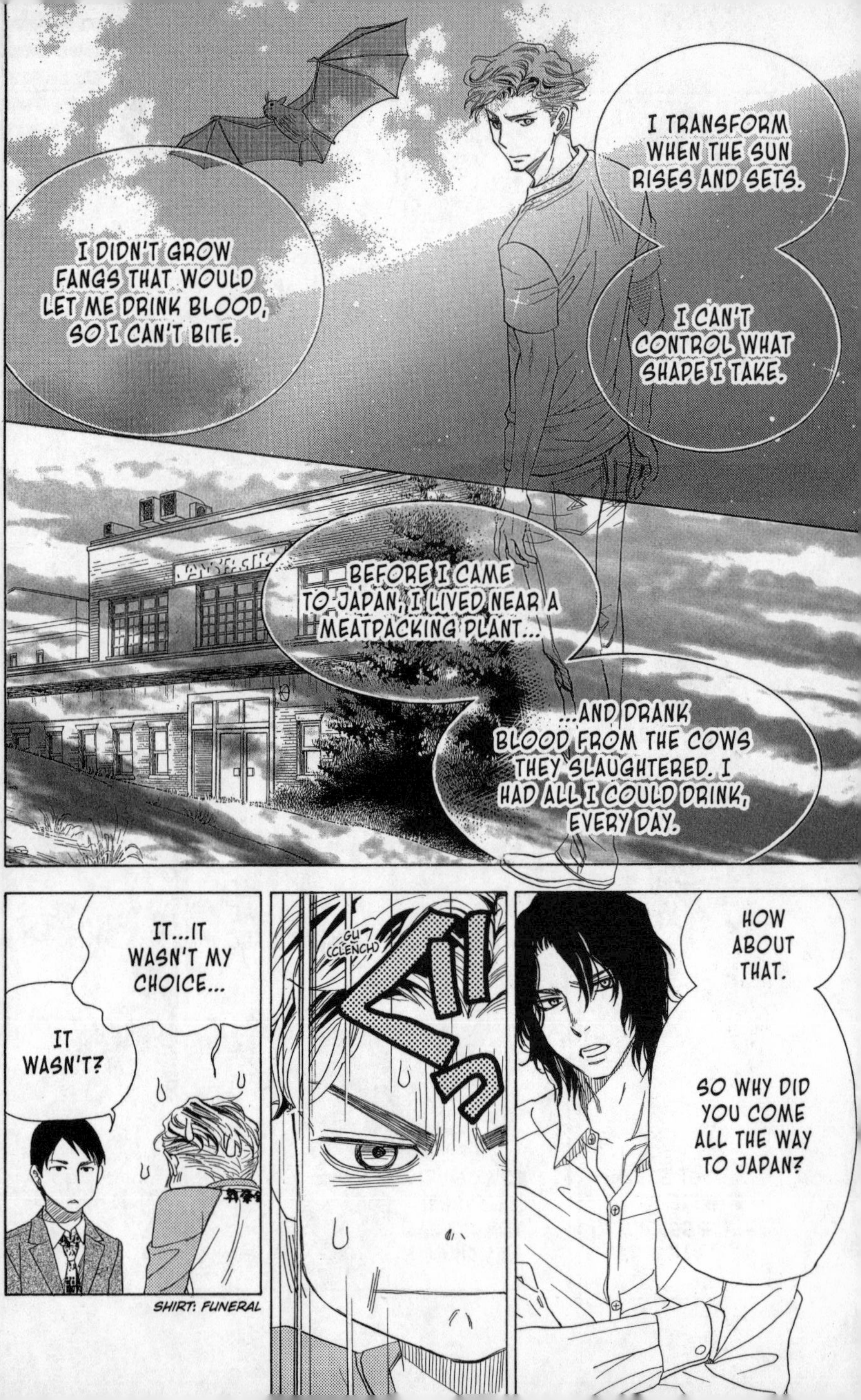
I TRANSFORM WHEN THE SUN RISES AND SETS.
I CAN'T CONTROL WHAT SHAPE I TAKE.
I DIDN'T GROW FANGS THAT WOULD LET ME DRINK BLOOD, SO I CAN'T BITE.
BEFORE I CAME TO JAPAN, I LIVED NEAR A MEATPACKING PLANT...
...AND DRANK BLOOD FROM THE COWS THEY SLAUGHTERED. I HAD ALL I COULD DRINK, EVERY DAY.
HOW ABOUT THAT.
SO WHY DID YOU COME ALL THE WAY TO JAPAN?
GU (CLENCH)
IT...IT WASN'T MY CHOICE...
IT WASN'T?
SHIRT: FUNERAL

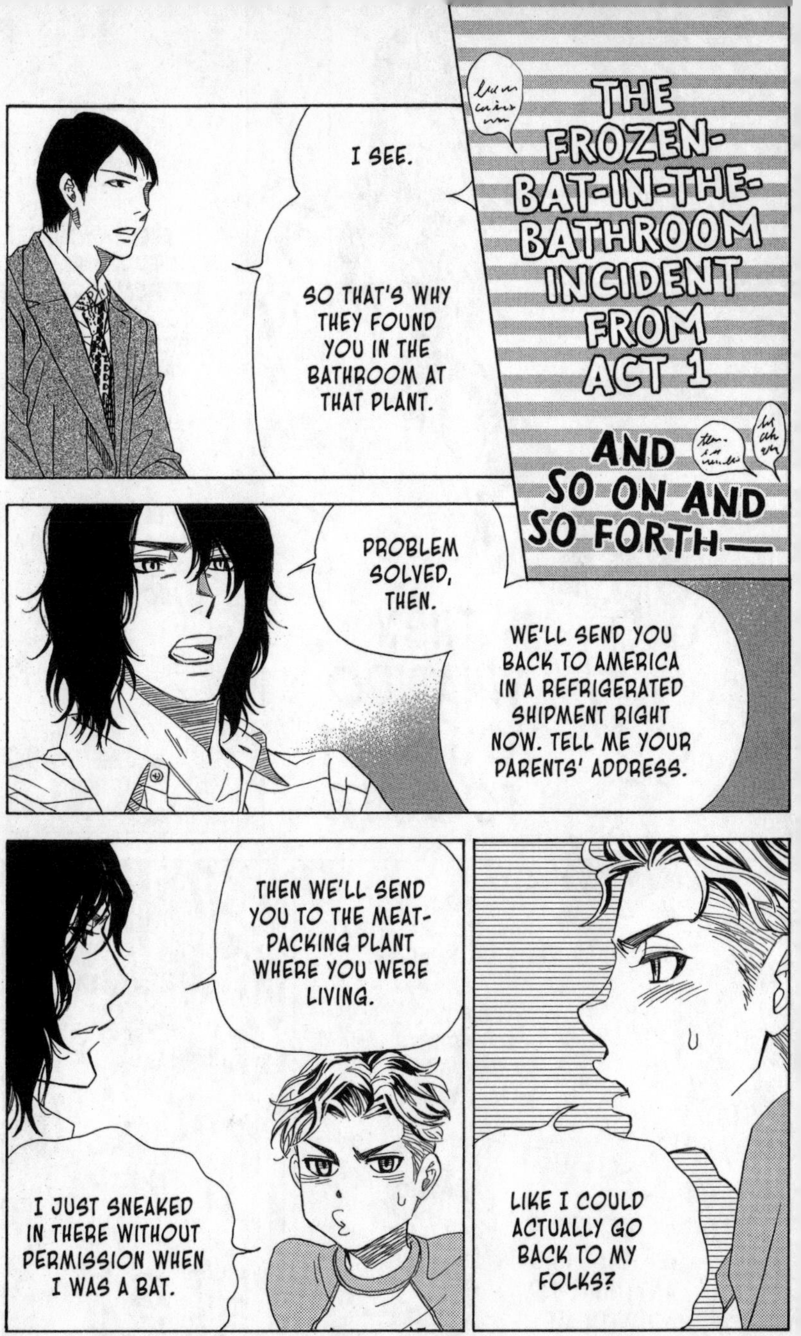
THE FROZEN-BAT-IN-THE-BATHROOM INCIDENT FROM ACT 1
AND SO ON AND SO FORTH—
I SEE.
SO THAT'S WHY THEY FOUND YOU IN THE BATHROOM AT THAT PLANT.
PROBLEM SOLVED, THEN.
WE'LL SEND YOU BACK TO AMERICA IN A REFRIGERATED SHIPMENT RIGHT NOW. TELL ME YOUR PARENTS' ADDRESS.
LIKE I COULD ACTUALLY GO BACK TO MY FOLKS?
THEN WE'LL SEND YOU TO THE MEAT-PACKING PLANT WHERE YOU WERE LIVING.
I JUST SNEAKED IN THERE WITHOUT PERMISSION WHEN I WAS A BAT.

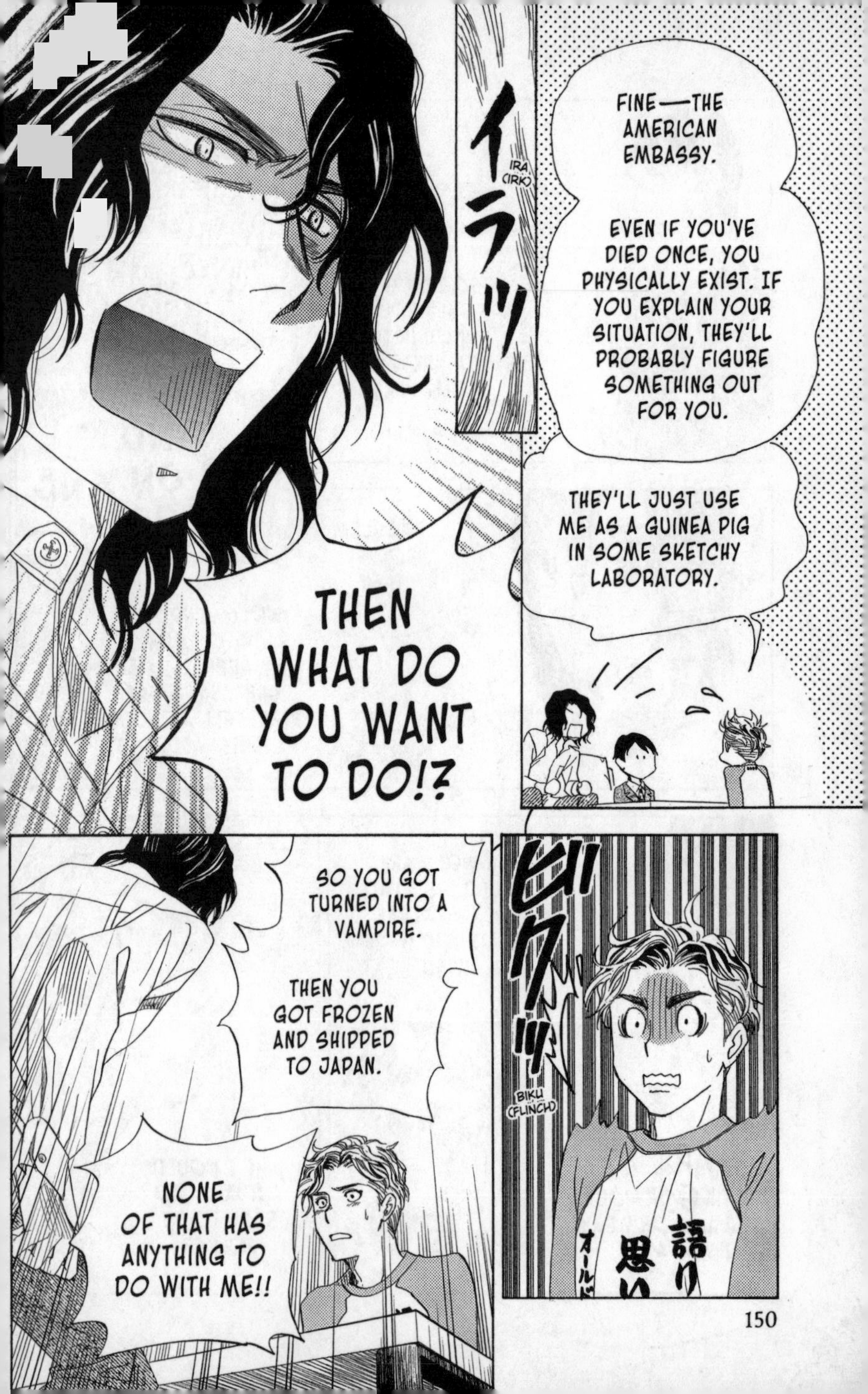

FINE—THE AMERICAN EMBASSY.
EVEN IF YOU'VE DIED ONCE, YOU PHYSICALLY EXIST. IF YOU EXPLAIN YOUR SITUATION, THEY'LL PROBABLY FIGURE SOMETHING OUT FOR YOU.
THEY'LL JUST USE ME AS A GUINEA PIG IN SOME SKETCHY LABORATORY.
イラッ
IRA (IRK)
THEN WHAT DO YOU WANT TO DO!?
ビクッ
BIKU (FLINCH)
語り
思い
SO YOU GOT TURNED INTO A VAMPIRE.
THEN YOU GOT FROZEN AND SHIPPED TO JAPAN.
NONE OF THAT HAS ANYTHING TO DO WITH ME!!

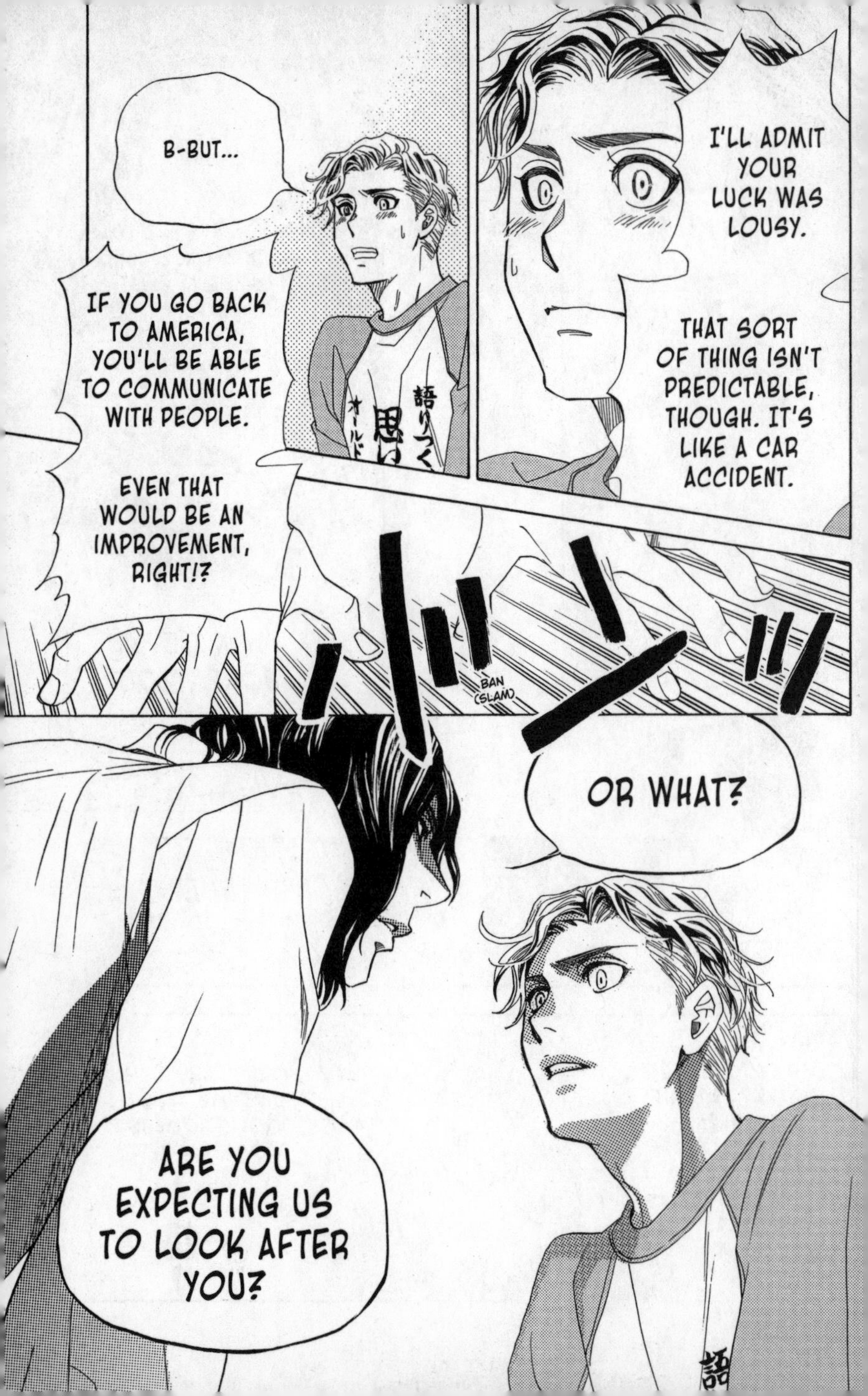
I'LL ADMIT YOUR LUCK WAS LOUSY.
THAT SORT OF THING ISN'T PREDICTABLE, THOUGH. IT'S LIKE A CAR ACCIDENT.
B-BUT...
IF YOU GO BACK TO AMERICA, YOU'LL BE ABLE TO COMMUNICATE WITH PEOPLE.
EVEN THAT WOULD BE AN IMPROVEMENT, RIGHT!?
BAN (SLAM)
OR WHAT?
ARE YOU EXPECTING US TO LOOK AFTER YOU?

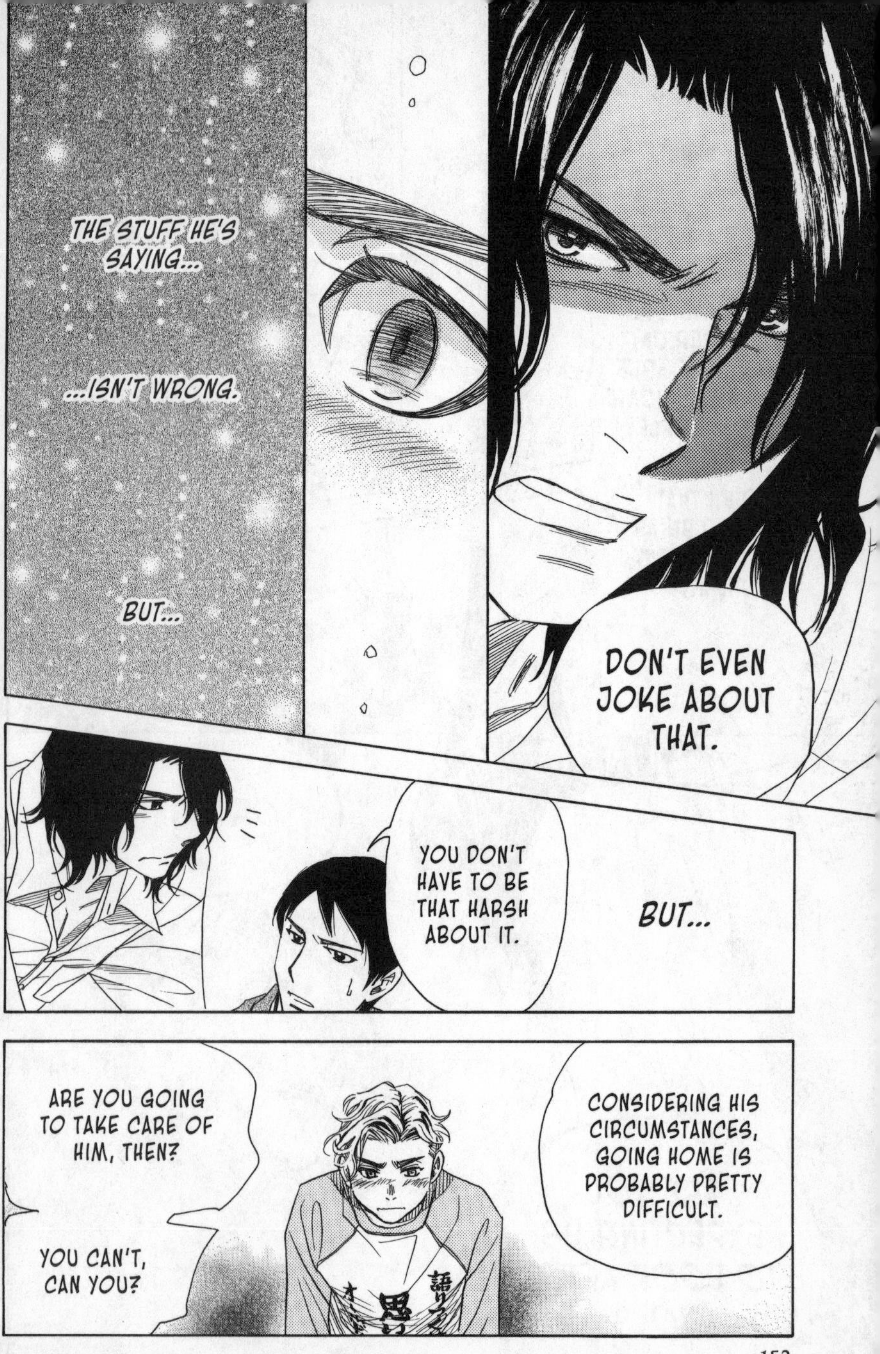
DON'T EVEN JOKE ABOUT THAT.
THE STUFF HE'S SAYING...
...ISN'T WRONG.
BUT...
YOU DON'T HAVE TO BE THAT HARSH ABOUT IT.
BUT...
CONSIDERING HIS CIRCUMSTANCES, GOING HOME IS PROBABLY PRETTY DIFFICULT.
ARE YOU GOING TO TAKE CARE OF HIM, THEN?
YOU CAN'T, CAN YOU?

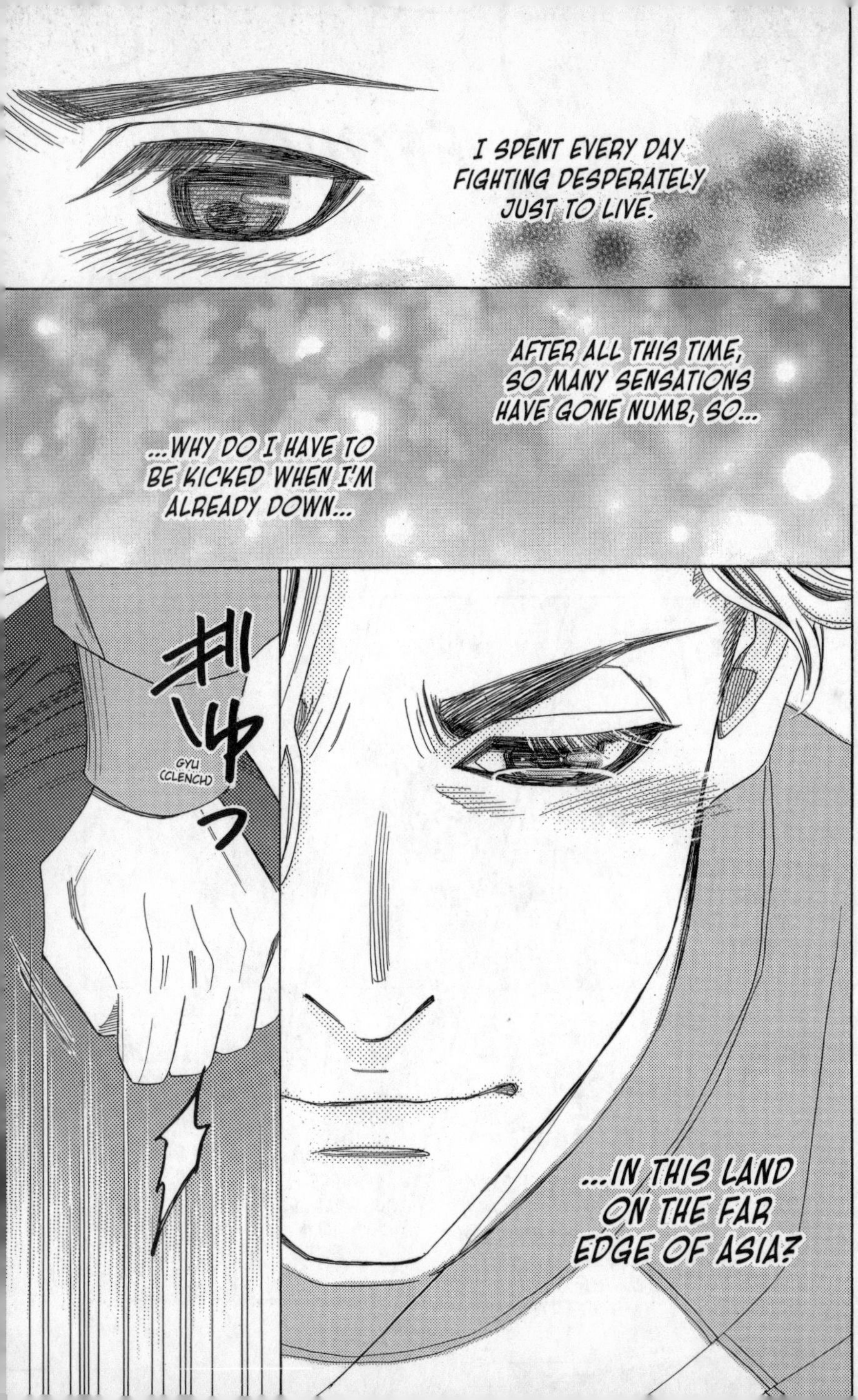
I SPENT EVERY DAY FIGHTING DESPERATELY JUST TO LIVE.
AFTER ALL THIS TIME, SO MANY SENSATIONS HAVE GONE NUMB, SO...
...WHY DO I HAVE TO BE KICKED WHEN I'M ALREADY DOWN...
...IN THIS LAND ON THE FAR EDGE OF ASIA?
ぎゅっ
GYU (CLENCH)

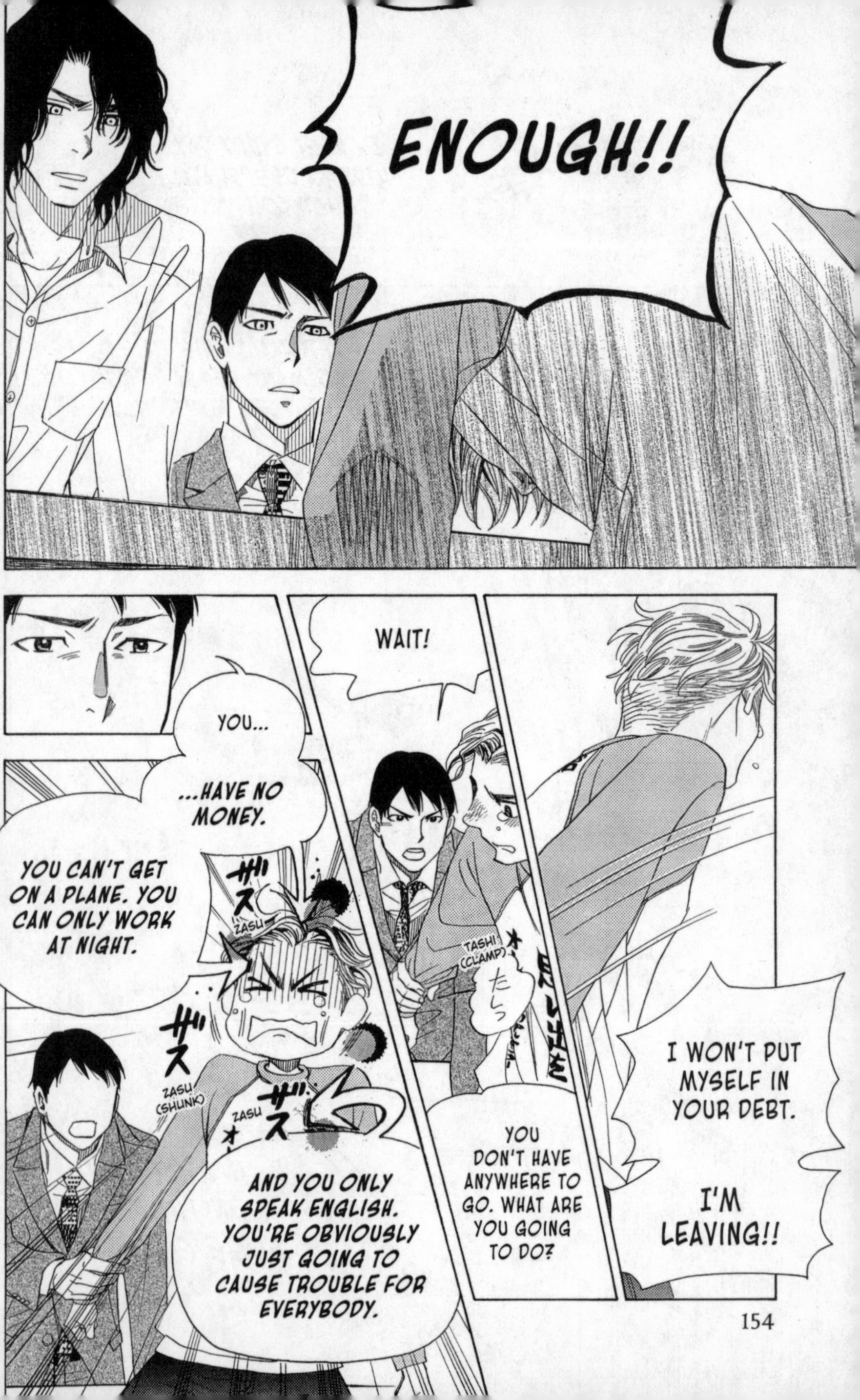
ENOUGH!!
I WON'T PUT MYSELF IN YOUR DEBT.
I'M LEAVING!!
WAIT!
TASHI (CLAMP)
YOU DON'T HAVE ANYWHERE TO GO. WHAT ARE YOU GOING TO DO?
YOU...
...HAVE NO MONEY.
ZASU
YOU CAN'T GET ON A PLANE. YOU CAN ONLY WORK AT NIGHT.
ZASU (SHUNK)
ZASU
AND YOU ONLY SPEAK ENGLISH. YOU'RE OBVIOUSLY JUST GOING TO CAUSE TROUBLE FOR EVERYBODY.

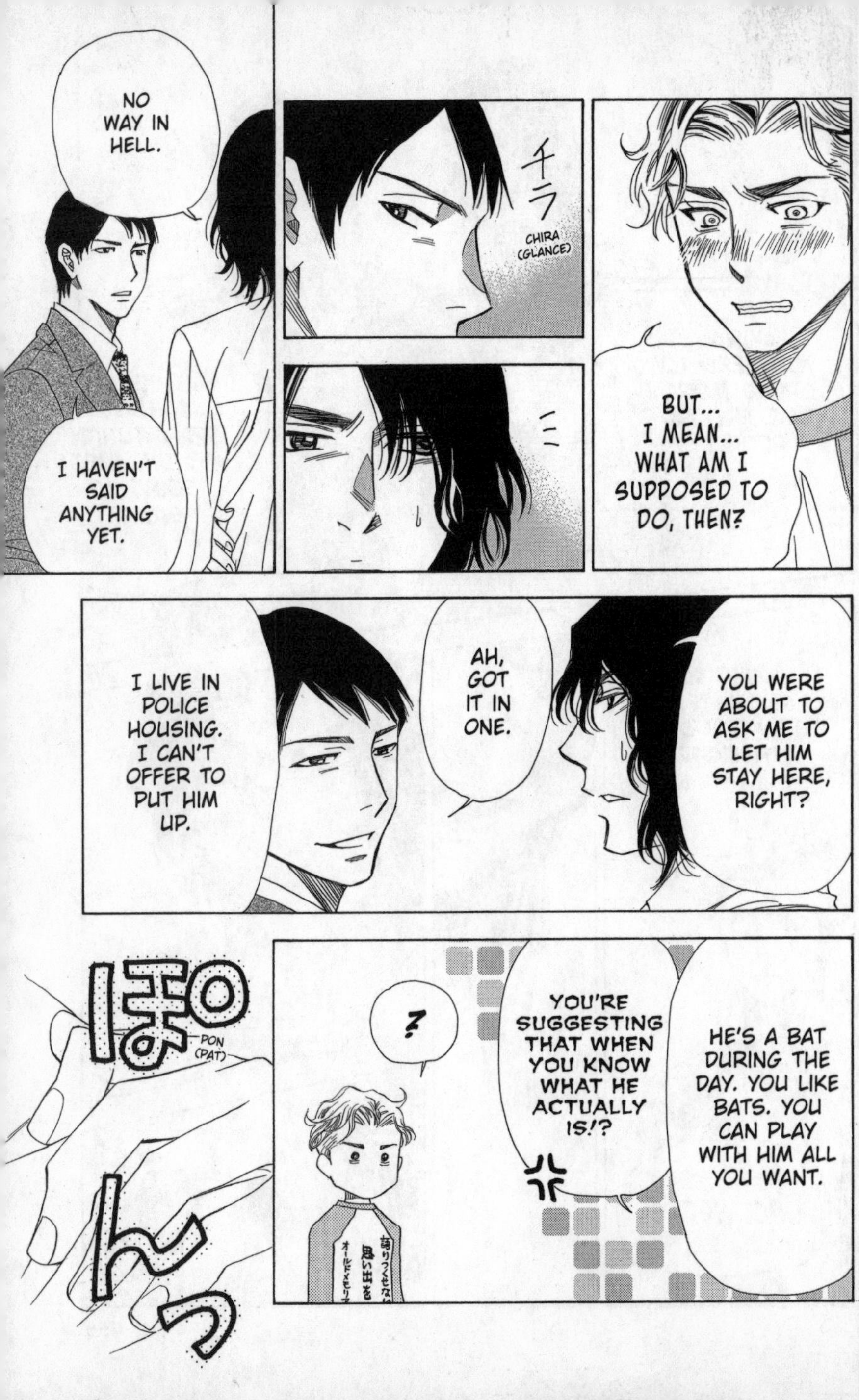
BUT... I MEAN... WHAT AM I SUPPOSED TO DO, THEN?
チラ
CHIRA (GLANCE)
NO WAY IN HELL.
I HAVEN'T SAID ANYTHING YET.
YOU WERE ABOUT TO ASK ME TO LET HIM STAY HERE, RIGHT?
AH, GOT IT IN ONE.
I LIVE IN POLICE HOUSING. I CAN'T OFFER TO PUT HIM UP.
HE'S A BAT DURING THE DAY. YOU LIKE BATS. YOU CAN PLAY WITH HIM ALL YOU WANT.
YOU'RE SUGGESTING THAT WHEN YOU KNOW WHAT HE ACTUALLY IS!?
?
ぽんっ
PON (PAT)

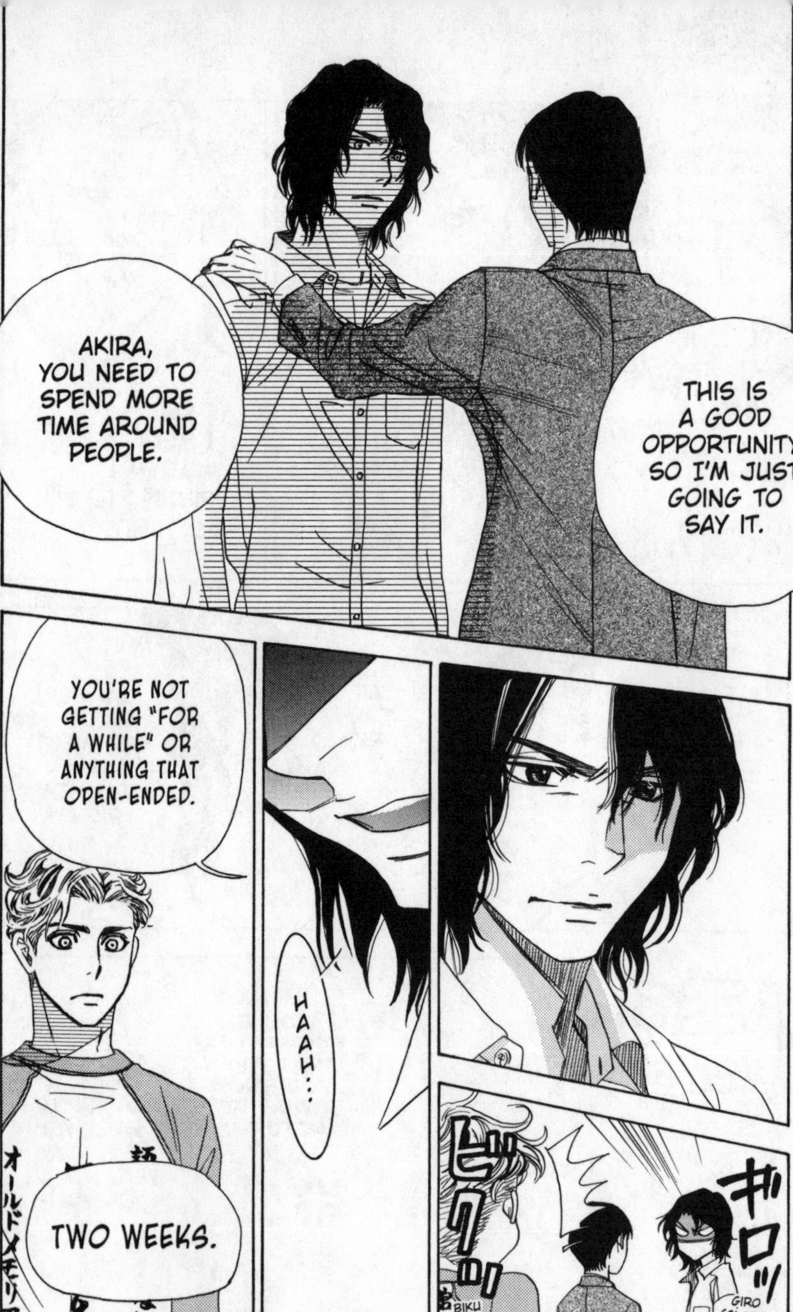
THIS IS A GOOD OPPORTUNITY, SO I'M JUST GOING TO SAY IT.
AKIRA, YOU NEED TO SPEND MORE TIME AROUND PEOPLE.
ギロッ
GIRO (GLARE)
ビクッ
BIKU (FLINCH)
HAAH...
YOU'RE NOT GETTING "FOR A WHILE" OR ANYTHING THAT OPEN-ENDED.
TWO WEEKS.
オールドメモリア

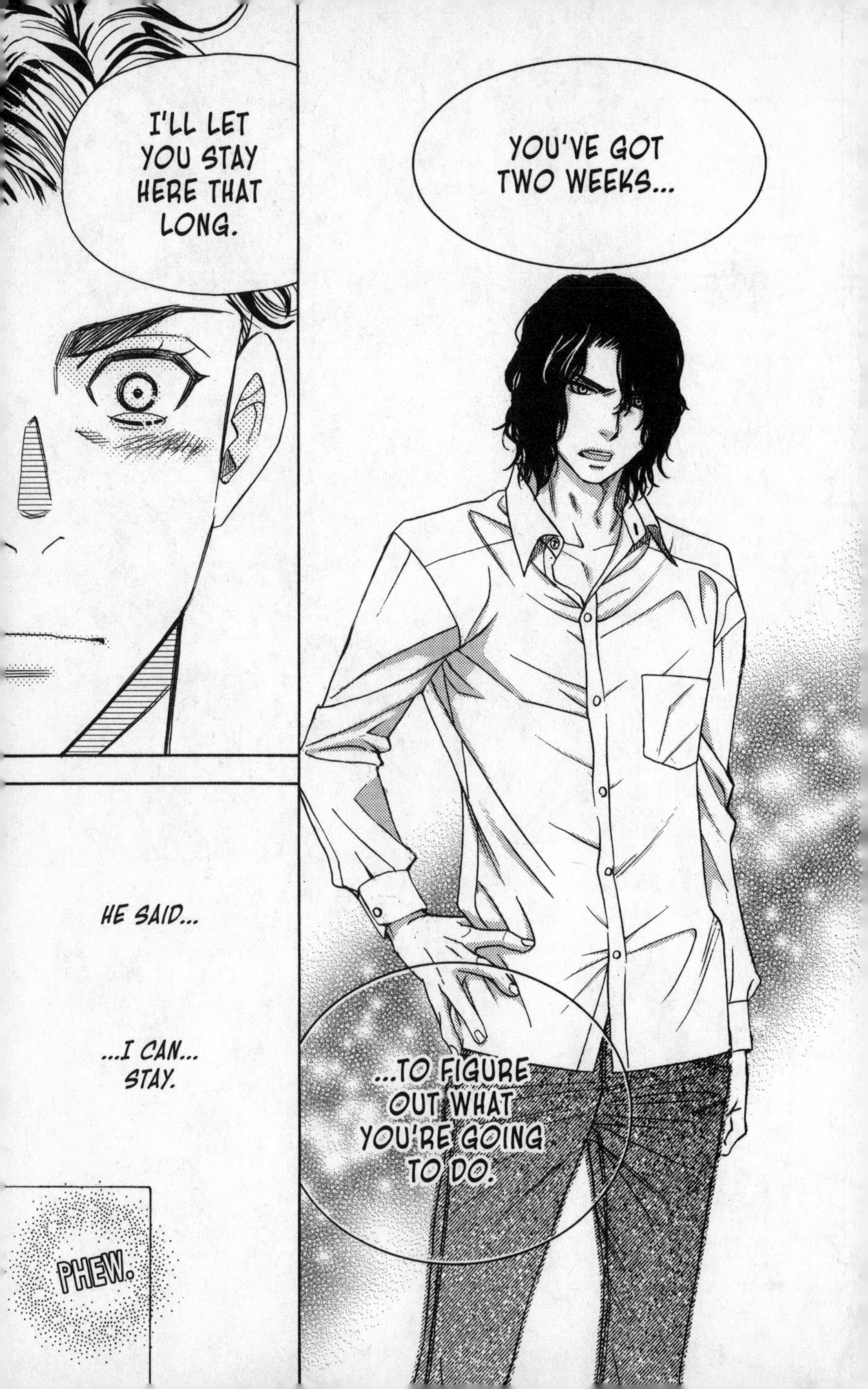
YOU'VE GOT TWO WEEKS...
...TO FIGURE OUT WHAT YOU'RE GOING TO DO.
I'LL LET YOU STAY HERE THAT LONG.
HE SAID...
...I CAN... STAY.
PHEW.

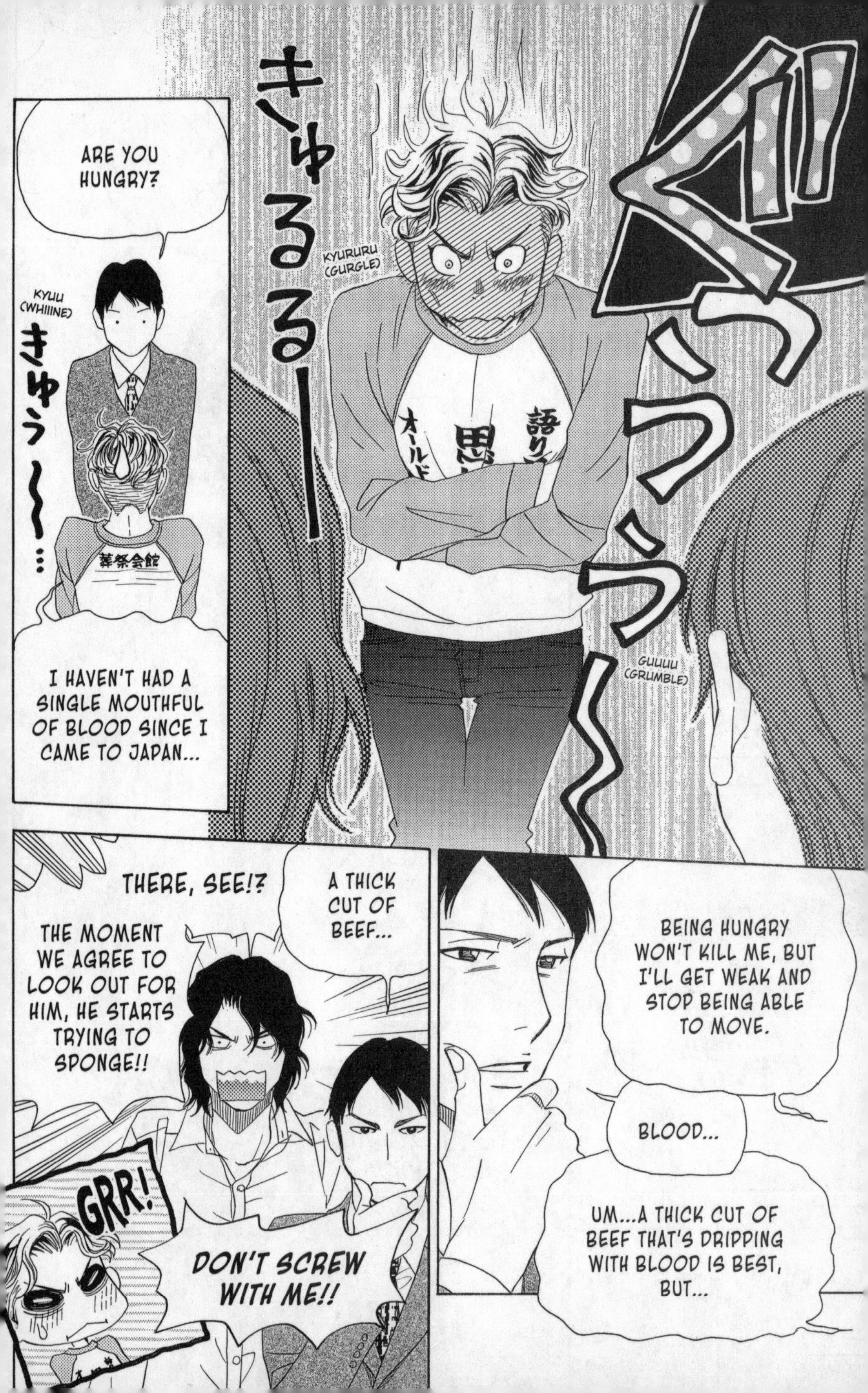
ぐぅぅぅ〜
GUUUU (GRUMBLE)
きゅるるー
KYURURU (GURGLE)
ARE YOU HUNGRY?
KYUU (WHIIINE)
きゅう〜〜…
葬祭会館
I HAVEN'T HAD A SINGLE MOUTHFUL OF BLOOD SINCE I CAME TO JAPAN...
BEING HUNGRY WON'T KILL ME, BUT I'LL GET WEAK AND STOP BEING ABLE TO MOVE.
BLOOD...
UM...A THICK CUT OF BEEF THAT'S DRIPPING WITH BLOOD IS BEST, BUT...
A THICK CUT OF BEEF...
THERE, SEE!?
THE MOMENT WE AGREE TO LOOK OUT FOR HIM, HE STARTS TRYING TO SPONGE!!
GRR!
DON'T SCREW WITH ME!!

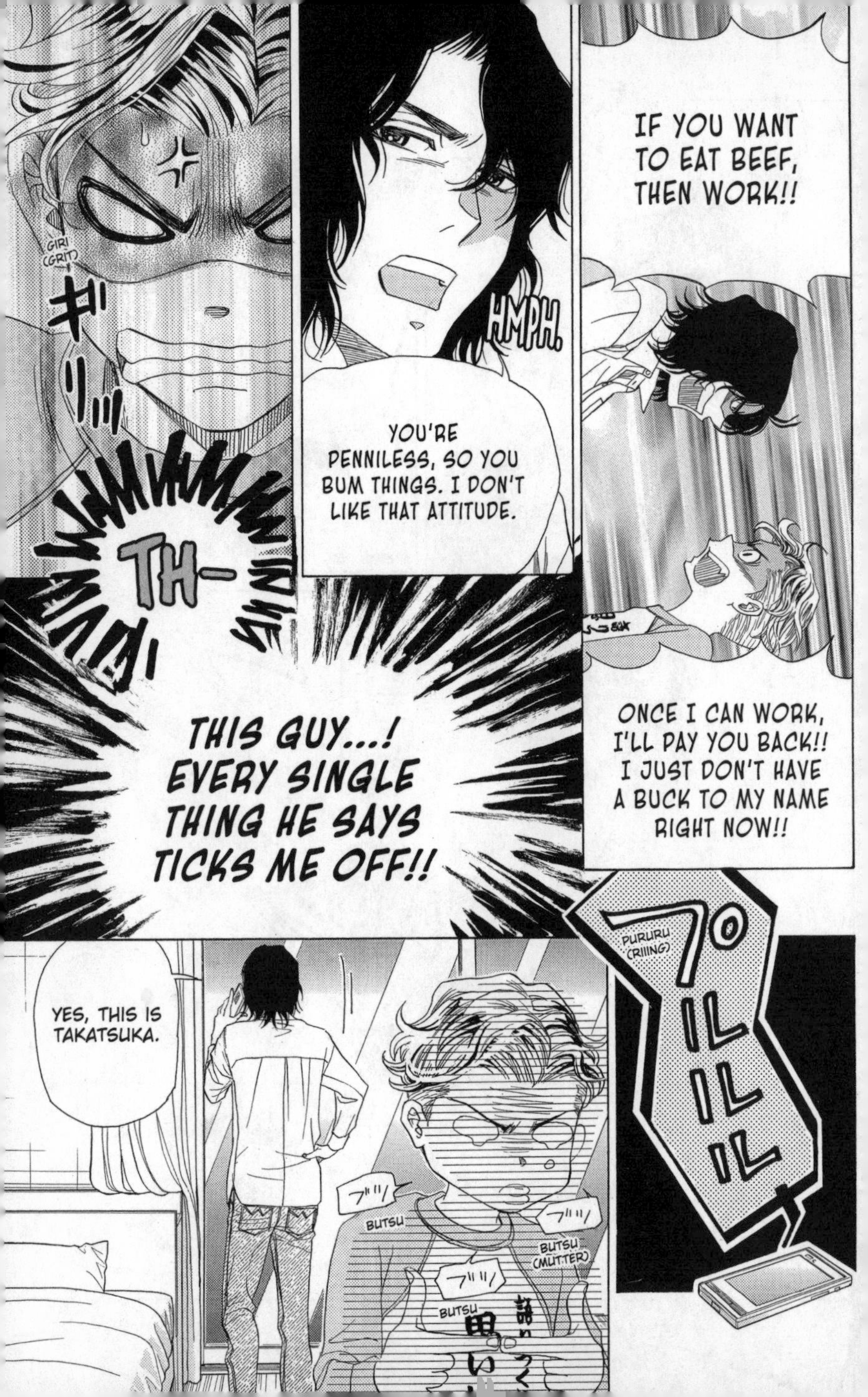

IF YOU WANT TO EAT BEEF, THEN WORK!!
ONCE I CAN WORK, I'LL PAY YOU BACK!! I JUST DON'T HAVE A BUCK TO MY NAME RIGHT NOW!!
HMPH.
YOU'RE PENNILESS, SO YOU BUM THINGS. I DON'T LIKE THAT ATTITUDE.
GIRI (GRIT)
TH-
THIS GUY...! EVERY SINGLE THING HE SAYS TICKS ME OFF!!
PURURU (RIIING)
YES, THIS IS TAKATSUKA.
BUTSU (MUTTER)
BUTSU
BUTSU

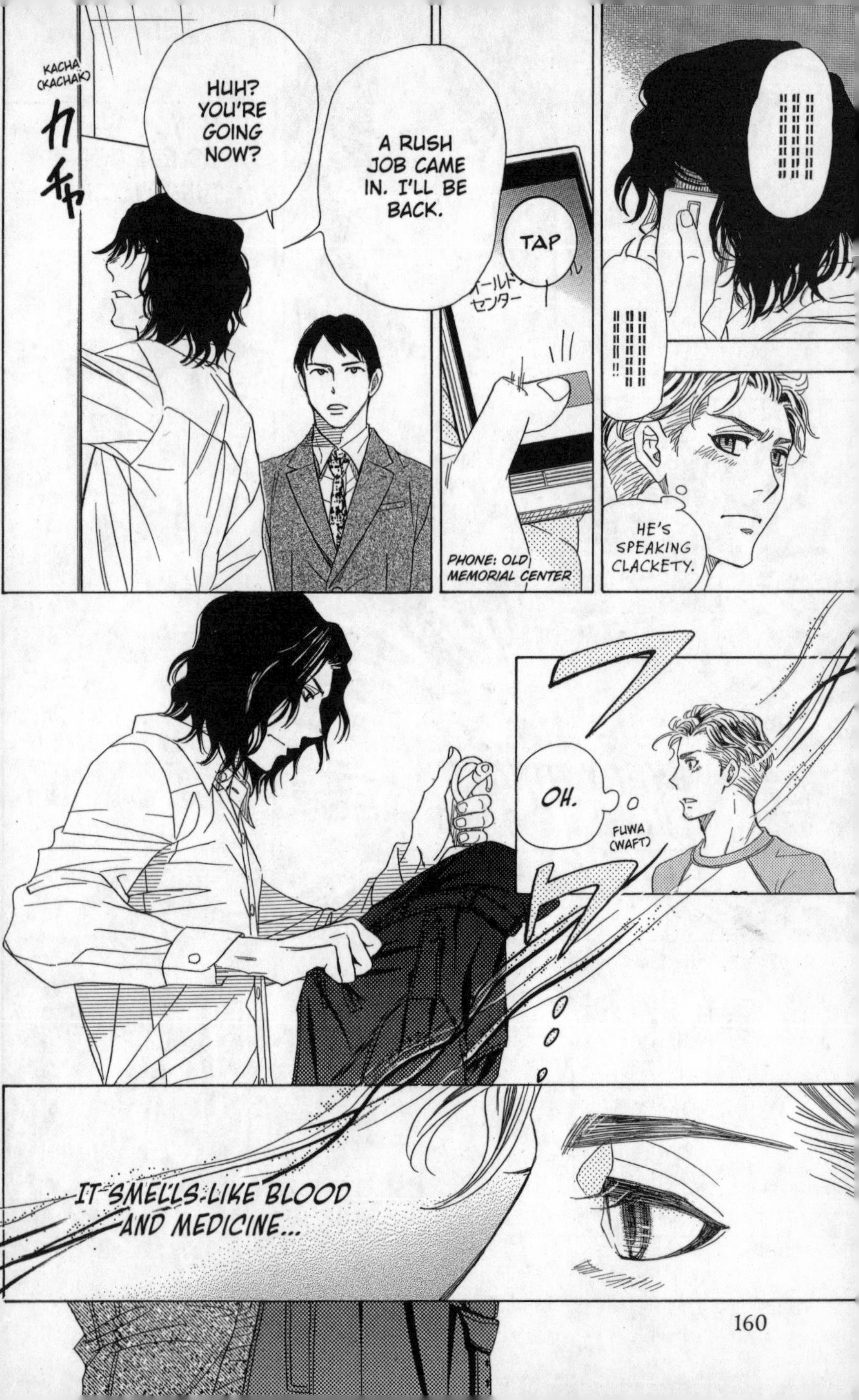
HE'S SPEAKING CLACKETY.
TAP
PHONE: OLD MEMORIAL CENTER
HUH? YOU'RE GOING NOW?
A RUSH JOB CAME IN. I'LL BE BACK.
KACHA (KACHA!)
カチャ
OH.
FUWA (WAFT)
IT SMELLS LIKE BLOOD AND MEDICINE...

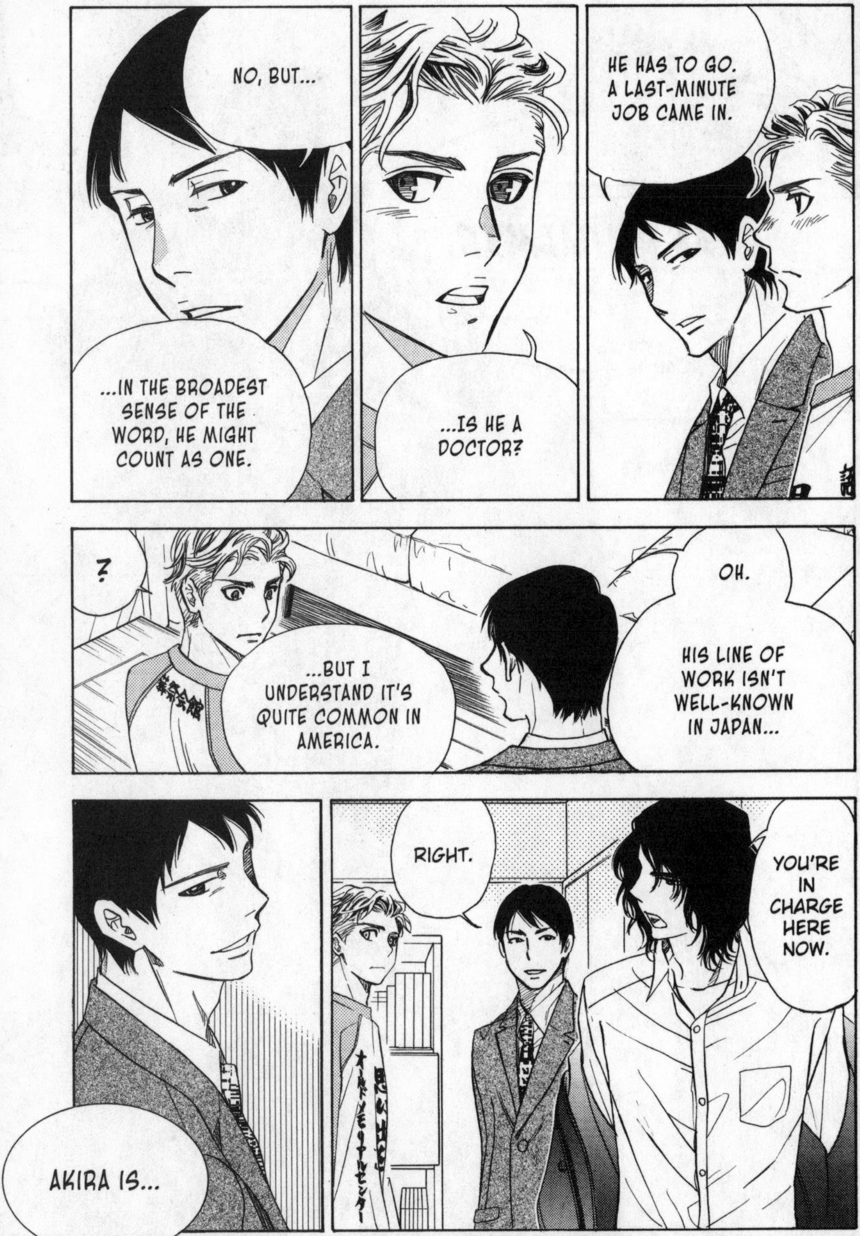
HE HAS TO GO. A LAST-MINUTE JOB CAME IN.
...IS HE A DOCTOR?
NO, BUT...
...IN THE BROADEST SENSE OF THE WORD, HE MIGHT COUNT AS ONE.
OH.
HIS LINE OF WORK ISN'T WELL-KNOWN IN JAPAN...
...BUT I UNDERSTAND IT'S QUITE COMMON IN AMERICA.
?
YOU'RE IN CHARGE HERE NOW.
RIGHT.
AKIRA IS...

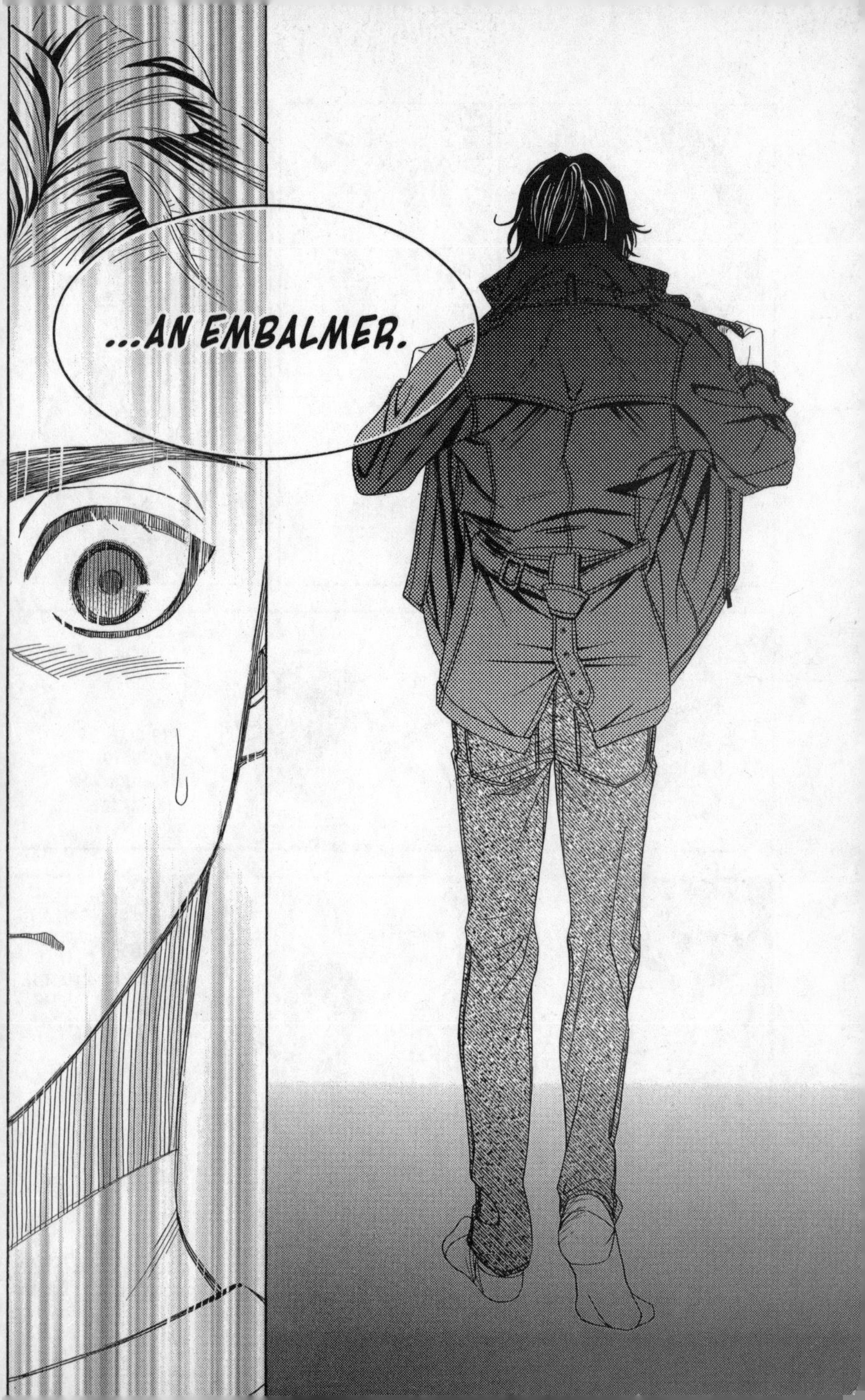
...AN EMBALMER.

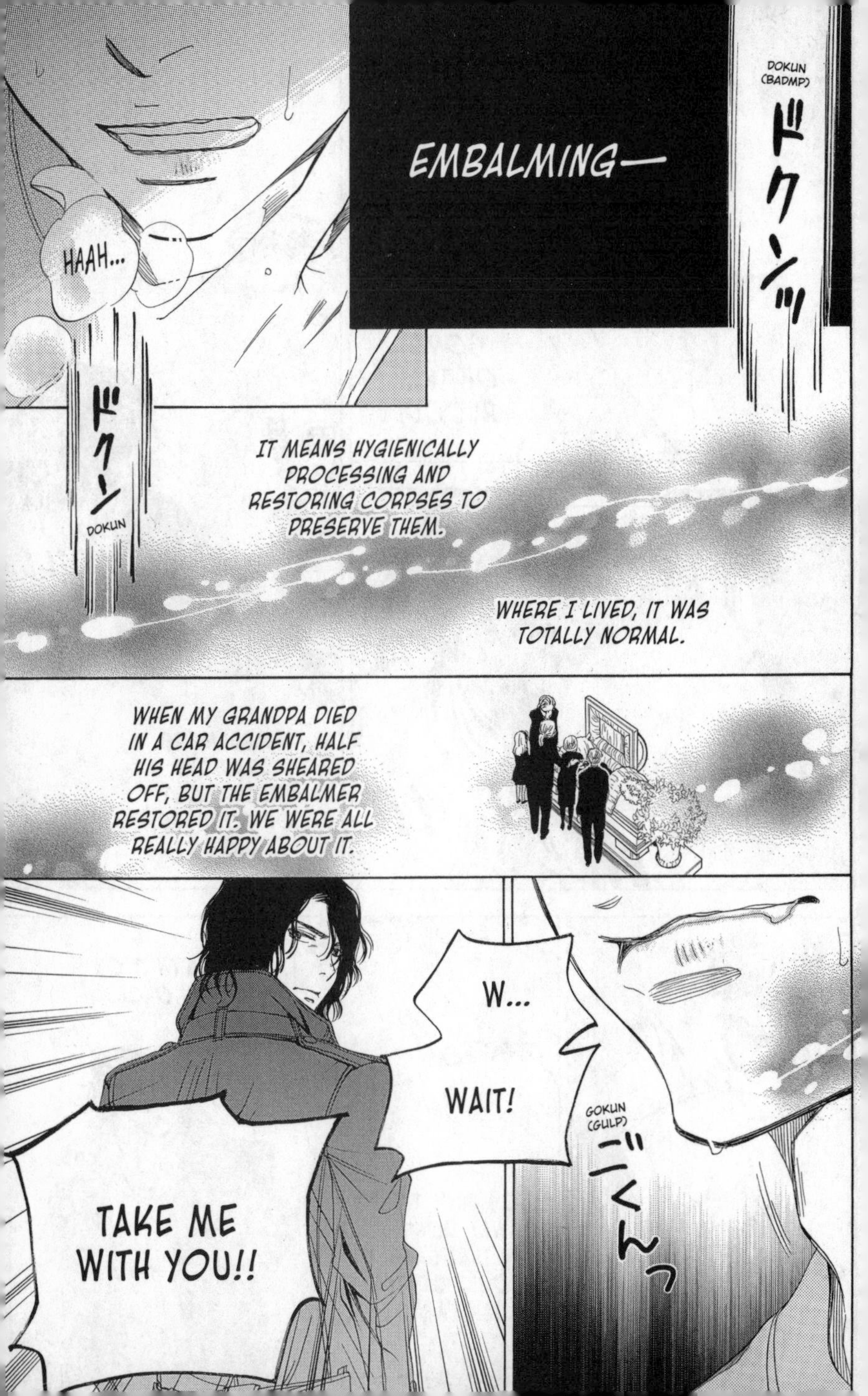
DOKUN (BADMP)
ドクンッ
EMBALMING—
HAAH...
ドクン
DOKUN
IT MEANS HYGIENICALLY PROCESSING AND RESTORING CORPSES TO PRESERVE THEM.
WHERE I LIVED, IT WAS TOTALLY NORMAL.
WHEN MY GRANDPA DIED IN A CAR ACCIDENT, HALF HIS HEAD WAS SHEARED OFF, BUT THE EMBALMER RESTORED IT. WE WERE ALL REALLY HAPPY ABOUT IT.
W...
WAIT!
GOKUN (GULP)
ごくんっ
TAKE ME WITH YOU!!

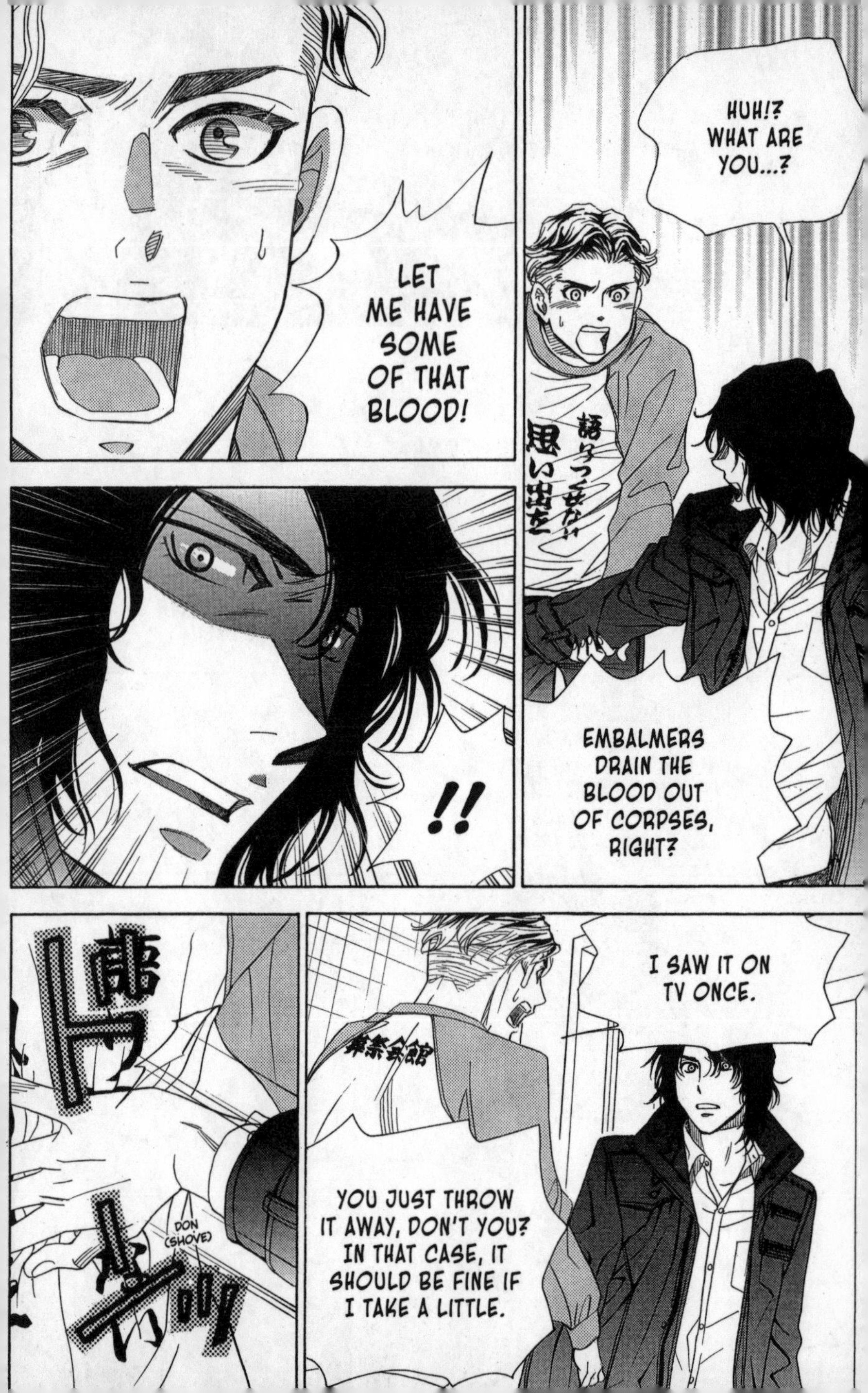
HUH!? WHAT ARE YOU...?
EMBALMERS DRAIN THE BLOOD OUT OF CORPSES, RIGHT?
LET ME HAVE SOME OF THAT BLOOD!
!!
I SAW IT ON TV ONCE.
YOU JUST THROW IT AWAY, DON'T YOU? IN THAT CASE, IT SHOULD BE FINE IF I TAKE A LITTLE.
DON (SHOVE)

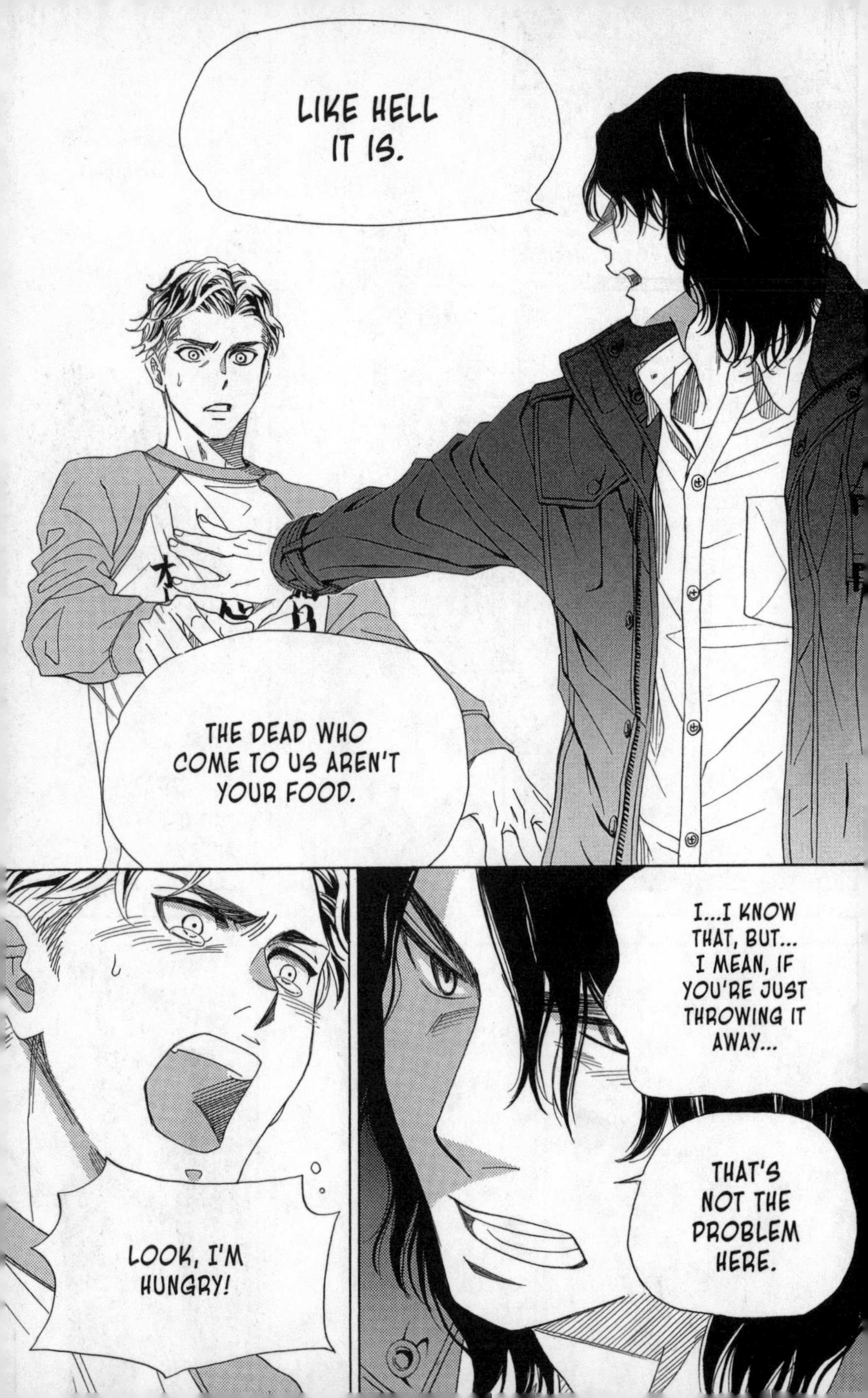
LIKE HELL IT IS.
THE DEAD WHO COME TO US AREN'T YOUR FOOD.
I...I KNOW THAT, BUT... I MEAN, IF YOU'RE JUST THROWING IT AWAY...
THAT'S NOT THE PROBLEM HERE.
LOOK, I'M HUNGRY!

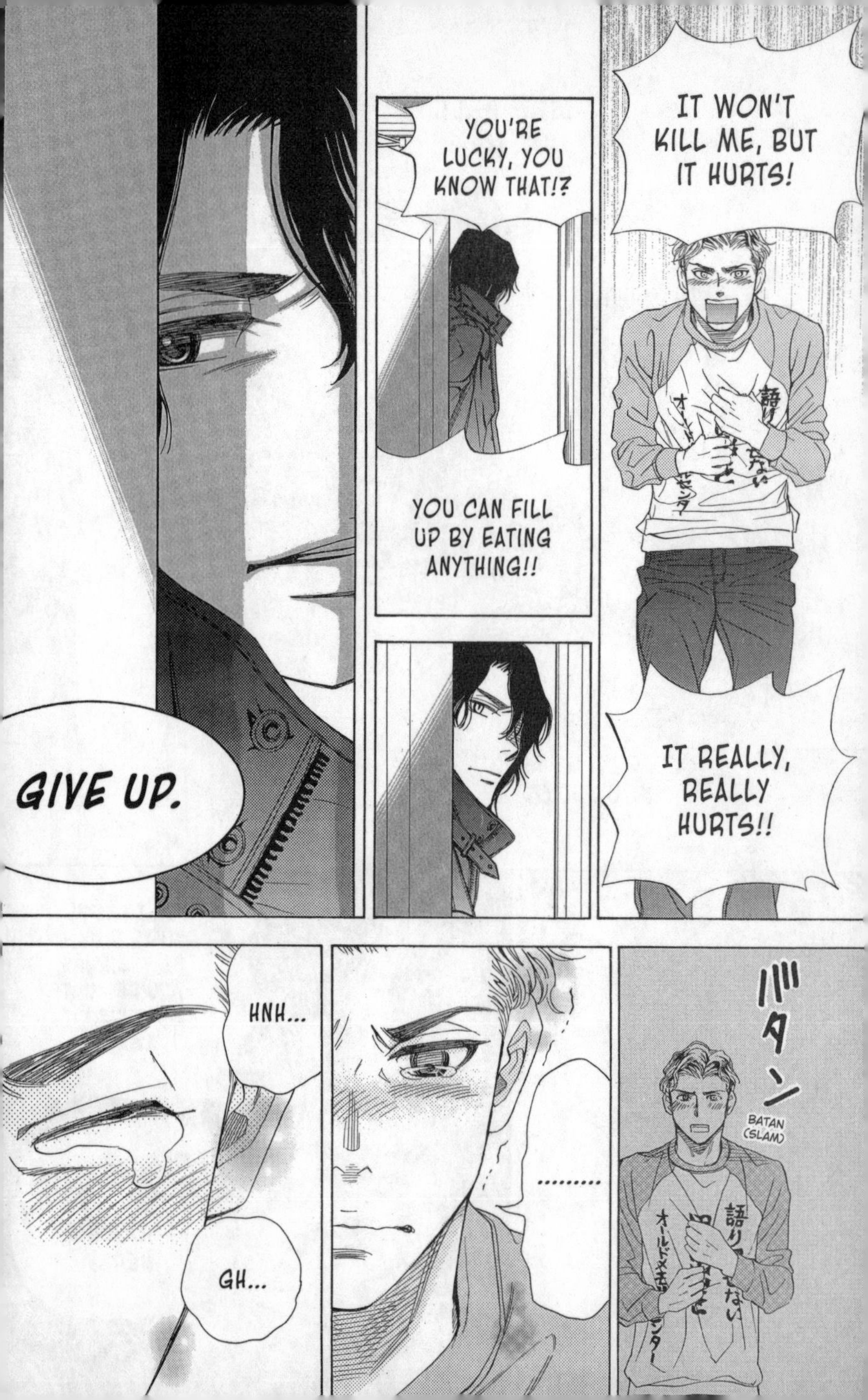
IT WON'T KILL ME, BUT IT HURTS!
IT REALLY, REALLY HURTS!!
YOU'RE LUCKY, YOU KNOW THAT!?
YOU CAN FILL UP BY EATING ANYTHING!!
GIVE UP.
バタン
BATAN (SLAM)
....
HNH...
GH...

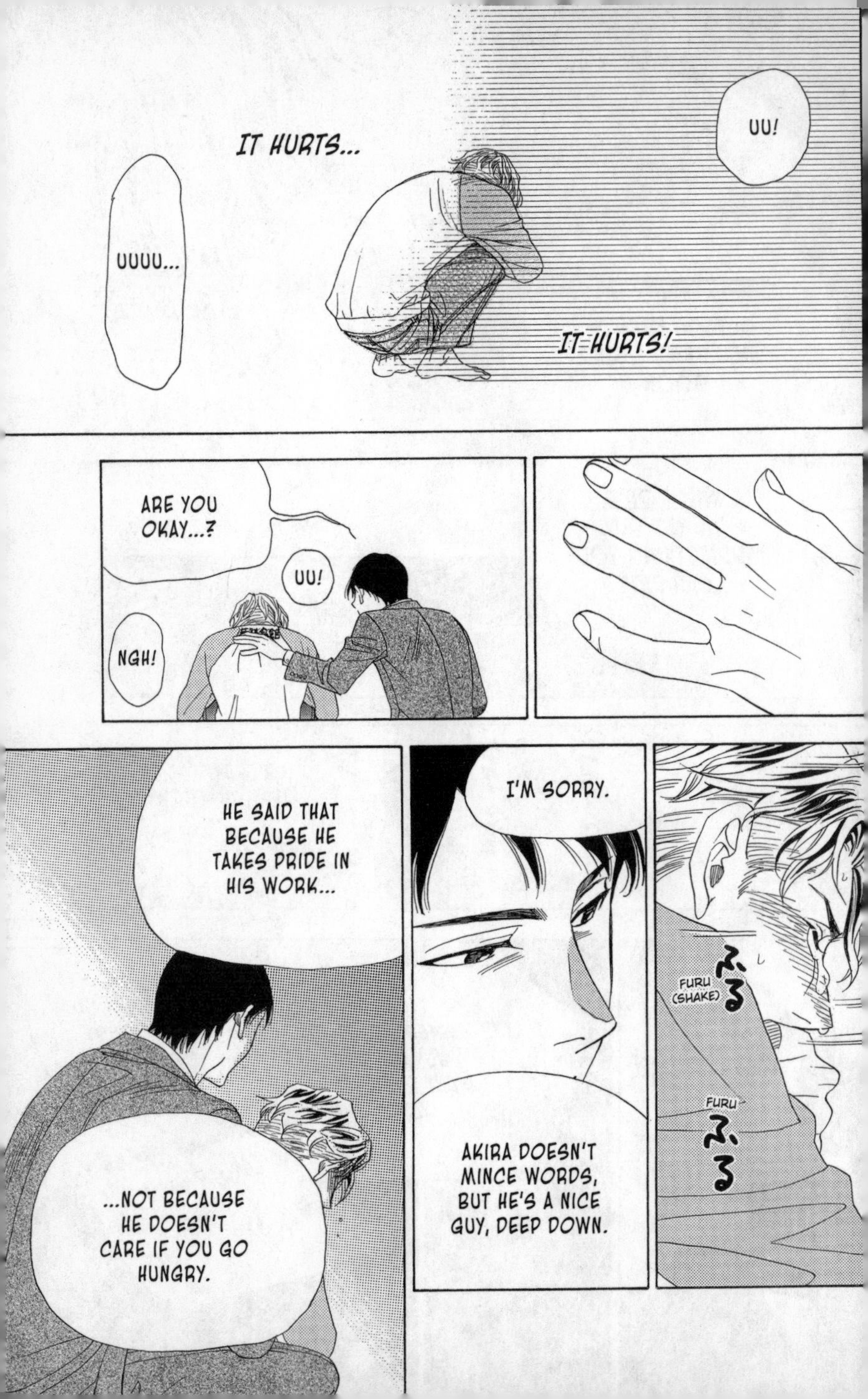
UU!
IT HURTS...
IT HURTS!
UUUU...
ARE YOU OKAY...?
UU!
NGH!
ふる
FURU (SHAKE)
ふる
FURU
I'M SORRY.
AKIRA DOESN'T MINCE WORDS, BUT HE'S A NICE GUY, DEEP DOWN.
HE SAID THAT BECAUSE HE TAKES PRIDE IN HIS WORK...
...NOT BECAUSE HE DOESN'T CARE IF YOU GO HUNGRY.

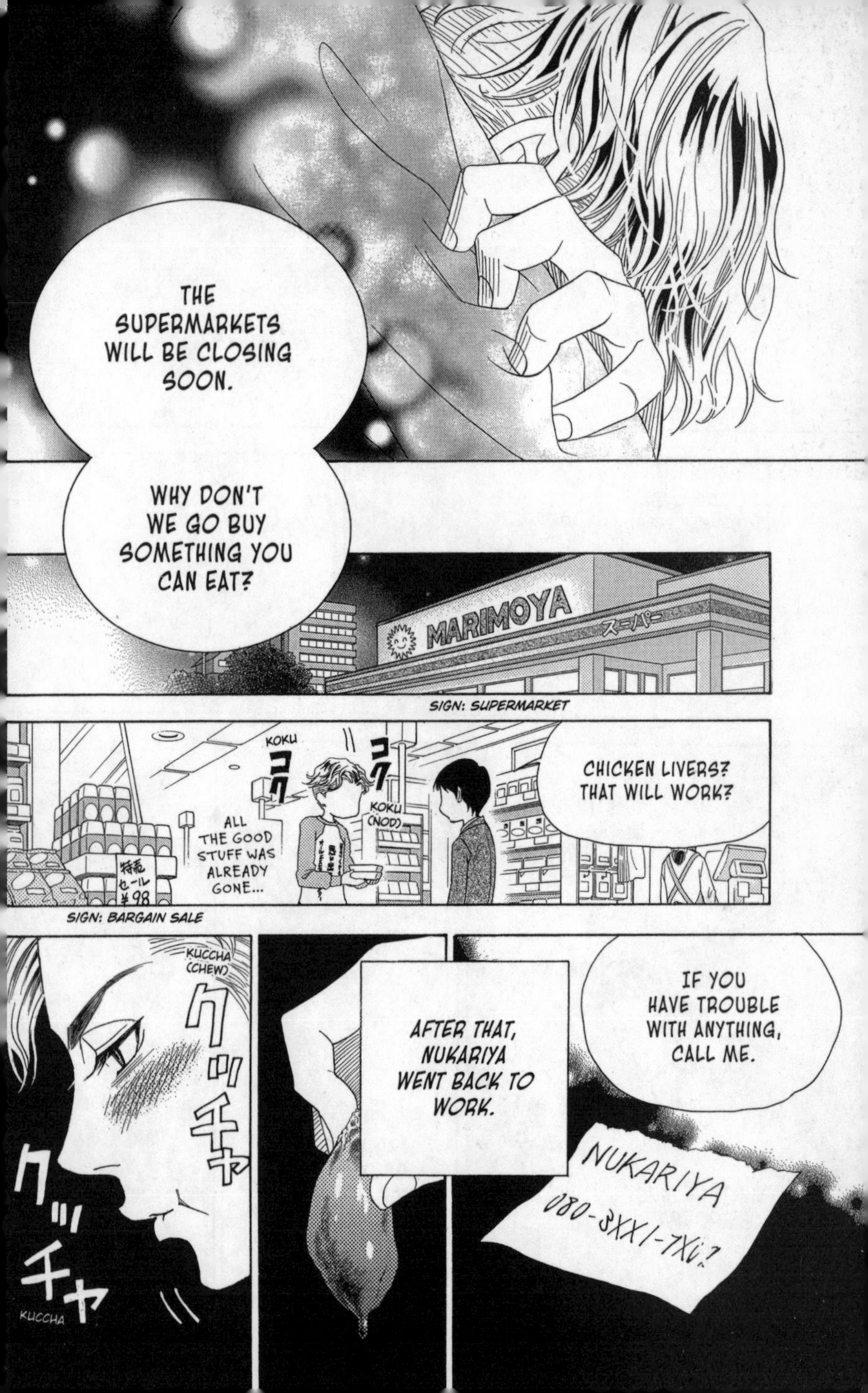
THE SUPERMARKETS WILL BE CLOSING SOON.
WHY DON'T WE GO BUY SOMETHING YOU CAN EAT?
MARIMOYA
スーパー
SIGN: SUPERMARKET
CHICKEN LIVERS? THAT WILL WORK?
コク
KOKU (NOD)
コク
KOKU
ALL THE GOOD STUFF WAS ALREADY GONE...
特売セール ¥98
SIGN: BARGAIN SALE
IF YOU HAVE TROUBLE WITH ANYTHING, CALL ME.
NUKARIYA
AFTER THAT, NUKARIYA WENT BACK TO WORK.
クッチャ
KUCCHA (CHEW)
クッチャ
KUCCHA

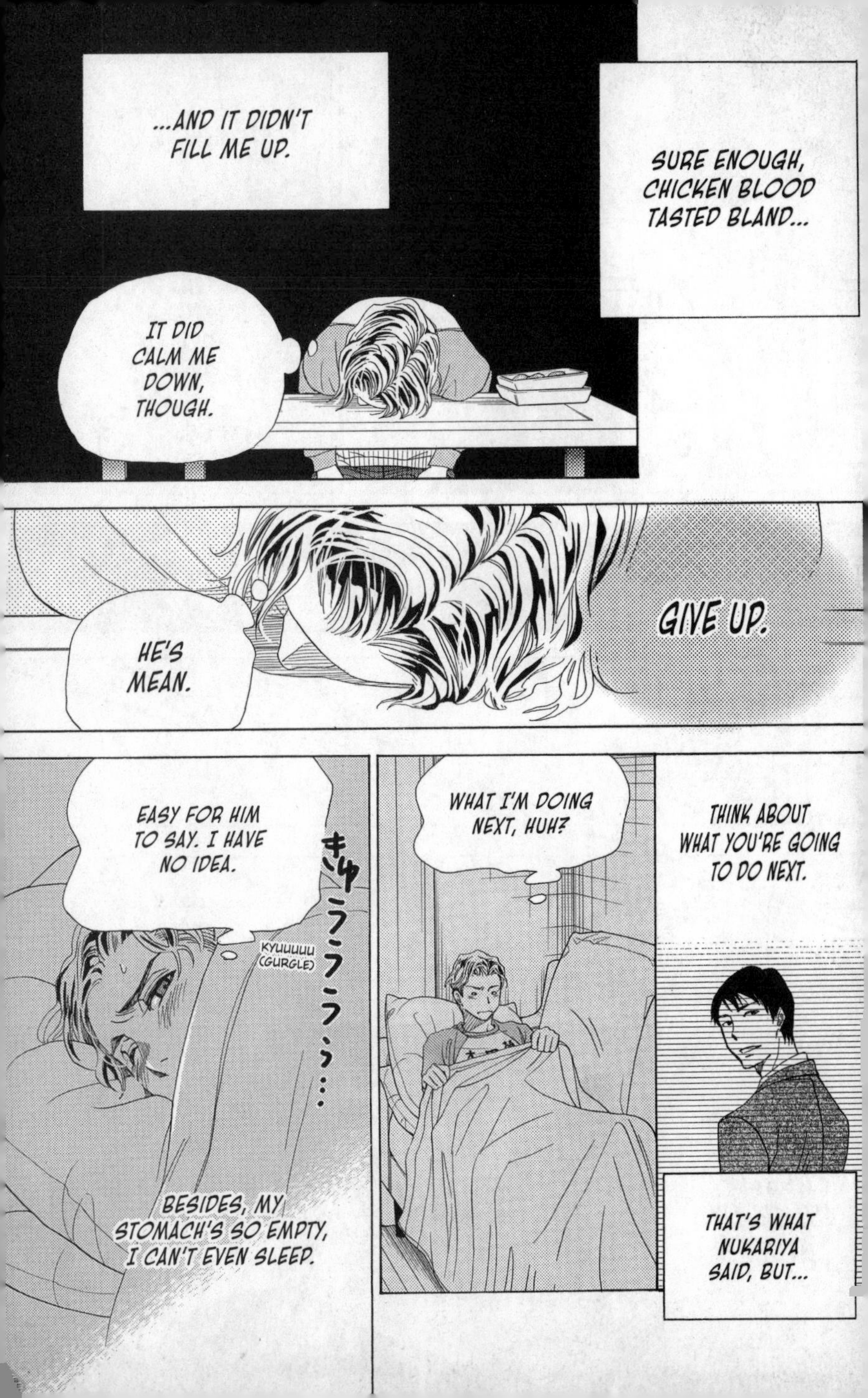
SURE ENOUGH, CHICKEN BLOOD TASTED BLAND...
...AND IT DIDN'T FILL ME UP.
IT DID CALM ME DOWN, THOUGH.
GIVE UP.
HE'S MEAN.
THINK ABOUT WHAT YOU'RE GOING TO DO NEXT.
THAT'S WHAT NUKARIYA SAID, BUT...
WHAT I'M DOING NEXT, HUH?
EASY FOR HIM TO SAY. I HAVE NO IDEA.
KYUUUUU (GURGLE)
BESIDES, MY STOMACH'S SO EMPTY, I CAN'T EVEN SLEEP.

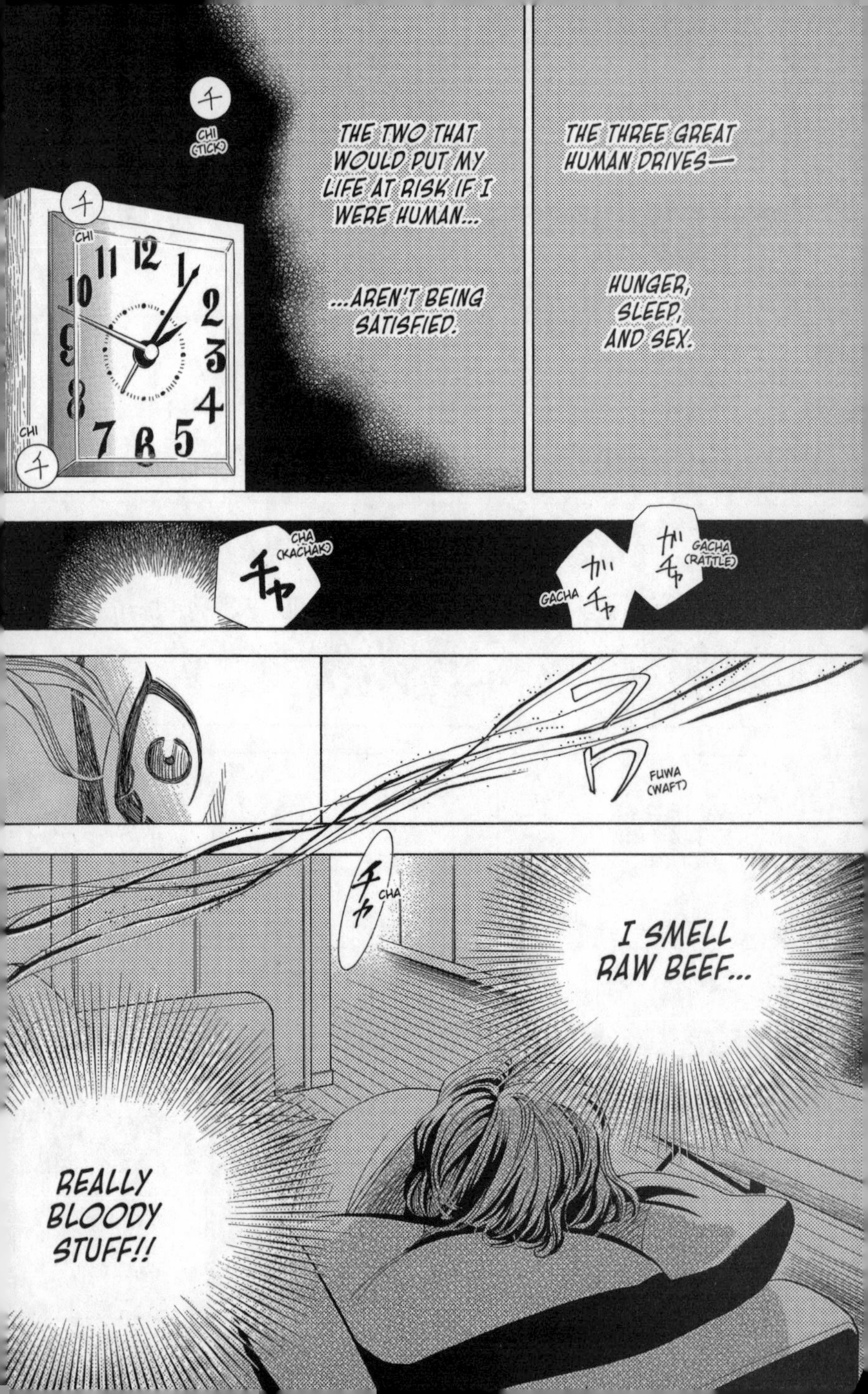
THE THREE GREAT HUMAN DRIVES—
HUNGER, SLEEP, AND SEX.
THE TWO THAT WOULD PUT MY LIFE AT RISK IF I WERE HUMAN...
...AREN'T BEING SATISFIED.
チ
CHI (TICK)
チ
CHI
CHI
チ
ガチャ
GACHA (RATTLE)
ガチャ
GACHA
チャ
CHA (KACHAK)
フワ
FUWA (WAFT)
チャ
CHA
I SMELL RAW BEEF...
REALLY BLOODY STUFF!!

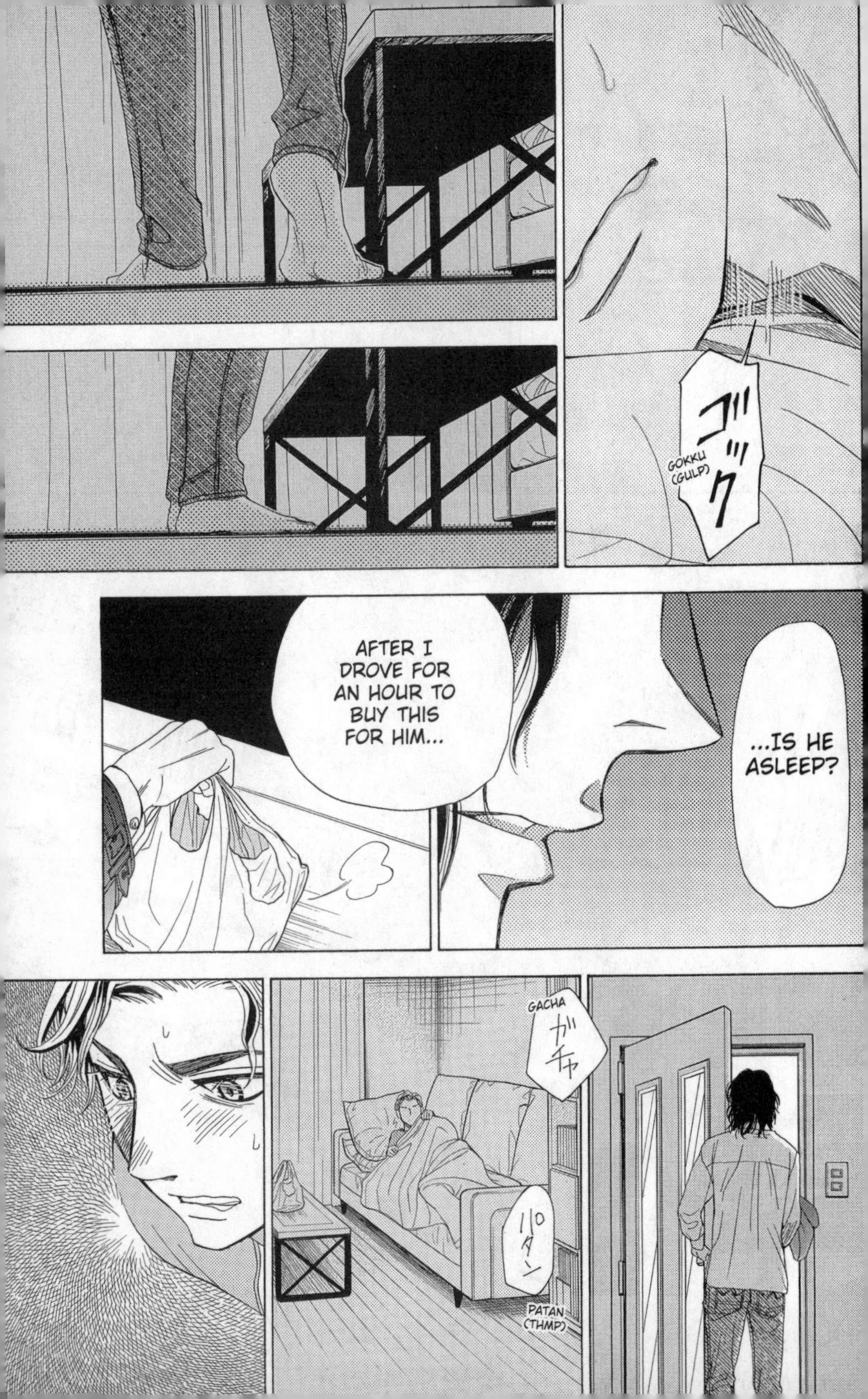
ゴック
GOKKU (GULP)
...IS HE ASLEEP?
AFTER I DROVE FOR AN HOUR TO BUY THIS FOR HIM...
GACHA
ガチャ
パタン
PATAN (THMP)

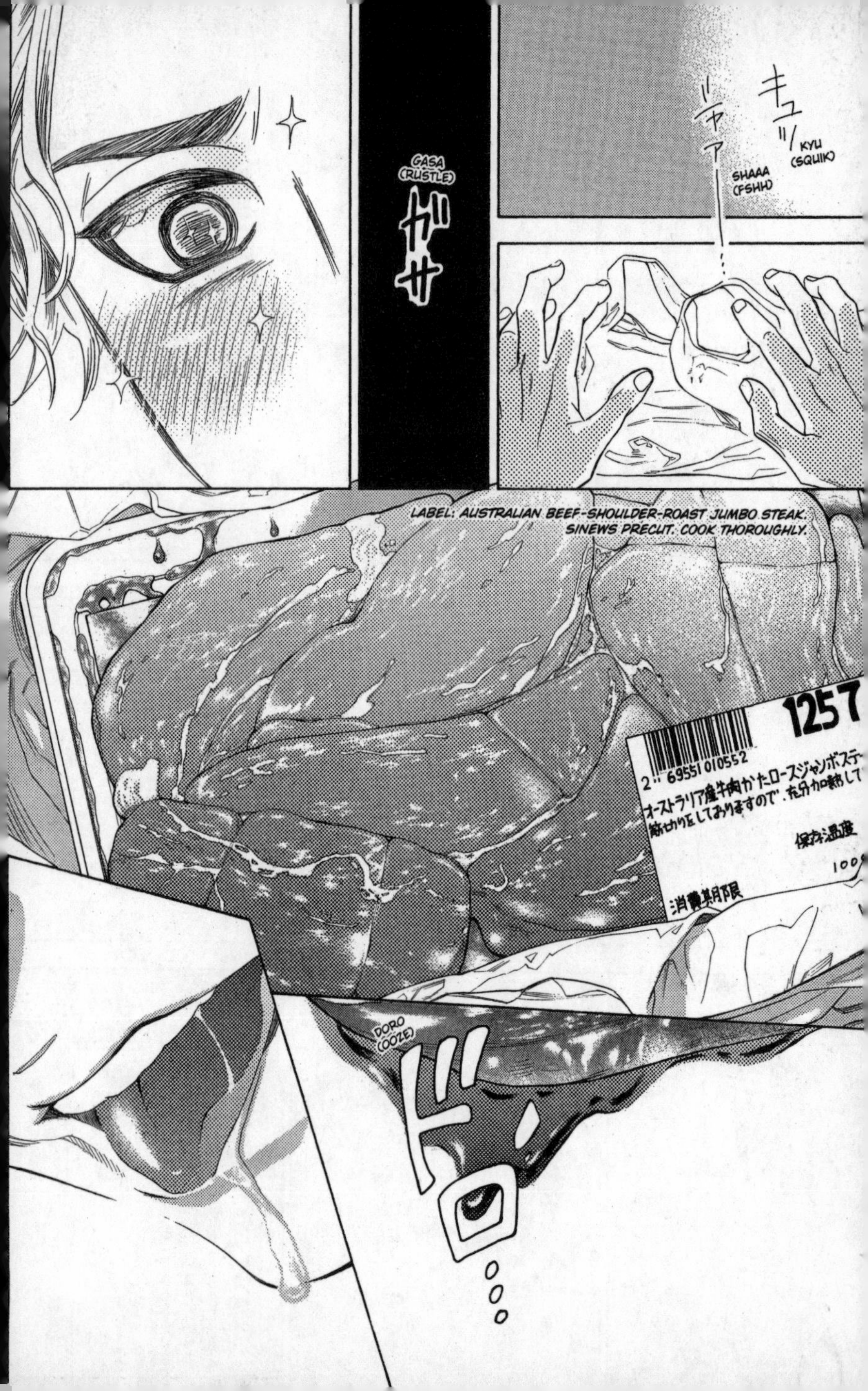
キュッ
KYU (SQUIK)
シャアー
SHAAA (FSHH)
GASA (RUSTLE)
ガサ
LABEL: AUSTRALIAN BEEF-SHOULDER-ROAST JUMBO STEAK. SINEWS PRECUT. COOK THOROUGHLY.
1257
2 69551 010552
オーストラリア産牛肉かたロースジャンボステ
筋切りしてありますので、充分加熱して
保存温度
消費期限
DORO (OOZE)
ドロ…

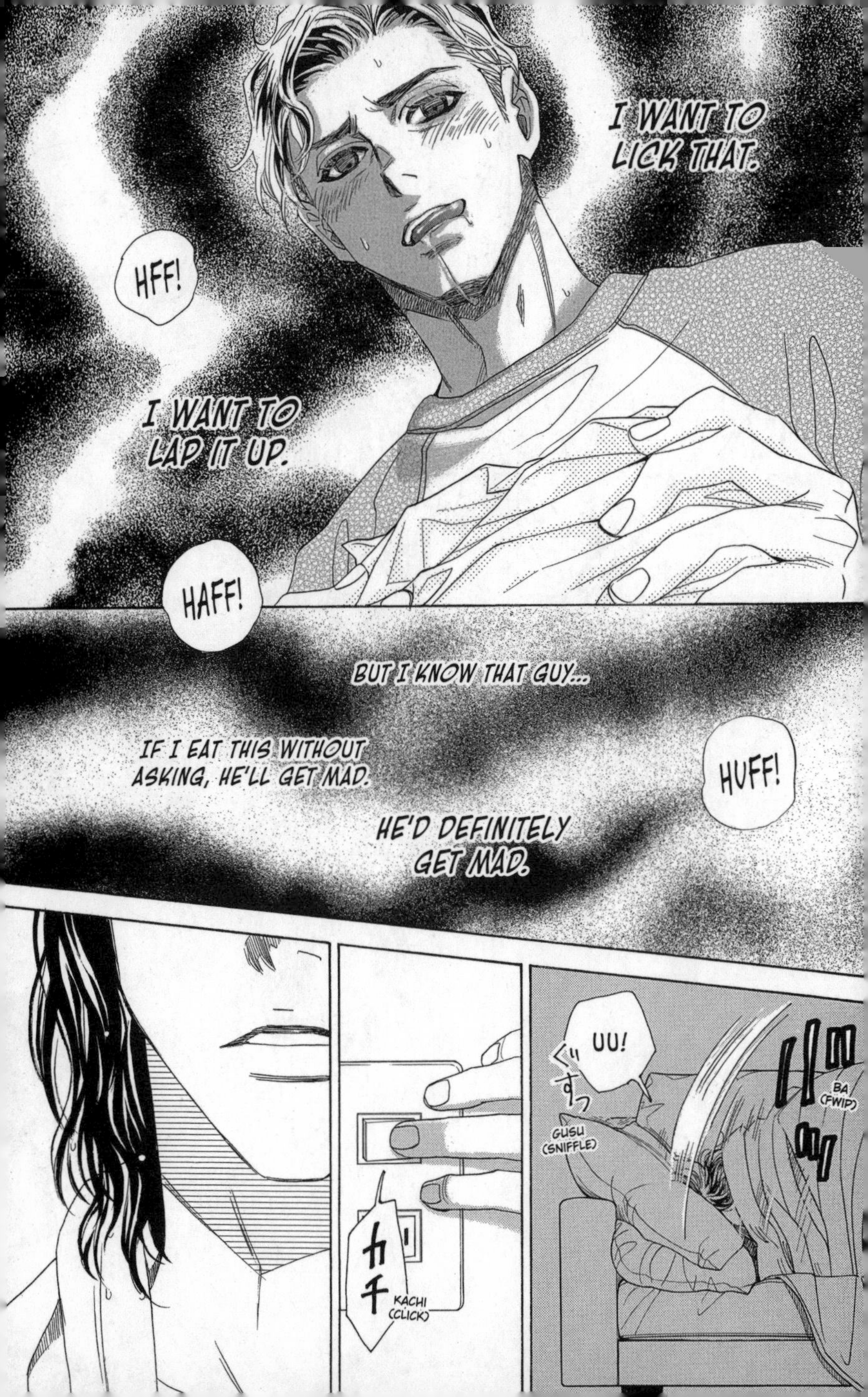
I WANT TO LICK THAT.
HFF!
I WANT TO LAP IT UP.
HAFF!
BUT I KNOW THAT GUY...
HUFF!
IF I EAT THIS WITHOUT ASKING, HE'LL GET MAD.
HE'D DEFINITELY GET MAD.
BA (FWIP)
UU!
GUSU (SNIFFLE)
カチ
KACHI (CLICK)

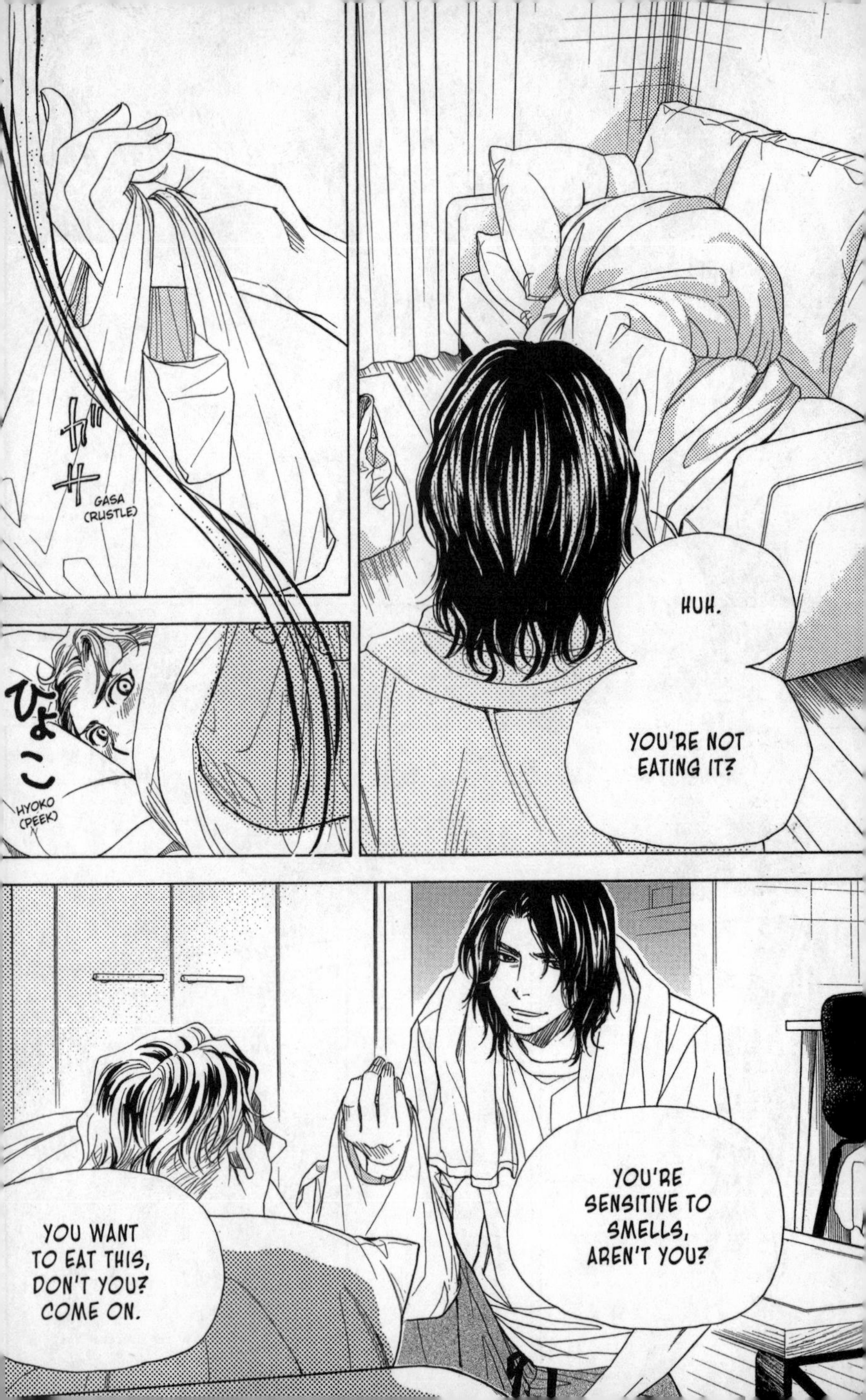
HUH.
YOU'RE NOT EATING IT?
ガサ
GASA (RUSTLE)
ひょこ
HYOKO (PEEK)
YOU'RE SENSITIVE TO SMELLS, AREN'T YOU?
YOU WANT TO EAT THIS, DON'T YOU? COME ON.

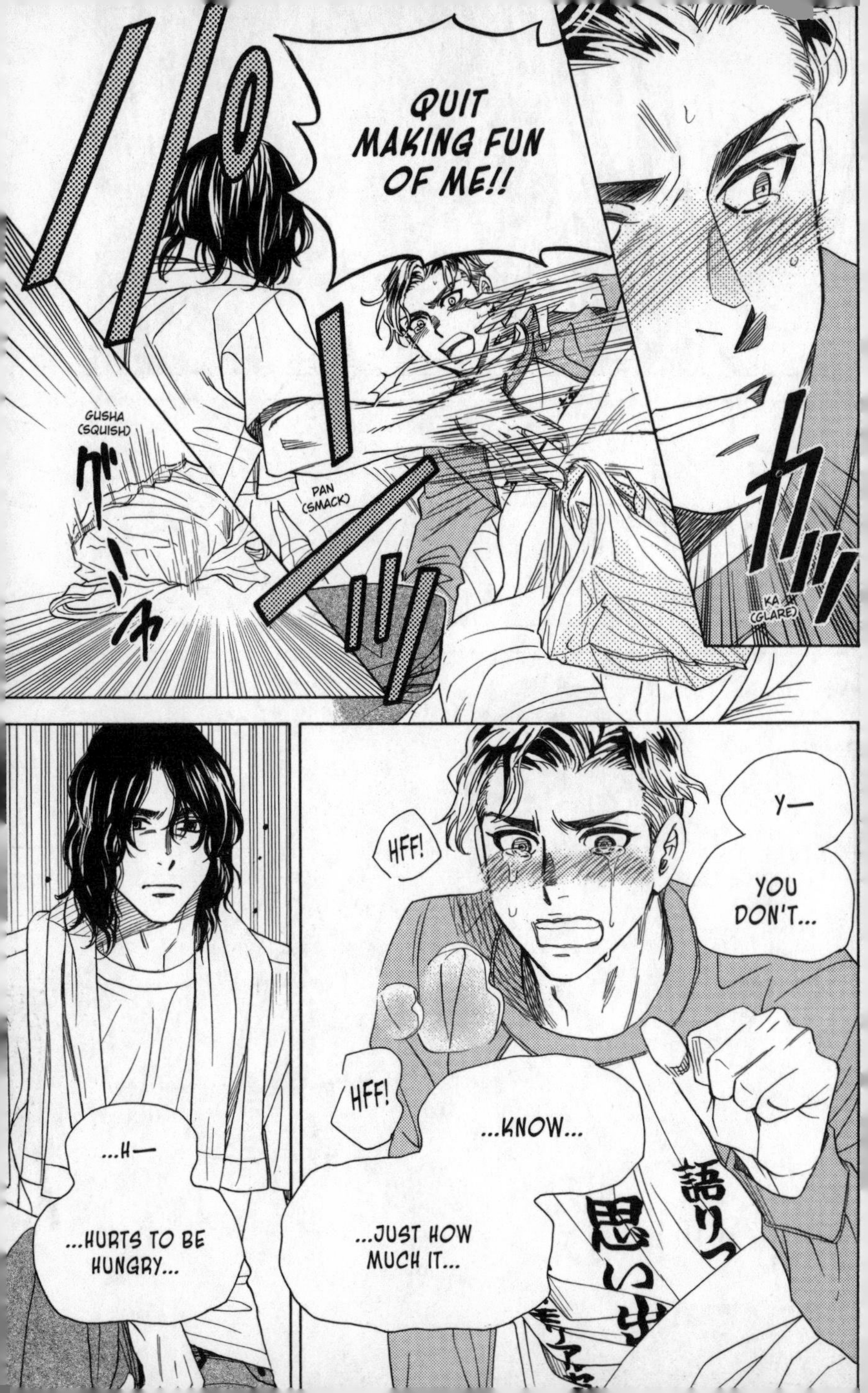
QUIT MAKING FUN OF ME!!
KA (GLARE)
PAN (SMACK)
GUSHA (SQUISH)
Y—
YOU DON'T...
HFF!
HFF!
...KNOW...
...JUST HOW MUCH IT...
...H—
...HURTS TO BE HUNGRY...

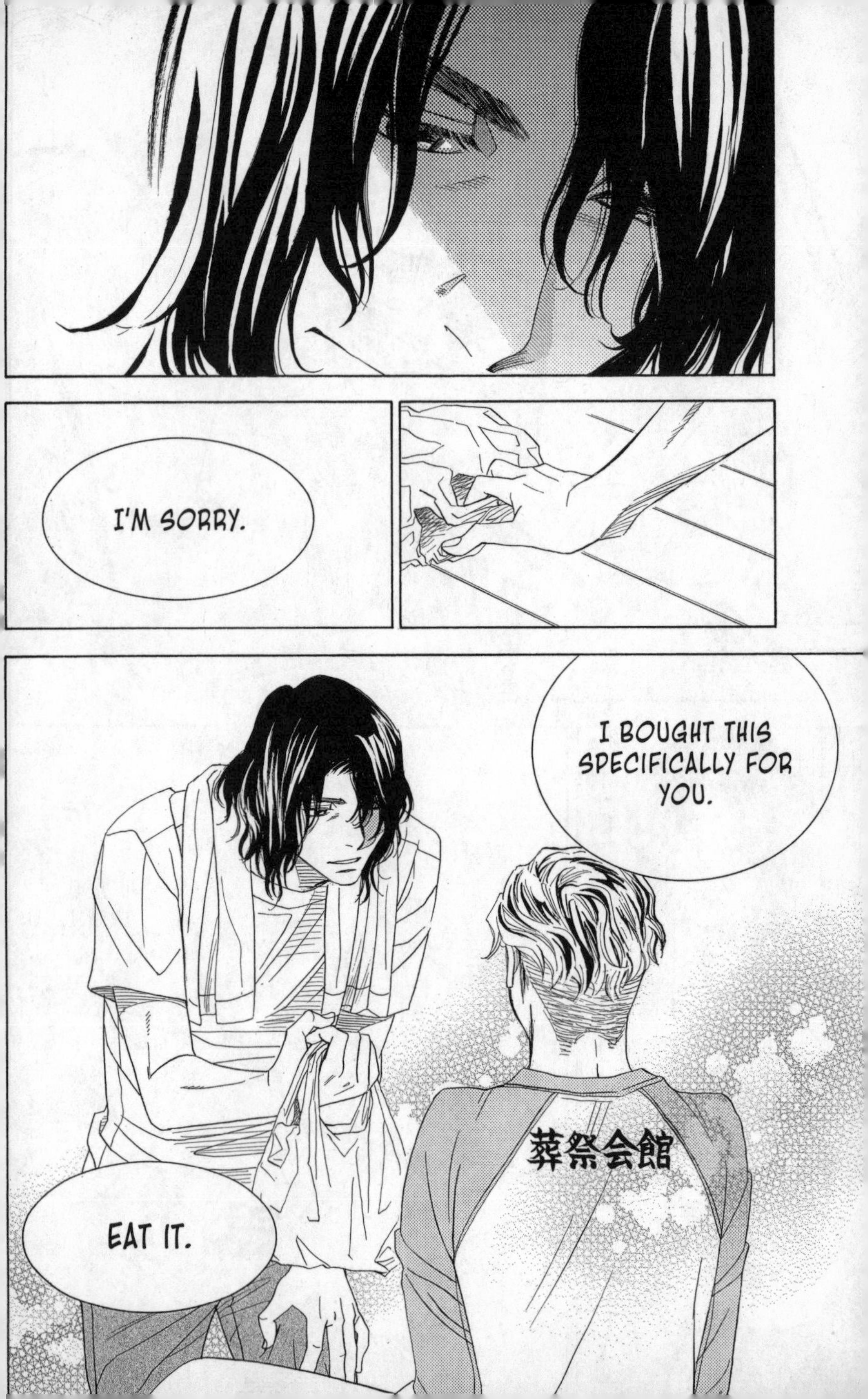
I'M SORRY.
I BOUGHT THIS SPECIFICALLY FOR YOU.
葬祭会館
EAT IT.

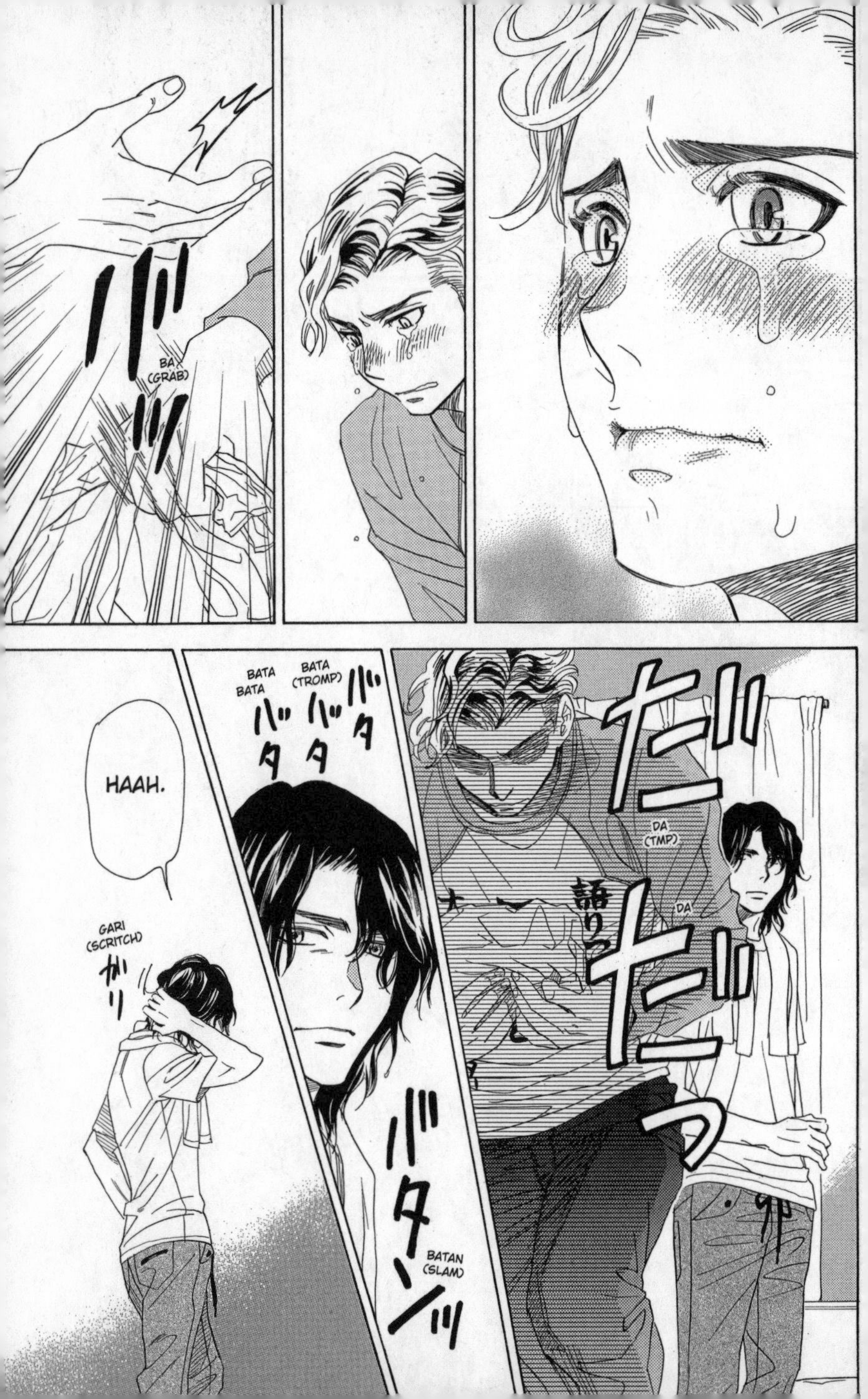
バッ
BA (GRAB)
だっ
DA (TMP)
だっ
DA
バタ
BATA (TROMP)
バタ
BATA BATA
バタンッ
BATAN (SLAM)
HAAH.
がり
GARI (SCRITCH)

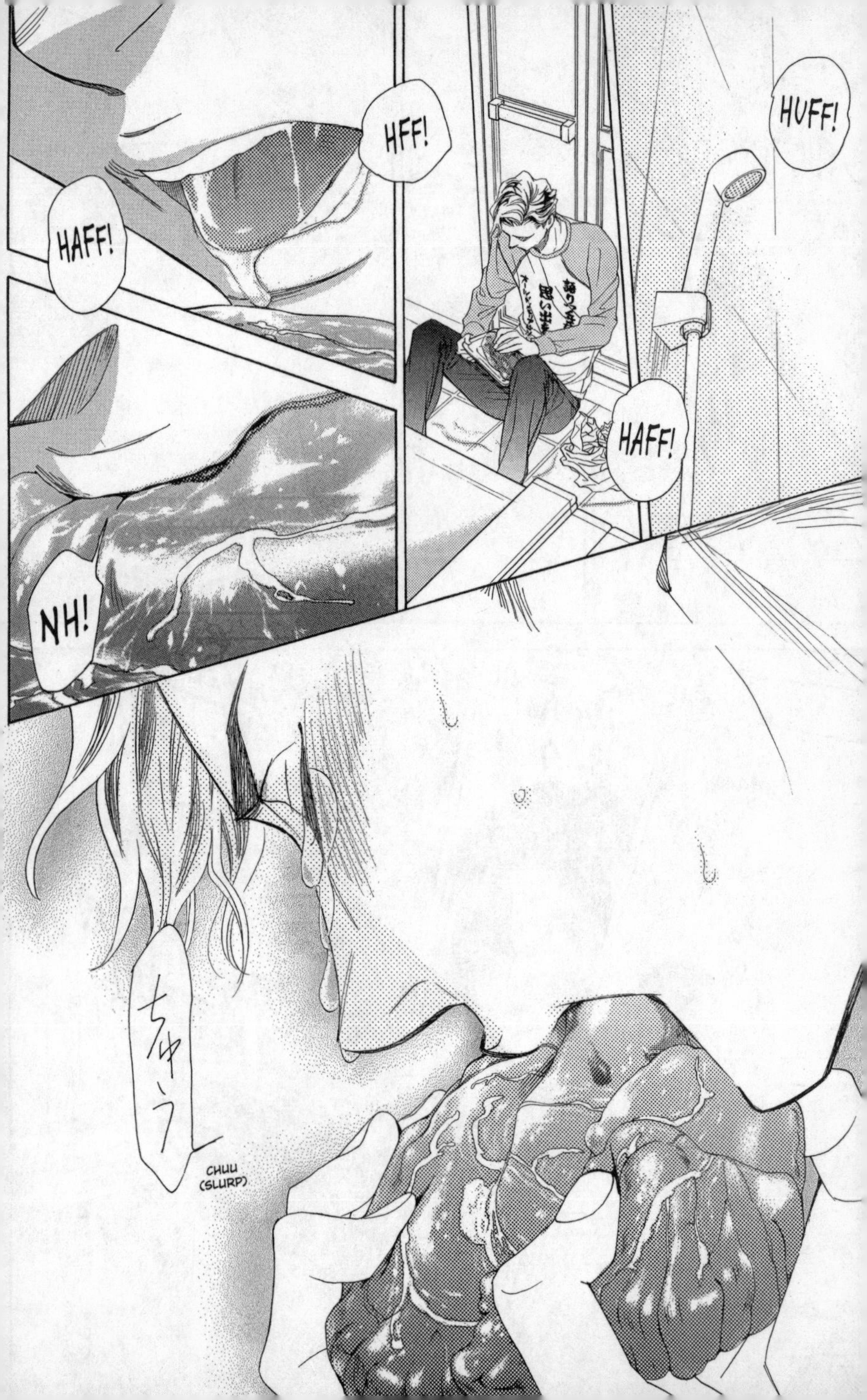
HUFF!
HAFF!
HFF!
HAFF!
NH!
ちゅ〜
CHUU
(SLURP)

PWAH!

HE'S A NICE GUY, DEEP DOWN.

IT'S NOT THAT HE DOESN'T CARE IF YOU GO HUNGRY.

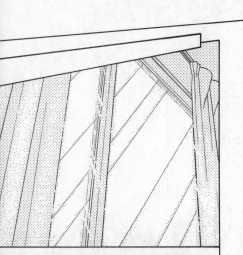

THAT MAY BE TRUE...

...BUT...

...IT'S NOT AS IF I CAN THANK HIM NOW.

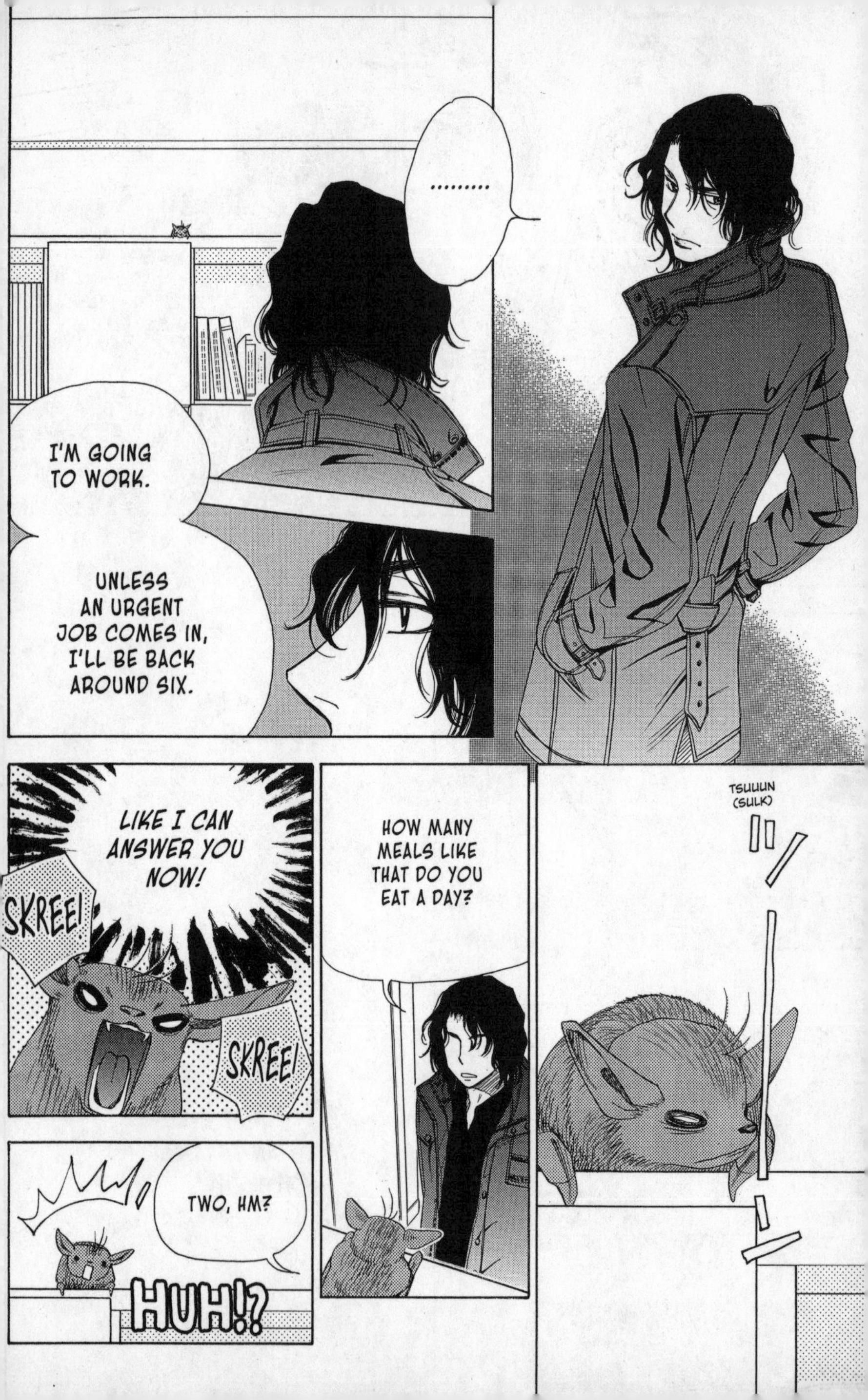
....
I'M GOING TO WORK.
UNLESS AN URGENT JOB COMES IN, I'LL BE BACK AROUND SIX.
TSUUUN (SULK)
HOW MANY MEALS LIKE THAT DO YOU EAT A DAY?
LIKE I CAN ANSWER YOU NOW!
SKREE!
SKREE!
TWO, HM?
HUH!?

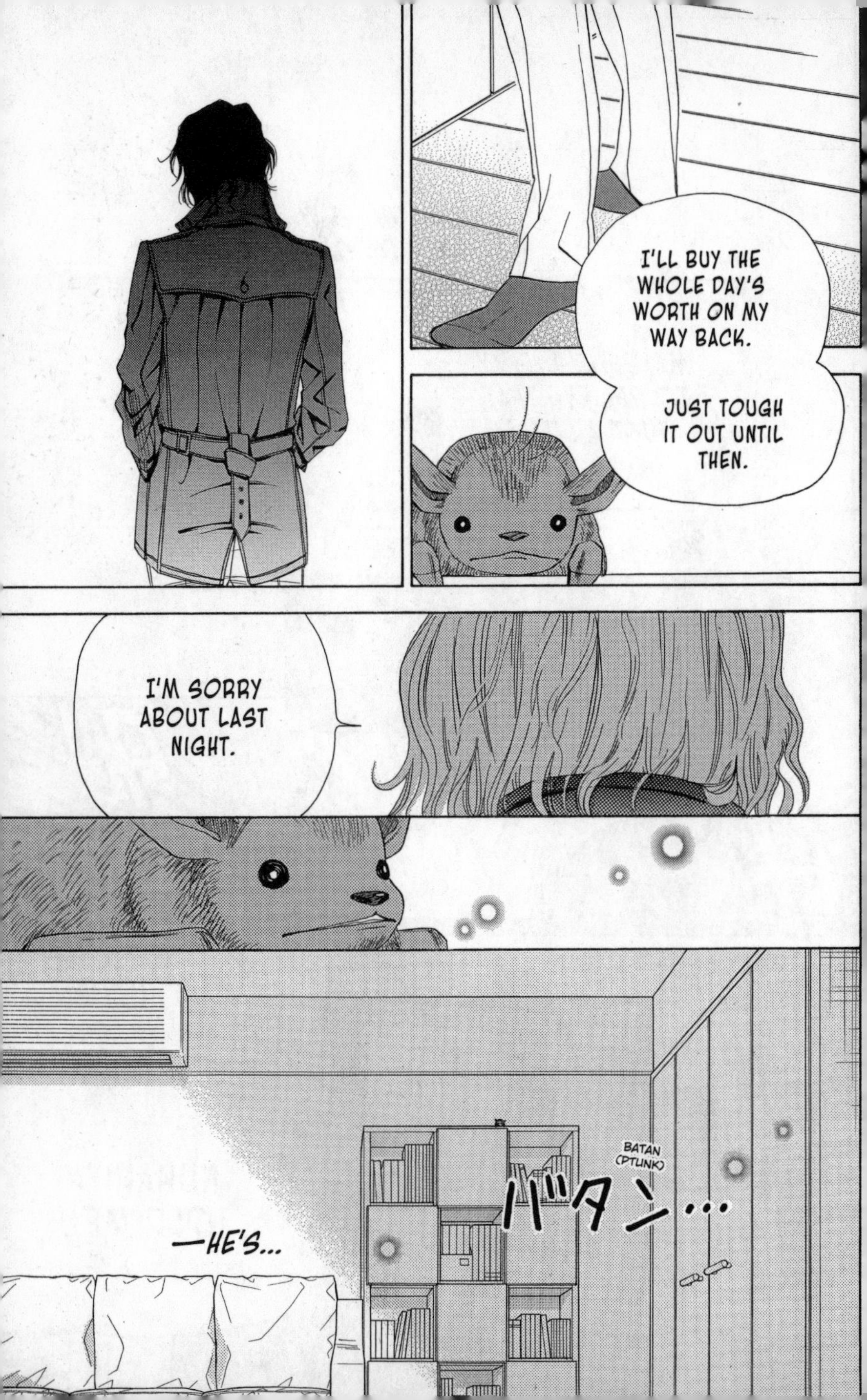
I'LL BUY THE WHOLE DAY'S WORTH ON MY WAY BACK.
JUST TOUGH IT OUT UNTIL THEN.
I'M SORRY ABOUT LAST NIGHT.
バタン…
BATAN (PTUNK)
—HE'S...

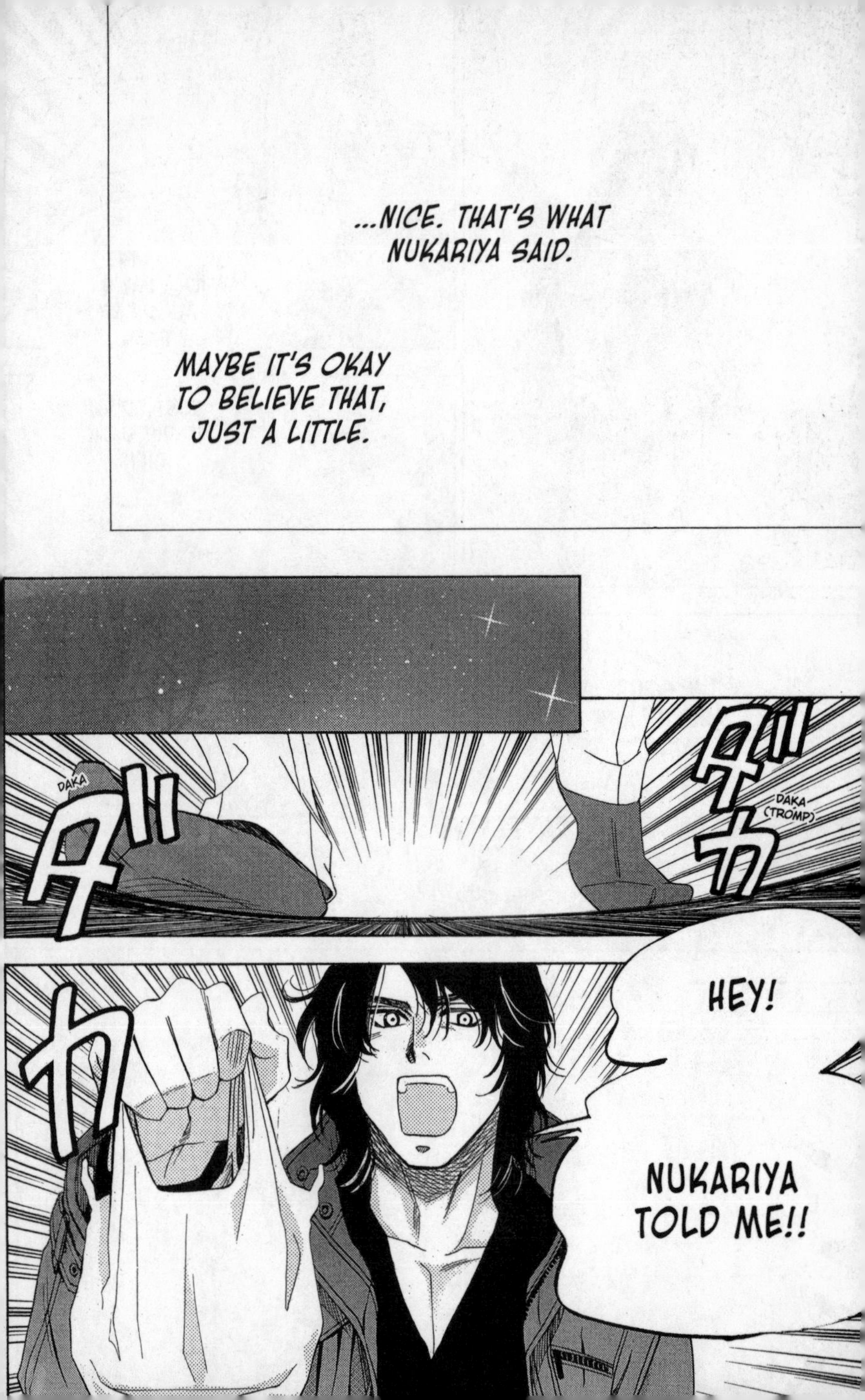
...NICE. THAT'S WHAT NUKARIYA SAID.
MAYBE IT'S OKAY TO BELIEVE THAT, JUST A LITTLE.
DAKA (TROMP)
DAKA
HEY!
NUKARIYA TOLD ME!!

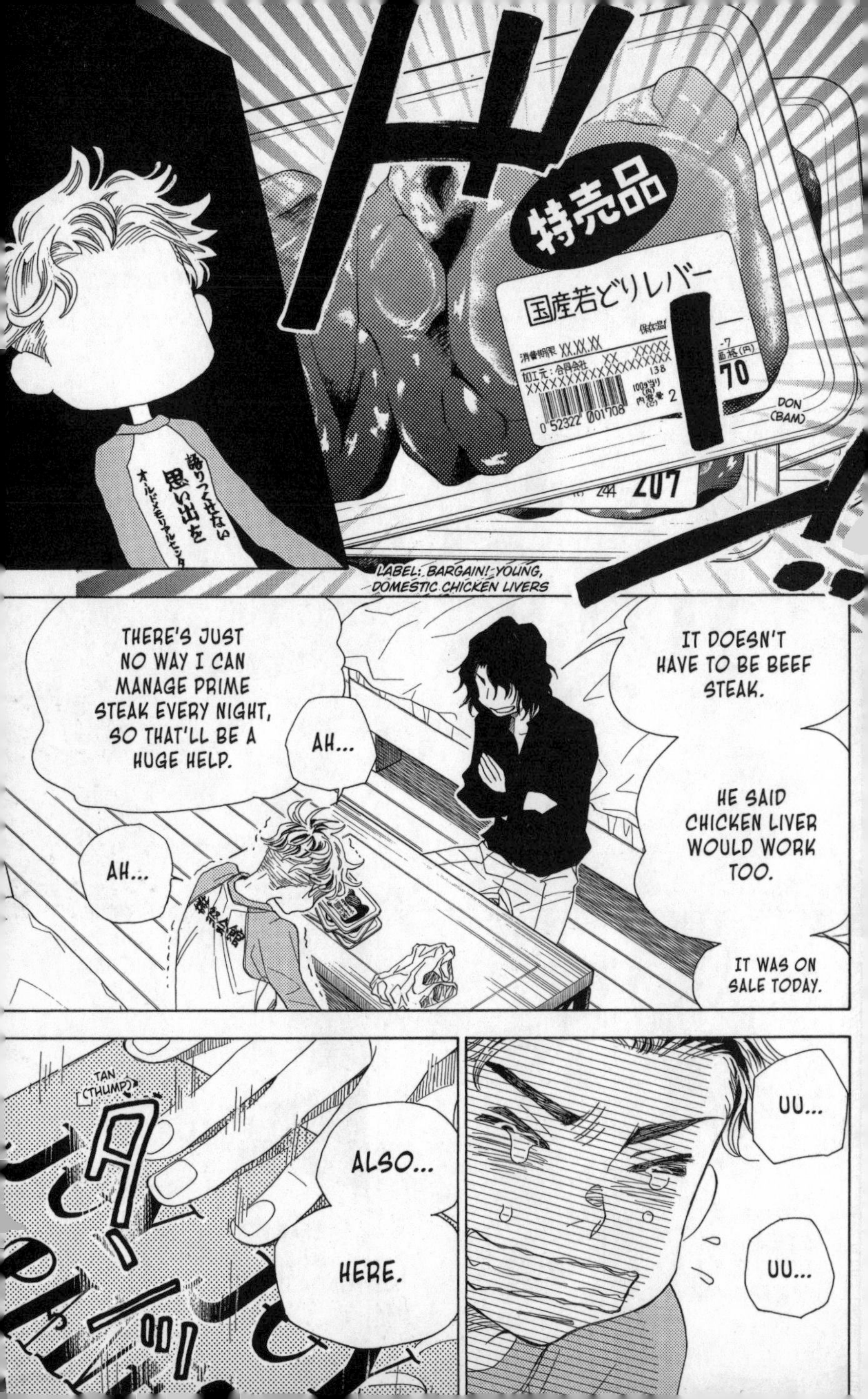
特売品
国産若どりレバー
DON
(BAM)
LABEL: BARGAIN! YOUNG, DOMESTIC CHICKEN LIVERS
語りつくせない
思い出を
IT DOESN'T HAVE TO BE BEEF STEAK.
HE SAID CHICKEN LIVER WOULD WORK TOO.
IT WAS ON SALE TODAY.
THERE'S JUST NO WAY I CAN MANAGE PRIME STEAK EVERY NIGHT, SO THAT'LL BE A HUGE HELP.
AH...
AH...
UU...
UU...
TAN
(THUMP)
ALSO...
HERE.

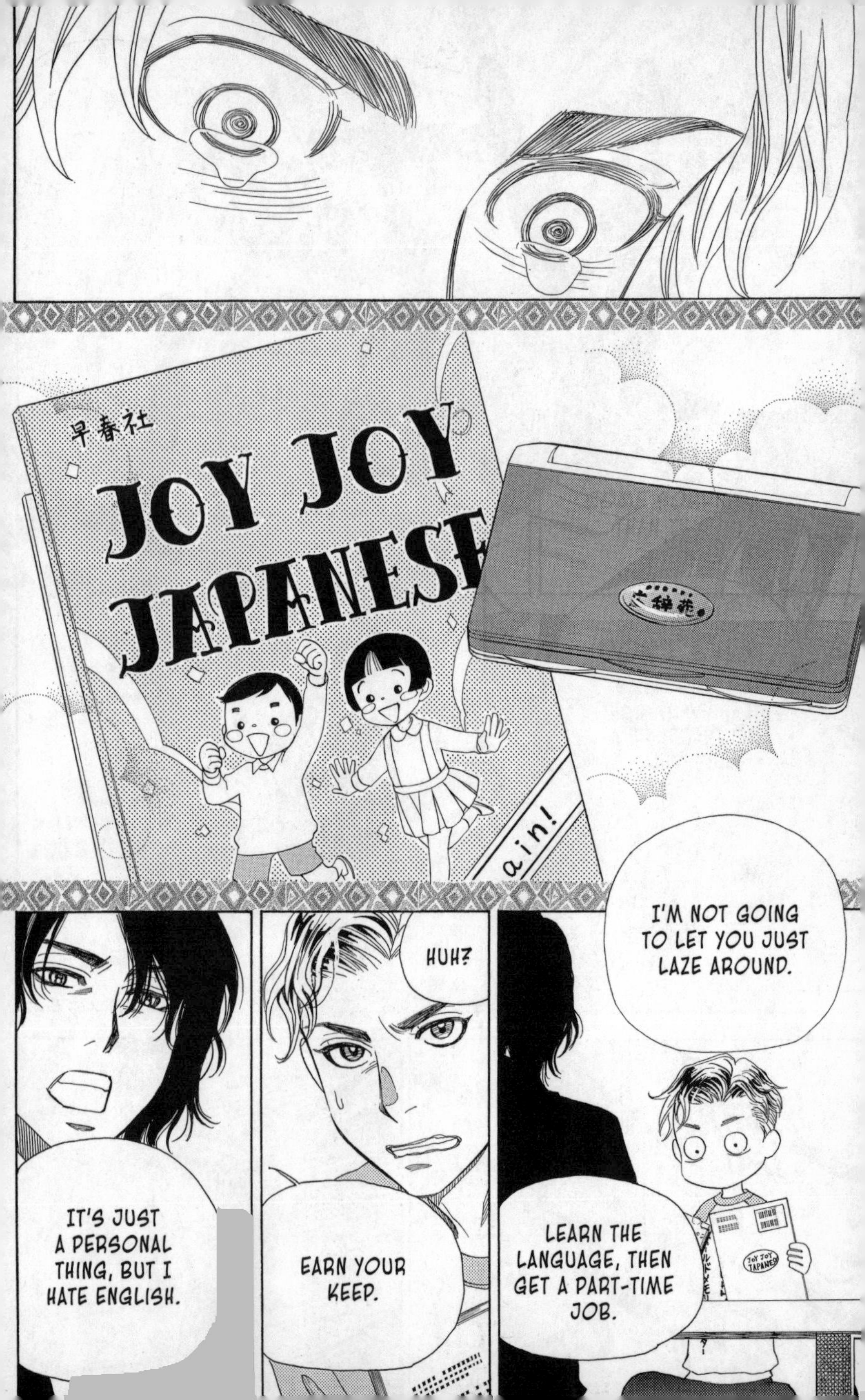
早春社
JOY JOY JAPANESE
I'M NOT GOING TO LET YOU JUST LAZE AROUND.
LEARN THE LANGUAGE, THEN GET A PART-TIME JOB.
JOY JOY JAPANESE
HUH?
EARN YOUR KEEP.
IT'S JUST A PERSONAL THING, BUT I HATE ENGLISH.

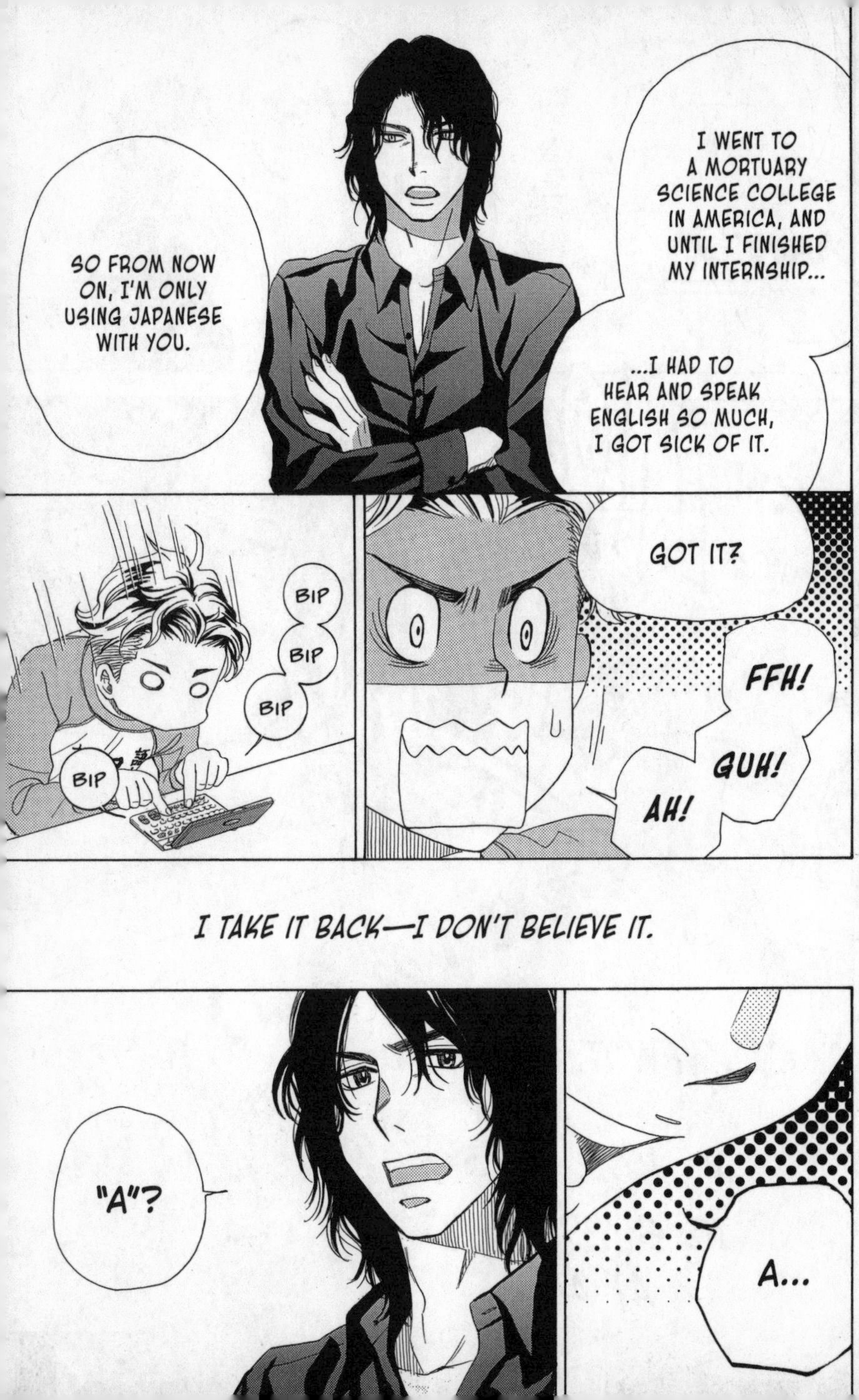
I WENT TO A MORTUARY SCIENCE COLLEGE IN AMERICA, AND UNTIL I FINISHED MY INTERNSHIP...
...I HAD TO HEAR AND SPEAK ENGLISH SO MUCH, I GOT SICK OF IT.
SO FROM NOW ON, I'M ONLY USING JAPANESE WITH YOU.
GOT IT?
FFH!
GUH!
AH!
BIP
BIP
BIP
BIP
I TAKE IT BACK—I DON'T BELIEVE IT.
A...
"A"?

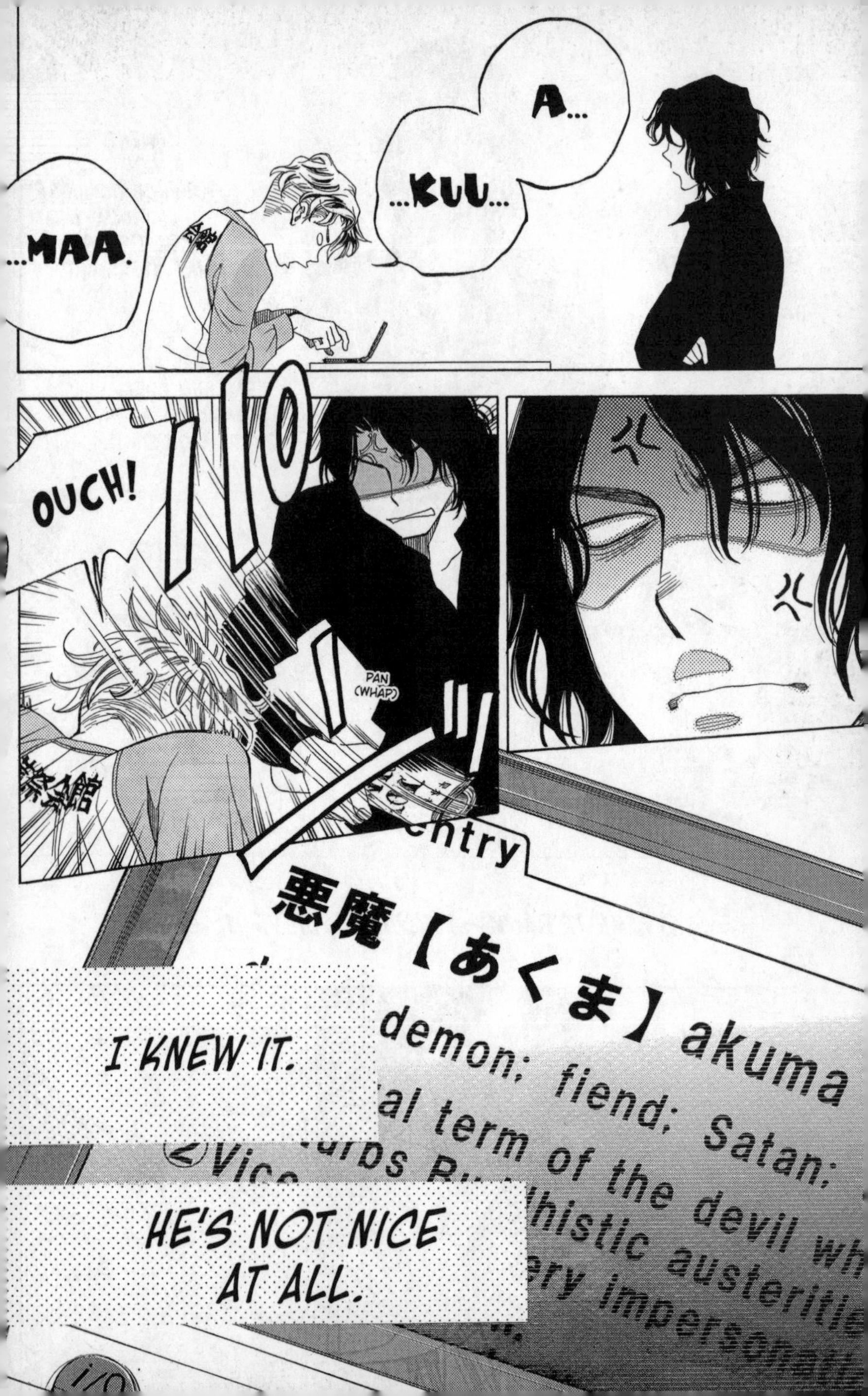
A...
...KUU...
...MAA.
OUCH!
PAN (WHAP)
entry
悪魔【あくま】akuma
demon; fiend; Satan;
I KNEW IT.
HE'S NOT NICE AT ALL.

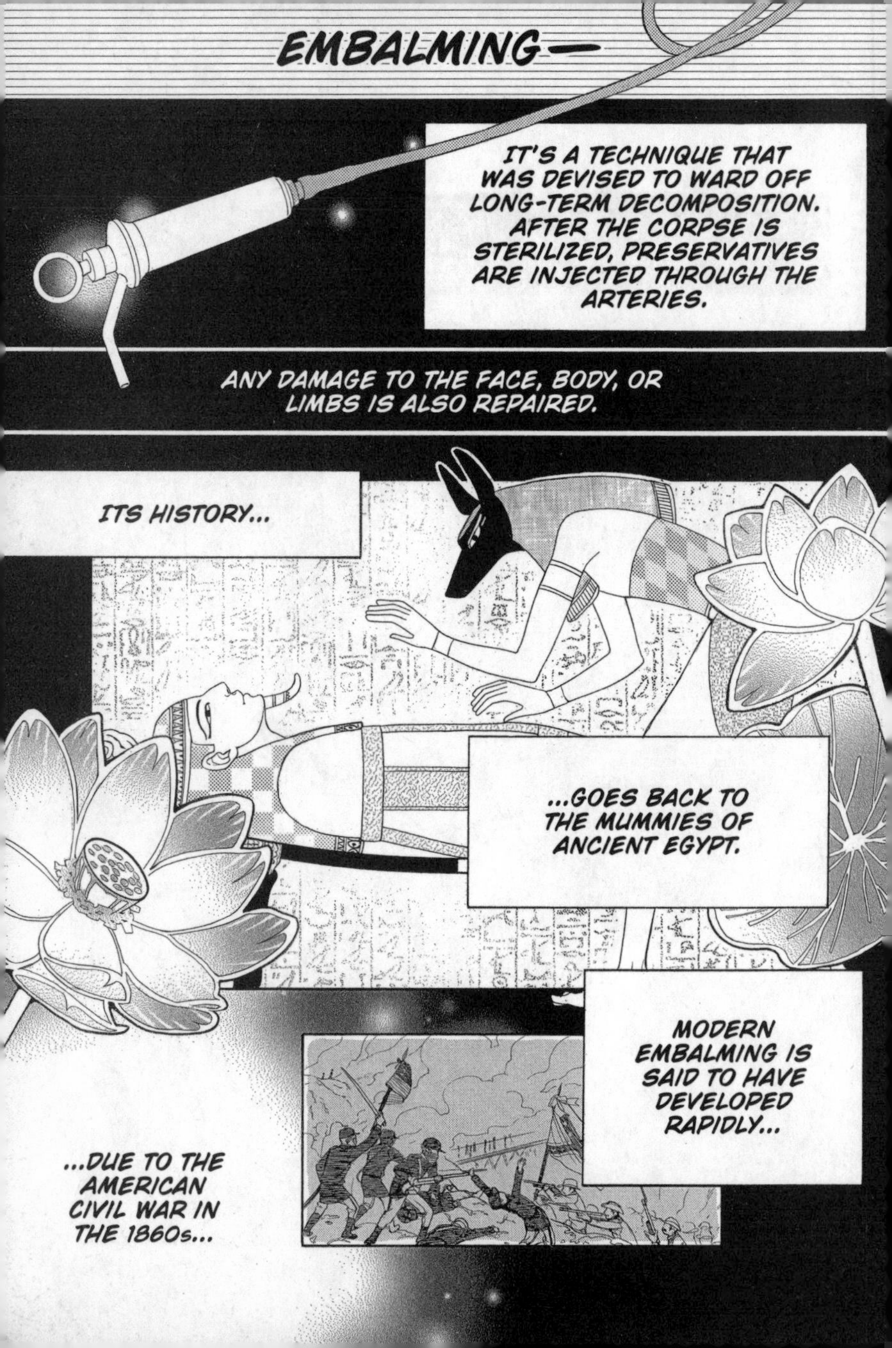
EMBALMING—
IT'S A TECHNIQUE THAT WAS DEVISED TO WARD OFF LONG-TERM DECOMPOSITION. AFTER THE CORPSE IS STERILIZED, PRESERVATIVES ARE INJECTED THROUGH THE ARTERIES.
ANY DAMAGE TO THE FACE, BODY, OR LIMBS IS ALSO REPAIRED.
ITS HISTORY...
...GOES BACK TO THE MUMMIES OF ANCIENT EGYPT.
MODERN EMBALMING IS SAID TO HAVE DEVELOPED RAPIDLY...
...DUE TO THE AMERICAN CIVIL WAR IN THE 1860s...

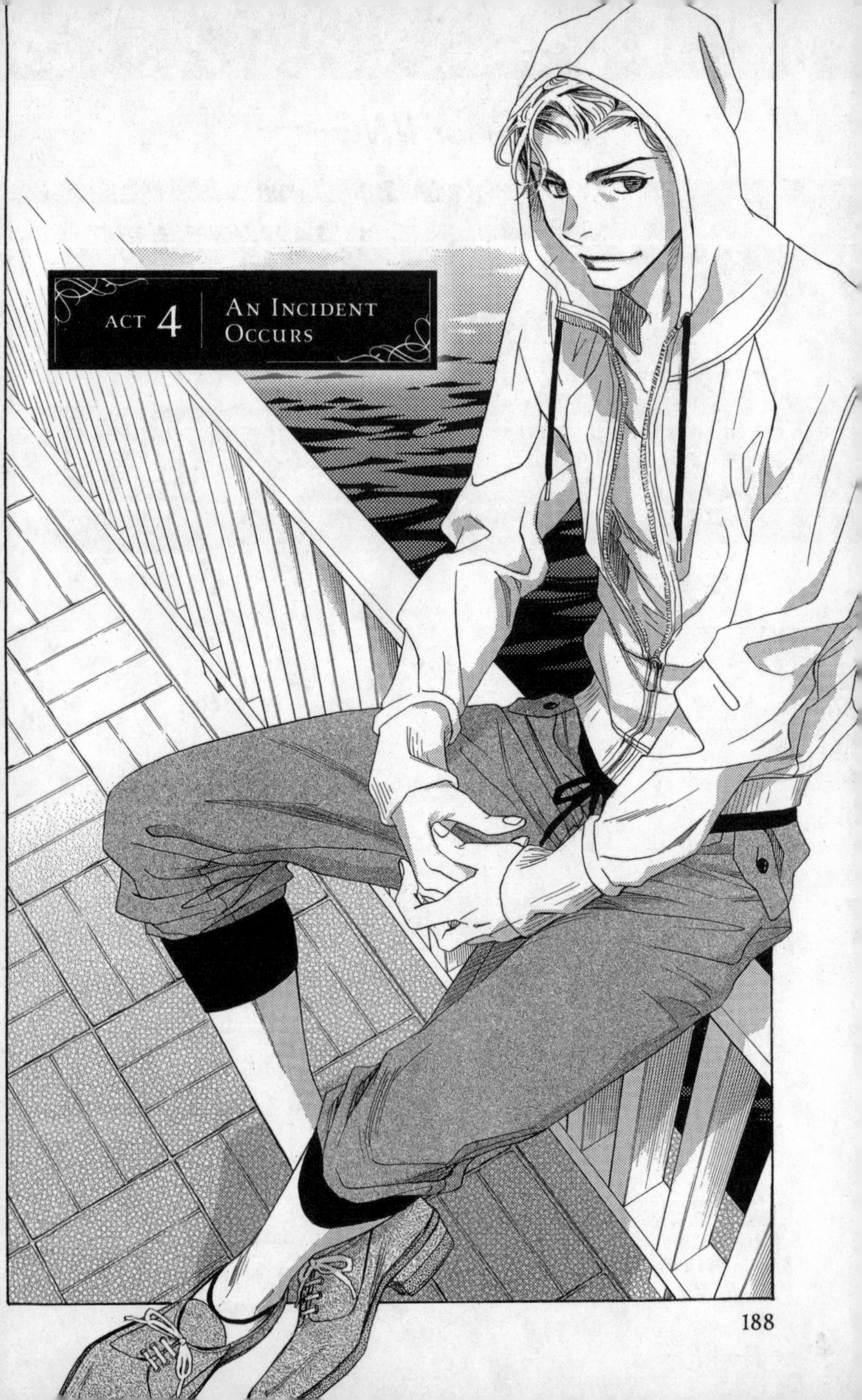
ACT 4
An Incident Occurs

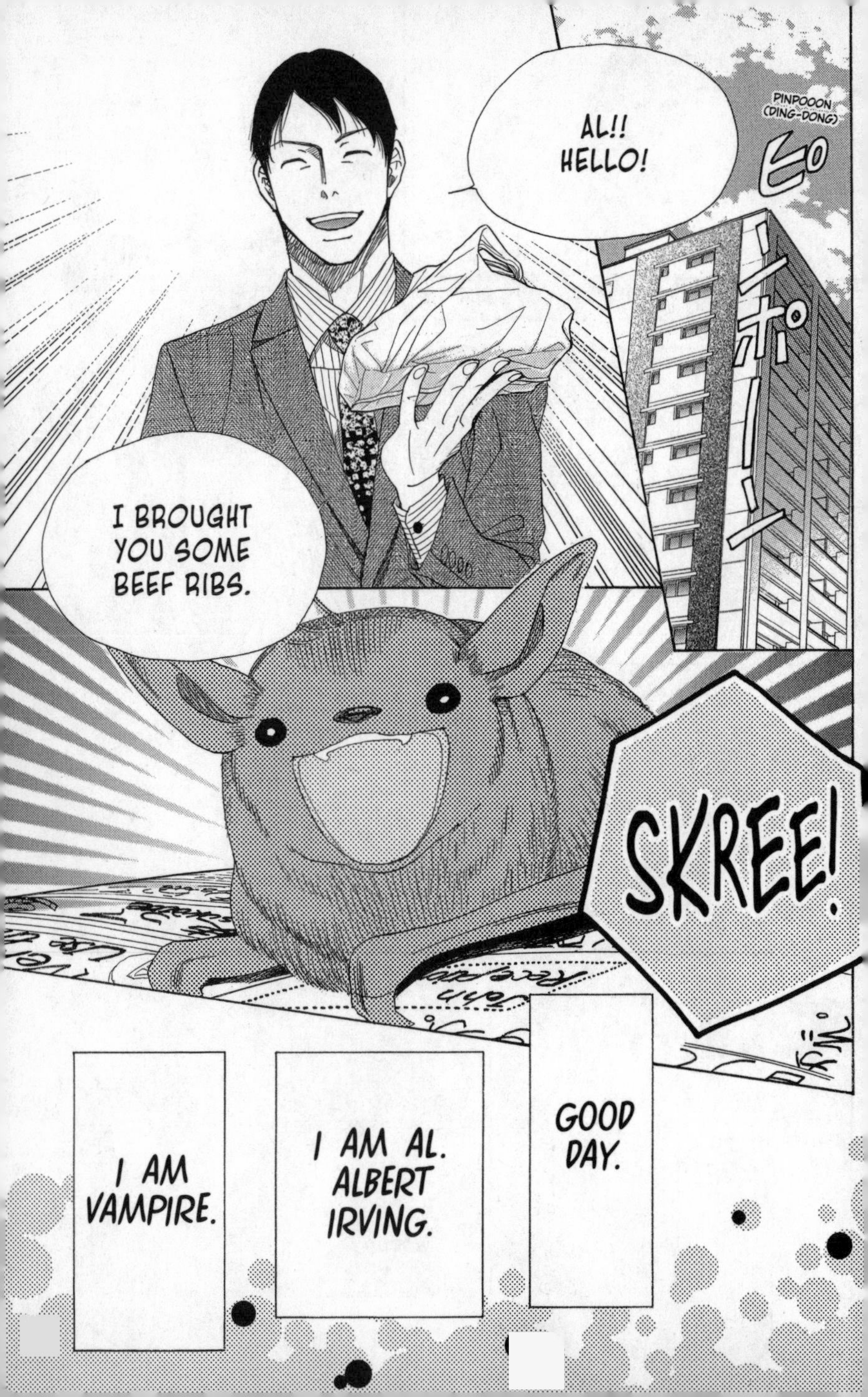
PINPOOON (DING-DONG)
ピンポーン
AL!! HELLO!
I BROUGHT YOU SOME BEEF RIBS.
SKREE!
GOOD DAY.
I AM AL. ALBERT IRVING.
I AM VAMPIRE.

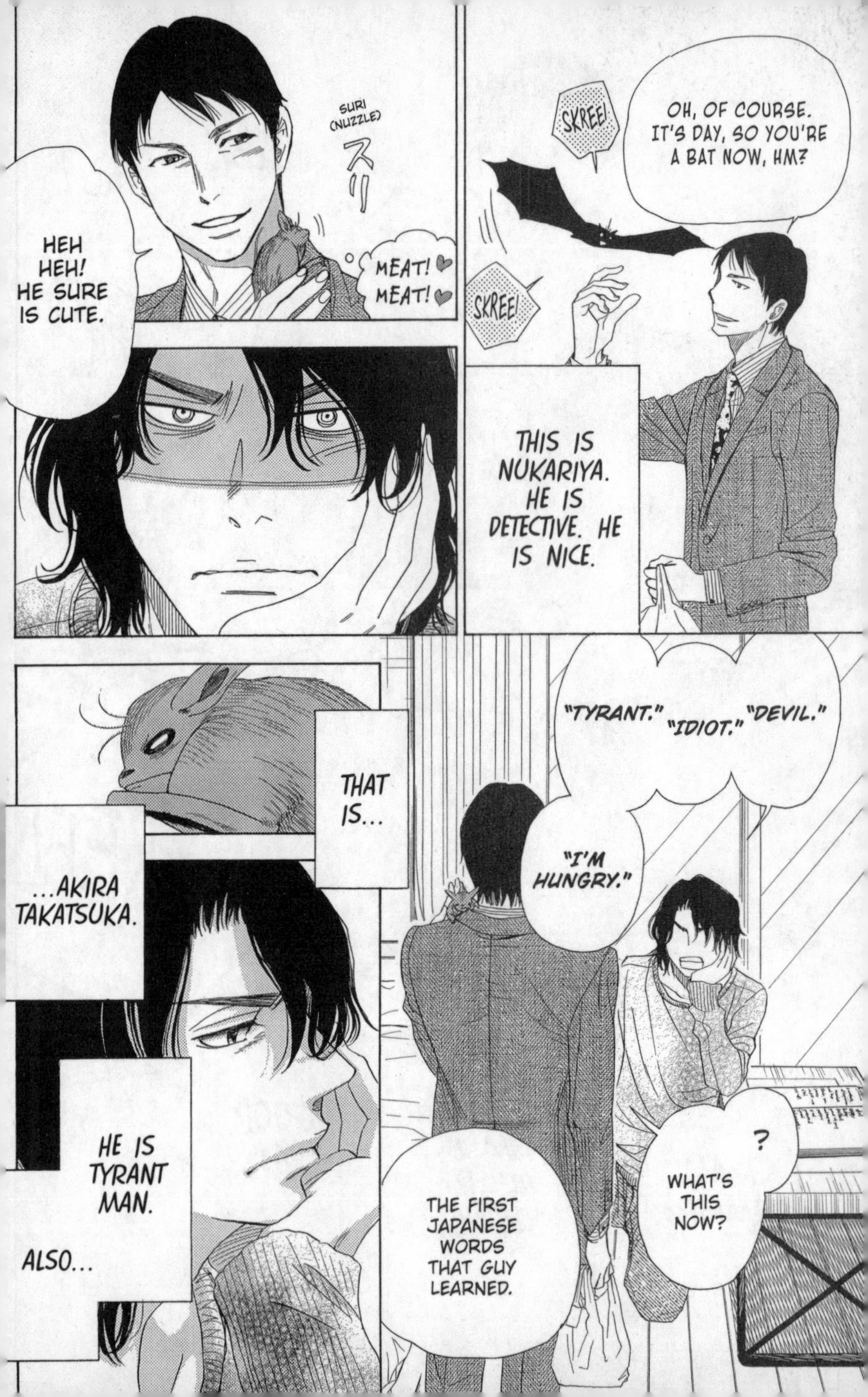
SKREE!
OH, OF COURSE. IT'S DAY, SO YOU'RE A BAT NOW, HM?
SKREE!
THIS IS NUKARIYA. HE IS DETECTIVE. HE IS NICE.
SURI (NUZZLE)
スリ
MEAT! MEAT!
HEH HEH! HE SURE IS CUTE.
"TYRANT." "IDIOT." "DEVIL."
"I'M HUNGRY."
?
WHAT'S THIS NOW?
THE FIRST JAPANESE WORDS THAT GUY LEARNED.
THAT IS...
...AKIRA TAKATSUKA.
HE IS TYRANT MAN.
ALSO...

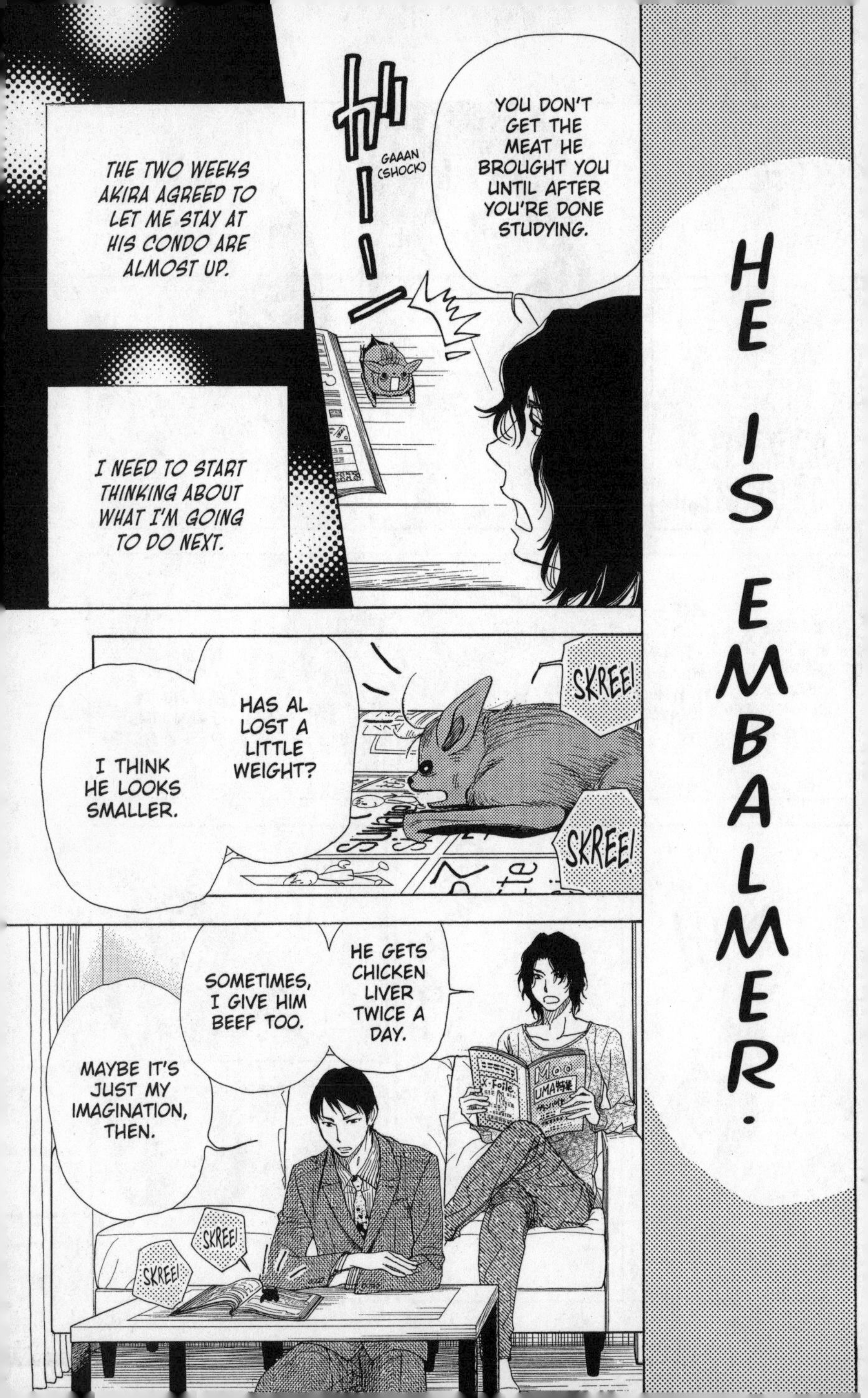
HE IS EMBALMER.
YOU DON'T GET THE MEAT HE BROUGHT YOU UNTIL AFTER YOU'RE DONE STUDYING.
GAAAN (SHOCK)
THE TWO WEEKS AKIRA AGREED TO LET ME STAY AT HIS CONDO ARE ALMOST UP.
I NEED TO START THINKING ABOUT WHAT I'M GOING TO DO NEXT.
SKREE!
SKREE!
HAS AL LOST A LITTLE WEIGHT?
I THINK HE LOOKS SMALLER.
HE GETS CHICKEN LIVER TWICE A DAY.
SOMETIMES, I GIVE HIM BEEF TOO.
MAYBE IT'S JUST MY IMAGINATION, THEN.
SKREE!
SKREE!

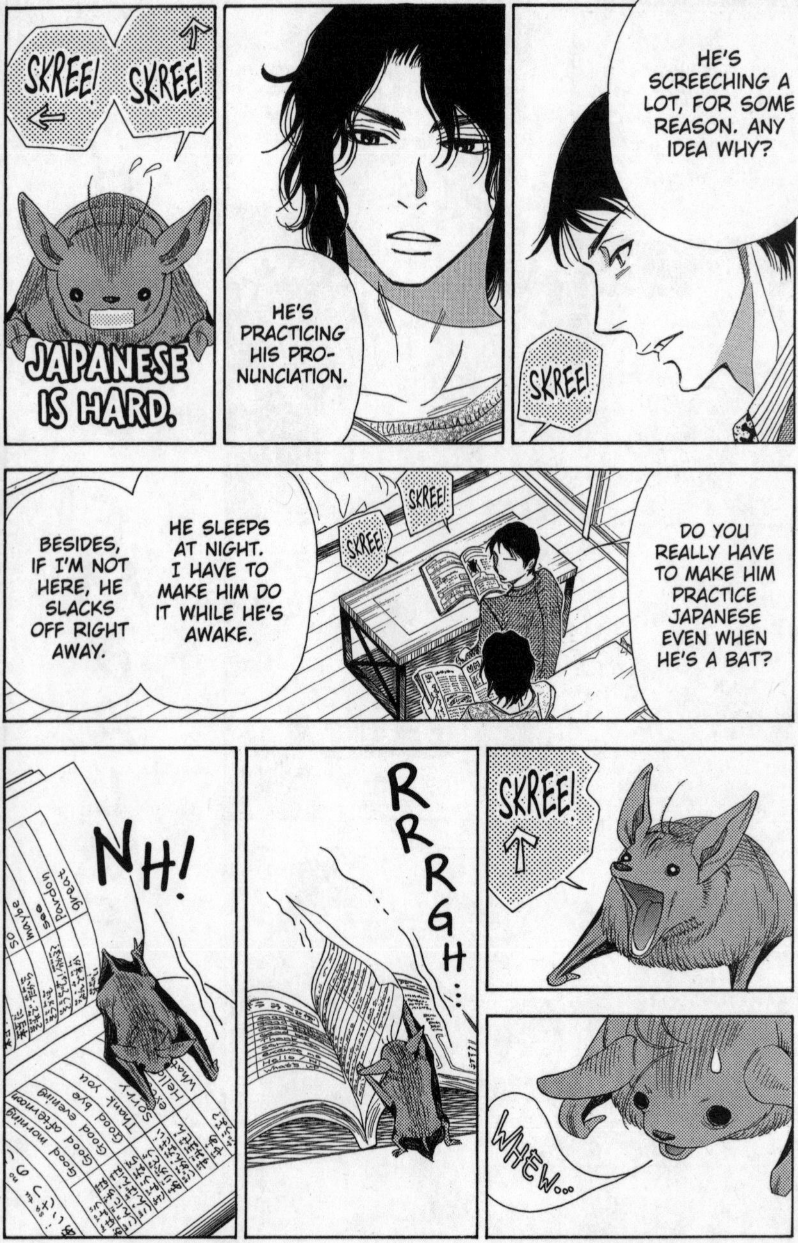
HE'S SCREECHING A LOT, FOR SOME REASON. ANY IDEA WHY?
SKREE!
HE'S PRACTICING HIS PRO-NUNCIATION.
SKREE!
SKREE!
JAPANESE IS HARD.
DO YOU REALLY HAVE TO MAKE HIM PRACTICE JAPANESE EVEN WHEN HE'S A BAT?
SKREE!
SKREE!
HE SLEEPS AT NIGHT. I HAVE TO MAKE HIM DO IT WHILE HE'S AWAKE.
BESIDES, IF I'M NOT HERE, HE SLACKS OFF RIGHT AWAY.
SKREE!
WHEW...
RRRGH...
NH!

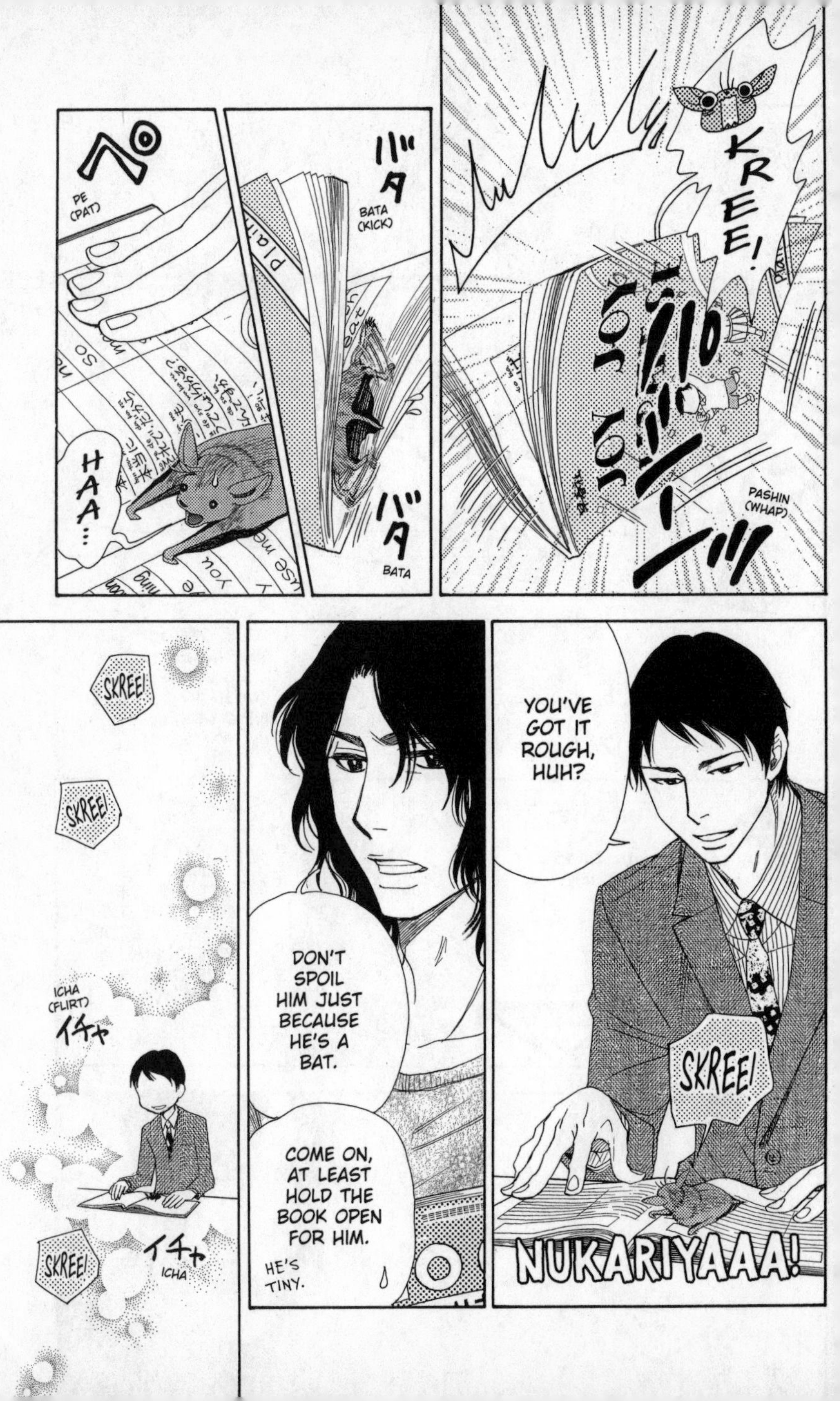
KREE!
パシンッ
PASHIN (WHAP)
バタ
BATA (KICK)
バタ
BATA
ペ
PE (PAT)
HAA...
YOU'VE GOT IT ROUGH, HUH?
SKREE!
NUKARIYAAA!
DON'T SPOIL HIM JUST BECAUSE HE'S A BAT.
COME ON, AT LEAST HOLD THE BOOK OPEN FOR HIM.
HE'S TINY.
SKREE!
SKREE!
イチャ
ICHA (FLIRT)
イチャ
ICHA
SKREE!

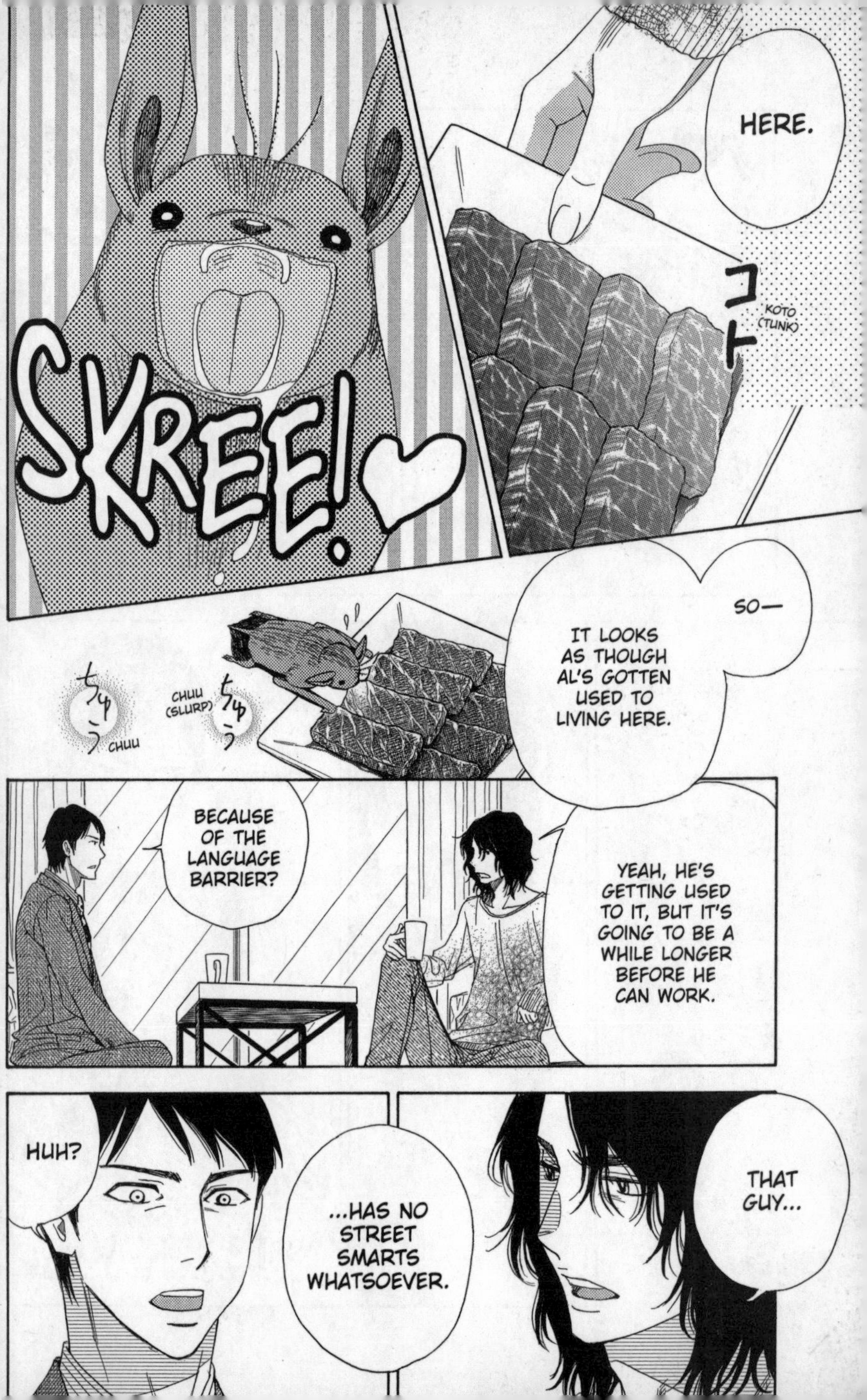
HERE.
コト KOTO (TUNK)
SKREE!
SO—
IT LOOKS AS THOUGH AL'S GOTTEN USED TO LIVING HERE.
ちゅう CHUU (SLURP)
ちゅう CHUU
YEAH, HE'S GETTING USED TO IT, BUT IT'S GOING TO BE A WHILE LONGER BEFORE HE CAN WORK.
BECAUSE OF THE LANGUAGE BARRIER?
THAT GUY...
...HAS NO STREET SMARTS WHATSOEVER.
HUH?

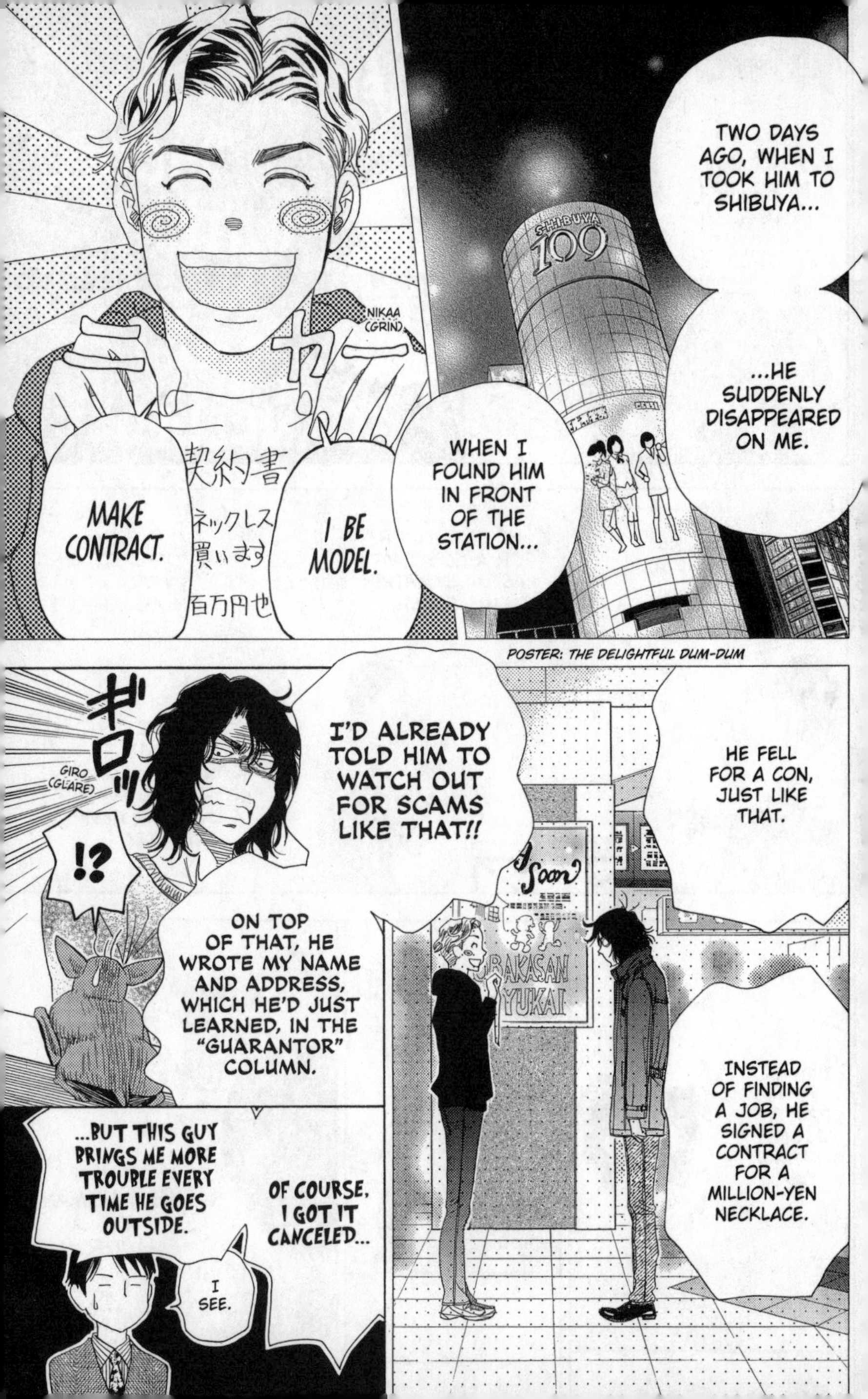
TWO DAYS AGO, WHEN I TOOK HIM TO SHIBUYA...
...HE SUDDENLY DISAPPEARED ON ME.
SHIBUYA 109
WHEN I FOUND HIM IN FRONT OF THE STATION...
NIKAA (GRIN)
I BE MODEL.
契約書
ネックレス
買います
百万円也
MAKE CONTRACT.
POSTER: THE DELIGHTFUL DUM-DUM
HE FELL FOR A CON, JUST LIKE THAT.
INSTEAD OF FINDING A JOB, HE SIGNED A CONTRACT FOR A MILLION-YEN NECKLACE.
Soon
BAKASAN YUKAI
I'D ALREADY TOLD HIM TO WATCH OUT FOR SCAMS LIKE THAT!!
GIRO (GLARE)
!?
ON TOP OF THAT, HE WROTE MY NAME AND ADDRESS, WHICH HE'D JUST LEARNED, IN THE "GUARANTOR" COLUMN.
OF COURSE, I GOT IT CANCELED...
...BUT THIS GUY BRINGS ME MORE TROUBLE EVERY TIME HE GOES OUTSIDE.
I SEE.

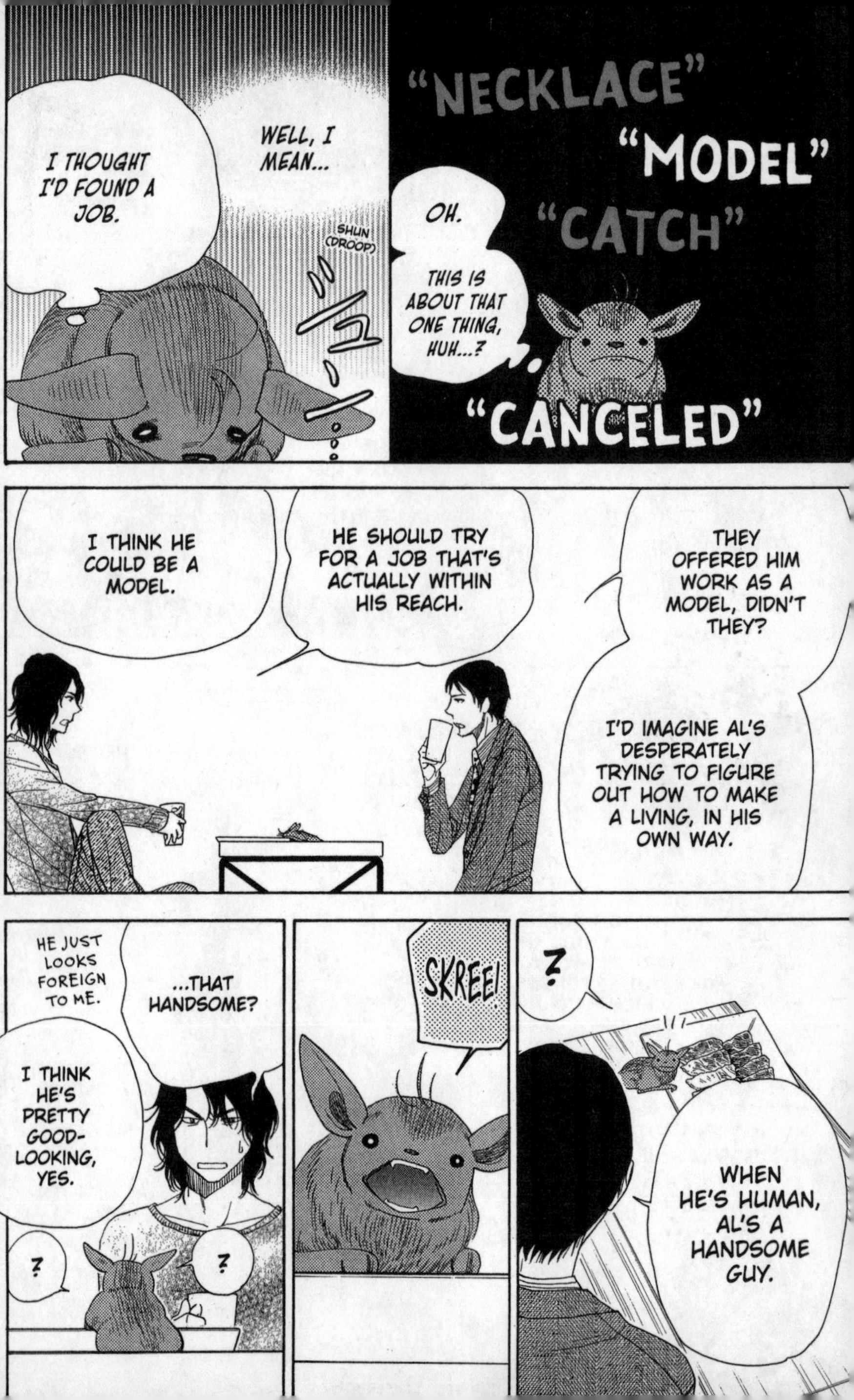
"NECKLACE"
"MODEL"
"CATCH"
OH.
THIS IS ABOUT THAT ONE THING, HUH...?
"CANCELED"
WELL, I MEAN...
I THOUGHT I'D FOUND A JOB.
SHUN (DROOP)
THEY OFFERED HIM WORK AS A MODEL, DIDN'T THEY?
I'D IMAGINE AL'S DESPERATELY TRYING TO FIGURE OUT HOW TO MAKE A LIVING, IN HIS OWN WAY.
HE SHOULD TRY FOR A JOB THAT'S ACTUALLY WITHIN HIS REACH.
I THINK HE COULD BE A MODEL.
?
WHEN HE'S HUMAN, AL'S A HANDSOME GUY.
SKREE!
...THAT HANDSOME?
HE JUST LOOKS FOREIGN TO ME.
I THINK HE'S PRETTY GOOD-LOOKING, YES.
?
?

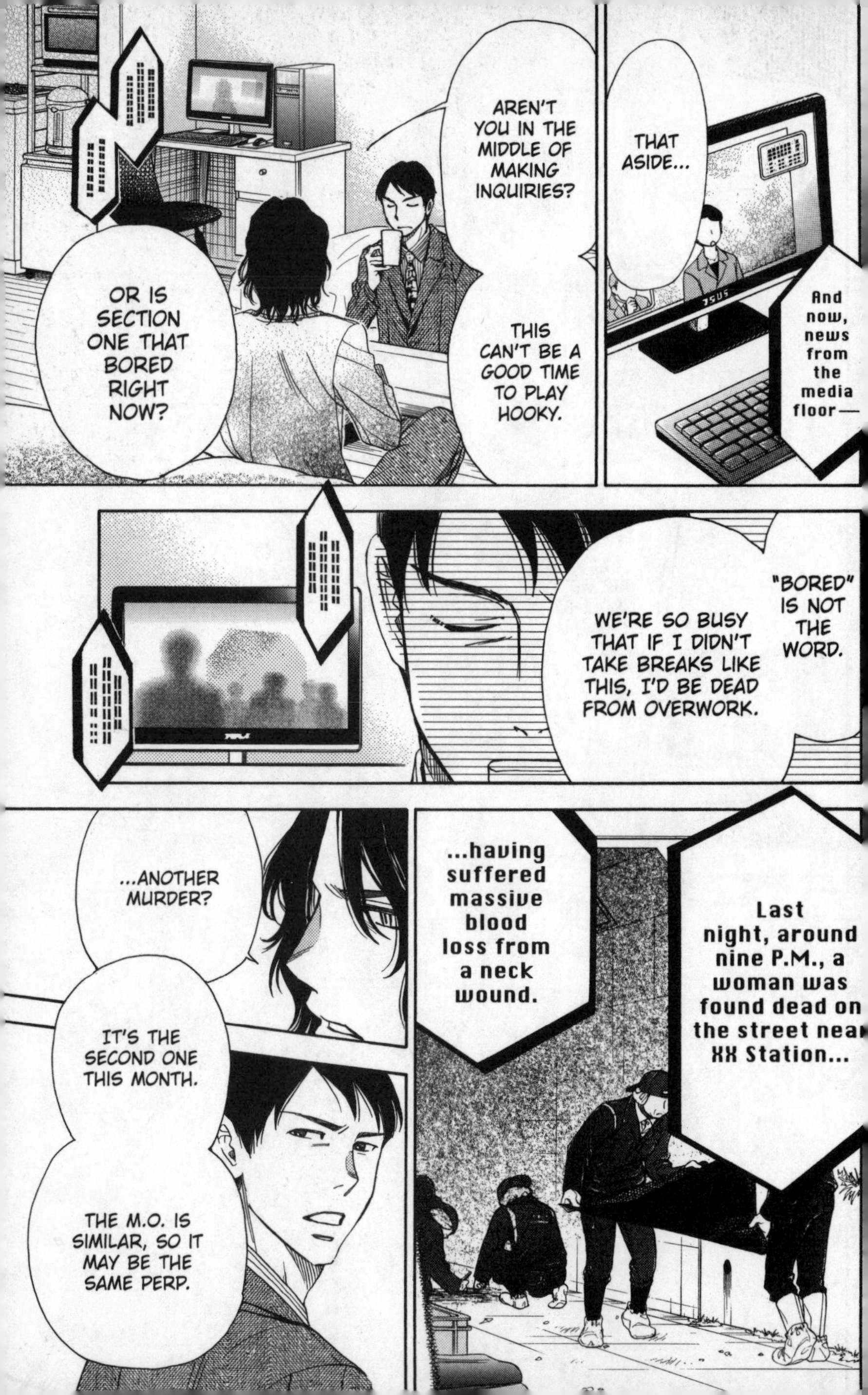
And now, news from the media floor—
THAT ASIDE...
AREN'T YOU IN THE MIDDLE OF MAKING INQUIRIES?
THIS CAN'T BE A GOOD TIME TO PLAY HOOKY.
OR IS SECTION ONE THAT BORED RIGHT NOW?
"BORED" IS NOT THE WORD.
WE'RE SO BUSY THAT IF I DIDN'T TAKE BREAKS LIKE THIS, I'D BE DEAD FROM OVERWORK.
Last night, around nine P.M., a woman was found dead on the street nea
XX Station...
...having suffered massive blood loss from a neck wound.
...ANOTHER MURDER?
IT'S THE SECOND ONE THIS MONTH.
THE M.O. IS SIMILAR, SO IT MAY BE THE SAME PERP.

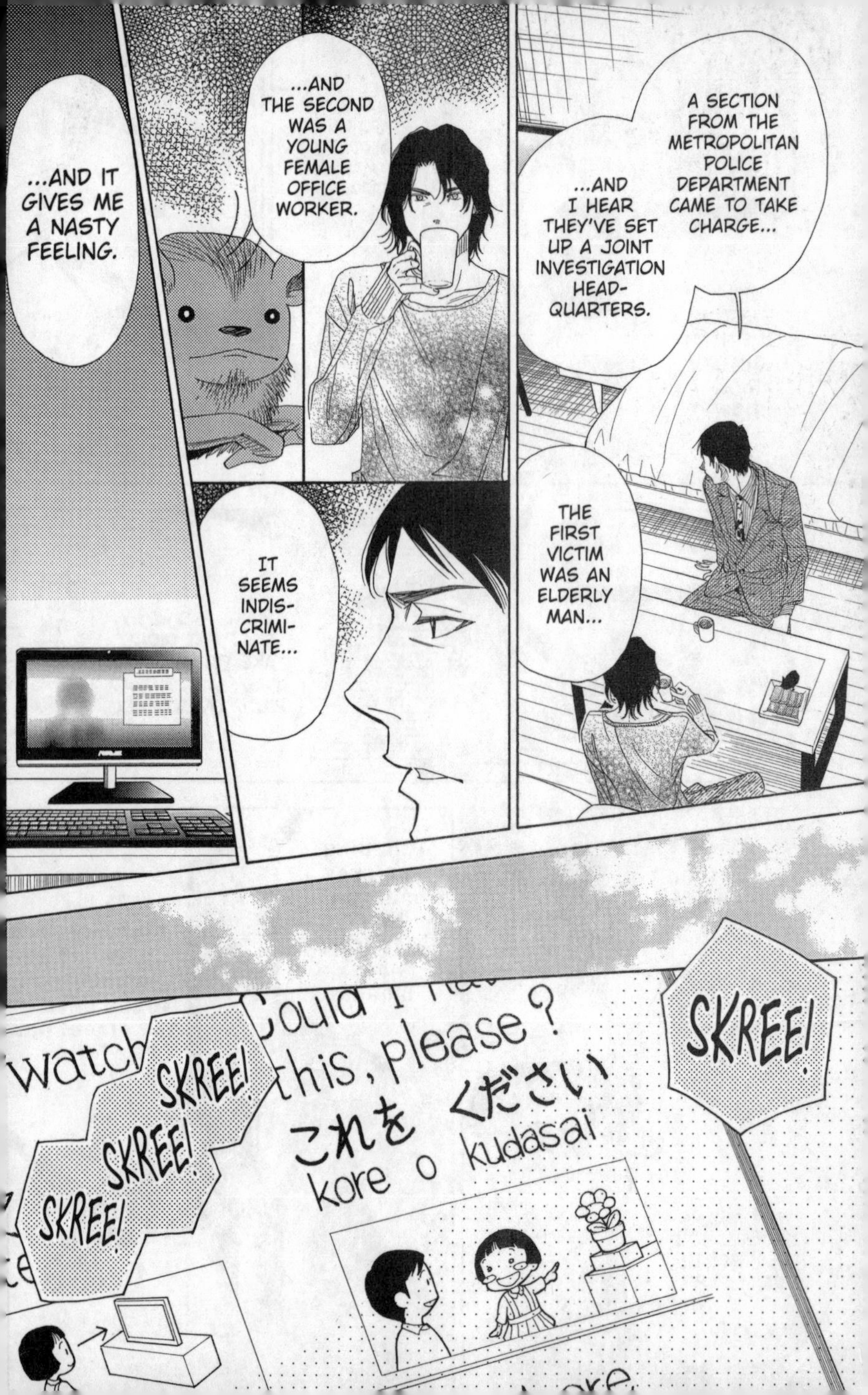
A SECTION FROM THE METROPOLITAN POLICE DEPARTMENT CAME TO TAKE CHARGE...
...AND I HEAR THEY'VE SET UP A JOINT INVESTIGATION HEAD-QUARTERS.
THE FIRST VICTIM WAS AN ELDERLY MAN...
...AND THE SECOND WAS A YOUNG FEMALE OFFICE WORKER.
IT SEEMS INDIS-CRIMI-NATE...
...AND IT GIVES ME A NASTY FEELING.
SKREE!
SKREE!
SKREE!
SKREE!
this, please?
これを ください
kore o kudasai

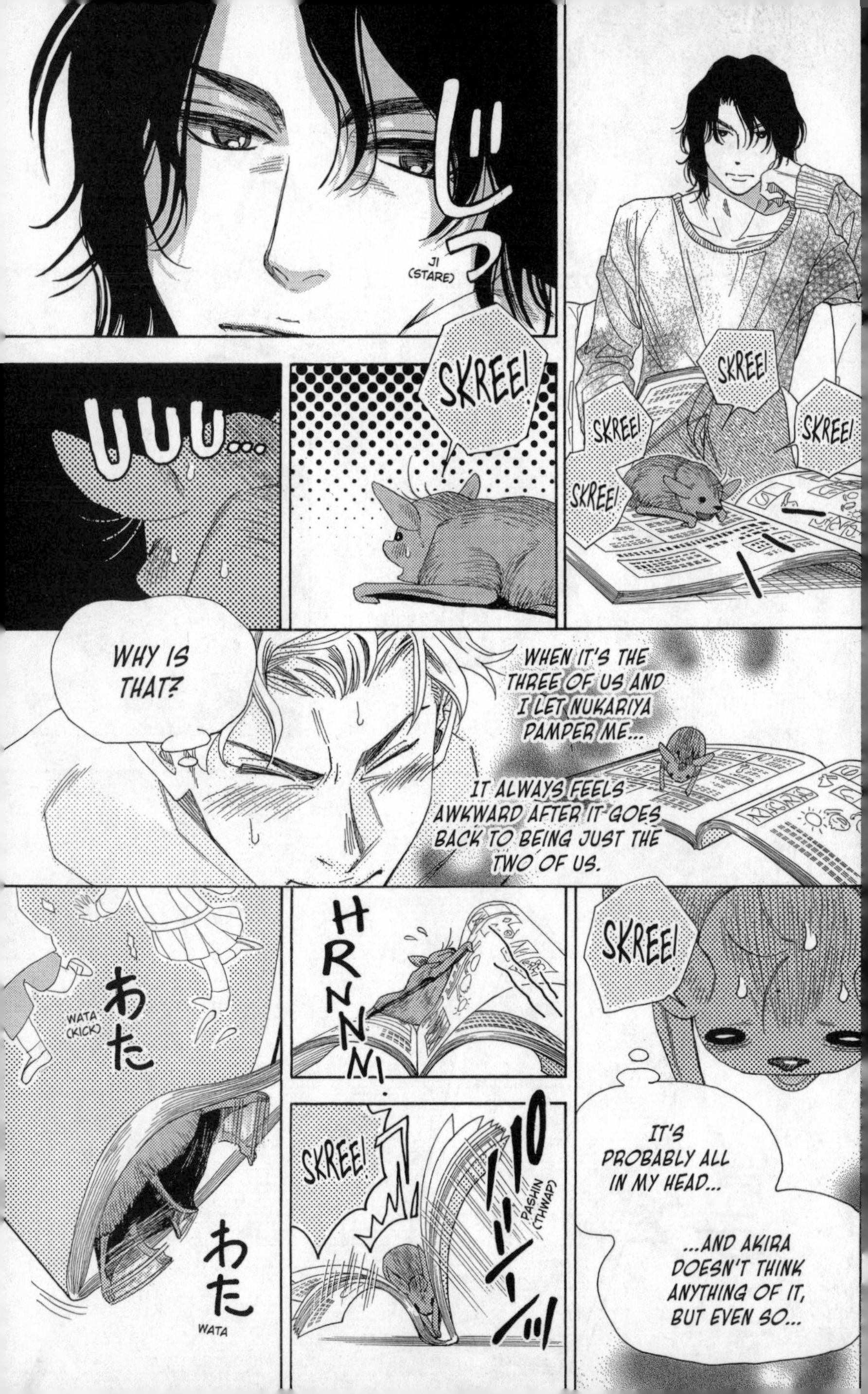
SKREE!
SKREE!
SKREE!
SKREE!
JI (STARE)
SKREE!
UUU...
WHEN IT'S THE THREE OF US AND I LET NUKARIYA PAMPER ME...
IT ALWAYS FEELS AWKWARD AFTER IT GOES BACK TO BEING JUST THE TWO OF US.
WHY IS THAT?
SKREE!
IT'S PROBABLY ALL IN MY HEAD...
...AND AKIRA DOESN'T THINK ANYTHING OF IT, BUT EVEN SO...
HRNNN!
SKREE!
PASHIN (THWAP)
WATA (KICK)
WATA

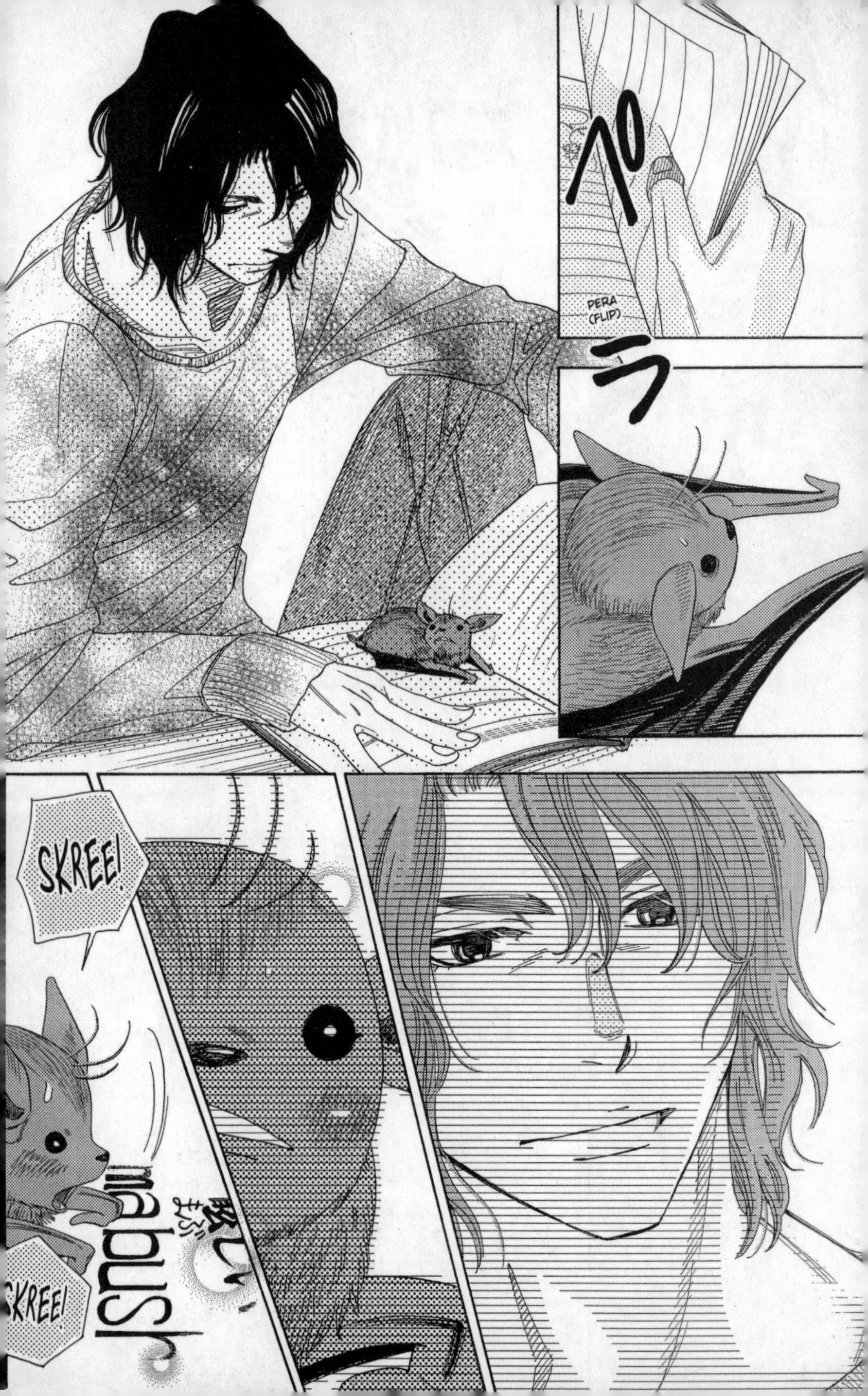

ペラ
PERA (FLIP)
SKREE!
SKREE!
眩しい
mabushi

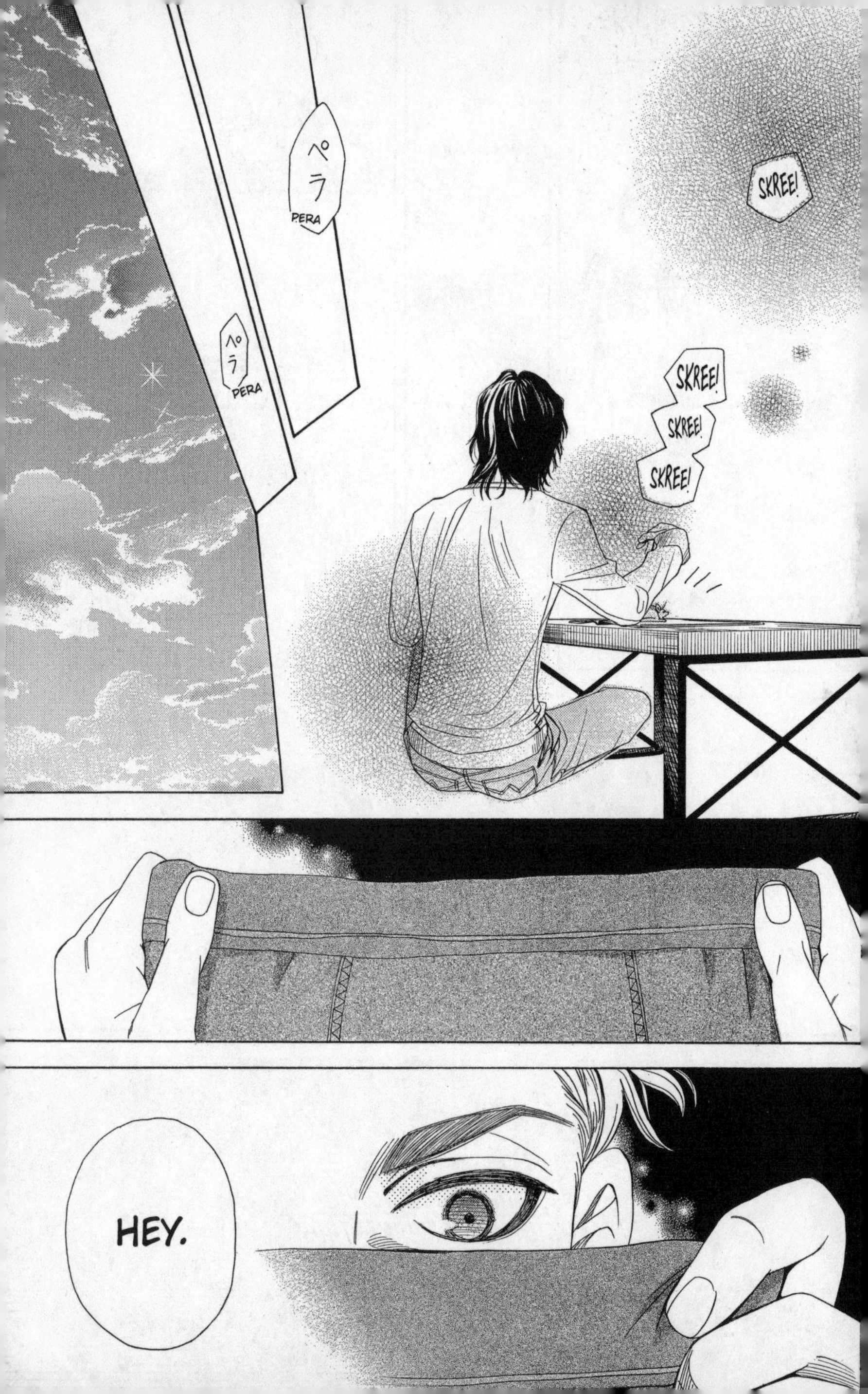
SKREE!
SKREE!
SKREE!
SKREE!
ペラ
PERA
ペラ
PERA
HEY.

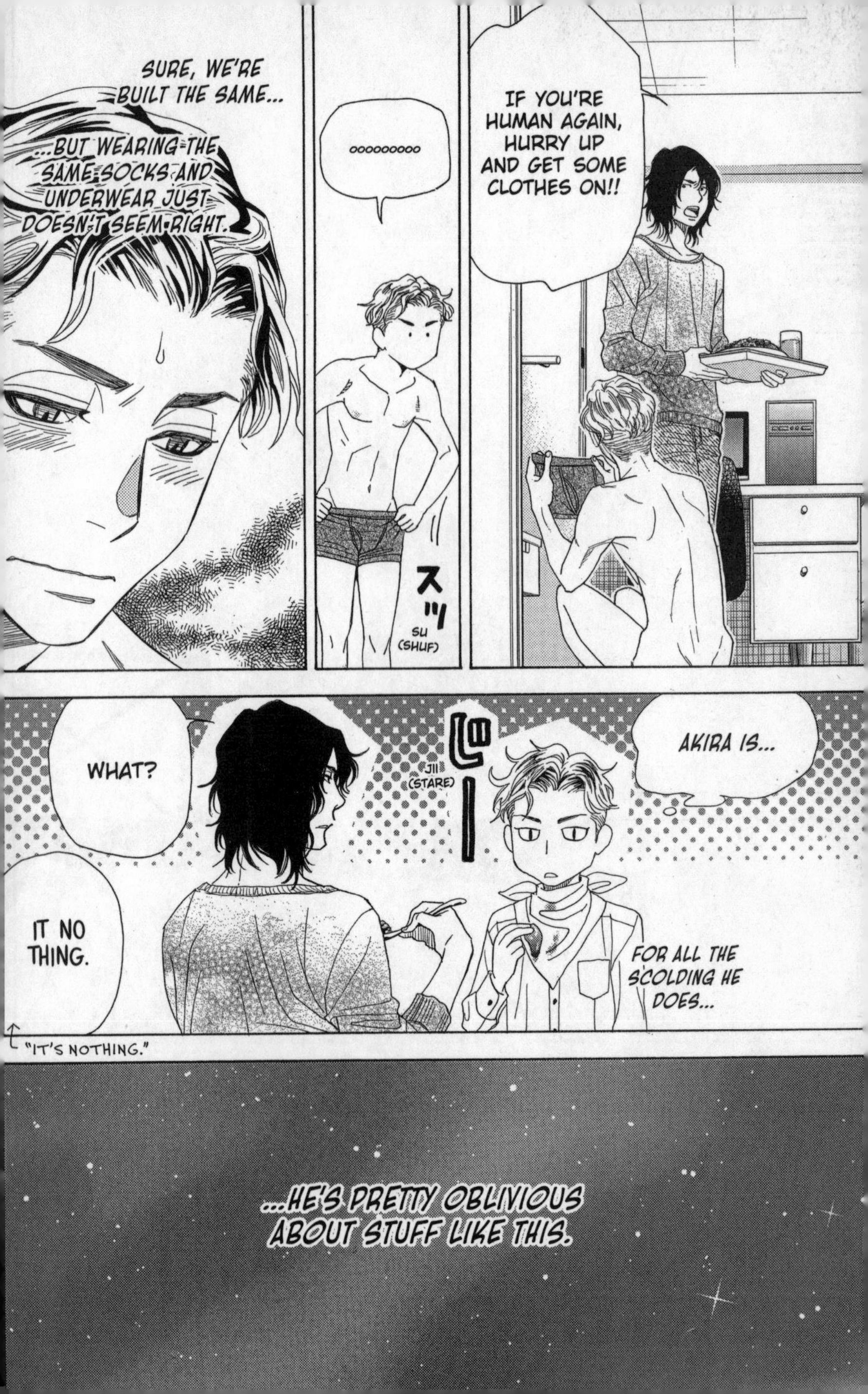
IF YOU'RE HUMAN AGAIN, HURRY UP AND GET SOME CLOTHES ON!!
ooooooooo
スッ
SU (SHUF)
SURE, WE'RE BUILT THE SAME...
...BUT WEARING THE SAME SOCKS AND UNDERWEAR JUST DOESN'T SEEM RIGHT.
AKIRA IS...
FOR ALL THE SCOLDING HE DOES...
じー
JII (STARE)
WHAT?
IT NO THING.
"IT'S NOTHING."
...HE'S PRETTY OBLIVIOUS ABOUT STUFF LIKE THIS.

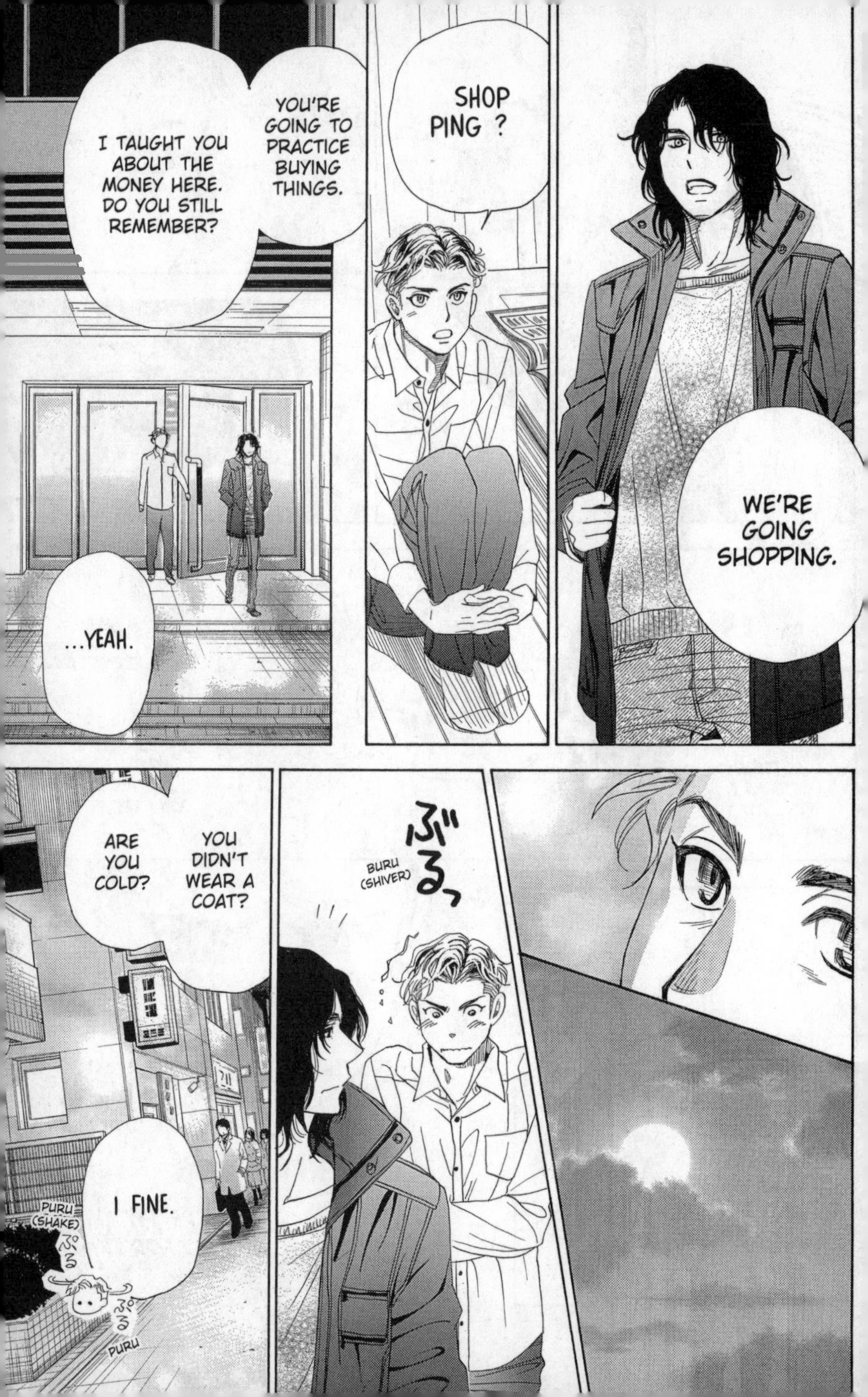
WE'RE GOING SHOPPING.
SHOP PING ?
YOU'RE GOING TO PRACTICE BUYING THINGS.
I TAUGHT YOU ABOUT THE MONEY HERE. DO YOU STILL REMEMBER?
...YEAH.
ぶるっ
BURU (SHIVER)
YOU DIDN'T WEAR A COAT?
ARE YOU COLD?
I FINE.
PURU (SHAKE)
ぷる
ぷる
PURU

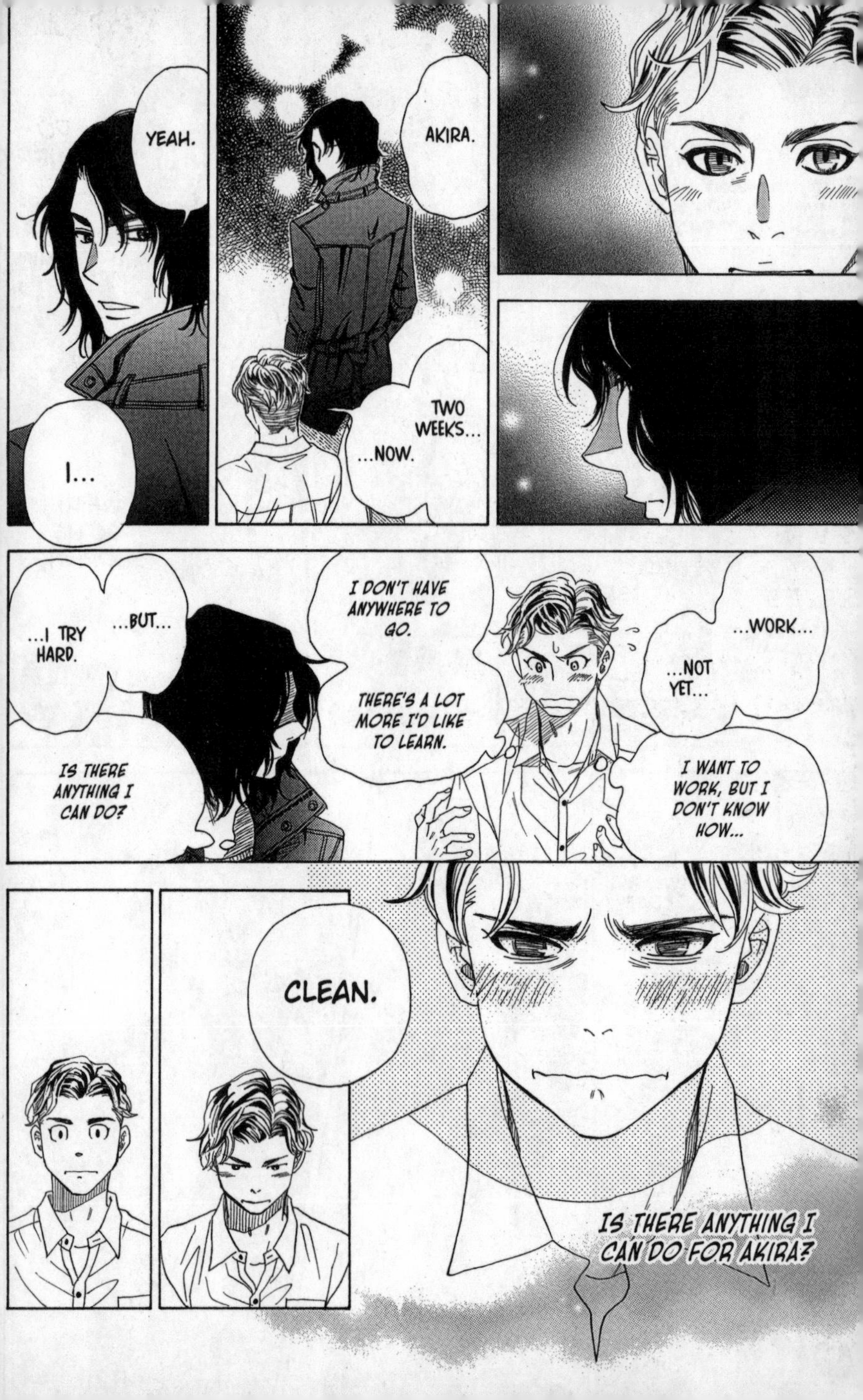
AKIRA.
TWO WEEKS...
...NOW.
YEAH.
I...
...WORK...
...NOT YET...
I WANT TO WORK, BUT I DON'T KNOW HOW...
I DON'T HAVE ANYWHERE TO GO.
THERE'S A LOT MORE I'D LIKE TO LEARN.
...BUT...
...I TRY HARD.
IS THERE ANYTHING I CAN DO?
IS THERE ANYTHING I CAN DO FOR AKIRA?
CLEAN.

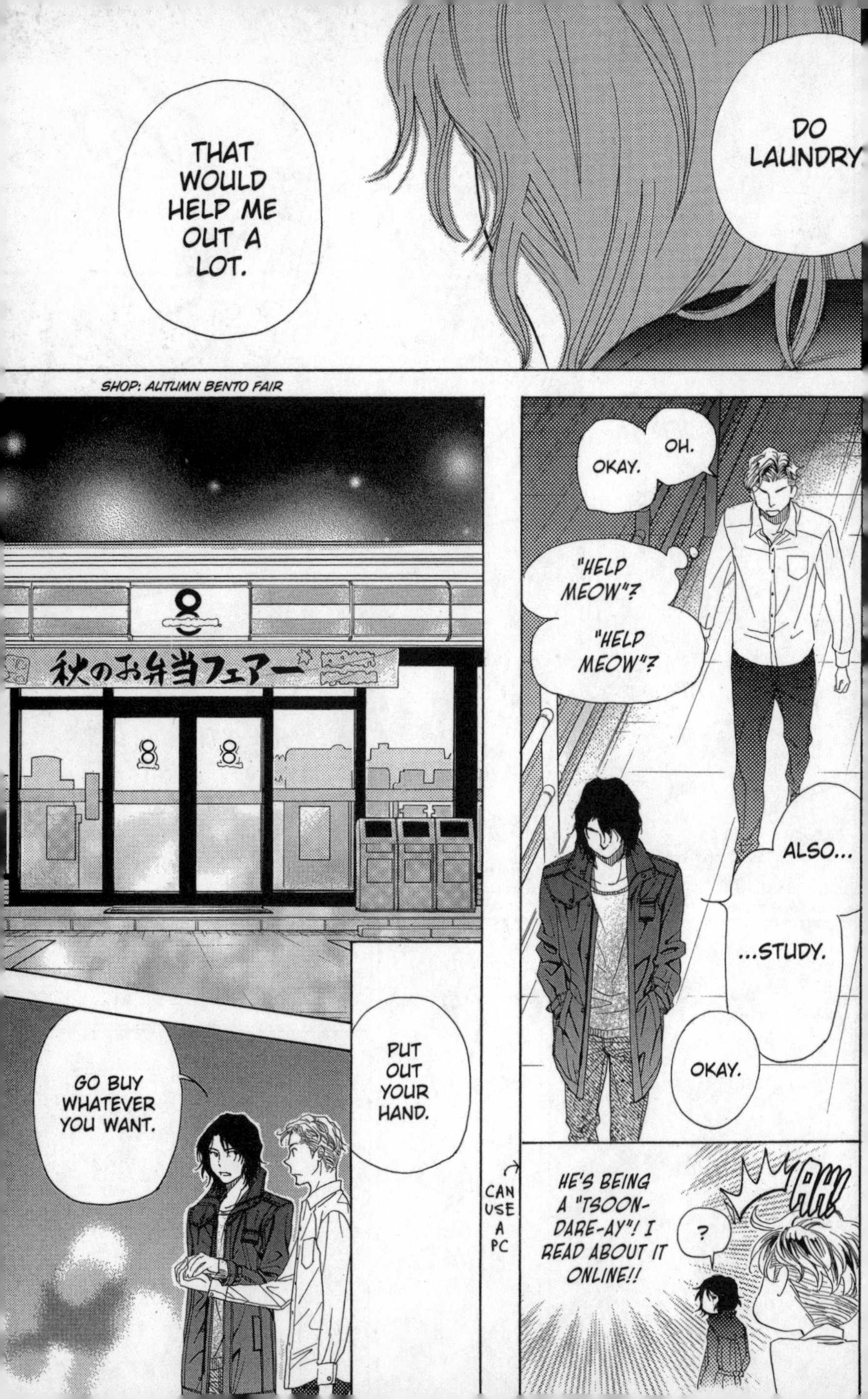
DO LAUNDRY
THAT WOULD HELP ME OUT A LOT.
OH.
OKAY.
"HELP MEOW"?
"HELP MEOW"?
ALSO...
...STUDY.
OKAY.
SHOP: AUTUMN BENTO FAIR
秋のお弁当フェアー
PUT OUT YOUR HAND.
GO BUY WHATEVER YOU WANT.
AH!
?
HE'S BEING A "TSOON-DARE-AY"! I READ ABOUT IT ONLINE!!
CAN USE A PC

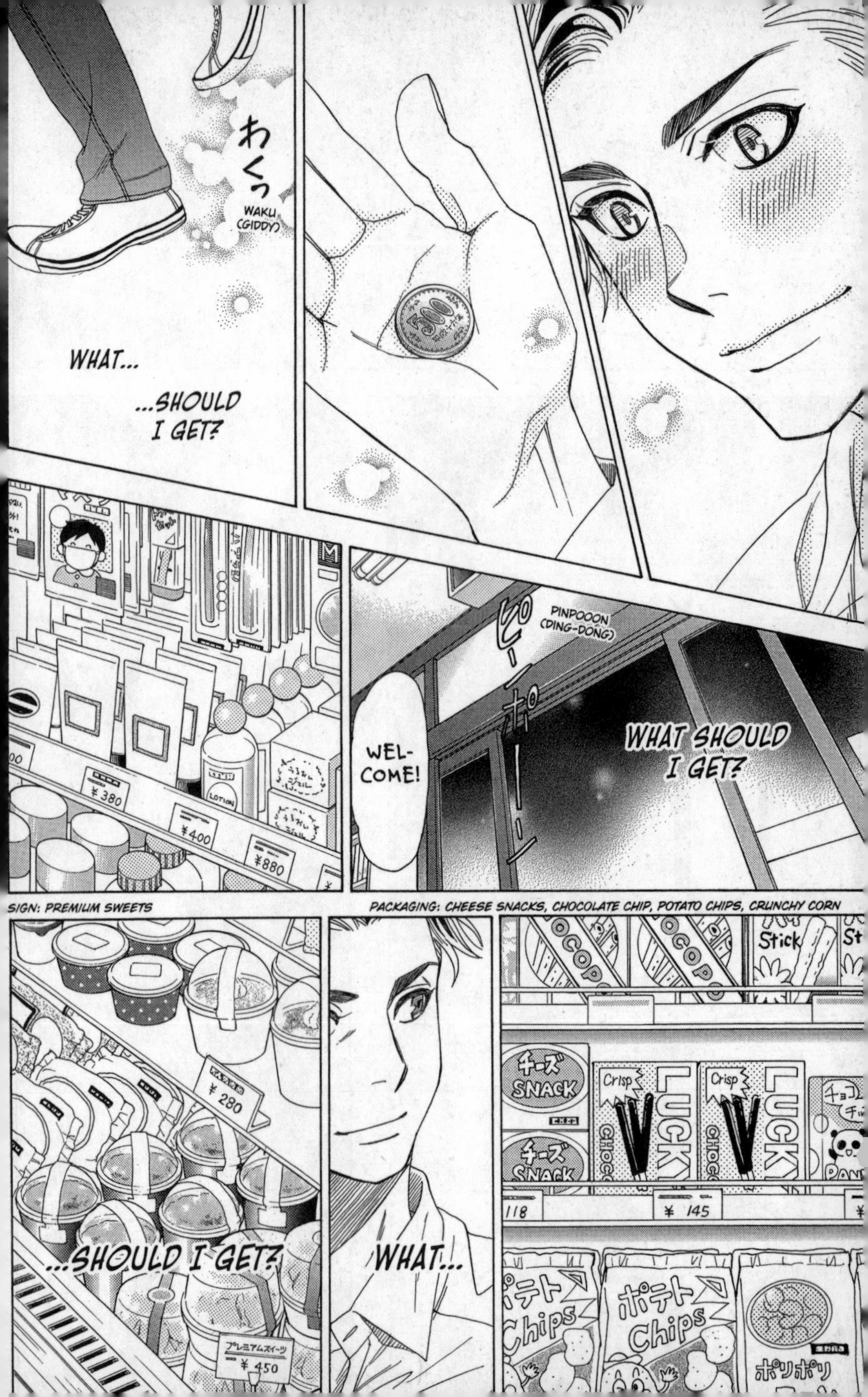
わくっ
WAKU (GIDDY)
WHAT...
...SHOULD I GET?
ピーポーーン
PINPOOON (DING-DONG)
WEL-COME!
WHAT SHOULD I GET?
¥380
LOTION
¥400
¥880
PACKAGING: CHEESE SNACKS, CHOCOLATE CHIP, POTATO CHIPS, CRUNCHY CORN
SIGN: PREMIUM SWEETS
Stick
チーズ SNACK
チーズ SNACK
Crisp
LUCKY
Crisp
LUCKY
118
¥ 145
ポテト Chips
ポテト Chips
ポリポリ
WHAT...
¥ 280
...SHOULD I GET?
プレミアムスイーツ
¥ 450

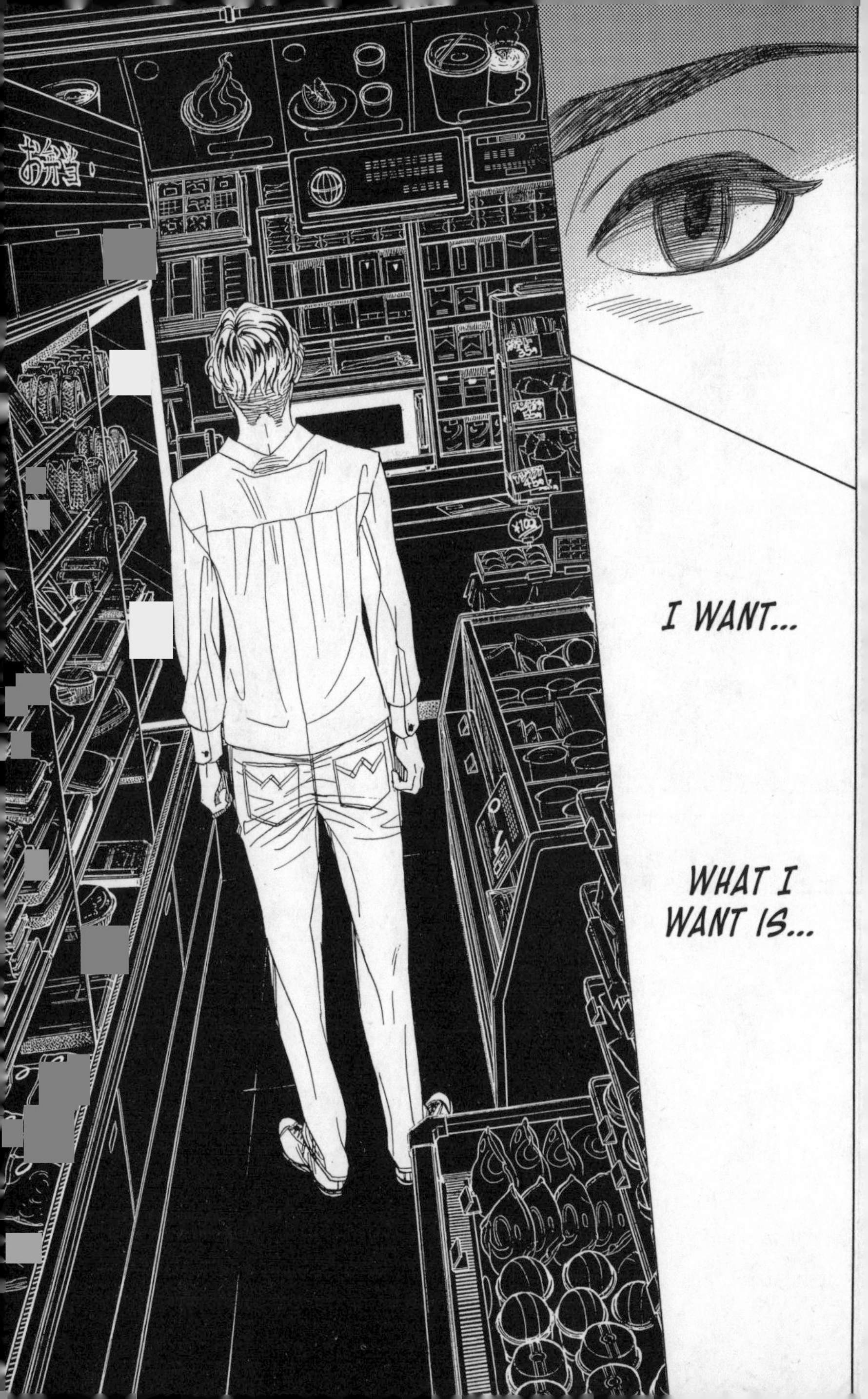
I WANT...
WHAT I WANT IS...
お弁当

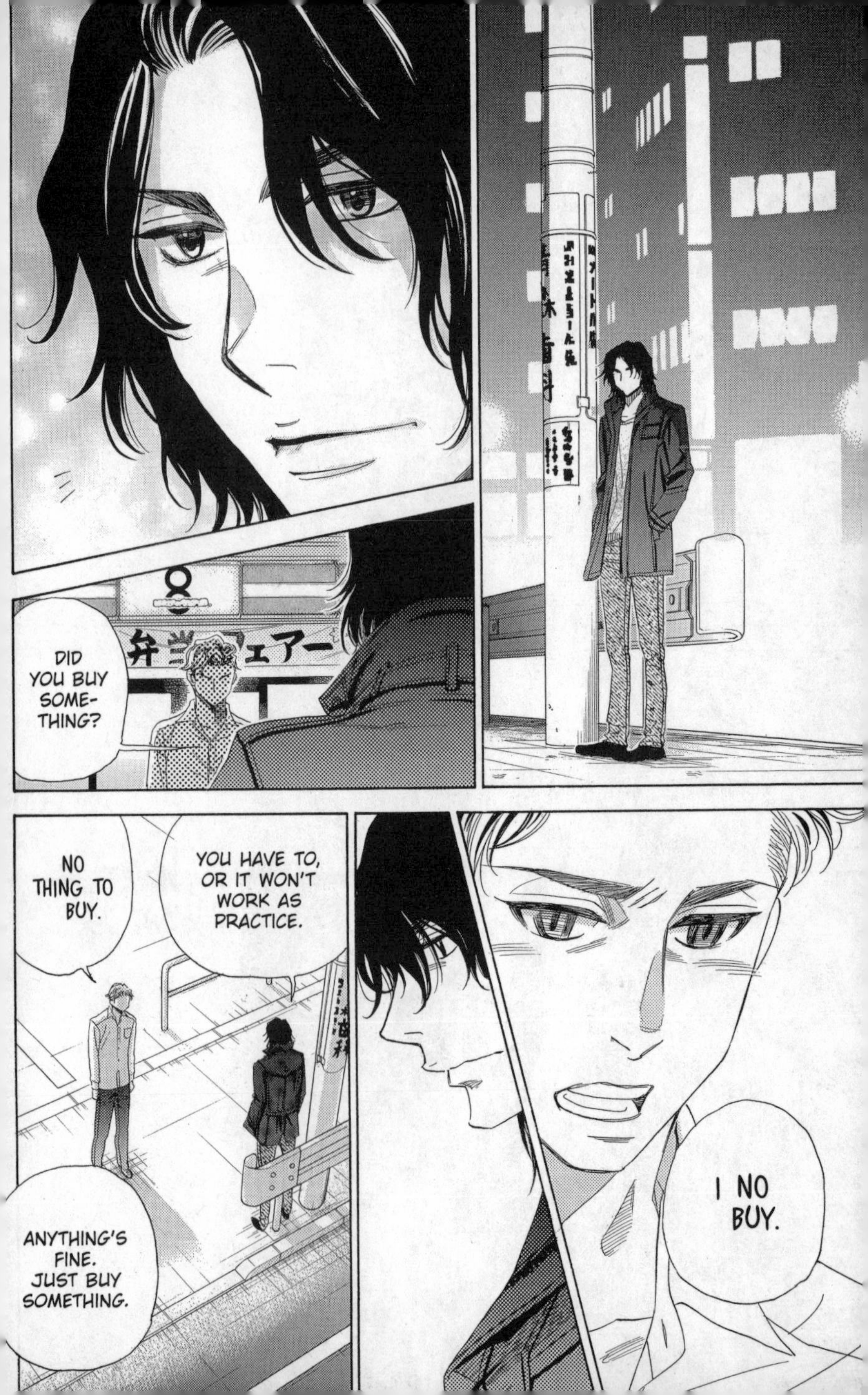
DID YOU BUY SOME-THING?
I NO BUY.
YOU HAVE TO, OR IT WON'T WORK AS PRACTICE.
NO THING TO BUY.
ANYTHING'S FINE. JUST BUY SOMETHING.

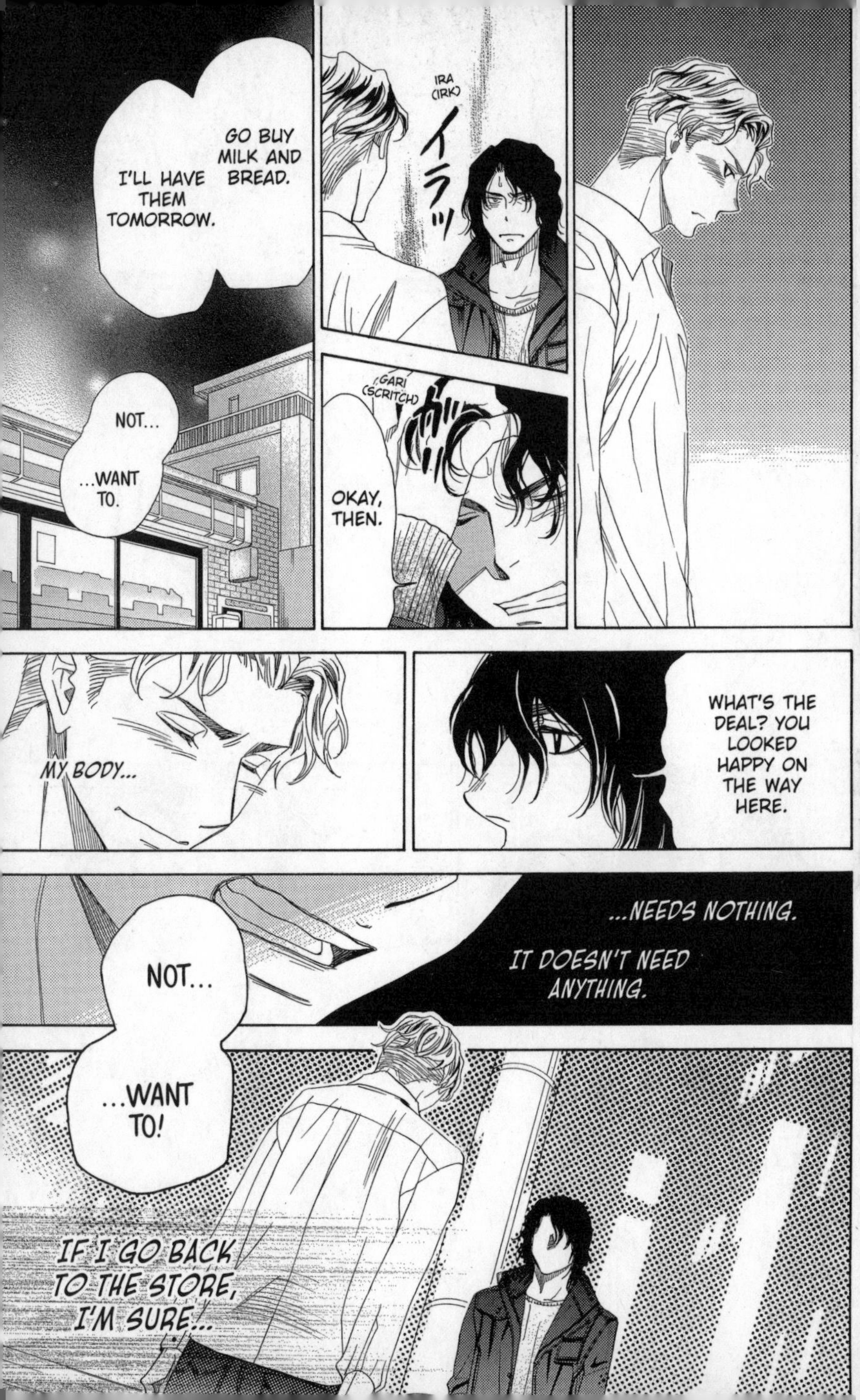
IRA
(IRK)
イラッ
GARI
(SCRITCH)
OKAY, THEN.
GO BUY MILK AND BREAD.
I'LL HAVE THEM TOMORROW.
NOT...
...WANT TO.
WHAT'S THE DEAL? YOU LOOKED HAPPY ON THE WAY HERE.
MY BODY...
...NEEDS NOTHING.
IT DOESN'T NEED ANYTHING.
NOT...
...WANT TO!
IF I GO BACK TO THE STORE, I'M SURE...

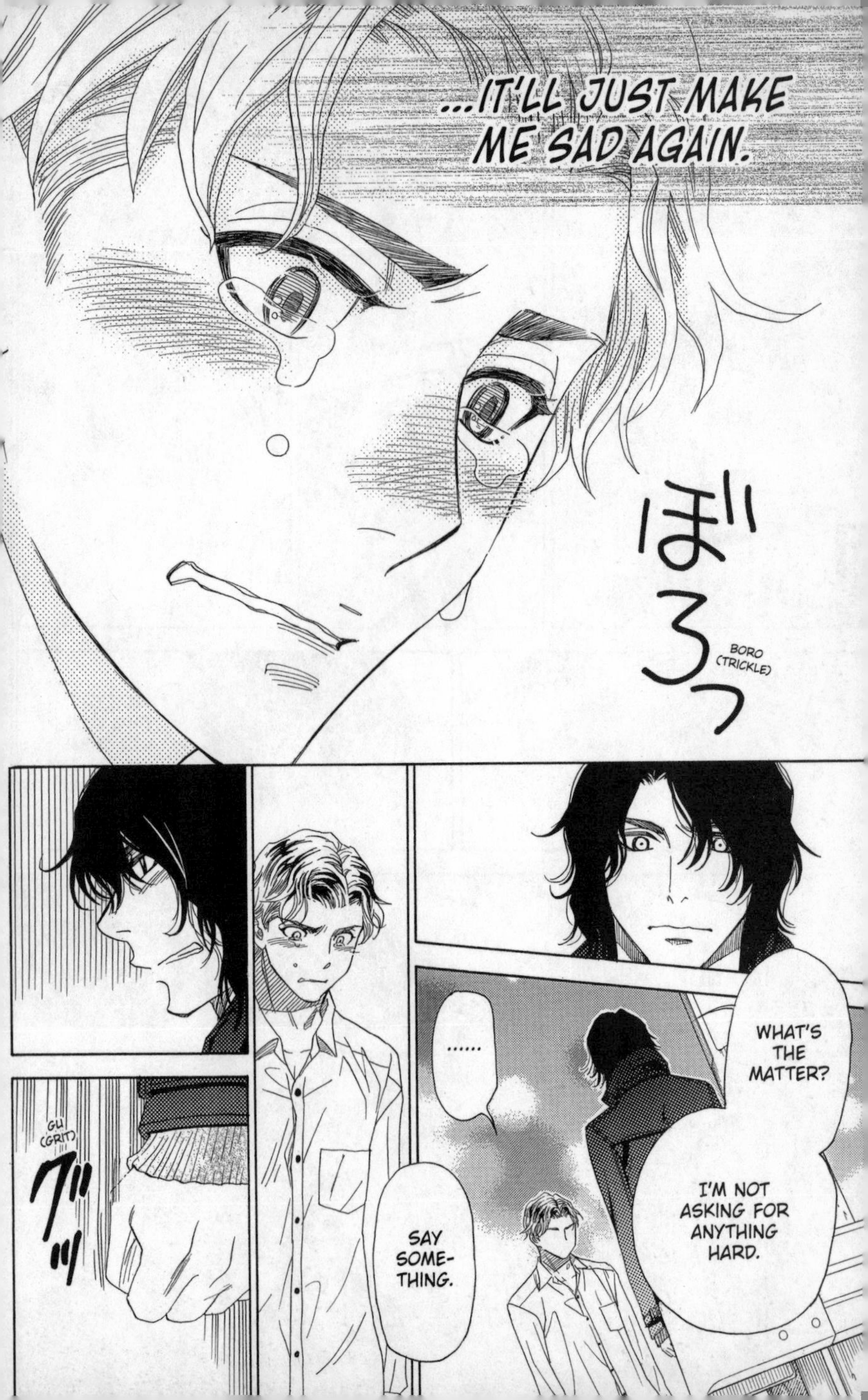
...IT'LL JUST MAKE ME SAD AGAIN.
ぼろっ
BORO (TRICKLE)
WHAT'S THE MATTER?
I'M NOT ASKING FOR ANYTHING HARD.
......
SAY SOME-THING.
グッ
GU (GRIT)

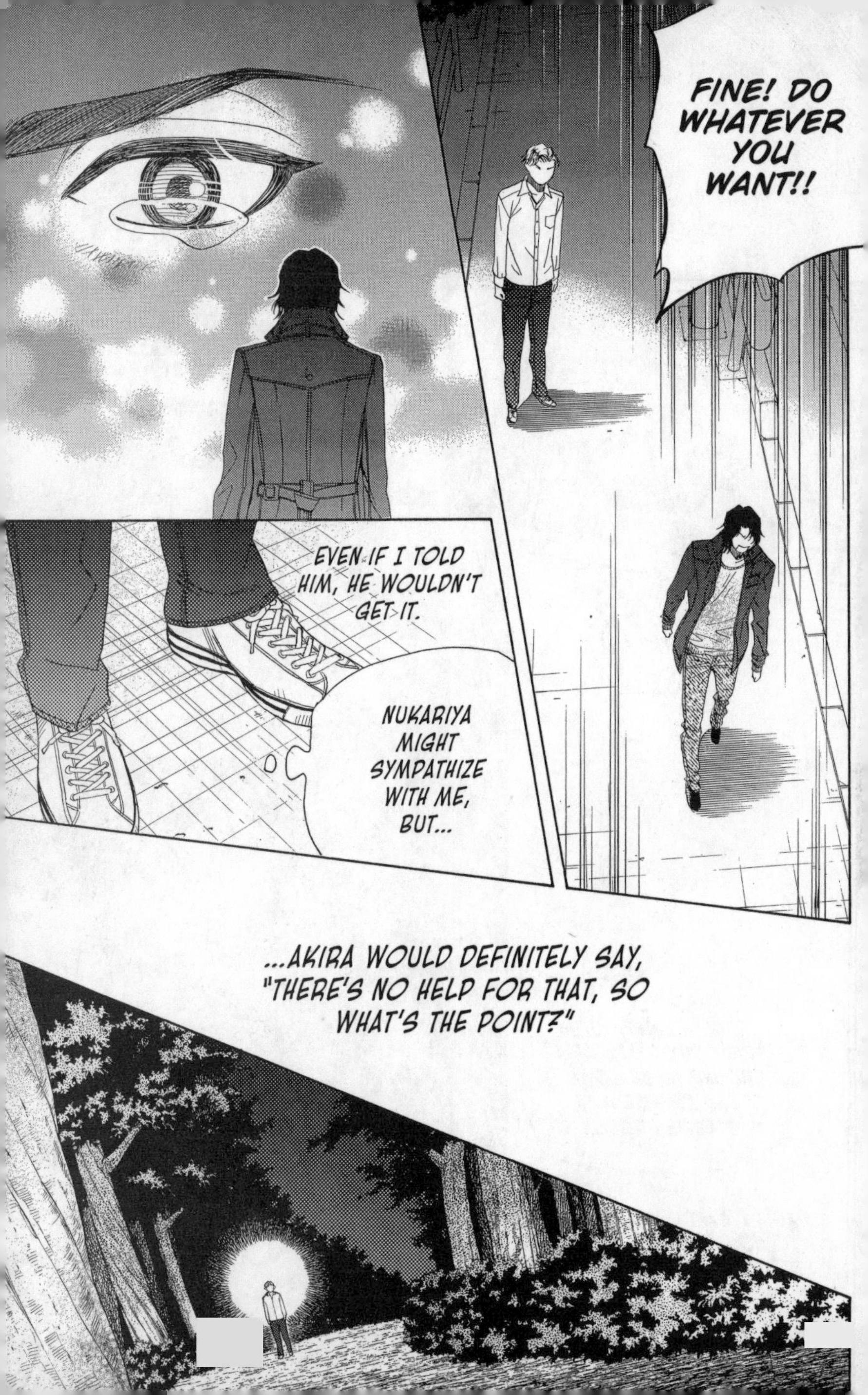
FINE! DO WHATEVER YOU WANT!!
EVEN IF I TOLD HIM, HE WOULDN'T GET IT.
NUKARIYA MIGHT SYMPATHIZE WITH ME, BUT...
...AKIRA WOULD DEFINITELY SAY, "THERE'S NO HELP FOR THAT, SO WHAT'S THE POINT?"

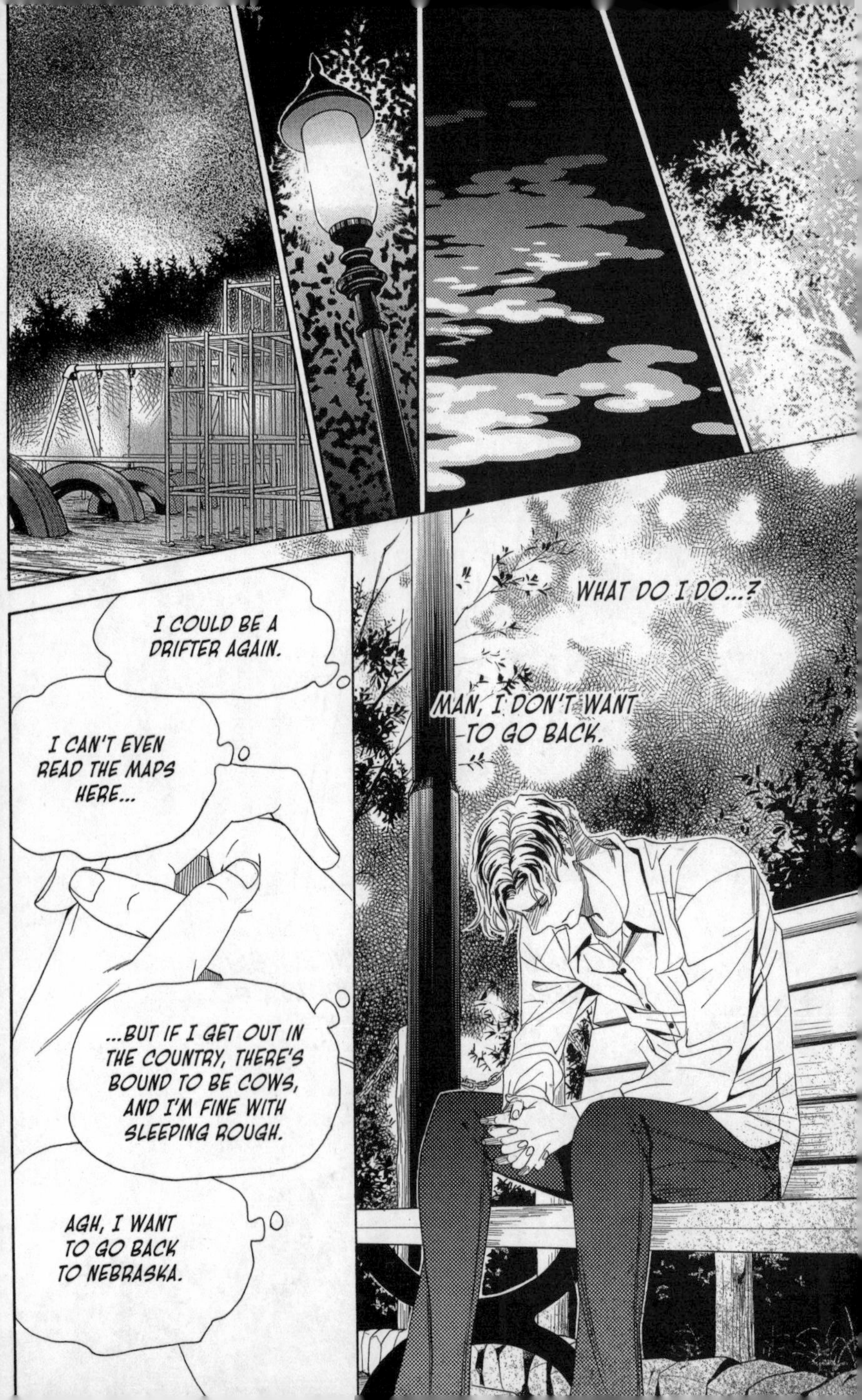
WHAT DO I DO...?
MAN, I DON'T WANT TO GO BACK.
I COULD BE A DRIFTER AGAIN.
I CAN'T EVEN READ THE MAPS HERE...
...BUT IF I GET OUT IN THE COUNTRY, THERE'S BOUND TO BE COWS, AND I'M FINE WITH SLEEPING ROUGH.
AGH, I WANT TO GO BACK TO NEBRASKA.

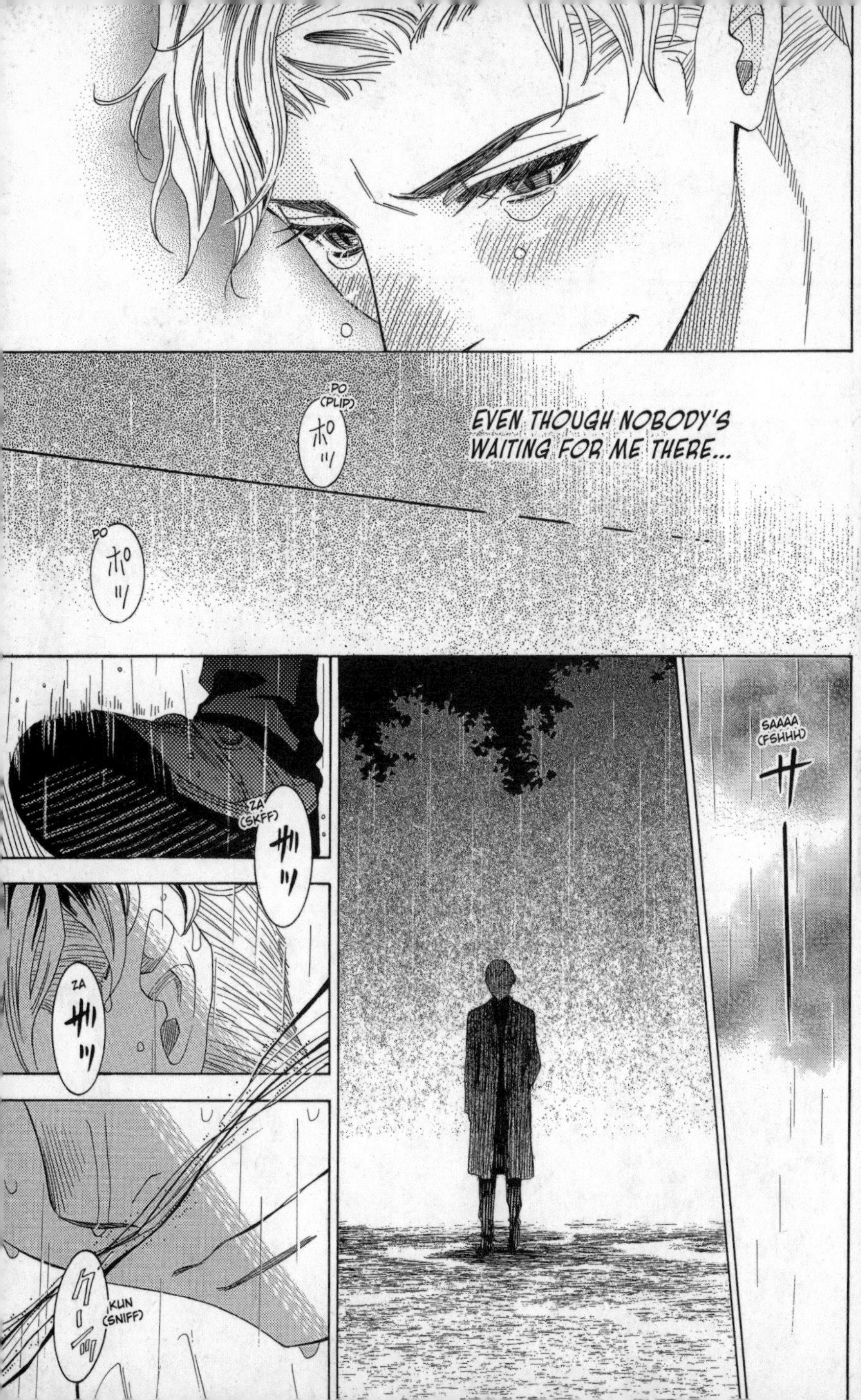
EVEN THOUGH NOBODY'S WAITING FOR ME THERE...
PO (PLIP)
ポッ
PO
ポッ
SAAAA (FSHHH)
サー
ZA (SKFF)
ザッ
ZA
ザッ
KUN (SNIFF)
クーッ

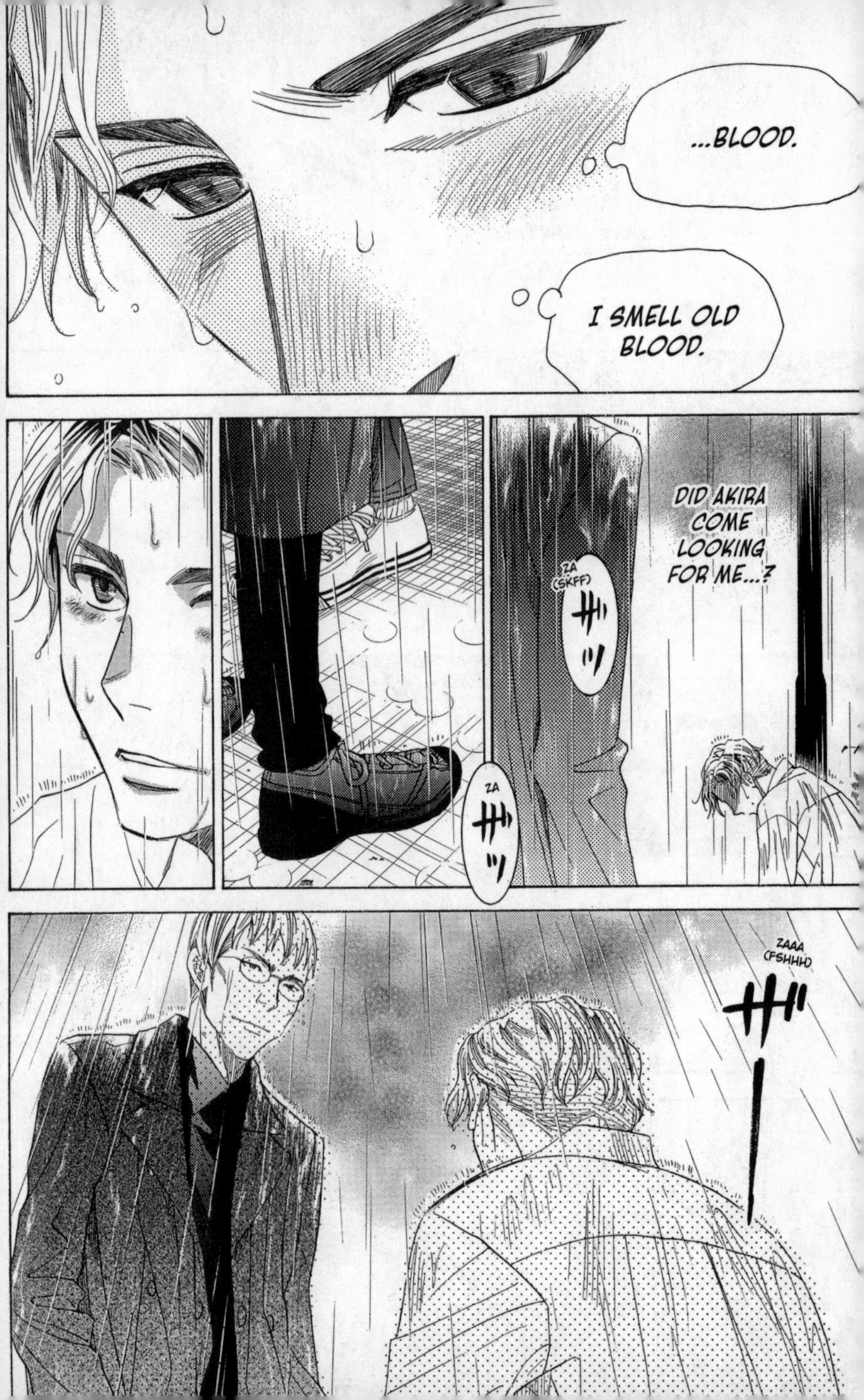
...BLOOD.
I SMELL OLD BLOOD.
DID AKIRA COME LOOKING FOR ME...?
ZA (SKFF)
ザッ
ZA
ザッ
ZAAA (FSHHH)
ザー

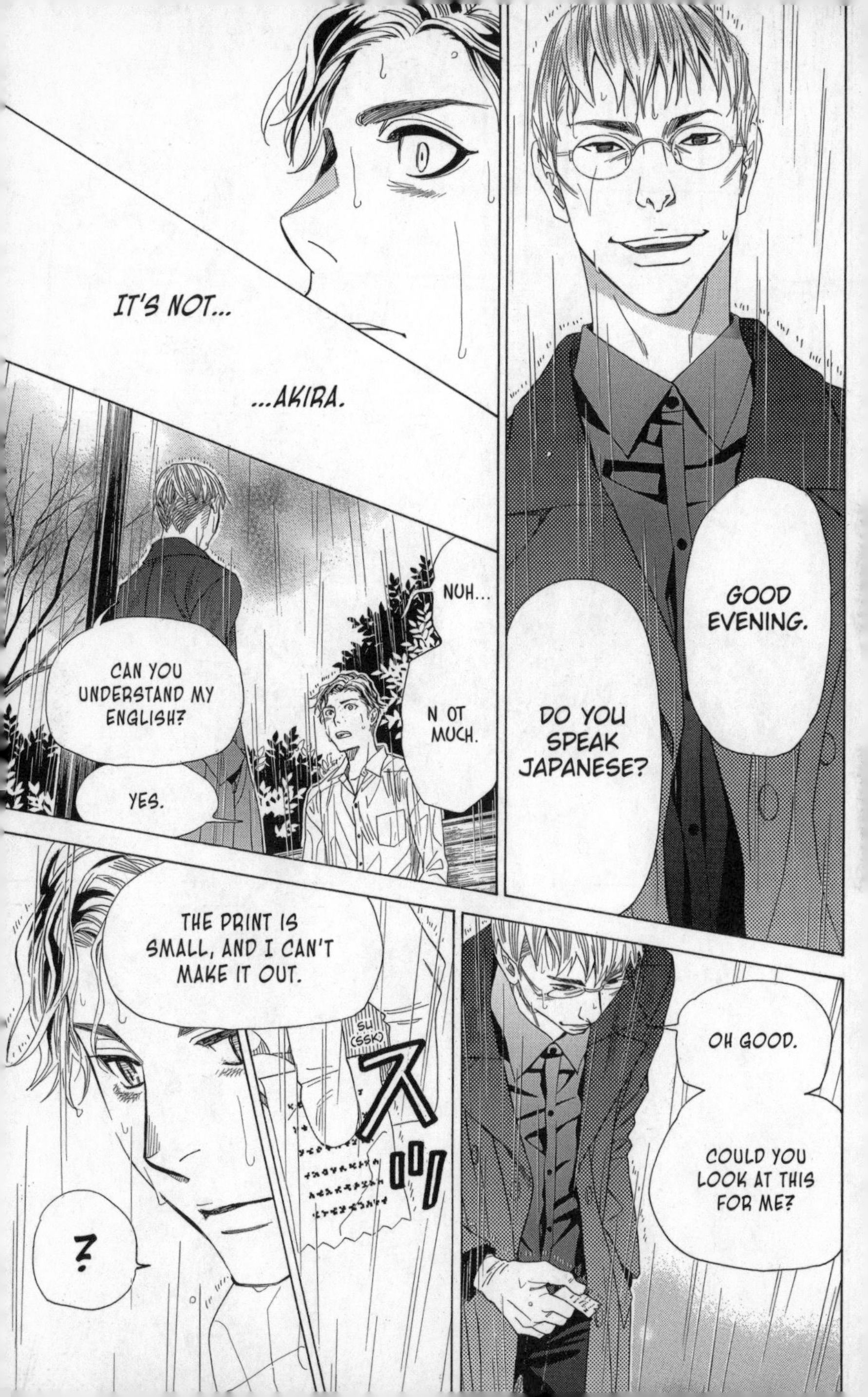
GOOD EVENING.
DO YOU SPEAK JAPANESE?
IT'S NOT...
...AKIRA.
NUH...
N OT MUCH.
CAN YOU UNDERSTAND MY ENGLISH?
YES.
OH GOOD.
COULD YOU LOOK AT THIS FOR ME?
THE PRINT IS SMALL, AND I CAN'T MAKE IT OUT.
SU (SSK)
?

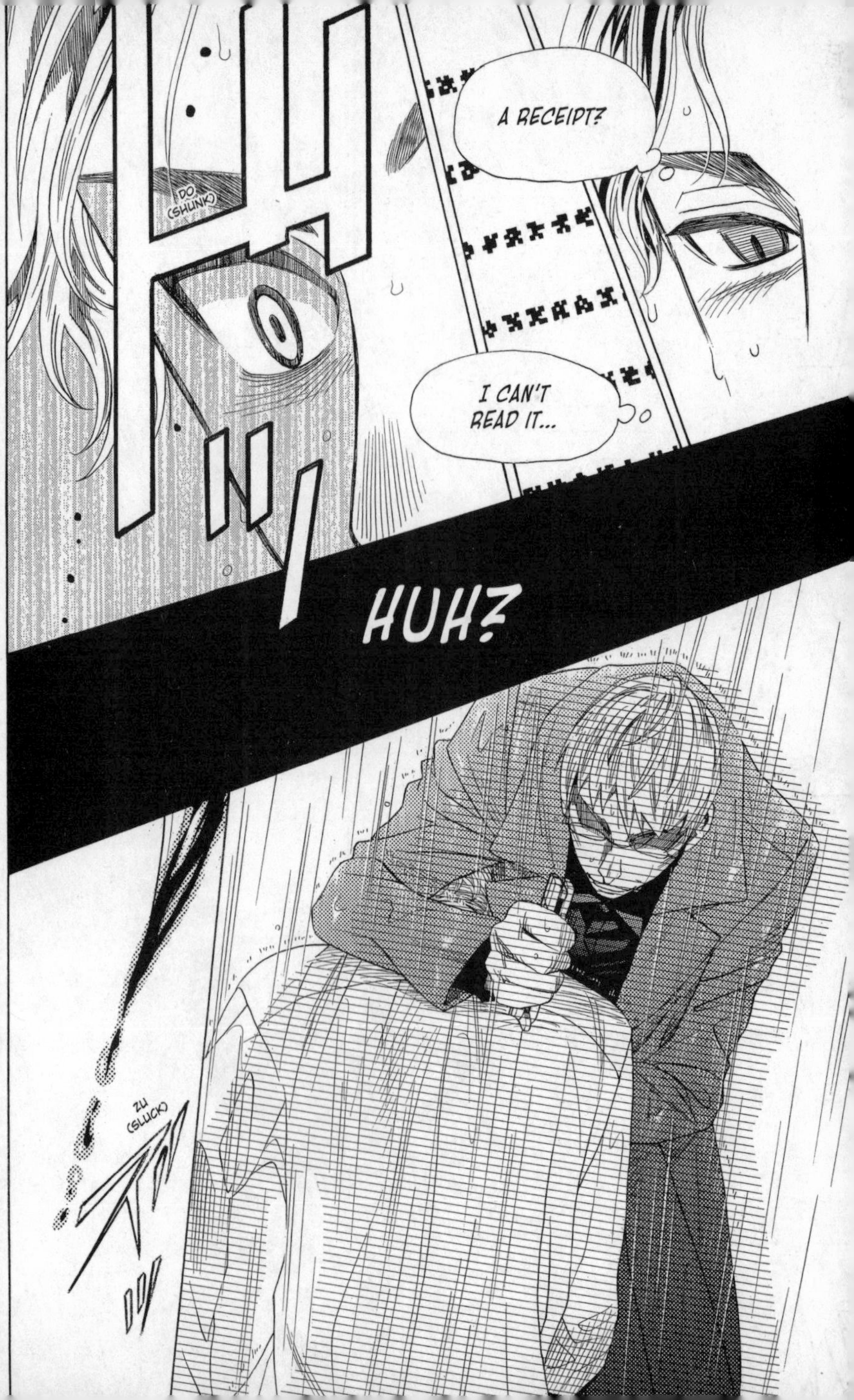
A RECEIPT?
I CAN'T READ IT...
DO (SHUNK)
HUH?
ZU (SLUCK)

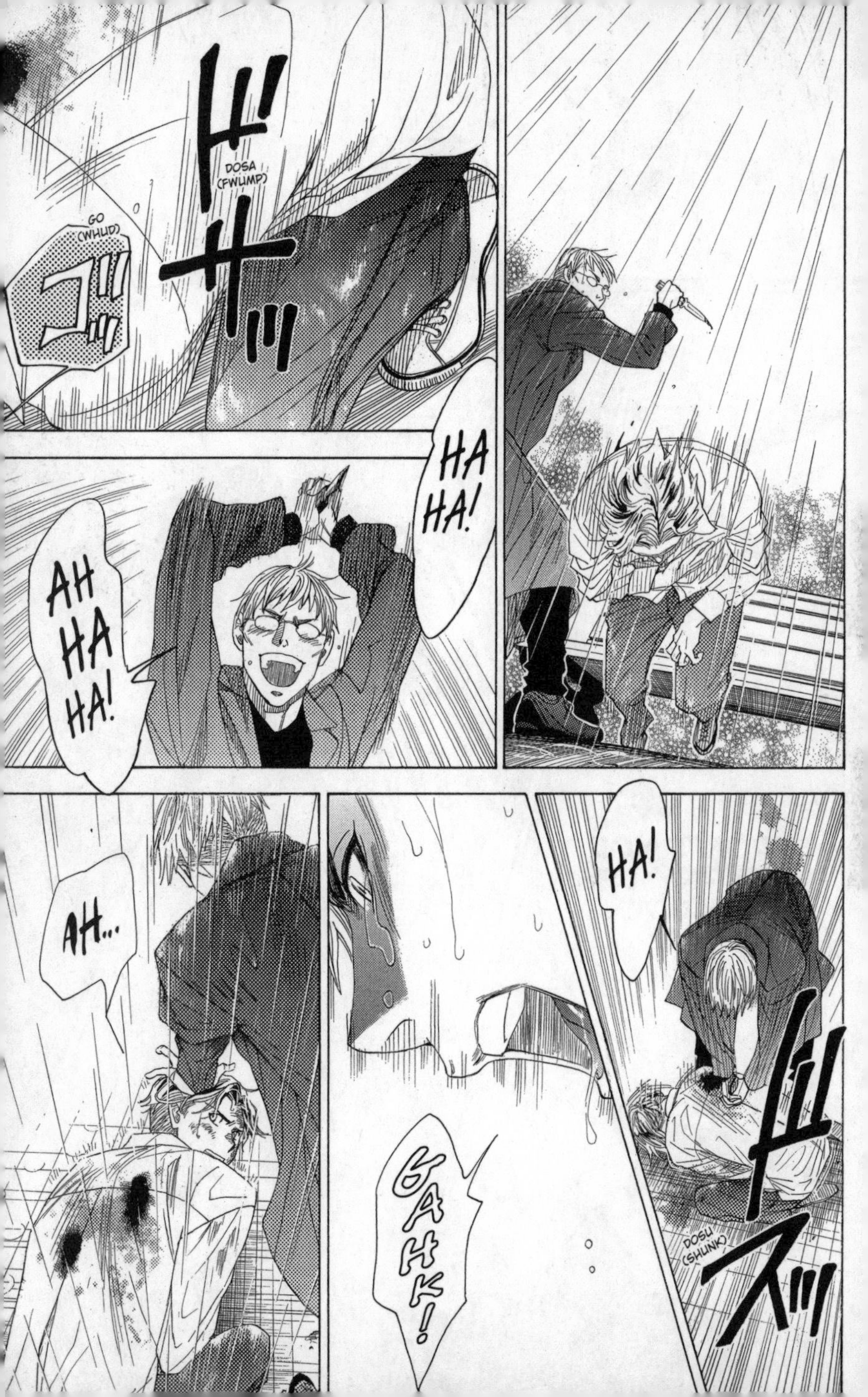
DOSA (FWUMP)
GO (WHUD)
HA HA!
AH HA HA HA!
HA!
DOSU (SHUNK)
GAHK!
AH...

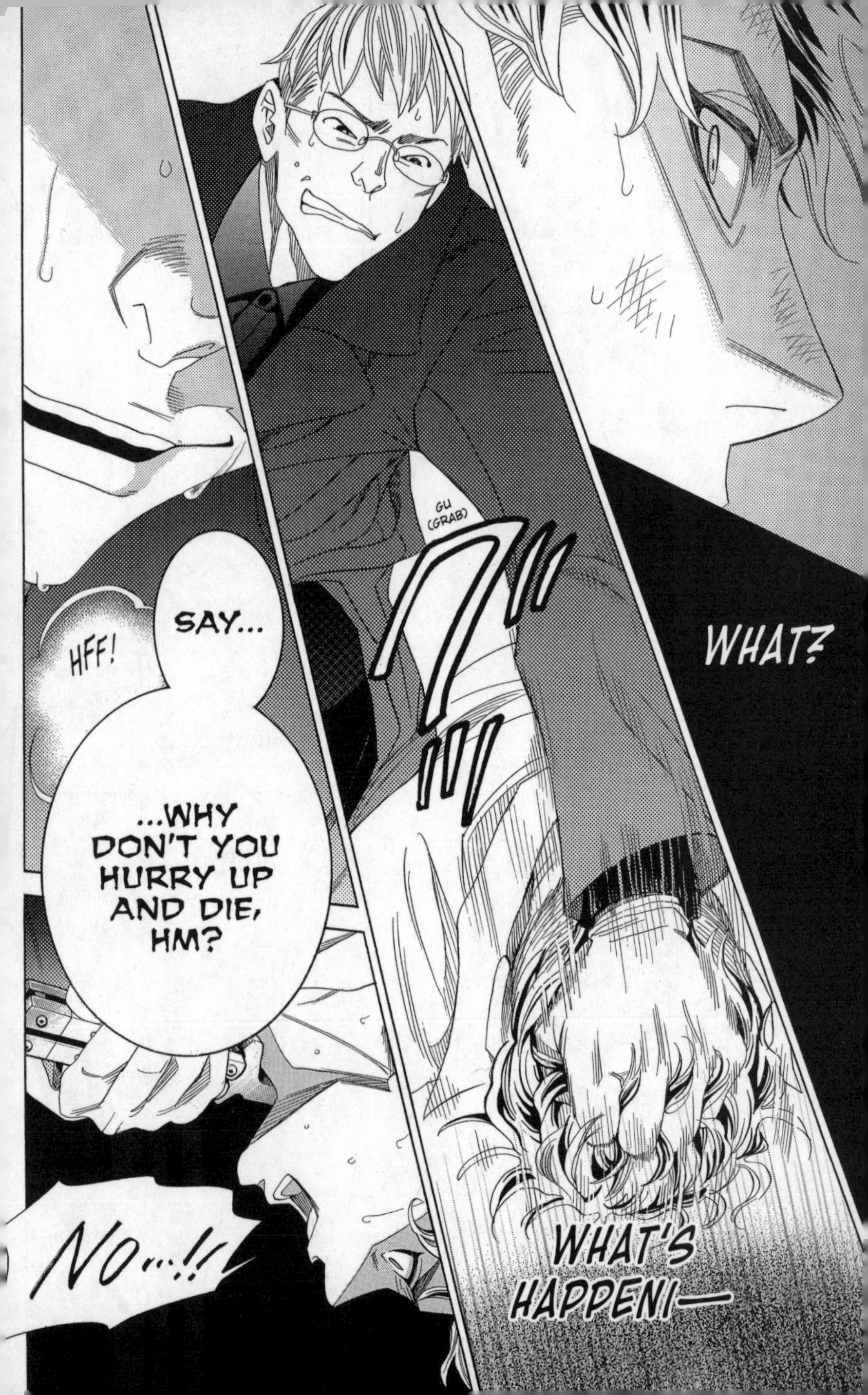
WHAT?
WHAT'S HAPPENI—
GU (GRAB)
SAY...
HFF!
...WHY DON'T YOU HURRY UP AND DIE, HM?
NO...!!

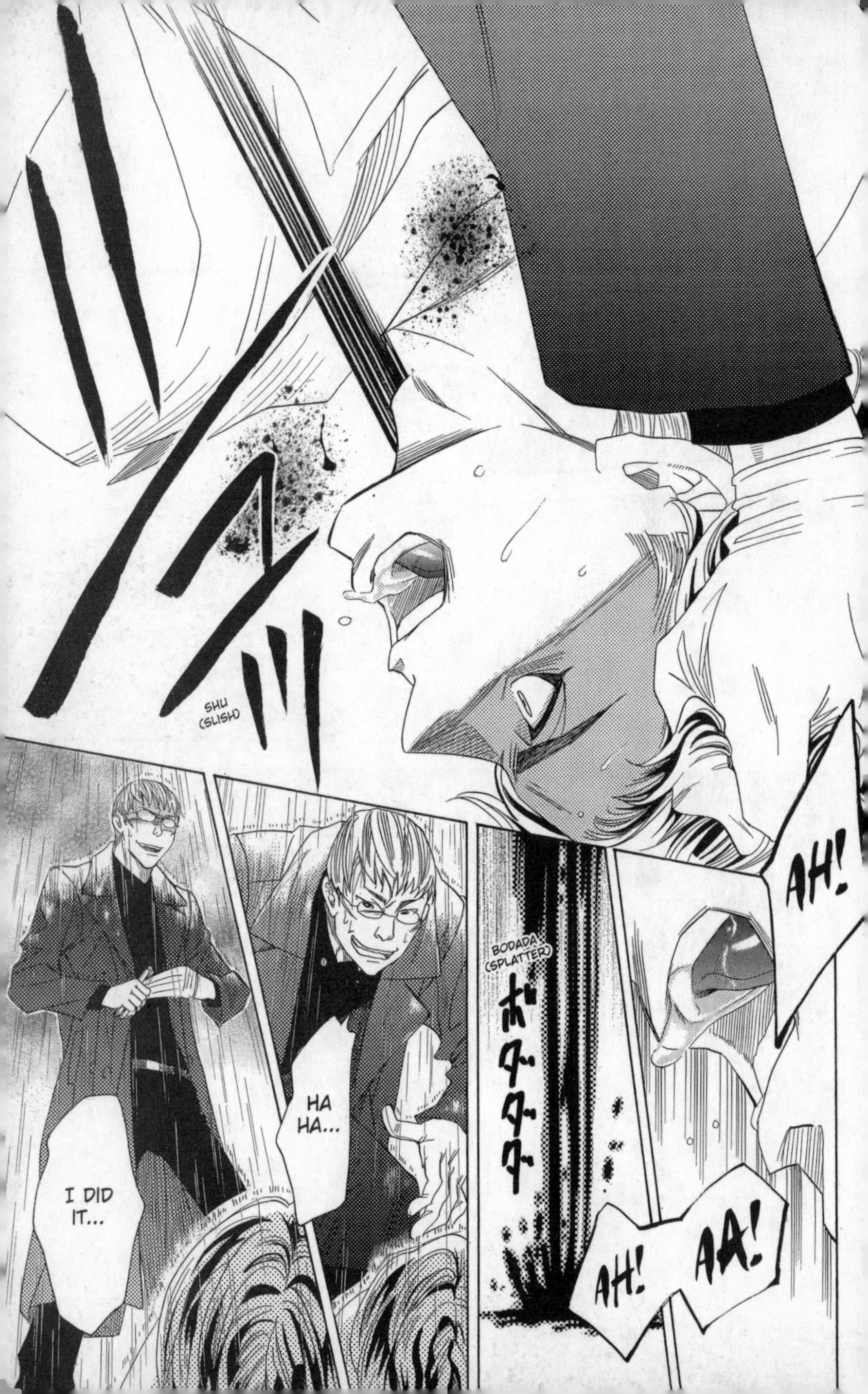
SHU
(SLISH)
AH!
AA!
AH!
BODADA
(SPLATTER)
ボダダダ
HA
HA...
I DID
IT...

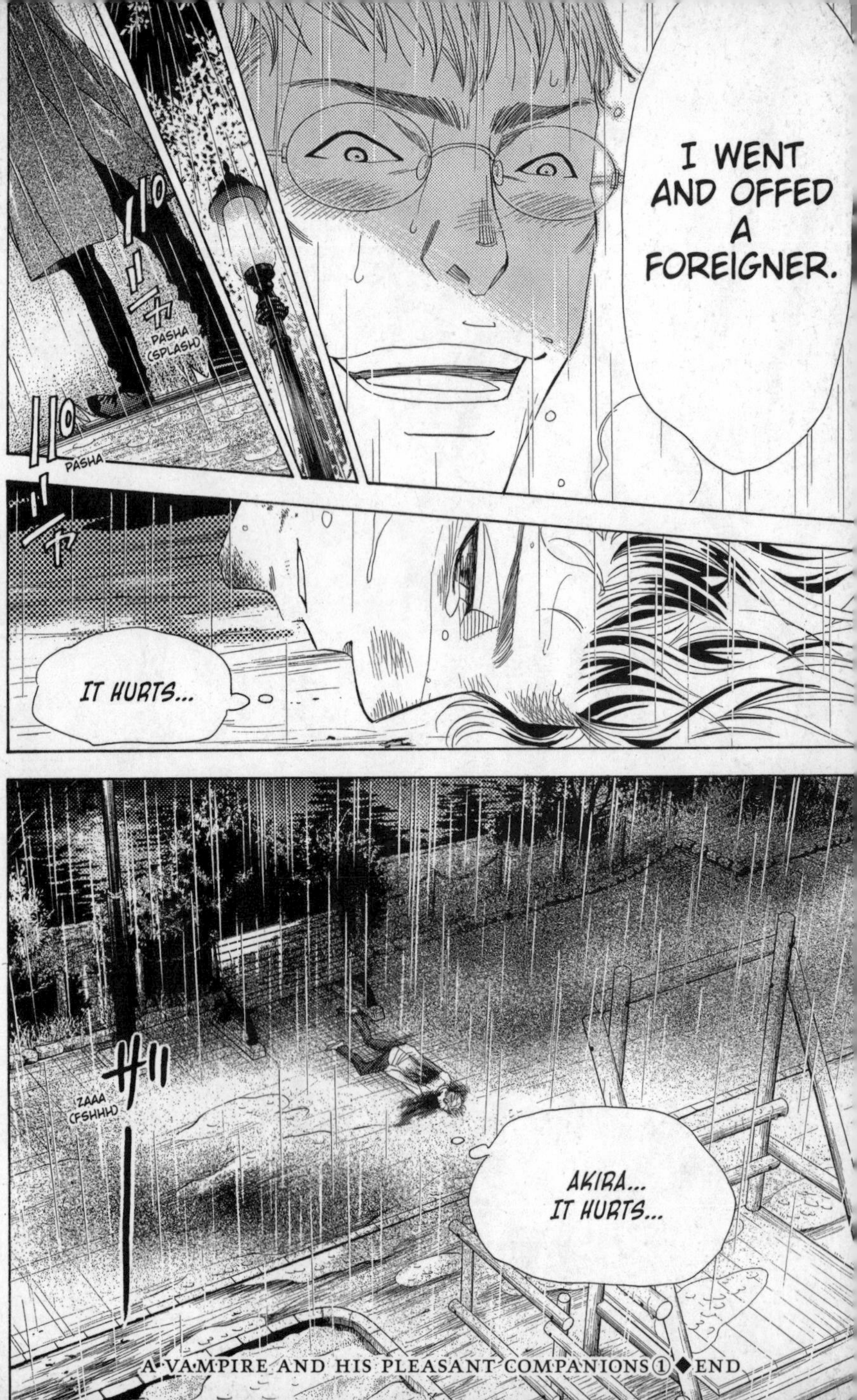
I WENT AND OFFED A FOREIGNER.
PASHA (SPLASH)
PASHA
IT HURTS...
ZAAA (FSHHH)
AKIRA... IT HURTS...
A VAMPIRE AND HIS PLEASANT COMPANIONS ① ◆ END

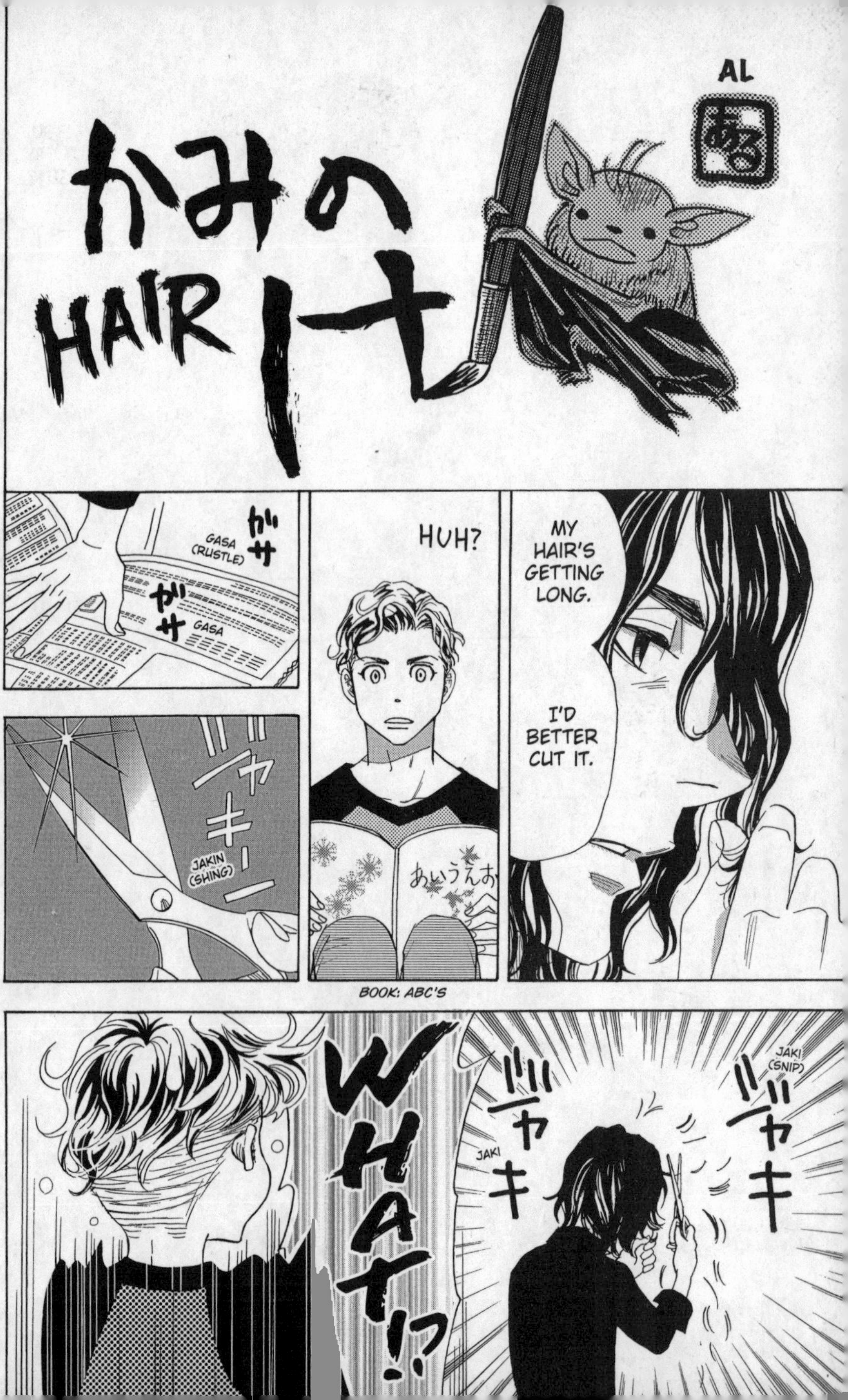

かみの
HAIR
AL
ある
MY HAIR'S GETTING LONG.
I'D BETTER CUT IT.
HUH?
あいうえお
ガサ
GASA (RUSTLE)
ガサ
GASA
ジャキーン
JAKIN (SHING)
BOOK: ABC'S
ジャキ
JAKI (SNIP)
ジャキ
JAKI
WHAT!?

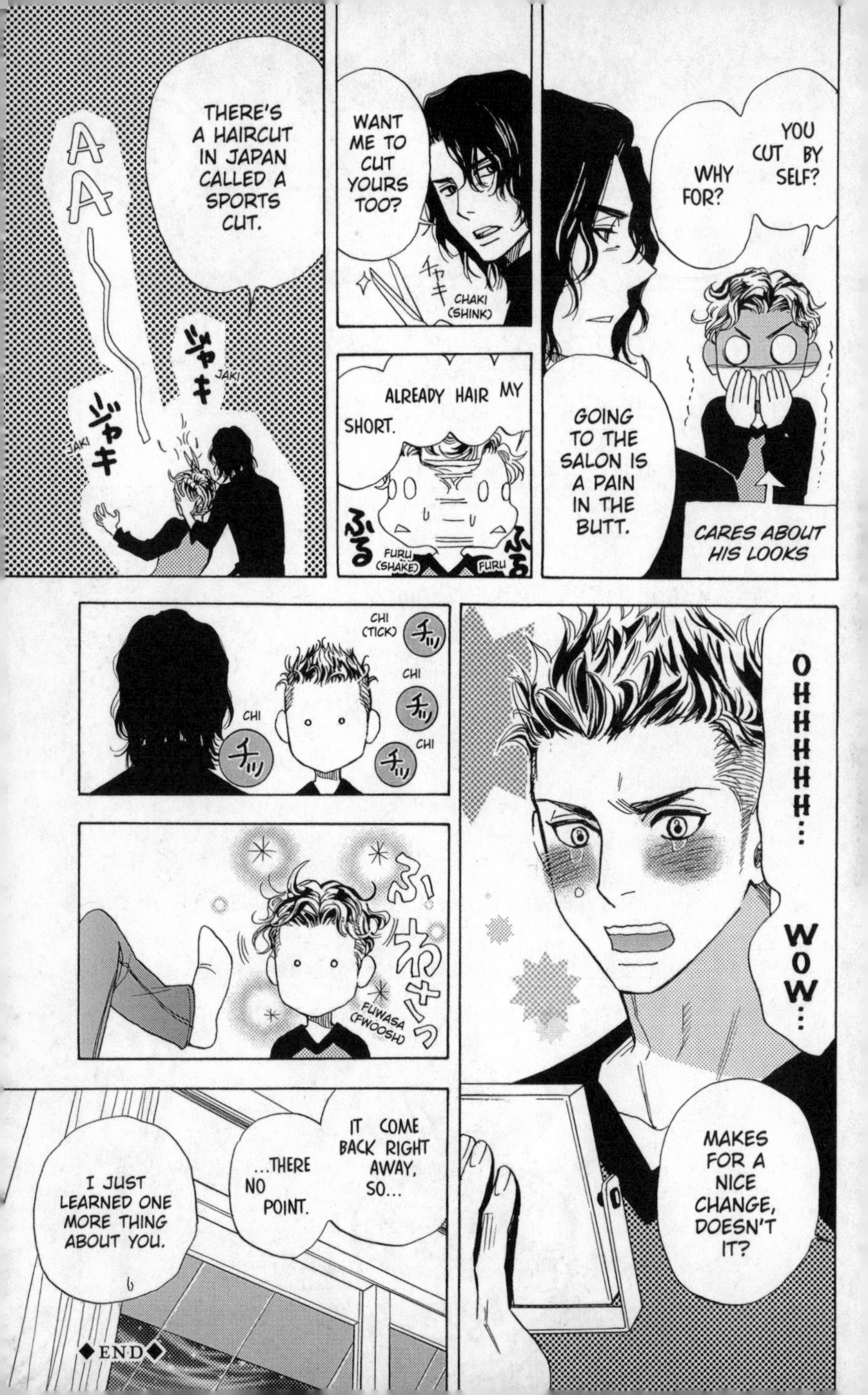
YOU CUT BY SELF? WHY FOR?
GOING TO THE SALON IS A PAIN IN THE BUTT.
CARES ABOUT HIS LOOKS
WANT ME TO CUT YOURS TOO?
チャキ
CHAKI (SHINK)
ALREADY HAIR MY SHORT.
ふる
FURU (SHAKE)
ふる
FURU
THERE'S A HAIRCUT IN JAPAN CALLED A SPORTS CUT.
AA
ジャキ
JAKI
ジャキ
JAKI
OHHHHHH...
WOW...
チッ
CHI (TICK)
チッ
CHI
チッ
CHI
チッ
CHI
ふわさっ
FUWASA (FWOOSH)
MAKES FOR A NICE CHANGE, DOESN'T IT?
IT COME BACK RIGHT AWAY, SO...
...THERE NO POINT.
I JUST LEARNED ONE MORE THING ABOUT YOU.
◆END◆

[Original Work] NARISE KONOHARA

A Vampire and His Pleasant Companions

[Art Staff] MORO-TAN · MIYA-SAN

KOMORING · AKAGAKI · OHNO

[Editor] SHIRAOKA   [Manager] ANEJA

[Design] K. NAWATA

[Comics Editor] NORO (Gendai Shoin)

[Special Thanks] [Original Work Editor] MIYAZAKI

......AND YOU!

Letters, please!

Attn: Marimo Ragawa

c/o Yen Press · 150 West 30th Street, 19th Floor · New York, NY 10001

Website: Crunchy Marimo Senbee http://www.ragawa.co.jp/

HOT   BATH

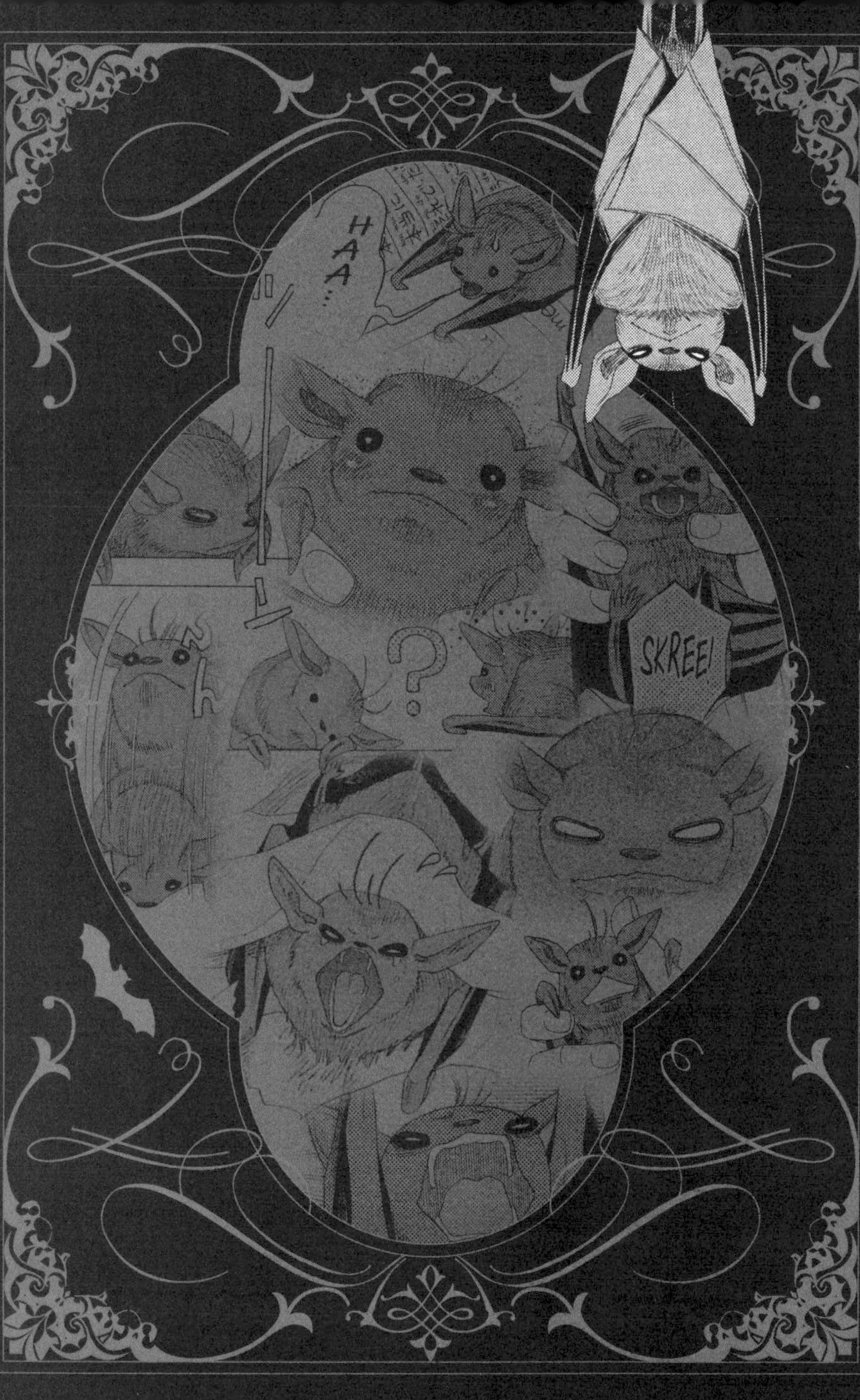
HAA...
SKREE!

TRANSLATION NOTES

CURRENCY CONVERSION
While exchange rates fluctuate daily, a good approximation is ¥100 to 1 USD.

PAGE 86
Torii is misinterpreting part of a saying that means, "Nothing good, or bad, lasts forever." It's a little more like saying, "This, too, shall pass," than having anything to do with evil being punished.

PAGE 155
In Japan, police officers can live in apartments provided by their station. Rent is pretty low, but the apartments are assigned to them, and they can either accept what they get or find their own housing. As such, although Nukariya's home isn't a dorm, it isn't technically his place, either.

PAGE 172
When you cook meat, the sinews shrink, which tends to make steaks curl up at the edges and cook unevenly. In Japan, it's common practice to make shallow cuts across the sinews before cooking meat, in order to minimize this shrinkage.

PAGE 191
Akira's *UMA* magazine is a parody of *Mu*, the paranormal magazine that appears in the Makoto Shinkai films *your name.* and *Weathering With You*.

PAGE 195
The con Al falls for is known as a "catch sale." (The term is made-in-Japan English.) The person running the con will "catch" people leaving crowded locations, such as train stations, take them to their office, and swindle them into signing expensive, hard-to-break contracts, sometimes by threatening them or physically preventing them from leaving until they sign. Akira is able to cancel the contract via the "cooling-off" system. Under Japanese consumer law, any purchase made through a door-to-door visit or direct solicitation on the street can be canceled for a full refund within eight days of signing the contract. If it's a scam and the contract "disappears," that eight-day period doesn't start until the document is found, which means the consumer can cancel at any time. Since this is the case, swindled people (who tend to be young and naive or old and not thinking clearly) are often pressured not to tell their guardians about the contract in hopes that the cooling-off period will run out before anyone tries to cancel it.

PAGE 196
All the words in the background of the first panel are loanwords that were imported into Japanese from English and still sound roughly the same. Al's managed to pick them out of the conversation and guess what Akira and Nukariya were talking about.

PAGE 205
A *tsundere* is someone whose initially hostile demeanor masks a softer side.

PAGE 222
Al's book reads, "AIUEO," which is the beginning of the *hiragana* and *katakana* syllabaries, so it's the Japanese equivalent of "ABC."

Please flip to back to read an
exclusive, new short story.

The VAMPIRE & HIS PLEASANT COMPANIONS

MARIMO RAGAWA
ORIGINAL STORY NARISE KONOHARA

1

Translation: **TAYLOR ENGEL**   Lettering: **ABIGAIL BLACKMAN**

This book is a work of fiction. Names, characters, places, and incidents are the product of the author's imagination or are used fictitiously. Any resemblance to actual events, locales, or persons, living or dead, is coincidental.

KYUKETSUKI TO YUKAI NA NAKAMA TACHI by MARIMO RAGAWA, NARISE KONOHARA
© Marimo Ragawa 2016
© Narise Konohara 2016
First published in Japan in 2016 by HAKUSENSHA, INC., Tokyo.
English translation rights arranged with HAKUSENSHA, INC., Tokyo through TUTTLE-MORI AGENCY, INC., Tokyo.

English translation © 2020 by Yen Press, LLC

Yen Press
150 West 30th Street, 19th Floor
New York, NY 10001

Visit us at yenpress.com
facebook.com/yenpress
twitter.com/yenpress
yenpress.tumblr.com
instagram.com/yenpress

First Yen Press Edition: December 2020

Yen Press is an imprint of Yen Press, LLC.
The Yen Press name and logo are trademarks of Yen Press, LLC.

The publisher is not responsible for websites (or their content) that are not owned by the publisher.

Library of Congress Control Number: 2020946726

ISBNs: 978-1-9753-1919-9 (paperback)
       978-1-9753-1920-5 (ebook)

10 9 8 7 6 5 4 3 2 1

BVG

Printed in the United States of America

The man's blunt attitude made Al break out in a cold sweat.

"My name is Albert Irving. I'll play any part."

He told the man his name, hoping he could at least get that to stick in his memory. Abruptly and with a serious expression, the man said, "Kid, you've got a good face." Al's expectations spiked.

"Th-thank you very much!"

"The thing is, though, Hollywood's lousy with good-looking kids like you... I hope we run into each other at an audition one of these days."

The redheaded man walked away. Al's gaze fell to the pavement. There were dreams lying all over the place in Hollywood. Bittersweet dreams. He hadn't managed to pick one up. No, he'd been turned down this time, but next time might work out. He'd told the man his name, too... Although the guy might not remember it.

Al raised his head. Even famous actors got rejected over and over at auditions. Maybe he'd tried to sell himself on the street and been shot down, but he couldn't afford to get discouraged on his first or second time out.

Abruptly, Mysterious's face flickered through his mind. The guy hadn't seemed to have any interest in the industry Al was dying to break into, and Al wondered what sort of work he'd end up doing. He couldn't even begin to imagine a job that would suit an excessively handsome, blunt guy who dressed from head to toe in monochrome.

<The End>

of the mural, which was a famous tourist attraction. Flat Face made a peace sign with his fingers, while Mysterious looked away sullenly. Wondering absently, *Are they a gay couple?* Al took the picture. Right after he pushed the button, a red-haired, middle-aged man walked into the frame.

"Hello there. Are you two in high school?"

Even when the redheaded man spoke to them, Mysterious didn't respond; apparently, he didn't understand English. Flat Face was the one who answered.

"We're college students."

"I see. Well, we're shooting a film nearby, and we're looking for extras. Would you tell your friend I was wondering if he'd come with me for a bit if he's got the time?"

Scouted! So it actually happens! His big break was right in front of him, but Mysterious grimaced, clicked his tongue, and briskly walked away.

"Whoa, Akira, hang on a second!" Flat Face said, running after him.

The redheaded man watched Mysterious go, looking disappointed. *Now's my chance!* Quickly, Al went up to him.

"Um, excuse me."

The man turned and looked at him.

"I overheard you just now. I'm an aspiring actor. I haven't been in anything yet, but could you use me? I'm fine with being an extra."

The red-haired man looked Al up and down appraisingly. It felt like an audition. The man asked for his agent's name, so Al told him.

"I've never heard of that one," he said; he sounded skeptical. "Where's your headshot and résumé?"

"Oh—I don't have them with me right now."

"Are you in a union?"

"Union?"

The redheaded man gave a light shrug.

"I think we're wasting our time here."

"Wait, are you an actor?! That's so cool! What have you been in so far? Tell me! I'm absolutely going to watch it."

"I-it was just a bit part, so I don't know if my name's in the credits. Besides, they might have cut my scene."

"I don't care."

"The title still hasn't been finalized."

"Tell me when they settle on one, then."

Since Jahne kept pushing for it, they traded e-mail addresses. Jahne smiled happily.

"You always did say you wanted to be an actor. I just knew you'd make your dream come true."

"I have a preproduction meeting to get to…" With yet another lie, Al slunk away. He hadn't expected to run into an old girlfriend at a time like this. Jahne seemed to have grown more sophisticated since he'd last seen her; she'd gotten used to city life. In contrast, he felt as if he'd faded somehow.

He kept walking, choosing places with relatively few people, until he found himself in front of a mural of old movie stars. Marilyn Monroe and Chaplin… He wanted to become the sort of actor who would stick in people's memories.

—No, he *would* become that sort of actor.

"Akira, wait a minute. I want to get a photo here."

His ears caught words in an unfamiliar language. It was a couple of high schoolers, probably Chinese kids. One of the guys had a flat face, but the other was handsome in a mysterious, intense way that made him do a double take. For a second, he'd thought he was a girl, but his chest was flat, and his gray T-shirt and black jeans were guys' clothes.

When Al made eye contact with the one with the flat face, the kid came running up to him.

"Could you take a picture for us, please?" he asked in oddly accented English.

"Yeah, sure."

Al took the camera. Flat Face and Mysterious stood in front

involuntarily, but he also saw tourist types in glaringly tacky T-shirts who were obviously just up from the country.

Al found a spot by the side of the road, then raised the brim of his cap. He waited, hoping some famous actor or producer would pass by, but there was no way it was going to go that well right from the start. As a matter of fact, everyone seemed pretty indifferent to him. In Nebraska, girls always tried to talk to him, but… Well, there were lots of other attractive people around here. But even so.

"Excuse me…"

There it was! A voice had spoken to him hesitantly. Was it a pickup? *No help for that, I guess*, he thought before turning around to see two girls. One had a blond pixie cut, and the other's chestnut hair was pulled back in a ponytail.

"I knew it," the girl with the chestnut ponytail said, clasping her hands in front of her face. "It's really Al! It's been ages!"

That smile and her husky voice made the lid on his memories pop open. She had changed quite a bit, but…

"Jahne? Is that you?"

"It most definitely is me."

He'd dated Jahne for two years, from when he was thirteen to fifteen. Cheerful, gorgeous Jahne had been popular in class, too. They'd gone to different high schools, which had made it harder to connect, and they'd ended up drifting apart.

"I haven't seen anyone from back home in forever. I'm going to UCLA now. What about you?"

It was the college that had rejected his application. Saying he'd come out here intentionally, hoping to get scouted, would have been embarrassing, so in an attempt to save a little face, he found himself lying.

"I'm here for work."

"Work? You're not a student?"

"It's, uh…movies and stuff."

As he mumbled, trying to duck the question, Jahne's brown eyes went wide.

were for local flyers, mail-order magazines, and posters. With nothing on his résumé and considering the agency specialized in modeling, there was really no help for that. Even so, being out in the middle of nowhere was a definite handicap. Al hated the idea of ending his teenage years without having done anything toward accomplishing his goals, so he took advantage of his summer vacation to go to Hollywood, the land of his dreams.

Yesterday evening, Al set foot on Californian soil for the very first time. The sight of the HOLLYWOOD sign up on the mountainside totally blew away the fatigue of driving all the way over from Nebraska, and he'd been so moved that he cried a little. Why hadn't he come here sooner? This was the world where he belonged. He was absolutely positive it was.

He hadn't managed to break into acting because he lived way out in the sticks in Nebraska. Because he hadn't gotten a chance. Because nobody had discovered him yet. He'd come to Hollywood in order to make that happen. If he wandered around Tinseltown, he might get lucky. Maybe a director would spot him and say, "You absolutely have to be in this film." There actually were actors who'd grasped the American dream that way. *Be confident!* he told his reflection. Throwing his shoulders back and sticking out his chest, Al triumphantly opened the motel door.

In California, even the sunlight glittered, shone, and dazzled. As he walked under the shady palm trees, the Dolby Theatre—a site of adoration for him—came into view. Al felt his body grow hot with excitement. Every year they held the Academy Awards here. From the time he was little, Al had believed he was meant to stand on the red carpet. *It hasn't happened yet, but I'm sure I'll be back! Wait for me...* He blew an ardent kiss to his fantasy lover, the Dolby Theatre.

In Hollywood & Highland, which he'd only ever seen on TV and online, he felt a power that seemed to roll through the whole city. There were beautiful people who made him catch his breath

Standing in front of a mirror with chipped edges, Albert Irving smiled, flashing gleaming-white, freshly brushed teeth. He was stylin' in black jeans and a shirt with a geometric pattern. Once he put on his cap, the finishing touch, the outfit would be perfect. Even his girlfriend had complimented him on this ensemble: "Absolutely anything looks good on you, doesn't it, Al?" He gave his reflection an enthusiastic thumbs-up. *No worries. You look awesome today, too.*

He'd gotten his blond hair and green eyes from his mom. For as long as he could remember, he'd been hearing, "What an adorable little angel," as a matter of course. He'd had too many girlfriends to count, starting as far back as kindergarten, and at the prom, his current girlfriend had been crowned prom queen. He'd been prom king; even though he and Michael from the football team had long shared the title of most popular guy in school, Al had beaten him in the end. It had been the greatest feeling ever. He didn't really shine at sports or at schoolwork, but God had given him the ultimate gift: good looks.

Al had planned to go to a college in California not far from Hollywood after graduating high school, but he hadn't been accepted. The only college he'd gotten into was a local one. When he told his family he wanted to go to acting school instead, they raised fierce objections and made him promise to stick with the local college till he got his degree.

As a first step toward breaking into show business, Al managed to get in with a local modeling agency, but even though he'd shelled out quite a bit, the only jobs he'd gotten

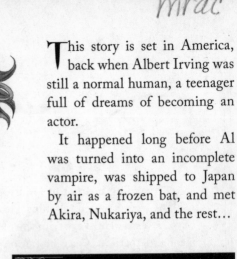

This story is set in America, back when Albert Irving was still a normal human, a teenager full of dreams of becoming an actor.

It happened long before Al was turned into an incomplete vampire, was shipped to Japan by air as a frozen bat, and met Akira, Nukariya, and the rest…

EXCLUSIVE, NEW SHORT STORY!

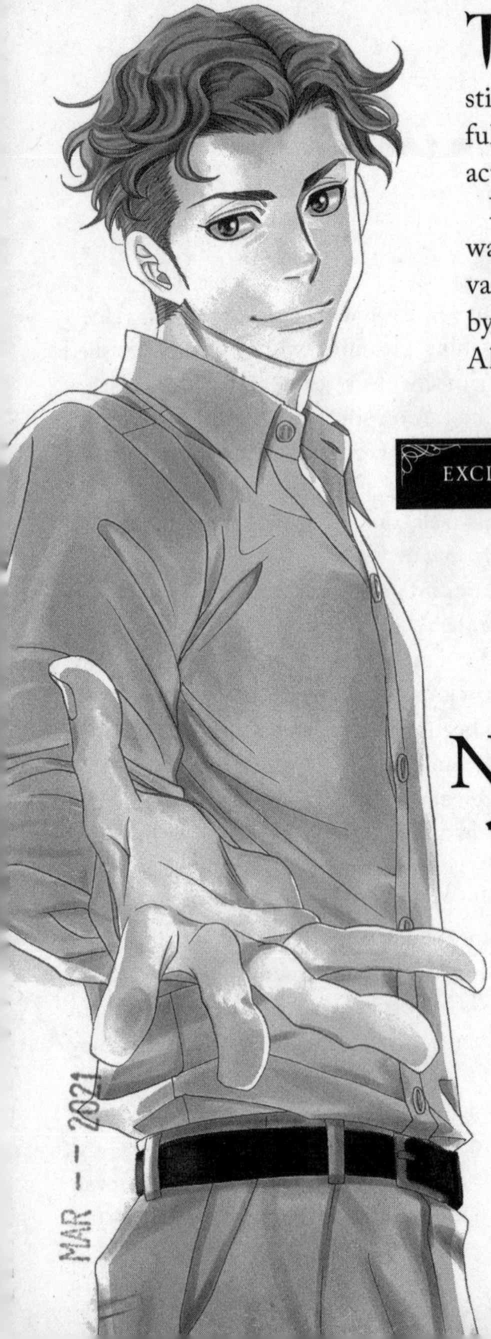

ALBERT IRVING, NINETEEN YEARS OLD

Narise Konohara